Forty Groundbreaking Articles from Forty Years of Biblical Archaeology Review

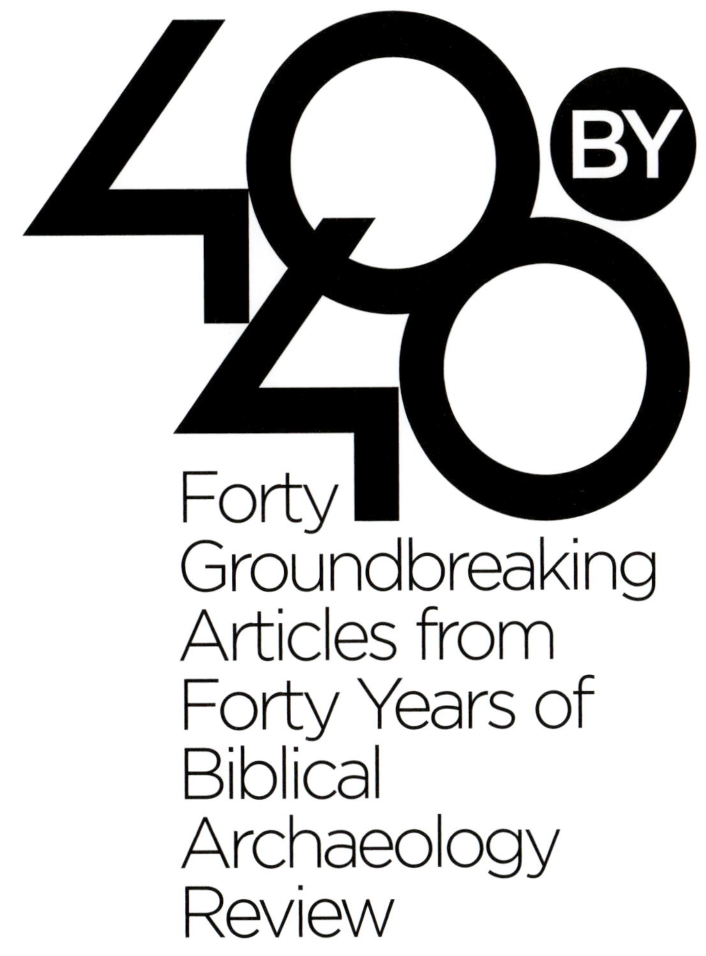

VOLUME ONE

HERSHEL SHANKS, EDITOR

BIBLICAL ARCHAEOLOGY SOCIETY
WASHINGTON, DC

Library of Congress Cataloging-in-Publication Data

40 by 40: forty groundbreaking articles from forty years of
Biblical archaeology review / edited by Hershel Shanks.
pages cm
Includes bibliographical references.
1. Bible—Antiquities. I. Shanks, Hershel.
II. Biblical archaeology review.
III. Title: Forty by forty
BS621.F65 2015
220.9'3—dc23
2014042393

4710 41st Street, NW
Washington, DC 20016

Printed in Canada
Design by AURAS Design, Silver Spring, MD

ISBN 978-0-9796357-7-9 for Soft Cover Set
ISBN 978-0-9796357-6-2 for Hard Cover Set

This book could not have been produced without the enthusiastic, encouraging and generous support of

George Blumenthal, USA

Major Jan Brown, Ret., USA

Lois England in memory of Richard (Dick) England, USA

Juergen Friede, Germany

Susie and Michael Gelman in memory of Avraham Biran, USA

Eugene and Emily Grant, USA

David and Jemima Jeselsohn, Switzerland

Marvin and Dolly Kay, USA

Atis and Lynda Krigers, USA

Lanier Theological Library, USA

P.E. MacAllister, USA

John and Carol Merrill, USA

Jeanette and Jonathan Rosen, USA

David Rosenstein, USA

Samuel D. Turner, USA

TABLE OF

VOLUME I

v Contributors

ix Acknowledgments

xi Introduction

CHAPTER 1
IN THE BEGINNING

3 Editor's Notes

4 The River Runs Dry—Creation Story Preserves Historical Memory JAMES A. SAUER

12 God Before the Hebrews—*Treasures of Darkness* Goes Back to the Mesopotamian Roots of Biblical Religion TIKVA FRYMER-KENSKY

20 How the Alphabet Was Born from Hieroglyphs ORLY GOLDWASSER

CHAPTER 2
IN FORMATION

36 Editor's Notes

40 3200-Year-Old Picture of Israelites Found in Egypt FRANK J. YURCO

60 Let My People Go and Go and Go—Egyptian Records Support a Centuries-Long Exodus ABRAHAM MALAMAT

66 Red Sea or Reed Sea?—How the Mistake Was Made and What *Yam Sûp* Really Means BERNARD BATTO

CHAPTER 3
ISRAEL EMERGING

78 Editor's Notes

80 BAR Interviews Yigael Yadin HERSHEL SHANKS

90 Who Destroyed Canaanite Hazor? AMNON BEN-TOR

102 Early Israel—An Egalitarian Society AVRAHAM FAUST

108/112 An Israelite Village from the Days of the Judges MOSHE KOCHAVI AND AARON DEMSKY

An Alphabet from the Days of the Judges AARON DEMSKY AND MOSHE KOCHAVI

120 Has Joshua's Altar Been Found on Mt. Ebal? ADAM ZERTAL

CHAPTER 4
ISRAEL'S RIVALS

141 Editor's Notes

142 What We Know About the Philistines TRUDE DOTHAN

168 When Canaanites and Philistines Ruled Ashkelon LAWRENCE E. STAGER

188 How Iron Technology Changed the Ancient World—And Gave the Philistines a Military Edge JAMES MUHLY

204 New Light on the Edomites ITZHAQ BEIT-ARIEH

CHAPTER 5
DAVID AND SOLOMON

222 Editor's Notes

224 "David" Found at Dan

238/251 Did I Find King David's Palace? EILAT MAZAR

The Interchange Between Bible and Archaeology NADAV NA'AMAN

256 Cow Town or Royal Capital?—Evidence For Iron Age Jerusalem NADAV NA'AMAN

CHAPTER 6
THE TEMPLE

266 Editor's Notes

268/275 Probable Head of Priestly Scepter From Solomon's Temple Surfaces in Jeruslem ANDRÉ LEMAIRE

Is This Inscription Fake? You Decide HERSHEL SHANKS

278 The New 'Ain Dara Temple—Closest Solomonic Parallel JOHN MONSON

CONTENTS

VOLUME II

v Contributors

CHAPTER 7

WATER AND BURIALS

299 Editor's Notes

301 How Water Tunnels Worked DAN COLE

320 Jerusalem Tombs from the Days of the First Temple GABRIEL BARKAY AND AMOS KLONER

CHAPTER 8

POWERFUL LIFE IN THE DIVIDED MONARCHY

340 Editor's Notes

342 Answers at Lachish DAVID USSISHKIN

364 The Persisting Uncertainties of Kuntillet 'Ajrud HERSHEL SHANKS

376 The Fury of Babylon—Ashkelon and the Archaeology of Destruction LAWRENCE STAGER

392 What Happened to the Cult Figurines?—Israelite Religion Purified After the Exile EPHRAIM STERN

404 The Riches of Ketef Hinnom—Jerusalem Tomb Yields Biblical Text Four Centuries Older than Dead Sea Scrolls GABRIEL BARKAY

CHAPTER 9

JERUSALEM IN FLAMES; AND THE DEAD SEA SCROLLS

423 Editor's Notes

424 Jerusalem in Flame—The Burnt House Captures a Moment in Time NAHMAN AVIGAD

432 The Dead Sea Scrolls and the People Who Wrote Them FRANK MOORE CROSS

CHAPTER 10

WHERE JESUS WALKED (AND SAILED)

444 Editor's Notes

446 Has the House Where Jesus Stayed in Capernaum Been Found? Italian Archaeologists Believe They Have Uncovered St. Peter's Home HERSHEL SHANKS AND JAMES STRANGE

458 Cast Your Net Upon the Water—Fish and Fisherman in Jesus' Time MENDEL NUN

470 The Galilee Boat—2,000-Year-Old Hull Recovered Intact SHELLY WACHSMANN

488 The Undiscovered Gate Beneath Jerusalem's Golden Gate JAMES FLEMING

502 The Siloam Pool—Where Jesus Cured the Blind Man HERSHEL SHANKS

CHAPTER 11

UNDERSTANDING THE DEATHS OF JOHN AND JESUS

515 Editor's Notes

516 Machaerus—Where Salome Danced and John the Baptist Was Beheaded GYÖZÖ VŐRŐS

528 Crucifixion—The Archaeological Evidence VASSILIOS TZAFERIS

CHAPTER 12

JEWS AND CHRISTIANS ABROAD

538 Editor's Notes

540 Financing the Collosseum LOUIS H. FELDMAN

556 Condemned to the Mines—Copper Production and Christian Persecution MOHAMMAD NAJJAR AND THOMAS E. LEVY

566 The Spade Hits Sussita ARTHUR SEGAL AND MICHAEL EISENBERG

580 Godfearers in the City of Love ANGELOS CHANIOTIS

ACKNOWLEDGMENTS

Creating these volumes really began 40 years ago. During these four decades, I have had the pleasure of knowing and working with the many eminent scholars whose articles are reproduced here. Equally important have been a series of devoted staff members who supported me in these efforts. I am deeply grateful to them, no less for their being unnamed.

More specifically, the entire production of this beautiful two-volume set has been directed by Biblical Archaeology Society president and BAR publisher Susan Laden. This could not have been done without her dedication and commitment, as well as her talent.

The manifold editorial questions that arose during the compilation of these volumes were creatively addressed by long-time managing editor and now contributing editor Dorothy Resig Willette.

Administrative editor Bonnie Mullin efficiently managed early editorial matters and coordinated the entire project.

The printing process was very competently supervised by production manager Heather Metzger.

Robert Sugar, who has led BAR's design team since 1977, continued in this capacity in connection with these volumes—to the often new creative designs of the articles. He was supported, as always, by his capable staff at AURAS Design—Sharri Wolfgang, David Fox and Andrew Chapman.

I am deeply grateful to all of you.

HERSHEL SHANKS
Editor, *Biblical Archaeology Review*
Washington, DC
2015

INTRODUCTION

This is a celebratory book—on two levels.

First, it celebrates the 40th anniversary of *Biblical Archaeology Review*, or BAR as it is universally called. BAR's first issue was published in March 1975, a 7-by-10-inch, 16-page (including cover) pamphlet printed on tan paper with brown ink and including a single black-and-white picture—or perhaps I should say a brown-and-tan picture.

Today, 40 years later, with a print run of more than 100,000, BAR is the largest circulation, most widely read, most widely cited, and most beautiful Biblical archaeology magazine in the world.

Second, and much more significant, this celebratory volume is a unique collection of 40 groundbreaking BAR articles by the world's leading scholars. The articles have been arranged in the order of the Hebrew Bible, then the New Testament and, finally, the years following the Roman destruction of the Jerusalem Temple in 70 C.E.

The articles in this volume are unique also in two other respects. Most importantly, each has been carefully edited to express the scholars' thoughts and ideas in language meant to be understood—yes, understood by laypeople—yet not watered down either. This is the hallmark of BAR articles. The other is the glorious color pictures that festoon each issue.

For these reasons, this book provides a marvelous teaching tool, both for students at all levels and for people who just want to learn. Try reading one article a week—or a day. You'll be surprised how easy and gratifying it is to learn.

For me, BAR's editor, it has been a wonderful ride. At the beginning of each chapter, I have included a few words about the articles' context and their original publication in BAR. I am equally grateful to the scholars who wrote for BAR and our readers—both of whom were necessary to make it possible.

HERSHEL SHANKS
2015

1

In the Beginning

From unexpected archaeological support for historical details in Genesis to the background of Israelite religion and the origins of the alphabet, these articles explored the foundations of the Bible.

Whether or not historical, the stories in Genesis—including the creation, the flood, the patriarchs Abraham, Isaac and Jacob, and Joseph in Egypt—preserve memories of their historical contexts. The Biblical authors incorporated these memories—and contemporaneous cultural practices—into stories that may not be literal.

JULY/AUGUST 1996
The River Runs Dry—Creation Story Preserves Historical Memory

In the first article below, an analysis of ancient climatic changes suggests intriguing results reflected in the creation story.

The author of the article, James Sauer, was president of the American Schools of Oriental Research (ASOR), the major American scholarly organization of Near Eastern archaeologists. And ASOR had been openly hostile to BAR, regarding us as a non-scholarly interloper in the archaeological world.

In an attempt to heal the rift between ASOR and BAR, and more specifically between Jim Sauer and me, billionaire Leon Levy invited us both to dinner at his elegant New York apartment, along with a few other ASOR leaders who were more sympathetic to what BAR was doing. Jim was pleasant, but he stood his ground: There was no room for BAR in his thinking.

A number of years later, Jim developed a fatal nerve disorder known as Huntington's disease. His attitude toward me inexplicably changed. He even agreed to write this article for BAR.

Jim Sauer died in 1996 at age 55.

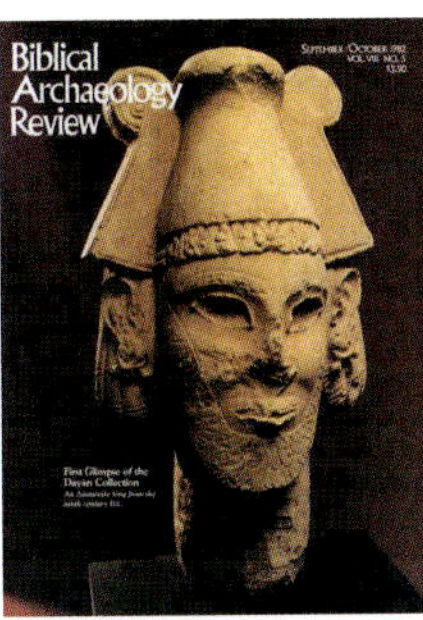

SEPTEMBER/OCTOBER 1982
God Before the Hebrews—*Treasures of Darkness* Goes Back to the Mesopotamian Roots of Biblical Religion

Tikva Frymer-Kensky was a brilliant young scholar who also died young (at 63). She taught at the University of Chicago Divinity School. In this article she surveyed four millennia of Mesopotamian religion that provided a background to Biblical religion, as reconstructed by Thorkild Jacobson, the "master-scholar of ancient Sumer and Assyria." In many ways, Frymer-Kensky observes, the ancient Israelites took the "religious torch" from early Mesopotamian religion, although adding their own unique contribution.

MARCH/APRIL 2010
How the Alphabet Was Born from Hieroglyphs

The invention of the alphabet ushered in "the most profound media revolution in history." Hebrew University Egyptologist Orly Goldwasser related how Semitic turquoise miners in the Sinai peninsula, perhaps precursors of the ancient Israelites, created letters from Egyptian hieroglyphs. This alphabetic innovation allowed them to record language with fewer than 30 signs instead of hundreds of hieroglyphic symbols.

THE RIVER RUNS DRY

CREATION STORY PRESERVES HISTORICAL MEMORY

JAMES A. SAUER

EVIDENCE OF CLIMATIC CHANGE HAS the potential, already partially realized, of dating the patriarchal age, the sojourn in Egypt (the Joseph story) and the origins of the Biblical Flood story. It may even enable us to locate at least one of the four rivers associated with the Garden of Eden.

I speak as a former skeptic. Every scholar (and many BAR readers) knows of the egregiously failed effort by the great William F. Albright in the heyday of Biblical archaeology to place the patriarchs in the Middle Bronze period, shortly after 2000 B.C.E. Today, the conventional wisdom—or at least the view of many mainstream scholars—is that the patriarchal stories do not have a setting in a particular archaeological period, that there is no patriarchal period as such. I too have written numerous papers noting that Albright and many of his students (including Nelson Glueck, G. Ernest Wright and John Bright) were too optimistic in making connections between archaeology and the Biblical sources before the emergence of Israel in Canaan in the 13th century B.C.E.

Now I am recanting. My current work on climate change had led me to conclude that Albright and his students were clearly correct to look for connections between the archaeological evidence and early Biblical traditions.[1]

Until very recently, the prevailing assumption among scholars had been that the climate of the Near East changed little, if at all, after about 9000 B.C.E., or the

EOSAT/BOSTON UNIVERSITY CENTER FOR REMOTE SENSING

PRECEDING PAGES: THE desert sands of Saudi Arabia appear in brilliant yellow-orange in this satellite photo of a 10,000-square-mile region northwest of Riyadh. Only 4 inches of rain fall annually in Saudi Arabia today, and scholars have assumed that the region was equally arid in ancient times. But the jagged seam cutting through the blue (indicating limestone) at top center suggests otherwise: The seam is part of a river channel, concealed by the sand dunes in the bottom half of the photo, that crossed the Arabian peninsula from about 10,000 B.C.E. until 3500-2000 B.C.E., when it dried up. Dubbed the Kuwait River, the river channel—along with evidence of floods in Mesopotamia, deep lakes in Africa, grasslands and lakes in Arabia, and heavy forest cover along the eastern Mediterranean coast—provides testimony to a lengthy wet period in the ancient Near East.

ALTHOUGH AUTHOR JAMES Sauer has long doubted that archaeology could uncover evidence of the earliest Biblical stories, he now suggests that the Flood story of Genesis 7:6-8:14 may preserve remembrances of this wet period. The Kuwait River, Sauer argues, may even be the model for the River Pishon, associated with the Garden of Eden (Genesis 2:12).

end of the last glacial period. This concept of climate stability has been held by the vast majority of scholars working in the Near East, including such leading Israeli archaeologists as the late Yohanan Aharoni[2] and Amihai Mazar.[3] But in the last few years, this situation has been changing, thanks to the work of such scholars as Aharon Horowitz,[4] Thomas Levy,[5] Paul Goldberg and Arlene M. Rosen.[6] My own work is simply an extension of theirs.

The evidence is unfortunately quite complex and technical, so here I will only summarize it, giving some examples.[7] The bottom line is that climatic changes have occurred in historic periods in the Near East; these climatic changes, which may explain widespread social changes, appear to have been a significant part of the Biblical memory.

Three boreholes, two from the Hula Lake (drained at the turn of the century and now partially refilled) in Israel and the other from the Mediterranean coast of Israel, provide us with pollen samples from various periods.[8] A high percentage of arboreal (tree) pollen results from a dense forest cover, which indicates a period of heavy rainfall. Percentages of arboreal

World Wide Wet

Evidence from throughout the Near East indicates that this region underwent a wet period from about 7500–3500 B.C.E.

How to Find a River— No Divining Rod Needed

Most people think little about pebbles, unless they're in their shoes, in which case that's probably all they think about. But for geologists, pebbles provide important, easily attained clues to an area's geologic composition and history. The pebbles of Kuwait offered Boston University scientist Farouk El-Baz (right) his first humble clue to detecting a river, identified in the accompanying article as the Pishon, that once flowed softly across the now-desiccated Arabian Peninsula. (See map, opposite.)

Geologists had long realized that pebbles of granite and basalt are abundant throughout Kuwait, even though these rocks are not indigenous to the area. The nearest rich source lies in the Hijaz Mountains, about 650 miles to the west, in Saudi Arabia. Trying to understand how the pebbles reached Kuwait, El-Baz examined photos of the region taken by satellites orbiting the earth.

In the photo on pages 4-5 and below, the blue indicates limestone, the yellow-orange denotes desert sand. (The region shown in the photo is outlined in red on the map.) Studying this satellite photo, El-Baz could easily detect a dried riverbed (today called Wadi Al-Batin) cutting through the limestone at top center and, apparently (but only apparently), petering out as it reached the sand. When he extended the line of the river across the sand dunes, as indicated in orange in the photo below, El-Baz noticed that the patterns of the desert's sand dunes changed precisely when they crossed this line. To the right (southeast), the dunes appear pockmarked, to the left (northeast) they are striated. Sand patterns like these are created by the circulation of the air in the desert, which in turn is influenced by the topography. Thus, El-Baz realized that something beneath the sand was the source of the variations in the sand. He determined that the river ran underground here, along a fault line.

EOSAT/BOSTON UNIVERSITY CENTER FOR REMOTE SENSING

On El-Baz's recommendation, a recent space shuttle mission probed the area with Shuttle Imaging Radar, which transmits radar waves to the ground and receives their echo. This method successfully detected subterranean river channels in the Sahara. He is awaiting their results.

Throughout the past several hundred thousand years, during wet periods (such as the one described in James Sauer's article), the river, in places 3 miles wide, dragged granite and basalt from the Hijaz mountains and dumped the pebbles along its fan-shaped delta, which covered two-thirds of modern Kuwait and part of southern Iraq. In memory of the pebble-strewn region that led him to the channel, El-Baz christened his discovery the Kuwait River.—MOLLY DEWSNAP

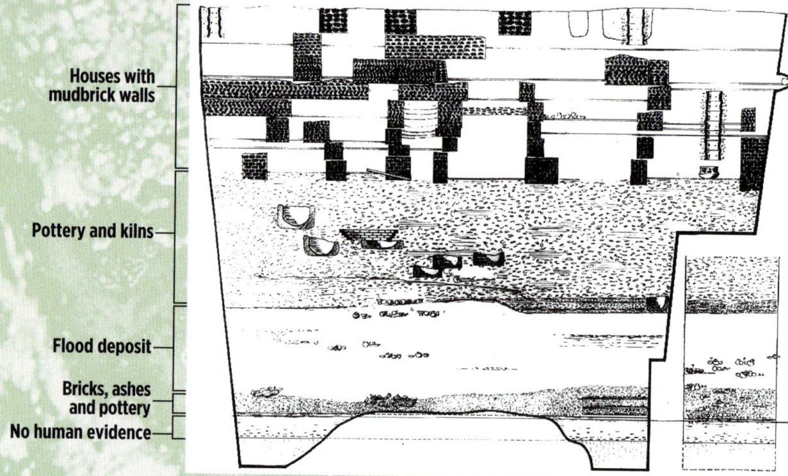

ILLUSTRATIONS COURTESY TRUSTEES OF THE BRITISH MUSEUM

Uncovering the Deluge

"Well, of course, it's the Flood," Lady Woolley casually remarked when her husband's excavation team uncovered an 8-foot-thick layer of soil that contained no evidence of human activity, sandwiched between two layers of pottery.* At lower left, two Arab workmen stand beside part of what came to be known as "the Flood deposit."

Sir Leonard Woolley excavated Ur, in southern Iraq, between 1922 and 1934. At left, he displays a second-millennium B.C.E. statuette discovered in one of the site's many wayside shrines.

Woolley first discovered evidence of what he and his wife called the Biblical flood in 1929 in a small shaft. Acknowledging that "one could scarcely argue for the Deluge on the strength of a pit a yard square," Woolley decided to cut a 75-by-60-foot pit, which eventually extended 64 feet down. As shown in his drawing of the various occupational layers discovered in the pit (center), the first eight layers, labeled A-H and running from 17 to 10 meters (55 by 33 feet) above sea level, contained mud-brick walls. These architectural ruins ended suddenly about 10 meters above sea level, and a 5.5-meter layer of broken pottery began. Scattered throughout this layer, Woolley discovered kilns and a potter's wheel, leading him to suggest this had been a pot factory.

Directly beneath the pottery layer came the so-called Flood deposit, measuring up to 12 feet thick and dating to the mid-fourth-millennium B.C.E. (The only intrusions into this layer were later graves.) Woolley observed that the silt had been deposited all at once, was water-laid and matched that of the Middle Euphrates region. During the Deluge, he speculated, the overflowing Euphrates had deposited the soil here.

Below the Flood deposit appeared a layer of mud bricks, ashes and potsherds that Woolley attributed to the prehistoric, pre-Flood community. About 3 feet below sea level, all traces of human occupation ended.

Woolley later retracted his identification of the Flood stratum, arguing that the deposit was too old to have resulted from the Biblical Deluge. Nevertheless, it offers strong evidence of flooding during the regional wet period that may have inspired the Flood story of Genesis 7:6–8:14.—MOLLY DEWSNAP

*See P.R.S. Moorey, *Ur of the Chaldees: A Revised and Updated Edition of Sir Leonard Woolley's Excavations at Ur* (Ithaca, NY: Cornell Univ., 1982).

pollen are markedly higher (indicating a wetter phase) in the Chalcolithic period (c. 4500-3500 B.C.E.), which ended with a dry oscillation before a wetter Early Bronze Age I (c. 3500-2850 B.C.E.), a somewhat drier but still moist phase during Early Bronze II-III (c. 2850-2350 B.C.E.) and a more arid phase in at least part of the Early Bronze IV period (c. 2350-2000 B.C.E.). This aridity peaks in Early Bronze IV (called by some Middle Bronze I). Middle Bronze Age I-II (c. 2000-1550 B.C.E.) witnesses a return to much wetter conditions, tapering off gradually through the Late Bronze Age (c. 1550-1200 B.C.E.) and the Iron Age (1200-586 B.C.E.). A slight increase in moisture appears in the Byzantine period (324-638 C.E.) and Islamic period (beginning in 638 C.E.), continuing until about 1400 C.E., and then declining until modern times.*

A wetter Chalcolithic period than we had previously supposed correlates beautifully with other evidence from Chalcolithic sites in Jordan and southern Israel. Teleilat el-Ghassul in the southeastern Jordan Valley and sites like Beersheba and Shiqmim in southern Israel are located in topographically low areas with little rainfall in modern times (generally between 0 and 200 millimeters annually—steppe-desert). These sites must have had more rainfall when they were occupied. Toward the end of the Chalcolithic period, however, there was a marked drop in arboreal pollens resulting from a decline in wooded vegetation, which indicates a decrease in rainfall.

My own studies in Yemen buttress this evidence.[9] In Wadi al-Jubah, we found dark paleosol (ancient soil), in places nearly 10 feet thick. This contrasts to the light, dry soil associated with arid climates. Studies of this dark soil revealed that it was full of decayed organic matter such as roots—a product of wetter conditions. We were able to date the layer of paleosol by carbon-14 tests. The test results show that the wetter period extended to the end of the Chalcolithic period, about 3500 B.C.E. After that, a drier period (but one still wetter than today) probably followed.

Similarly, in southern Saudi Arabia ancient lakes existed in the Empty Quarter (today, the largest sand desert in the world) until about 3500 B.C.E.

A core sample from the Arabian Sea not far from Yemen gave clear evidence of a wetter environment from about 7000 to 5000 B.C.E., followed by what appears to have been a drier climate after about 3000 B.C.E.[10] Other consistent evidence comes from African lakes.[11]

*Interestingly, the decline after 1400 C.E. has sometimes been attributed to Ottoman tax policies or unregulated wood cutting, but in fact the process began even earlier, with a period of greater aridity in Late Mamluk times.

PHOTOS COURTESY OF RICHARD B. CARTEN

THE CRADLE OF GOLD (MAHD EDH-DHAHAB), one of the richest gold mines in Saudi Arabia or Africa (upper photo), may have been worked as early as 1000 B.C.E., causing some to identify it as King Solomon's mine (1 Kings 9:26-28). The fissures on the hillside are remnants of ancient mining. Rediscovered in 1932 by American mining engineer Karl Twitchell, the mine currently produces more than 5 tons of gold a year. This quartz-sulfide-gold vein (lower photo) is still mined today.

The river that watered the Garden of Eden split into four rivers, Genesis 2:10-12 relates, including the Pishon, which flowed "around the whole land of Havilah, where there is gold; and the gold of that land is good; bdellium and onyx stone are there." Bible scholars have identified Havilah with the Arabian peninsula because it is rich with bdellium (fragrant resins) and precious stones, but they have been unable to pinpoint the location of the river in this arid region. The recent discovery of the Kuwait River adjacent to the Cradle of Gold, the only Arabian source for such "good gold," has led James Sauer to suggest that this dry riverbed may be the Pishon.

Some especially striking but very different kind of evidence comes from the Arabian Peninsula. With the use of remote sensing technology, Farouk El-Baz has traced a major, partially underground, sand river channel from the mountains of Hijaz to Kuwait, which he has named the Kuwait River. Dated by associated geology, the dry river channel is clearly a relic of a wetter phase in Arabia during this period. It gradually dried up sometime after 3500 B.C.E.[12]

All this evidence (and much more that I have not cited here) supports the view that a global wet phase began around 7500 B.C.E. This phase, though probably interrupted by some drier periods, was predominantly wet until at least 3500 B.C.E., around the end of the Chalcolithic period. Water filled major lakes, at least one river flowed in Arabia and part of Arabia was grassland.

In Mesopotamia, the mid-fourth-millennium B.C.E. evidence probably corresponds to the Biblical and other ancient Near Eastern traditions of floods. True, these floods were localized phenomena, not global catastrophes. Several localized floods from this period have been found. At Ur, Leonard Woolley discovered an almost 3-meter-thick sterile layer that he originally considered evidence of the Flood, though he eventually abandoned that viewpoint because the level in question dated too early. But other flood deposits were later found at higher levels at several sites.[13]

The Kuwait River also has a probable Biblical connection. It may well be the Pishon River, one of the four rivers, according to the Bible, associated with Eden:

> The name of the first is Pishon; it is the one that flows around the whole land of Havilah, where there is gold; and the gold of that land is good; bdellium and onyx stone are there.
>
> Genesis 2:11-12

Although the meaning of some of the details in this passage is uncertain, it does seem to describe a river flowing into the head of the Persian Gulf from the low mountains of western Arabia, the path followed by the recently discovered Kuwait River. An important key is the Biblical phrase "the gold of that land is good." Only one place in Arabia has such a deposit—the famous site of Mahd edh-Dhahab, the "Cradle of Gold."* This ancient and modern gold mining site is located about 125 miles south of Medina, near the headwaters of the Kuwait River.

The Biblical text also mentions bdellium and onyx. Aromatic resins (bdellium) are known in Yemen to the southwest, and, although they are not thought to have been produced in the vicinity of Medina, they could easily have been brought there. Semiprecious stones such as alabaster also come from these areas, but it is uncertain whether other precious stones, such as onyx, do.

In any event, no other river would seem to fit the Biblical description. I am therefore inclined to think that the Kuwait River could well be the Pishon of the Bible. If so, it implies extraordinary memory on the part of the Biblical authors, since the river dried up sometime between about 3500 and 2000 B.C.E.

At the end of the third millennium B.C.E., say around 2000 B.C.E., most major urban sites in Israel and Jordan were abandoned for about 300 years. As Arlene Rosen has persuasively argued, a period of great aridity occurred at the end of the third millennium B.C.E.[14]

Harvey Weiss has recently shown that, in Northern Syria, the climate was drier from about 2200 to 1900 B.C.E., suggesting that the collapse at the beginning of that period may have been caused primarily by prolonged drought.

In Egypt, historical records attest to serious famines in this same period.

The aridity of this period explains some of the shifts in settlement in Israel and Jordan as well as in Syria, Mesopotamia and Egypt. Climatic change was probably the main cause of these shifts.

In my opinion, the descriptions of the severe famines at the time of Joseph (Genesis 41-47) reflect this period of aridity. The famine reported at the time of Joseph is probably another accurate fragment of climatic memory reflected in the early Biblical traditions.

If this is correct, we may place the patriarchal age sometime in the third millennium B.C.E. Proceeding from these considerations is the likely conclusion that the Early Bronze Age sites of Bab edh-Dhra, Numeira and other places adjacent to the Dead Sea in Jordan were indeed some of the Biblical Cities of the Plain (Genesis 14), as was suggested early on by the excavators but lately is rarely mentioned.[15]

I do not mean to imply that the early Biblical stories are literally true. Clearly, the Biblical traditions are very much cast in the worldview of the Iron Age. But that has led too many scholars to ignore the possibility that the Biblical texts accurately preserve many earlier traditions. Since the memories of climatic change and of early geography seem so accurate, some of these traditions may have been written down for the first time, not in the tenth century B.C.E. (the earliest date given by most scholars) but very much earlier.

These conclusions not only agree with Albright's views, but they also push back even further his dates

*See Lois Berkowitz, "Has the U.S. Geological Service Found King Solomon's Mines?" BAR, September 1977.

for the historical backgrounds of the Biblical traditions. He and his students opted for a patriarchal age in the Middle Bronze period. The evidence I have just rehearsed would place it in the Early Bronze period. David Noel Freedman was right, but for the wrong reasons, when he proposed a third-millennium B.C.E. date for the patriarchs.

I thus disagree with archaeologists like William Dever in their treatment of the Bronze Age and the preceding Chalcolithic period. I think we can expect more archaeological, climatic, geographical, literary and artistic evidence from these periods that will buttress my position. "Biblical archaeology" can and should be extended back to these periods and to regions as far afield as Mesopotamia and Egypt, as Albright originally maintained.

[1] I thank Dr. Lawrence E. Stager for my research associate position at the Harvard Semitic Museum. The funding to support this research came from Richard J. Scheuer, Eugene M. Grant, Leon Levy, Shelby White and P.E. MacAlister. Thanks to Dr. Lawrence T. Geraty, the president of La Sierra University in Riverside, California, this university has provided the institutional base for these donations.

[2] Yohanan Aharoni, *The Archaeology of the Land of Israel* (Philadelphia: Westminster, 1982).

[3] Amihai Mazar, *Archaeology of the Land of the Bible, 10,000-586 B.C.E.* (New York: Doubleday, 1990).

[4] Aharon Horowitz, "Climatic and Vegetational Developments in Northeastern Israel During Upper Pleistocene-Holocene Times," in *Pollen et Spores* 13 (1971), pp. 255-278; "Preliminary Palynological Indications as to the Climate of Israel During the Last 6,000 Years," in *Paleorient* 2 (1974), pp. 407-414; "Human Settlement Patterns in Israel," in *Expedition* 20:4 (1978), pp. 55-58; and *The Quaternary of Israel* (New York: Academic Press, 1979).

[5] Thomas E. Levy "The Chalcolithic Period," in *Biblical Archaeologist* 49 (1986), pp. 82-108.

[6] Paul Goldberg and Arlene M. Rosen, "Early Holocene Palaeoenvironments of Israel," in *Shiqmim 1: Studies Concerning Chalcolithic Societies in the Northern Negev Desert, Israel (1982-1984)*, British Archaeological Reports International Series 356(i-ii) (1987), ed. Thomas E. Levy, pp. 23-33.

[7] For details, see James A. Sauer, "A New Climatic and Archaeological View of the Early Biblical Traditions," in *Scripture and Other Artifacts*, eds. Michael D. Coogan et al. (Louisville, KY: Westminster/John Knox, 1994).

[8] See Horowitz, "Human Settlement Patterns," figure 1.

[9] See Sauer and J.A. Blakely, "Archaeology Along the Spice Route of Yemen," in *Araby the Blest*, ed. Daniel T. Potts, (Copenhagen: Carsten Niebuhr Institute, 1988), pp. 90-115.

[10] F. Sirocko, M. Sarnthein, H. Erlenkeuser, H. Lange, M. Arnold and J.C. Duplessy, "Century-Scale Events in Monsoonal Climate over the Past 24,000 Years," in *Nature* 364 (1993), pp. 322-364.

[11] Karl W. Butzer, Glynn L. Isaac, Jonathan L. Richardson and Celia Washbourn-Kamau, "Radiocarbon Dating of East African Lake Levels," in *Science* 175 (1972), pp. 1069-1076.

[12] See Farouk El-Baz, "Boston University Scientist Discovers Ancient River System in Saudi Arabia," in *Boston University News*, March 25, 1993, pp. 1-2; and "Gulf War Disruption of the Desert Surface in Kuwait," in *Gulf War and the Environment* (New York: Gordon and Breach, 1994).

[13] See Max E. L. Mallowan, "Noah's Flood Reconsidered," in *Iraq* 26 (1964), plate 20, pp. 62-82.

[14] Arlene M. Rosen, "Environmental Change at the End of the Early Bronze Age," in *L'urbanisation de la Palestine à l'age du Bronze ancien*, British Archaeological Reports International Series 527 (1989), ed. Pierre de Miroschedji, pp. 247-256.

[15] See "Have Sodom and Gomorrah Been Found?" BAR, September/October 1980; also see Walter E. Rast and Richard T. Schaub, "Survey of the Southeastern Plain of the Dead Sea 1973," in *Annual of the Department of Antiquities of Jordan* 19 (1974), pp. 5-53; "The Southeastern Dead Sea Plain Expedition: An Interim Report of the 1977 Season," in *Annual of the American Schools of Oriental Research* 46 (1981); "Preliminary Report of the 1981 Expedition to the Dead Sea Plain, Jordan," in *Bulletin of the American Schools of Oriental Research* 254 (1984), pp. 35-60; and "Reports of the Expedition to the Dead Sea Plain, Jordan 1," in *Bab edh-Dhra: Excavations in the Cemetery Directed by Paul W. Lapp (1965-1967)* (Winona Lake, IN: Eisenbrauns, 1989); see also Michael D. Coogan, "Numeira 1981," in the *Bulletin of the American Schools of Oriental Research* 255 (1984), pp. 75-81.

Related Reading

Edwin M. Yamauchi, "Historic Homer," BAR, March/April 2007.

Jeremy McInerney, "Did Theseus Slay the Minotaur?" BAR, November/December 2006.

God Before the Hebrews

Treasures of Darkness *goes back to the Mesopotamian roots of Biblical religion*

TIKVA FRYMER-KENSKY

What, if anything, can we learn about Biblical religion from the vast quantities of material relating to Mesopotamian religion? The answer is: a great deal. No single volume provides better evidence for this conclusion than the recently published and widely acclaimed book by Thorkild Jacobsen, *The Treasures of Darkness—A History of Mesopotamian Religion.**

Jacobsen is the revered master-scholar of ancient Sumer and Assyria. At 75, he has had an enormously fruitful and prolific scholarly life. *Treasures of Darkness* is a moving distillation of Jacobsen's sensitive understanding of Mesopotamian religion.

But this book is not directed to a Biblical audience. Jacobsen has not set out to demonstrate what a study of Mesopotamian religion can teach us about Biblical religion, although he sometimes makes references to similarities and parallels. His primary concern is with the civilizations he has spent a lifetime studying.

Yet the resonances are there. Much of ancient Mesopotamian religion is reflected, although in a perhaps refined form, in later Israelite religion. In a sense, the Israelites can be said to have taken the religious torch from early Mesopotamian religions. To these they of course added their own unique contribution. But many of the abstract attributes of the divine were already in place, developed in Sumerian and Assyrian civilizations of the fourth, third and second millennia B.C.

In 1980, Jacobsen was the recipient of the prestigious George Foote Moore Award conferred at the gala centennial celebration of the Society for Biblical Literature. Why was a Sumerologist/Assyriologist getting an award from the Society for *Biblical* Literature? The citation accompanying the award recognized that Jacobsen's "area of major concentration has been outside [Biblical scholarship]. Nevertheless," the citation continued, "he has brought immense riches and value to the field of Biblical research." In *Treasures of Darkness*, he

*New Haven: Yale University Press, 1976.

THE URUK VASE. Carved from alabaster, this elegant vase dates from the end of the fourth millennium B.C. Standing 41 inches tall, it depicts the rite of sacred marriage, in which the god (identified by Jacobsen as Amaushumgalanna, the god of the date palm) approaches the gate of his bride, Inanna. Amaushumgalanna leads a long procession bearing wedding gifts. The sacred marriage was believed to bring fertility to the land. The upper register shows the meeting between Amaushumgalanna and Inanna. Only the back of Inanna is visible on the far left where she stands in front of the gateway. Behind Inanna, above the animals, is the sanctuary of her temple with its altar and sacred furniture, including (far right) two tall vases. Scholars believe that the Uruk Vase may have stood in such a sanctuary.

makes these immense riches, at least as they relate to Mesopotamian religion, available in a popular and understandable format.

Jacobsen traces three major stages in the development of Mesopotamian religion, corresponding, conveniently enough, to the fourth, third, and second millennia B.C. Each of these three stages reflects a different social and political milieu, which in turn resulted in a different religious orientation.

The earliest Mesopotamian myths provide the keys to understanding the world of the fourth millennium B.C. Compared to later periods, the fourth millennium was a relatively peaceful time during which political power was diffused. Naturally, there were occasional threats to the peace and even military confrontations, but this was not the norm. Sumer was ruled by an ad-hoc, crisis-determined assembly which met at Nippur and conferred offices for the duration of the occasional emergencies.

Gradually all this changed during the third millennium B.C. Conditions then were more accurately reflected in the surviving epics, rather than in the myths. War became the common condition. The "temporary" rulers of the broadly based crisis assemblies of the fourth millennium were replaced by more permanent rulers who were needed for their societies to build massive city walls, erect large public buildings for the administration of the bureaucracy, and raise standing armies to guard the city and defend it. In the third millennium, popular assemblies faded into the background. In their place royal rule developed and was institutionalized. Gradually these new kings extended their rule over increasingly vast areas.

In this setting the religious concepts of the fourth and third millennia differed widely. One way to understand the central religious concern of each period is to ask what the central fear of the age was: in the fourth millennium, characterized by a relatively primitive economy, it was the fear of famine, of not having enough food; in the third millennium, it was the fear of war.

This social setting had major implications for the development of religious consciousness in both periods. In the fourth millennium the attitude toward the divine was one of awe at first perceiving the will behind natural phenomena. The gods were seen as kings and lords of their city, guarding it against attack from without and against corruption from within.

In the fourth millennium, worship centered on the numerous powers that dwelt in natural phenomena and were vital to human survival. These powers were experienced as intransitive (not reaching beyond the phenomena in which they were perceived). Because there was a variety of natural phenomena, religion took a pluralistic, polytheistic form. The cult revolved around ways to ensure the presence and protection of powers beneficial to the early economies, and the absence of harmful ones. Various families of Sumerian gods corresponded to the ecological conditions prevalent in their home areas. There were, for example, gods of the marsh and gods of the pastureland.

By the third millennium, however, the human metaphor for the gods had become predominant: the gods were seen as rulers rather than as the natural phenomena themselves. The divine was more often conceptualized in anthropomorphic terms, as super ruler.

The change, however, was gradual rather than abrupt. Beginning in the Early Dynastic period (end of the fourth millennium) the non-human forms of the divine began to recede, becoming emblems, and even, at times, enemies of the newer anthropomorphic god.

The Sumerian cult of Dumuzi typifies Mesopotamian religion in the fourth millennium—both in the religious metaphors that define it and the social and political conditions to which it relates. Dumuzi is basically an "intransitive" figure, the *élan vital* in nature. Indeed, originally there were several distinct Dumuzi figures—Dumuzi of the date palm, Dumuzi of the shepherds, Dumuzi of the grain, and the allied figure of Damu, the power in the rising sap. As economies grew more complex, several of these distinct manifestations of Dumuzi, characteristic of the early economies, were amalgamated.

Literary texts dealing with Dumuzi are relatively abundant. They focus on the great cycle of the year. In some texts, the passing of the fertile spring into the hot, dry summer is represented by Dumuzi's death. Other texts relating to Dumuzi's death include simple laments by Dumuzi's wife, mother and sister. Myths describe the search for the lost Dumuzi, a search that ultimately proves successful: he is found. Other texts have a ritual background: they describe the courtship and marriage of Dumuzi. In the "sacred marriage," Dumuzi, the power for fertility and yield, is "married" to Inanna, who represents the power of the storehouse. The powers of nature are thus humanized in order to satisfy the need for a meaningful relationship with these often uncontrollable powers.

In the complex tale of "Inanna's descent," Inanna is trapped in the netherworld. The forces imprisoning Inanna agree to release her on the condition that she provide a substitute. In her anger that Dumuzi has not mourned her "death," she names Dumuzi, thus dooming him to the netherworld. Inanna is revived and Dumuzi is doomed to the netherworld in her stead. (Ultimately Dumuzi is rescued for half of each year by his sister's descent to the netherworld in his place.) Jacobsen explains this involved story as a mythic perception of the relationship between the food in the storehouses and the plants and animals killed to provide this food. The revival (replenishing) of community storehouses is at the expense of the living plants and animals (represented by Dumuzi), which must be killed to replenish the stores.

The Dumuzi cult was not confined to the fourth millennium. Indeed, much of the literary evidence by which we reconstruct the Dumuzi cult is considerably later than the fourth millennium. But there is enough evidence to reflect its fourth-millennium origins, including the great Uruk vase, dating to that period, which depicts the sacred marriage between Dumuzi and Inanna.

Dumuzi himself survived, however, even into the first millennium, under the name Tamuz. In one of Ezekiel's visions the prophet sees the women of Jerusalem—even at the gateway of the Lord's temple—sitting and wailing for the death of Tamuz (Ezekiel 8:14), not much differently than the women of Sumer wailed 2,500 years earlier.

If the threatening power of nature was the dominant concern of the fourth millennium, the threatening power of man was the dominant concern of the third millennium. The archaeological record reveals that wars and military raids became commonplace. City walls were built for protection and cities grew in size and number as more people sought refuge behind their walls. This development transformed the dominant political system of the third millennium. No longer were "temporary emergency leaders" adequate. Permanence was needed in the wake of permanent emergency.

War and victory were the overriding subjects of contemporary thought and became important topics in art. Epic tales celebrated the new rulers, giving man (as represented by the ruler) a prominence to rival the gods.

Conversely, the new idea of "ruler," drawn from the then current political situation, was used to suggest the divine aspects of "majesty" and "energy." The metaphor of god as ruler appropriately expressed the power of the gods, and of the earthly setting in which mankind experienced this power. In the third millennium, important gods became

BAGHDAD MUSEUM/DR. GEORG GERSTER, PHOTO RESEARCHERS

THE GOD NINURTA—the god of thundershowers and floods of Spring. This figure is from a group of statues discovered in ancient Eshnunna (modern Tell Asmar) by the Iraq expedition of the Oriental Institute of the University of Chicago. It dates from shortly after 3000 B.C. and stands about 2.5 feet tall.

BRITISH MUSEUM

THE SEAL OF ADDA. The small incised cylinder seal (left) with a hole in the middle was probably worn about the neck. The seal was used as identification. When rolled across a receptive surface, such as moist clay, the seal produced the impression seen on the right.

The cuneiform at the upper left of the impression identifies the seal as belonging to a scribe named Adda. The design depicts the rising of the sun god Utu at the place of sunrise in the mountains (at the bottom center). At the right of the sun god is Enki, the god of the fertile sweet waters. From his shoulders flows the water filled with swimming fish; he holds a bird that may be the thunderbird. Behind Enki is his vizier Isimud, who (like Janus) looks forward and back. The god at the left of the sun is probably Inanna, and behind her the storm god, probably Ninurta, identified by his bow and arrow (lightning) and accompanied by a lion (which, according to Jacobsen, roars like the thunder).

understood as manorial lords of their temple estates. Like their earthly counterparts, such estates were focal points of economic activity; they had large staffs of lesser gods as well as human workers. Like earthly rulers, the divine lords provided protection against external enemies and administered justice within their realms.

This new "ruler" metaphor also provided a new perspective on the universe. The whole cosmos became understood in terms of political organization. Each god had a role to play in this political entity, a role granted by the assembly of all the gods. In the fourth millennium, the gods' immanence in natural phenomena had been perceived as an expression of their innate nature; in the third millennium, the gods assumed the roles and duties given them by the assembly of the gods, an essentially political body. This assembly of the gods was the highest authority in the universe. It met in Nippur and served as a court that passed sentence on wrongdoers, both human and divine. It elected and deposed kings (human and divine) and could condemn whole cities to destruction. These gods, now politically conceived, were active shapers of history.

The four most important gods in the third millennium were An, Enlil, Ninhursaga and Enki. Their powers corresponded to the four great cosmic elements: air, storms, rocky ground, and flowing fresh waters.

An was the power in the sky, the father of the gods, the procreator of vegetation. He was thus the image of paternal authority, who presided over the assembly of the gods and conferred earthly kingship.

Enlil was the god of the moist spring rains and of storms. Enlil was thus the embodiment of energy and force, the executive manager of the gods. Unfortunately, his power was not always beneficent. He could easily unleash fearful storms on man and thus destroy him.

Ninhursaga, the female of the supreme triad, was a many-faceted goddess. Originally, she was the power in the stony soil. She was also closely associated with wildlife and herd animals. She is preeminently the birth-giving mother (often under the name Nintur). Jacobsen suggests that the connection between birth and the "rocky ground" may be that the birth of herd animals normally occurred in the spring when the herds were pastured in the stony soil that rings Mesopotamia in the foothills of the Iranian ranges and in the Arabian desert. As birthgiver, Ninhursaga was the great midwife and the one who gave birth to kings. She did not, however, develop a political function in the organization of the gods and therefore progressively lost rank among the gods.

Enki, the rival third member of the divine triad, was the power in the sweet waters in rivers, marshes and rain. His was thus the power to fertilize and the power to cleanse. Because water moistens clay before it is shaped, Enki was also the god of artists and craftsmen, the most cunning of the gods.

Powers in the lesser cosmic elements were seen as the grandchildren and great-grandchildren of An.

In the second millennium, we see a critical change in religious orientation. For the first time, a concern for self predominates which gives rise to personal religion. Jacobsen is not clear what social and political changes account for this shift or what new fears provided the impetus. But that religion redirected itself to areas of personal concern is unquestionable.

And in Mesopotamian religion of the second millennium we find the clearest connections with Biblical religion. For example, compare Jacobsen's definition of personal religion in second millennium Mesopotamia with Psalms 25 and 38. Jacobsen describes personal religion as the "religious attitude in which the religious individual sees himself as standing in close personal relationship to the divine, expecting help and guidance in his personal life and personal affairs, expecting divine anger and punishment if he sins, but also profoundly trusting to divine compassion, forgiveness and love for him if he repents."

Now listen to the Psalms:

"Remember, Lord, thy tender care
and thy love unfailing,
shown from ages past.
Do not remember the sins and offences
of my youth,
but remember me in thy unfailing love.
The Lord is good and upright;
therefore he teaches sinners the way they
should go....

Turn to me and show me thy favor,
for I am lonely and oppressed.
Relieve the sorrows of my heart
and bring me out of my distress.
Look at my misery and my trouble and
forgive my every sin." (Psalm 25)

And from Psalm 38:

"On thee, O Lord, I fix my hope;
thou wilt answer, O Lord my God.
I said, 'Let them never rejoice over me
who exult when my foot slips.'
I am indeed prone to stumble,
and suffering is never far away.
I make no secret of my iniquity
and am anxious at the thought of my sin....

But, Lord, do not thou forsake me;
keep not far from me, my God.
Hasten to my help, O Lord my salvation."

The attitude reflected here is basic to both Judaism and Christianity. It finds its roots in second-millennium Mesopotamia.

Jacobsen is careful to note, however, that the typical humility and self-abasement of penitence presuppose a remarkable, almost arrogant feeling of human importance. We believe that we matter to God, that what we do is important to Him, that God cares about our deeds, our sins, and our repentance.

This second-millennium concept of God as intimately concerned with the daily affairs of the individual is a radically different religious perspective from the awe-struck perception of the mystery of natural phenomena which characterized fourth-millennium religion and the perception of the majesty of the organized universe which characterized third-millennium religion. In the second millennium, God is brought into the close personal world of the individual, who, for the moment, ignores the holiness and awesomeness of the Maker of the Universe.

But man cannot long ignore the non-personal aspect of God. Psalm 8 is a classic statement:

"When I look up at thy heavens, the work
of thy fingers,
The moon and the stars set in their place
by thee,
What is man that thou shouldst remember
him, mortal man that thou shouldst care
for him?

The coexistence of these two aspects of God is a basic paradox: The worshipper is overwhelmed by God's majesty and holiness, and yet at the same time he approaches God on a very personal level, appealing to God for his personal salvation.

The origins of these conflicting attitudes are to be found in Mesopotamia, where the concept of personal religion originated. For example, listen to this Mesopotamian prayer.

I have cried to thee, (I) thy suffering, wearied
distressed servant.
See me, O my lady, accept my prayers!
Faithfully look upon me and hear my
supplication!

Say "A pity!" about me, and let thy mood
be eased.
"A pity!" about my wretched body
that is full of disorders and troubles,
"A pity!" about my sore heart
that is full of tears and sobbings.

Texts reflecting this attitude toward personal religion appear early in Mesopotamia, toward the beginning of the second millennium, and there are no examples elsewhere in the Near East until half a millennium later. It seems clear that the concept of personal religion spread from Mesopotamia to Israel and Egypt, although we do not know how this occurred or the paths it took.

In Mesopotamia, however, the concept of a personal god was not perceived as contradictory to the idea of divine holiness and majesty because God's personal aspect was reflected in personal gods rather than cosmic gods. In Mesopotamia an individual worshipped his personal god or goddess, as well as the great national gods with their cosmic offices; an individual's personal god was in many ways a personification of the power for personal success in that individual. When one attained luck and good fortune, one "acquired a god." The god inspired the individual to act and generally lent success to his plans. The personal god was the divine parent of the individual who cared for him as a mother and a father: he provided for his children, protected them, and interceded on their behalf with the higher powers. The god dwelt within the man's body, was present even at the act of conception, and thus in a way engendered his children, who accordingly held the same personal god throughout the generations. Man dwelt in the "[protective] shadow of his god." If the god got angry at the individual, however, he would leave, and with him went the individual's power to succeed. Man therefore placated his personal god and induced him to return by penitence and penitential prayers. The humility of penitence—and the assurance of the god's concern—is logical in the context of a "personal god."

In Mesopotamian religion, this idea of the personal god as "parent" served as a psychological bridge to the many gods' awesome powers. But even the great cosmic powers could be personal gods—although only of great men and royalty. These great cosmic gods too had loving concern for their children. All gods could thus be viewed as concerned and approachable, as the "parents" of man. A familiar filial attitude toward all the gods began to permeate religion, resulting in the general attitude called "personal religion."

Another paradox familiar to the student of the Bible, which can also be found in Mesopotamian religion of the second millennium, is the paradox of the righteous sufferer; he finds himself in trouble despite his blamelessness. This problem is dealt with in two notable Babylonian works, the so-called Babylonian Job ("I will Praise the Lord of Wisdom") and the Babylonian Theodicy. Neither of these compositions can provide the answer to a problem that is essentially unresolvable. As Jacobsen points out, however, in the Babylonian Job, for the first time the personal egocentric view of the righteous sufferer is rejected. The Babylonian Job is overwhelmed; he realizes how great the distance is between God in his cosmic majesty and individual man in his littleness; in this context, man cannot demand justice. This realization does not, however, result in the rejection of personal religion. With the help of the concepts of personal religion, man has become the son of God and can confront him on an intimate level.

A number of major Mesopotamian religious works developing the concept of personal religion were produced in the second millennium: the Atrahasis story, Enuma Elish, and the Gilgamesh Epic. According to Jacobsen, all are existential critiques of the universe; that is, each of them deals in a sophisticated way with basic questions of existence and the nature of the universe.

The Atrahasis story focuses on the destructive capacity of the power of the gods. Atrahasis' response to this power is that man should increase his devotion to the gods and take care not to disturb them.

Enuma Elish is an attempt to understand the universe. It does this by telling us how Marduk became king of the gods. The story begins with the birth of successive generations of gods. One of the older gods, Apsu (god of sweet water, the progenitor god), rebels against the exuberant energy of the younger gods (which is their essence), but is defeated by Ea/Enki. Tiamat (god of the salt waters and also a progenitor) is then roused by an assembly of her children and she too rebels. The general assembly of the gods meets and confers kingship on Marduk (the state god of Babylonia). Marduk defeats Tiamat and then, by creating the universe, converts his temporary "kingship" into a permanent monarchy. Enuma Elish operates on many levels: It reflects the rise of Babylon as ruler over a united Babylonia; it is an account of how the universe is ruled; and it explains how monarchy evolved. According to Enuma Elish, the universe is grounded in divine power and divine will; both nature and society are characterized by political order.

The third great Mesopotamian religious work is

Thorkild Jacobsen

Thorkild Jacobsen is one of the pioneers in the study of Sumerian literature and civilization; he has made enormous contributions to our knowledge of Mesopotamia. As an archaeologist, he organized the excavations at Nippur. As an administrator, he directed the University of Chicago's Oriental Institute as well as the Chicago Assyrian Dictionary project. Jacobsen is best known, however, for his many clear and precise scholarly articles in which he demonstrates his mastery of meticulous scholarship and attention to detail. But he is not satisfied only with technical precision; his articles also have a philosophical depth and synthesizing scope that take them beyond technical mastery. Many of his most important articles have been collected in a volume *Toward the Image of Tammuz* (ed. W. Moran); these include seminal articles on the textile industry, on the irrigation system of Ur, and on major grammatical studies of both Sumerian and Akkadian. But, above all, in the realm of cultural history and in the study of political systems, law and religion, Jacobsen has illuminated Mesopotamian civilization and influenced future scholarship.

the Gilgamesh Epic, a magnificent humanistic tale based on legends concerning a supposedly "historical Gilgamesh" (a ruler of Uruk circa 2600 B.C.). The subject of the story is man's relationship to death. The story contains two sets of legends: One recounts the valor of the historical Gilgamesh; the other involves magical tales, such as "The Death of Gilgamesh" and "Gilgamesh, Enkidu and the Netherworld," both dealing with death.

As Jacobsen points out, almost diametrically opposed attitudes toward death are reflected in these stories. In some, Gilgamesh seeks to avoid death. In the magical tales, however, Gilgamesh almost recklessly courts death, but death nevertheless remains the great unavoidable evil. These antithetical attitudes are the theme of the epic, reflecting the development from an early disdain of death to an obsessive fear of it. When the story opens, Gilgamesh shares a heroic attitude of his time: he aspires to immortality through immortal fame. When death takes his friend Enkidu, however, Gilgamesh begins to comprehend the reality of death and realizes that he himself must die. His previous value system collapses; immortal fame now means nothing to him. He becomes obsessed instead with the quest for real immortality.

Ultimately, his ancestor Utnapishtim—who is immortal—tells him the story of the flood to demonstrate that Utnapishtim's own achievement of immortality was unique and is not available to Gilgamesh. Utnapishtim then offers Gilgamesh a parting gift, the rejuvenating plant. But the plant is stolen from him by a serpent when Gilgamesh carelessly leaves it on the bank of a pool. According to Jacobsen, Gilgamesh's very lack of heroic stature brings him to his senses. He cannot defy human nature, he must accept reality; only the relative immortality of lasting achievement can be his.

For Jacobsen, the second millennium was the high point of Mesopotamian religious achievement. He devotes only a short epilogue to the first millennium; these were disturbed times. Mesopotamia was invaded both by Arameans and the Sutu. Faced with the possibility of sudden death, Mesopotamian society reflected an increased interest in the powers of death and in the netherworld, and stories about them became increasingly popular. The religious outlook reflected the turmoil and increasing brutalization of the times. The gods of political enemies themselves became enemies, and were treated as such in rituals, in which these gods were maimed and killed.

But even in the first millennium the three major metaphors that Jacobsen discerns in Mesopotamian thought survived—god as provider (fourth millennium), god as ruler (third millennium), and god as parent (second millennium). God as provider was an official in charge of the beneficent phenomena of nature. The ruler metaphor justified the trend toward absolutism in earthly kingship. The parent metaphor continued to flourish not only in the penitential psalms and in rites of contrition, but in the idea of quietistic piety as well. Thus the torch of Mesopotamian religion was passed on.

Related Reading

William W. Hallo, "The Origin of Israelite Sacrifice," BAR, November/December 2011.

Bill T. Arnold, "Nebuchadnezzar and Solomon," BAR, January/February 2007.

How the ALPHABET
HIE

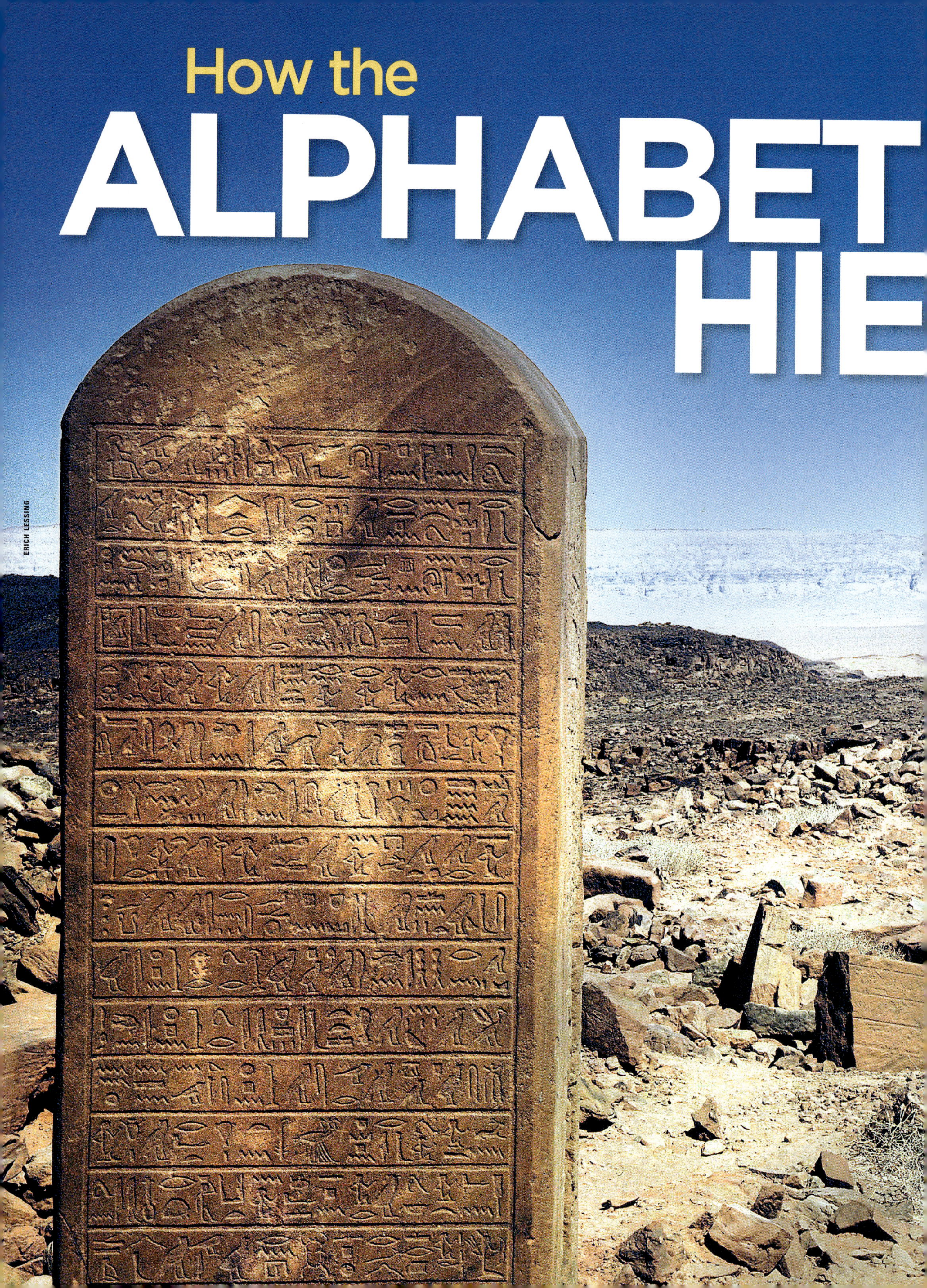

ERICH LESSING

Was Born from
ROGLYPHS

ORLY GOLDWASSER

PREVIOUS PAGES: SITE OF THE REVOLUTION. Amid the desolate, windswept hills of southern Sinai stand the jumbled remains of Serabit el-Khadem. Trailing out from the ruins of the site's temple of Hathor are stelae and stones inscribed with the names and prayers of countless officials, laborers and itinerant travelers who worked the rich turquoise mines during the Egyptian Middle Kingdom (c. 1950–1800 B.C.E.). While many of the messages were carved in arcane Egyptian hieroglyphs, others were inscribed in Canaanite using, for the first time, a simple but ingenious alphabetic script made up of only a few dozen hieroglyphic-inspired signs. This invention, developed by humble workmen in the turquoise mines of Sinai, would forever change human communication.

TO THE ASIATICS, AS THEY were called, the lush Nile Delta, with its open marshlands rich with fi sh and fowl, was a veritable Garden of Eden. From earliest times, Canaanites and other Asiatics would come and settle here. Indeed, this is the background of the Biblical story of the famine in Canaan that led to Jacob's descent into Egypt (Genesis 46:1–7).

By the beginning of the Egyptian Middle Kingdom (a few years after 2000 B.C.E.), the pressure of immigrants on the eastern Delta was so strong that the Egyptian authorities built a series of forts at strategic points to "repel the Asiatics," as the story of Sinuhe tells us.[1]

MEDITERRANEAN SEA
NILE DELTA
•Avaris (Tell el-Daba)
CANAAN/RETENU
DEAD SEA
SINAI
•Timna
EGYPT
Serabitel-Khadem
Nile River
RED SEA
Wadi el-Hôl
N
0 100 m

More than a century later, however, Egyptian policy toward the Asiatics changed. Instead of trying to prevent them from coming in, the Egyptians cultivated close relations with strong Canaanite city-states on the Mediterranean coast and allowed select Asiatic populations to settle in the eastern Delta. The last of the great pharaohs of the XIIth Dynasty, Amenemhet III (c. 1853–1808 B.C.E.) and Amenemhet IV (c. 1808–1799 B.C.E.), even established a new town for them.

The XIIth Dynasty was followed by the much weaker XIIIth Dynasty. Thousands of immigrants from Syria, Lebanon and Canaan then flooded into the eastern Delta, creating the large Canaanite settlement that would become Avaris (modern Tell el-Daba), the capital of the famous Hyksos. The Hyksos were Canaanites who seized power from the Egyptian pharaohs and ruled all Egypt for more than a hundred years (c. 1638–1530 B.C.E.).

But before this, at the end of the XIIth Dynasty during the reigns of Amenemhet III and Amenemhet IV, Egypt was at the height of its power. A lively trade was conducted with Nubia to the south. Imports from the Levant entered Egypt by land and sea. Gold and precious stones were quarried in the eastern desert. And a large-scale enterprise was regularly conducted to search for turquoise in the high mountains of southern Sinai, at a site today called Serabit el-Khadem.

On this mountain deep in the Sinai desert, prey to merciless winds and scorching heat, are the remains of an ancient Egyptian temple to the goddess Hathor, "The Mistress of Turquoise." Founded by Sesostris I, the second king of the XIIth Dynasty (c. 1953–1908 B.C.E.), the temple continued in existence, with some interruptions, until the end of the New Kingdom—for about 800 years.

Building on the work of Sesostris I, pharaohs Amenemhet III and Amenemhet IV exploited Serabit's rich turquoise mines. The precious blue stone was a much-sought-after luxury item in royal

HERSHEL SHANKS

A POWERFUL MINORITY. This colorful but worn painting from the Beni Hassan tomb of an Egyptian official of the XIIth Dynasty shows a family of "Asiatic" nomads entering Egypt with their animals and belongings. During the Middle Kingdom, similar groups of Semitic Asiatics from Syria and Canaan poured across Egypt's borders to settle in the well-watered and fertile regions of the eastern Nile Delta, the Biblical land of Goshen. By the end of the period, Asiatics were involved in nearly every aspect of Egyptian society and, for a time, even managed to gain political control over much of Egypt.

RECONSTRUCTING THE SERABIT SANCTUARY. Although Serabit's temple is today little more than a jumble of ruins, for nearly 800 years the site was continually maintained and expanded by the pharaohs of Egypt's Middle and New Kingdoms. The site was surrounded by a large enclosure wall that was entered through a small gate (see above). Upon entering the temple complex, worshipers walked along a processional way that was outfitted with numerous chapels, the walls and courtyards of which were adorned with the stelae and carvings of earlier generations. At the end of the processional way was an open courtyard that gave access to the temple's inner sanctum, a small grotto hewn into the hillside dedicated to the Egyptian goddess Hathor, mistress of turquoise. A number of stelae at Serabit are decorated with depictions of the goddess and her distinctive curling hairdo (right).

Z. RADOVAN/WWW.BIBLELANDPICTURES.COM

circles. No fewer than 28 expeditions to the Serabit turquoise mines are recorded during the reign of Amenemhet III alone.

To ensure the blessing of the gods, the earlier temple was dramatically enlarged by Amenemhet III and Amenemhet IV. Shrines and numerous commemorative stelae with hieroglyphic inscriptions were erected on the path leading to the temple, especially honoring Hathor, the goddess of turquoise.

Where did all the people who engraved these inscriptions come from? Most were probably from the Delta. The turquoise expeditions to Serabit brought together high officials, scribes, priests, architects, physicians, magicians, scorpion charmers, interpreters, caravan leaders, donkey drivers, miners, builders, soldiers and sailors.

And many members of the expeditions left inscriptions in the temple precinct. Some contain only a name or a drawing. All sought the blessing of the gods for success in their dangerous enterprise—as well as for a safe journey home. These records also tell us of the hundreds of miners and stone workers active during the mining seasons,

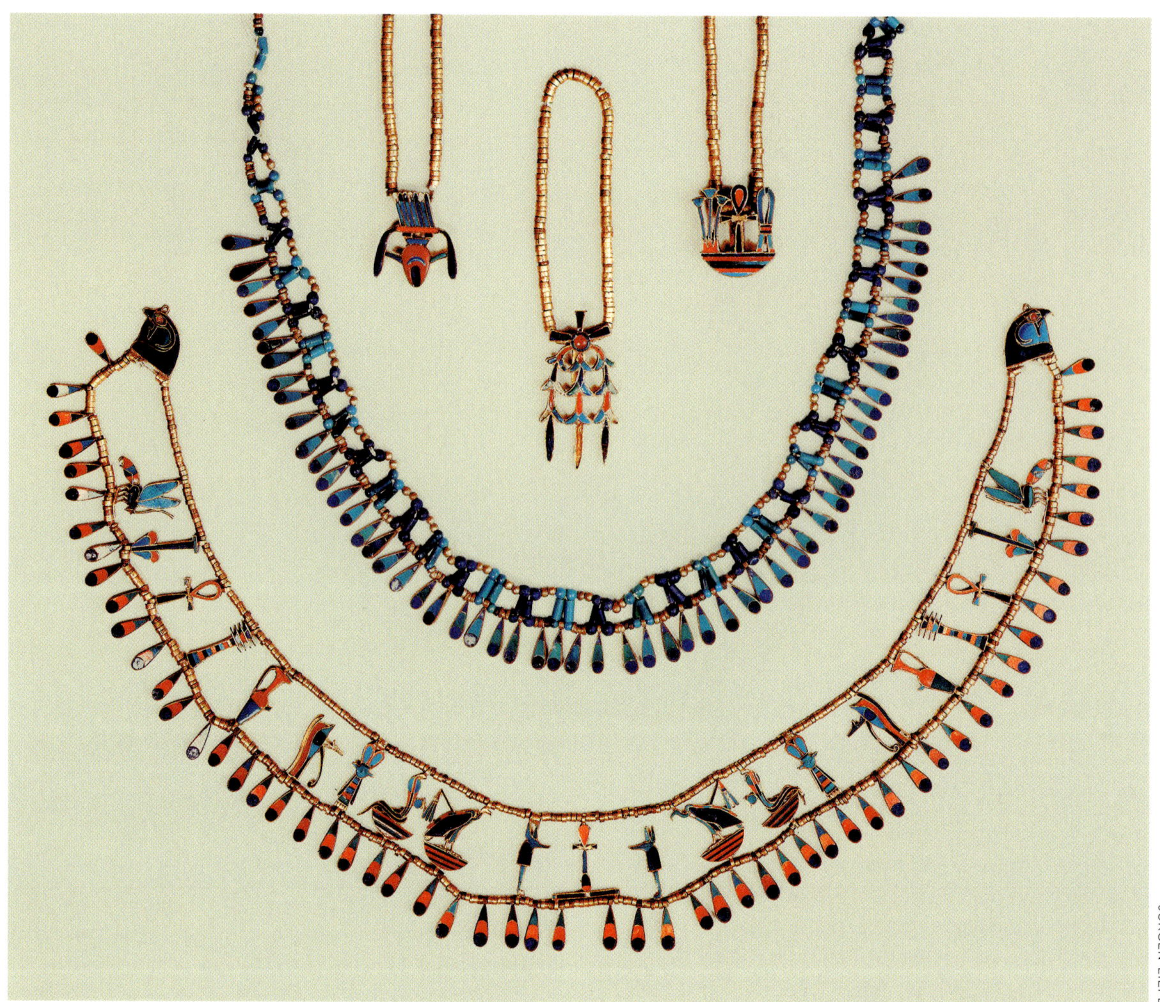

JÜRGEN LIEPE

EGYPTIAN TIFFANY'S. During the Middle Kingdom, Egyptian pharaohs like Amenemhet II and his successors supported mining expeditions to the mountains of southern Sinai in search of turquoise, a semiprecious blue-greenish stone that had become a prized commodity in royal circles across Egypt and the Near East. These gold necklaces and armlets, once worn by Amenemhet II's daughter Khnumet, include hieroglyphic-shaped pendants and accents made of turquoise.

as well as those who were engaged in the building projects at the temple.

Were these miners and workmen Egyptian? Canaanite? Both?

Egyptian society at this time was relatively tolerant, so foreigners were quickly accepted and integrated into Egyptian society, as long as they were not political enemies of the state. Some high officials who left inscriptions at the Serabit temple present themselves as Egyptians, yet they also mention that they are Asiatic in origin or have an Asiatic mother. Despite this ancestry, they consider themselves Egyptian. Only Asiatics who came from outside Egypt are identified as such. Canaanites from Egypt who arrived with the Egyptian expeditions from the Delta were not labeled Canaanites in the inscriptions; they are simply regarded as Egyptians.

The expedition lists at Serabit also contain the names of many "interpreters." The presence of these dragomans is strong evidence that some language barrier must have existed. The hundreds of recorded donkeys that served as pack animals were probably driven by Asiatic caravan experts, who would be able to direct turquoise shipments back to Egypt. And no doubt Asiatic soldiers in Egyptian service escorted these caravans. The bottom line: There were surely many more Canaanites at Serabit than are listed as such in the hieroglyphic inscriptions at the site.

One final note: Nowhere in the many inscriptions at the site is there a mention of slaves. Canaanites, yes; slaves, no.

It was here at Serabit, I believe, that the alphabet was invented—by Canaanites!

The invention of the alphabet ushered in what was probably the most profound media revolution in history. Earlier writing systems, like Egyptian hieroglyphic and Mesopotamian cuneiform with its curious wedge-shaped characters, each required a knowledge of hundreds of signs. To write or even to read a hieroglyphic or cuneiform text required familiarity with these signs and the complex rules that governed their use.

By contrast, an alphabetic writing system uses fewer than 30 signs, and people need only a few relatively simple reading rules that associate these signs with sounds.

This great invention had far-reaching social and cultural implications. With the alphabet, writing broke out of the "golden cage" of the professional scribal world. Writing was no longer their monopoly. When many more members of society could learn to read (and write), access to information and knowledge was no longer as limited as it had been. Alphabetic writing eventually gave many more people control over their lives and enabled larger segments of the population to take a more active role in the cultural and administrative affairs of their respective societies.

But how was it done?

ALTHOUGH, AS I BELIEVE, the alphabet was invented by Canaanites, we still owe a significant debt to the Egyptians, for it was Egyptian hieroglyphs that provided the trigger and the means that made the invention of the alphabet possible.

To understand how this came about, we must first examine some very odd Serabit inscriptions—just a few dozen that markedly differ from the hundreds of hieroglyphic inscriptions at the site. The credit for first noticing one of these unusual inscriptions in Serabit goes to Hilda Petrie, wife of the famous Egyptologist Sir William Matthew Flinders Petrie, who was leading an archaeological expedition to Serabit in 1905. It was she who called attention to some fallen stones on the ground by one of the mines, bearing several awkward signs that seemed not to be real hieroglyphs.

Then more of these inscriptions began turning up on rocks by the turquoise mines, and even inside the mines. A few came from the desert roads leading to the temple. From the temple precinct itself, however, only two small statues and a sphinx bore inscriptions in this strange new script.

Petrie studied these crude inscriptions and observed that they appeared to be a kind of imitation of hieroglyphic signs. Yet the repertoire of signs was very small. Petrie ingeniously identified these awkward signs as an alphabetic script, different from the Egyptian hieroglyphic system with its hundreds of signs. Yet Petrie was unable to read these strange inscriptions.

UNIVERSITY COLLEGE LONDON, PETRIE MUSEUM OF EGYPTIAN ARCHAEOLOGY

A WOMAN'S TOUCH. During William Matthew Flinders Petrie's archaeological expedition to Serabit in 1905, his wife Hilda, herself an Egyptologist, noticed some fallen stones inscribed with unusual signs that were clearly not typical Egyptian hieroglyphs. Although Petrie determined that the signs represented an alphabetic script based on hieroglyphic pictograms, he was unable to decipher the curious inscriptions. This photo shows the Petries at the ancient Egyptian capital of Memphis in 1910.

In 1916, some ten years later, Sir Alan Gardiner, the famous English Egyptologist, noticed a group of four signs that was frequently repeated in these unusual inscriptions. Gardiner correctly identified the repetitive group of signs as a series of four letters in an *alphabetic* script that represented a word in a Canaanite language: *b-ʿ-l-t*, vocalized as *Baalat*, "the Mistress." Gardiner suggested that *Baalat* was the Canaanite appellation for Hathor, the goddess of the turquoise mines. Were these inscriptions carved by Canaanite workmen?

An important key to the decipherment was a unique bilingual inscription. It is inscribed on a small sphinx from the temple and features a short inscription in what appears to be parallel texts in

© THE TRUSTEES OF THE BRITISH MUSEUM

THE RIDDLE OF THE SPHINX. This 10-inch-long sphinx fashioned from sandstone proved to be the key to deciphering the Proto-Sinaitic script. It was discovered by Petrie amid the ruins of Serabit's Hathor temple and includes dedicatory inscriptions on both sides of the base (underlined in yellow in the photos above and below) and on the right shoulder (shown in photo above). Both inscriptions on the base are written in the Proto-Sinaitic alphabetic script. The inscription on the right shoulder is written in Egyptian hieroglyphs, The hieroglyphic text identifies the name of the goddess to whom the sphinx is dedicated as Hathor, "the mistress of turquoise." The famous Egyptologist Alan Gardiner observed that each of the signs in the Proto-Sinaitic texts represented not an entire word, as in hieroglyphic, but only its initial sound. Four of these strange signs (written left-to-right) spelled the name *Baalat*, a Canaanite word also meaning "the Mistress." Thus was Gardiner able to translate *Baalat*, the first word deciphered in alphabetic script. In the drawing (above right) of the Proto-Sinaitic inscriptions on the base, the letters forming the key word, *Baalat*, are highlighted in blue.

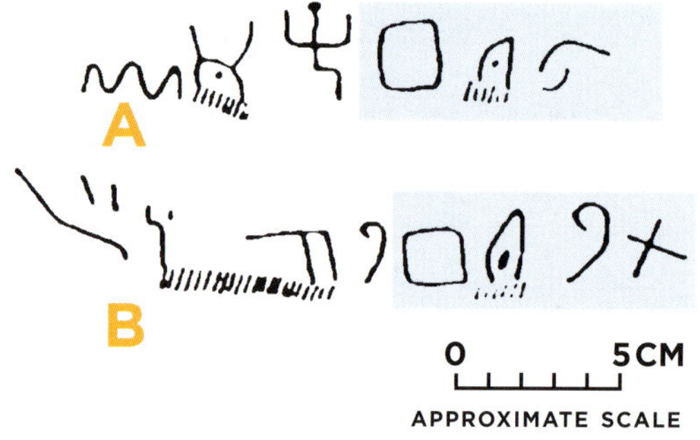

COURTESY ORLY GOLDWASSER, AFTER GARDINER

Egyptian and in the new script.

The Egyptian hieroglyphic inscription on the sphinx reads:

"The beloved of Hathor, the mistress of turquoise."

The text in the strange script, now identified as a Canaanite text, reads:

m-'-h-(b) B-'-l-[t], "The beloved of Baalat" (see drawing A above).

Each of the critical letters in the word *Baalat* is a picture—a house, an eye, an ox goad and a cross.

Gardiner correctly saw that each pictograph has a single acrophonic value: The picture stands not for the depicted *word* but only for its *initial sound.* Thus the pictograph *bêt*, "house," drawn as the four walls of a dwelling (shown at upper left, on p. 27) represents only the initial consonant *b*. *Baalat* is written as shown in the drawing above, in the blue highlighted areas (although the final *tav* is not legible in line A).

This ingenious principle is at the root of all of our alphabetic systems. Each sign in this script

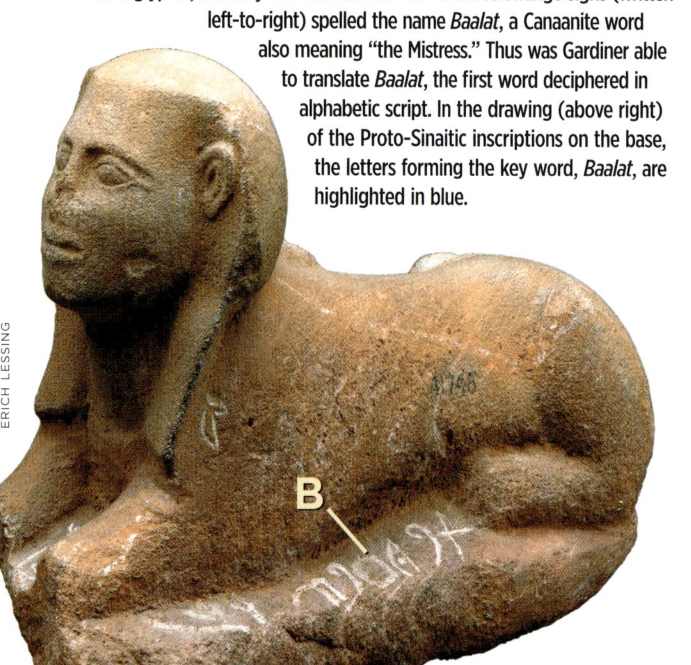

ERICH LESSING

stands for one consonant in the language. (Vowels were not represented. The representation of vowels came later, and in different ways in different alphabetic systems.)

The alphabet was invented in this way by Canaanites at Serabit in the Middle Bronze Age, in the middle of the 19th century B.C.E., probably during the reign of Amenemhet III of the XIIth Dynasty.

We are reasonably confident about the place of the invention because almost all of the examples of the new script—which we may now identify by the name scholars call it, Proto-Sinaitic—come from this one site.[2]

We are also confident about the time of the invention because there are some very specific connections between the Middle Kingdom Egyptian hieroglyphs in Sinai and the new script.[3] There is one hieroglyph that appears to have a special use, with very few exceptions, only in Egyptian hieroglyphic inscriptions in the Sinai during the Middle Kingdom. We might call this the "Sinai Hieroglyph." The sign looks like a striding man with bent, upraised arms (shown in middle at left). In the Egyptian hieroglyphic inscriptions in Sinai, this sign is a logogram; that is, it stands for an entire word, not just part of a word. It probably means something like "foreman." This hieroglyph appears dozens of times in Egyptian Middle Kingdom inscriptions at Serabit. (Its phonetic reading in Egyptian in this specific use in Sinai, however, is unknown.) This hieroglyph is rare even in later New Kingdom Egyptian inscriptions at Serabit. And it hardly ever appears anywhere else in Egypt.[4]

A letter in the new Proto-Sinaitic alphabet looks very much like this Middle Kingdom Egyptian hieroglyph. The Proto-Sinaitic sign (shown at right in upper left) almost certainly stems directly from the Egyptian hieroglyph.

The Canaanites at Serabit probably connected this pictogram, which they saw everywhere at the site, with a loud call or order emitted by an official when he raised his hands to assemble the people, a typical shout such as *Hoy!* (also known in Biblical Hebrew),[5] which may be the origin of the letter *h* in the Proto-Sinaitic script.

If I am correct that the first alphabetic script was invented at Serabit el-Khadem in the reign of Amenemhet III (mid-19th century B.C.E.), I believe

THIS SHORT EGYPTIAN HIEROGLYPHIC INSCRIPTION from Serabit (below) includes five examples of a figure with two raised arms (highlighted in orange). This sign was possibly used to designate the Egyptian word for "foreman." Goldwasser believes that the Canaanite inventors of the alphabet, who must have associated this sign with the foreman's loud calls to work (*Hoy!*), modeled both the shape and phonetic value of the Proto-Sinaitic letter "H" (shown at right, above) after this sign.

FROM GARDINER, *THE INSCRIPTIONS OF SINAI, PART I*

DANIEL BERTI

HERSHEL SHANKS

HERSHEL SHANKS

MINING WITH A PRAYER. During the Egyptian Middle Kingdom, countless workers toiled in Serabit's dark, cavernous mines (shown above) searching for turquoise. Working in cramped, poorly ventilated caves supported by only a handful of stumpy rock-hewn pillars, the miners no doubt looked to their gods for protection and guidance. Were the inscriptions they carved on the walls of the mines meant to secure the eternal blessing of the gods as the miners searched for the precious turquoise?

Their inscriptions, which number only a few dozen, are crudely and often haphazardly carved into Serabit's stones and rock faces, with little or no attention given to the scribal "rules" that govern more formal writing traditions. In this inscription (shown above right), which W.F. Albright read as "Thou, O Shaphan, collect from 'Ababa eight(?) *minas* (of turquoise). Shime'a, groom of the chief of the car[avaneers(?)]," the first half of the text is oriented vertically, while the second half continues in a horizontal direction. This casual method of writing suggests that the miners who invented the alphabet did not know how to read or write the highly formalized, rule-governed hieroglyphic script they saw all around them.

I can plausibly explain the process by which it was invented—not by sophisticated scribes, but by comparatively unlettered Asiatic workers.

The inventors at Serabit clearly used models of hieroglyphs taken from the Egyptian Middle Kingdom inscriptions around them. The Proto-Sinaitic pictograms were adapted from the hieroglyphic pictograms and appear mostly in the area of the turquoise mines and the roads leading to the mines.

It may seem strange, but I believe the inventors of the alphabet were illiterate—that is, they could not read Egyptian with its hundreds of hieroglyphic signs. Why do I think so? The letters in the Proto-Sinaitic inscriptions are very crude. They are not the same size. They are not written in a single direction: Some are written left to right, others right to left and some from top to bottom. This suggests that the writers had mastered neither Egyptian hieroglyphic nor any other complex, rule-governed script.

For these illiterate Canaanites the *pictorial* meanings of the new letters were paramount. The iconic meaning of the hieroglyphs (what they actually pictured) served as an important mnemonic tool for the Canaanite adopters. The iconic meaning of the hieroglyphs was so important that even today, when the Hebrew letters have lost all iconic connection to the old pictorial models (we can't recognize what the letters are supposed to picture), most letters are still named after the old pictures!

The modern Hebrew letter *aleph* is the *'alp*, the word for "ox"; the letter *bêt* is the *bayt* or "house"; the letter *'ayin*, "eye," is the name of the old pictorial letter in Proto-Canaanite script (see drawings at upper right on page 33). But looking at a modern Hebrew *aleph*, *bêt* or *'ayin*, we can no longer see the ox, house or eye (nor are these original pictograms evident in the Latin letters A or B).

Mostly by taking Egyptian hieroglyphs as pictorial models, the Canaanite inventors of the alphabet used the small selection of pictograms they chose

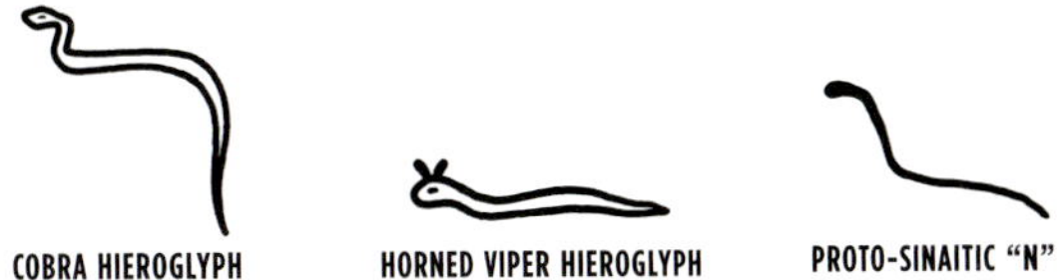

in a completely new way, with no reference to (and no knowledge of) the correct reading of the signs in Egyptian!

Confirming their ignorance of the meaning of Egyptian hieroglyphs, the Canaanite inventors of the alphabet would sometimes conflate two different hieroglyphic pictograms. For example, Egyptian hieroglyphic distinguishes two different kinds of snakes. One sign pictures a cobra generally; the other depicts a horned viper (both signs are shown above). These different pictograms are signs for different sounds in Egyptian, the first for the sound "DG" and for the second, "F." These two snakes are never confused in Egyptian writing. The Canaanite inventors of the alphabet, however, failed to note the distinction and simply conflated the two snakes into a single Proto-Sinaitic sign that they used for the letter "N," from their word for "snake," probably *naḥash* (shown above, far right).

For a few letters, the Canaanites took as models not hieroglyphs, but important objects from their own world.[6] For example, a drawing of the palm of the hand represents "K," *kaf* in Canaanite (see top right on p. 33); there is no pictogram of a palm of the hand in Egyptian hieroglyphic. Similarly with the Proto-Sinaitic sign depicting a composite bow;

AN EVOLVING ALPHABET

HIEROGLYPHIC	PROTO-SINAITIC	PHOENICIAN & PALEO-HEBREW	EARLY GREEK	GREEK	LATIN	MODERN HEBREW
[illegible]	[illegible]	[illegible]	[illegible]	A	A	א
[illegible]	[illegible]	[illegible]	[illegible]	B	B	ב
[illegible]	[illegible]	[illegible]	[illegible]	E	E	ה
	[illegible]	[illegible]	[illegible]	K	K	כ
[illegible]	[illegible]	[illegible]	[illegible]	M	M	מ
[illegible]	[illegible]	[illegible]	[illegible]	N	N	נ
[illegible]	[illegible]	o	o	O	O	ע
[illegible]	[illegible]	[illegible]	[illegible]	P	R	ר
	[illegible]	W	[illegible]	Σ	S	ש
+	+	×	T	T	T	ת

CHARTING THE HISTORY OF THE ALPHABET. The ABCs have come a long way since they were invented more than 3,500 years ago. The workmen of Serabit adapted most of the original Proto-Sinaitic letters from pictographs found in Middle Egyptian hieroglyphs. This easily learned alphabetic script survived relatively unchanged for hundreds of years until, around 1200 B.C.E., a more linear, abstracted script developed among the cities and kingdoms of Iron Age Syria and Palestine. As the alphabet was adopted for Phoenician, Greek and then Latin, the letters became ever more abstracted, and in the end, no longer bore any resemblance to the original pictorial characters invented by the Serabit miners. Modern Hebrew letters (shown at far right) developed through the Aramaic alphabetic tradition, although they retain the names of many of the original Proto-Sinaitic letters.

ALPHA MALE. This Canaanite warrior depicted on the walls of the Beni Hassan tomb carries a compound bow (called a *ša-na-nu-ma* in Canaanite), which was used as the model for the Proto-Sinaitic letter "SH" (see next to last row, second column of chart at left).

SANCTUAIRE D'HATHOR

GARDINER, *INSCRIPTIONS OF SINAI, PART I*

SANCTUAIRE D'HATHOR

INVENTOR OF THE ALPHABET? On one of the Serabit el-Khadem stelae (shown at right), Khebeded, "the brother of the Ruler of Retenu," is shown proudly seated atop a donkey being led by two attendants (see detail and drawing above). While such a depiction would have been considered an insult by most Egyptians, for the Canaanites who labored at the mines, it was a sign of Khebeded's elevated, even royal, status and, most probably, his high rank within the Canaanite workforce. Was he the Canaanite who invented the alphabet?

there is no comparable sign in Egyptian. In Proto-Sinaitic it stands for "SH"; the word for a composite bow in Canaanite was *ša-na-nu-ma* or the like.[7] These examples represent independent creativity on the part of the Canaanite inventors of the alphabet and tend to confirm that they took the Egyptian hieroglyphic signs idiosyncratically and without regard to their function or value in Egyptian.

We might be even more specific about who the inventors of the alphabet were: We may even know their names. They apparently emerged from among the circle of one Khebeded. He is mentioned in several Egyptian hieroglyphic inscriptions at the site and is referred to as the "Brother of the Ruler of Retenu." Retenu was the area between Gaza and the Baqaa in Lebanon. "Ruler of Retenu" was the title carried by rulers in this area of the Levant. When Asiatic rulers migrated to the eastern Delta, it seems that they kept the title "Ruler of Retenu." It is clear that this "Khebeded, brother of the Ruler of Retenu" is a Canaanite. In one stela at Serabit (Stela 112), Khebeded pictures himself proudly riding on a donkey with an attendant both fore and aft. No Egyptian would picture himself riding on a donkey. On another stela at the site, Khebeded is pictured with the typical Canaanite "mushroom" hair dress. From the references in these stelae, it appears that Khebeded was involved with Egyptian expeditions to Serabit for more than a decade. He is clearly the highest-ranking Canaanite who left a hieroglyphic inscription in the Serabit temple. He was probably a leader of the Canaanite workforce.

The quality of the hieroglyphs in an inscription that Khebeded added on a stela (he only added his inscription to an existing stela with much better hieroglyphs) in the temple is very poor. His inscription on Stela 92 would have been an embarrassment for an educated Egyptian scribe (see drawings at bottom of p. 33).[8] Hieroglyphic signs of different sizes are crammed next to each other, and vacant spaces appear at the end of the line. But the hieroglyphic pictograms in Stela 92 bear a remarkable resemblance to the signs in the Proto-Sinaitic inscriptions. Perhaps most striking is the pictogram for "house," (shown on the left below) in the Egyptian hieroglyphic text of Stela 92. The resemblance to the house in the Proto-Sinaitic inscriptions representing *bêt* (shown in the middle at left) is unmistakable and is very different from the original Egyptian hieroglyph (shown on the right at left).

The only Egyptian inscriptions where the square house is consistently used come from this area of Sinai and from the Middle Kingdom. And it appears unequivocally several times in Stela 92, which is probably a hieroglyphic Egyptian text made by Canaanites who were familiar with the Proto-Sinaitic inscriptions. They confused the picture of their own "house"-letter with the correct Egyptian hieroglyph!

The Proto-Sinaitic alphabet may well have been invented in the circle of the Canaanite Khebeded and his followers, many of whose names appear in his stela.

John Darnell, who discovered a two-line inscription in the Wadi el-Hôl (near Thebes) similar to the Proto-Sinaitic inscriptions from Serabit (see box on p. 34), has suggested that the alphabet must have been invented in Egypt in a location with "a plurality of cultural contexts."[9] But isn't "a plurality of contexts" an exact description of

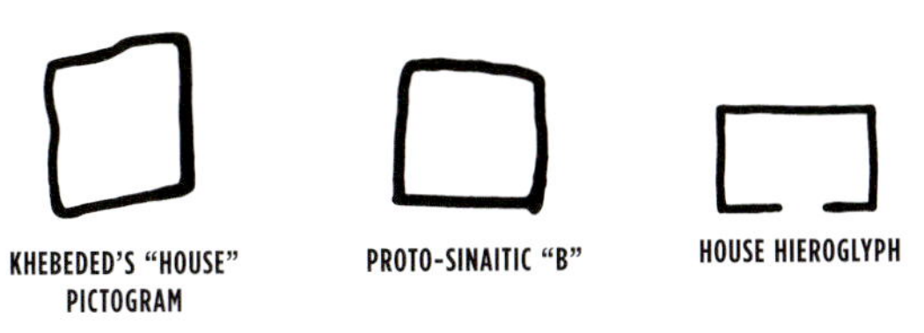

MUSHROOM HAIRDO. This drawing of a hieroglyphic stela inscription (below) shows a procession of Egyptian officials, of whom the Canaanite Khebeded (shown last in line, at left) is depicted with the typical mushroom-shaped headdress sported by "Asiatic" men. The same hairstyle adorns the head of a large monumental statue (right) of a Canaanite ruler found at the Hyksos capital of Avaris (Tell el-Daba) in Egypt's eastern Delta. Together these mushroom hairdos confirm Khebeded's identity as a proud Canaanite.

GARDINER, *INSCRIPTIONS OF SINAI, PART I*

The Wadi el-Hôl Inscription: Earlier than Serabit?

In 1993 Egyptologist John Darnell discovered in the Wadi el-Hôl near Luxor, Egypt, an alphabetic inscription similar to those at Serabit el-Khadem discussed in the accompanying article. Initially, it was thought that this inscription might be earlier than the Serabit inscriptions. If so, was the alphabet invented earlier than the Serabit inscriptions and somewhere other than Serabit, perhaps near the Wadi el-Hôl?

Although there was some early scholarly speculation that this indeed might be the case, this view has now been largely abandoned. The el-Hôl inscription is faintly carved into a limestone wall on the ancient road between Thebes and Abydos. The inscription could be read "(The) besieger עותי, 'El's Trickle,'" (see drawing at upper and lower right).* On the same rock face as this alphabetic inscription are some Egyptian cursive hieroglyphic inscriptions that can be dated paleographically. If the alphabetic inscription can be dated by the date of the Egyptian inscriptions, perhaps we can determine whether Serabit or el-Hôl is earlier. However questionable this dating procedure might be, this is all we have to go on. But even if the hieroglyphic inscriptions are used as a basis for dating the alphabetic inscription at el-Hôl, the latter would be slightly later than alphabetic inscriptions from Serabit. Almost all scholars, including John Darnell, now agree that the adjacent hieroglyphic inscriptions at el-Hôl date to the late Middle Kingdom (18th century B.C.E.). This would place the el-Hôl alphabetic inscription slightly later than the alphabetic inscriptions from Serabit.

The alphabetic inscription from el-Hôl represents an early and slightly deviating version from its origins at Serabit. The el-Hôl inscription exhibits features of influence from the Egyptian writing system, as well as the inscription's Canaanite communicators. Here is an example of each:

In the vertical portion of the el-Hôl text (pictured above right; see drawing at right), the "seated man" sign is used as an unpronounced determinative or classifier; this sign is not a letter, but rather tells the reader that the following word belongs to a particular category or classification [MAN]. This is a typical hieroglyphic characteristic. It is not used in any alphabetic writing system. In this respect, the el-Hôl inscription is not as "purely" alphabetic as the Serabit inscriptions.

The pictorial style of the el-Hôl letters, however, indicates that the Serabit system was communicated (probably by a Canaanite) to the Wadi el-Hôl scribe.

The letter *resh*, for example, (fourth letter from the top) was carved in the shape of a head with the typical Canaanite "mushroom" headdress (see image above left) and does not follow the model of the Egyptian hieroglyphic head (see image above right). Most probably the el-Hôl alphabetic inscription was brought here by some Canaanites who used the typical Canaanite head. After all, it is "their" script.—**O.G.**

PHOTOGRAPH BY BRUCE ZUCKERMAN AND MARILYN LUNDBERG, WS RESEARCH. COURTESY DEPARTMENT OF ANTIQUITIES, EGYPT.

CANAANITE "MUSHROOM" HEADDRESS

EGYPTIAN HIEROGLYPHIC HEAD

	M	מ
	K	כ
	T	ת
	R	ר
	[CLASSIFIER FOR MAN]	
	ʿ	ע
	W	ו
	T	ת
	P	פ
	K	כ
	ʾ	א
	L	ל

*I would like to thank Professor Steve Fassberg, Caspar Levias Chair in Ancient Semitic Languages at the Hebrew University in Jerusalem, for his help in reading the inscription.

Serabit in the Middle Kingdom?

It was indeed a world unto itself. The workers in the mines spent long days and nights in the isolated desert, secluded in their camps. The difficult, dangerous work and the long expeditions no doubt cost lives. The Canaanites watched the Egyptians praying, worshiping and *writing* to the gods. When a name was written, it remained with the god forever. When a blessing was sought, it remained with the god long after the moment of prayer.

The isolation, fear, pressure and the sudden appreciation of "eternalizing the name" would naturally lead the Canaanites to try to write their own calls to their own gods (Baalat and El) in their own language.[10]

Was it the cognitively seductive nature of the hieroglyphic script, with its hundreds of little pictures, that made some Canaanite workers at

Serabit feel that they could "almost read" and that gave them the feeling of "Yes, we can"?

As already noted, the vast majority of the inscriptions in this alphabet come from the Serabit area—more than 30 of them. Only one has come from elsewhere in Egypt (the two-line Wadi el-Hôl inscription). Some few, very short inscriptions (most only a couple of letters) have been found in Canaan dating to the end of the Middle Bronze Age and the Late Bronze Age (c. 1750–1200 B.C.E).

THE ALPHABET WAS NOT an instant success—at least based on the existing examples. One thing is certain: It did not travel fast. Only rarely did a Canaanite caravaneer or soldier bring the alphabet elsewhere. For a half millennium after its invention, this alphabet was rarely used—at least as far as it is reflected in the archaeological record.

As the Semitist Seth Sanders has observed: "In this earliest phase, the alphabet is a quick and dirty tool of foreign workers, scrawled in desolate places: the mines, the gush of terror. There is no high culture there ... The alphabet's first documented use boils down to the most basic and touching form of communication—'I was here.'"[11]

AN HONEST MISTAKE? On another Khebeded stela (two faces of which are shown below and right), our author noted an interesting scribal mistake that suggests the Canaanite prince Khebeded already knew the first alphabet. Although Khebeded wrote this text in Egyptian, many of the hieroglyphic signs he used are either poorly carved or incorrect. One sign in particular (highlighted in orange) bears a remarkable resemblance to the box-like Proto-Sinaitic letter *bêt* (B), rather than its hieroglyphic character. Did Khebeded confuse the new letter *bêt* with the original hieroglyphic "house" sign on whose shape it had been based?

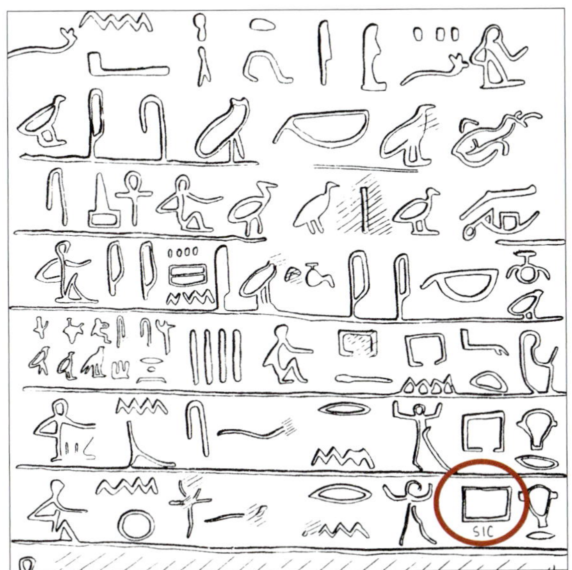

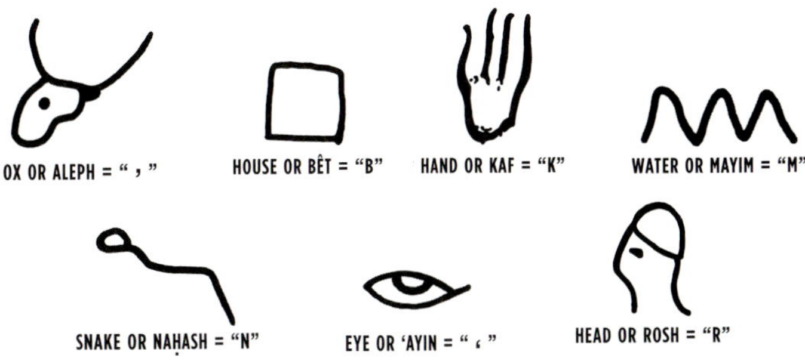

The Middle Kingdom in Egypt was followed by what is known as the Hyksos period (the XVth–XVIIth dynasties: 17th–16th centuries B.C.E.). In the Hyksos period, Canaanites ruled Egypt. (This period is sometimes cited as a model for Joseph's rise to power in Egypt, as described in Genesis 37–47.) As noted earlier, the Hyksos capital at Tell el-Daba has been intensively excavated for almost 40 years by Viennese archaeologist Manfred Bietak and his team. Not a single Proto-Sinaitic inscription has been found there. The Canaanite rulers of Avaris would never adopt such an undeveloped, "primitive," low-class script for their own records. When they presented themselves in inscriptions (which are scarce in Avaris), it was naturally in prestigious Egyptian hieroglyphs.

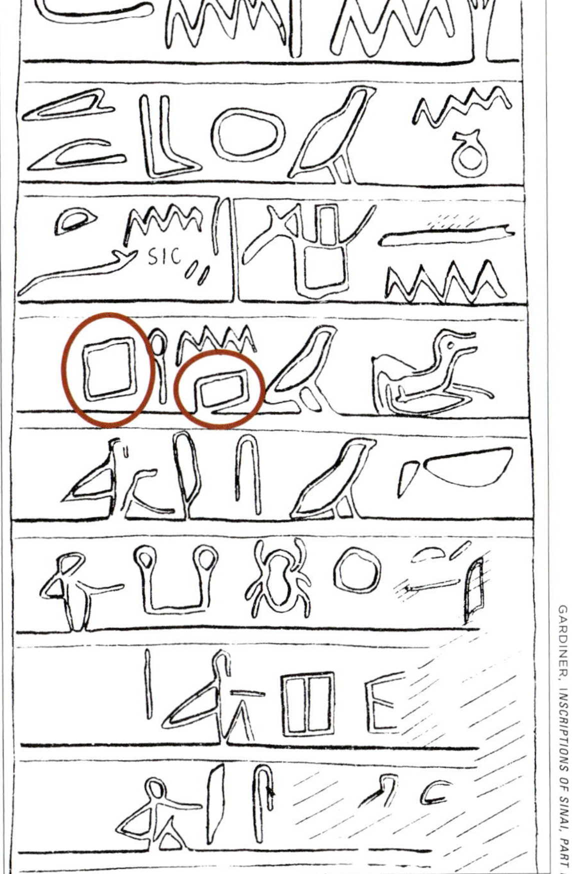

GARDINER, *INSCRIPTIONS OF SINAI, PART I*

A Cuneiform Alphabet at Ugarit

DIFFERENT SCRIPT, SAME ALPHABET. This cuneiform clay tablet found at the ancient Syrian coastal city of Ugarit is in fact impressed with wedge-shaped alphabetic signs. Was the alphabet invented twice?

During the 14th and 13th centuries B.C.E., many of the royal scribes in the Canaanite coastal city of Ugarit (modern Ras Shamra in Syria) were trained in a unique form of the wedge-shaped cuneiform script. Unlike the normal cuneiform script, which includes hundreds of signs, the new Ugaritic script is made up of only a couple dozen.

After studying the script, scholars realized that Ugaritic is, in fact, an "alphabetic" cuneiform script that adapted the techniques of cuneiform writing (i.e., clay tablets, stylus and wedge-shaped signs) to an alphabetic system. Thirty cuneiform characters were used to write all sorts of documents, from letters to literary texts.

Toward the end of the Late Bronze Age, the Ugaritic alphabet spread to Canaan. Single tablets in this special cuneiform script have been found at Canaanite Beth Shemesh, Taanach, Nahal Tabor and other locations.

In Canaan, during the 13th and 12th centuries B.C.E., two alphabetic writing systems lived side by side: the cuneiform Ugaritic alphabet, practiced by educated scribes in the urban centers, and the "script of the caravaneers" born in the mines of Serabit el-Khadem and practiced occasionally and in a limited form (mostly for writing names) by the non-urban Canaanite populations who inhabited the hill country and the urban fringes.

Does this mean that the alphabet was invented again, independently, by the learned scribes in Ugarit, several hundred years after the Canaanite miners of Serabit had already come up with the same idea?

The answer is no. The sophisticated scribes of Ugarit only domesticated the brilliant traveling innovation of the miners and caravaneers of Serabit that they somehow learned. The scribes of Ugarit "translated" what probably looked to them like weird iconic (pictorial) signs into their own "civilized" wedge-shaped script.

The proof that we are not dealing with an independent alphabetic invention is twofold. First, the order of the cuneiform alphabetic signs is essentially the same as the order of the iconic Proto-Canaanite alphabetic signs. Second, the names of the alphabetic cuneiform signs go back to the iconic meanings of the signs of the Proto-Canaanite script.[1] In other words, the names of these wedge-shaped signs are very similar to the names of the Proto-Canaanite pictorial letters, although the Ugaritic cuneiform is not pictorial at all. All this is evidenced in abecedaries like this one found in Ugarit (pictured above).

During the "translation" process, the wedge characters of the Ugaritic script renounced the iconic relationship between the name of the letter and its appearance. In this way, the mnemonic power of the Proto-Canaanite alphabet was completely lost to the Ugaritic scribes.

Ultimately, the cuneiform alphabet of Ugarit disappeared from the historical stage, probably during the 12th century B.C.E. It ceased to exist a few decades after the city-based schools, scribes and institutions that promoted it vanished with the fall of the great Late Bronze Age civilizations.

[1]See Frank Moore Cross and Thomas Lambdin, "A Ugaritic Abecedary and the Origins of the Proto-Canaanite Alphabet," *Bulletin of the American Schools of Oriental Research* 160 (1960), pp. 21–26, now conveniently available in Frank Moore Cross, *Leaves from an Epigrapher's Notebook* (Winona Lake, IN: Eisenbrauns, 2003), pp. 313–316.

As the alphabetic script wandered with Canaanite caravans, it piously retained its pictorial forms for hundreds of years. People learned the letters from one another orally. For this kind of use, the *pictorial* nature of the signs was very important. It was easy to learn the alphabet simply by memorizing the pictures. The first sound of the picture was the letter. To remember the alphabet, all one had to do was memorize the pictures. The rest followed from that: The "name" of the letter leads one to a picture, which helps to recreate the *form* of the letter: At the top of page 33 you can see the ox-shaped head of the letter *aleph*, the box-shaped house (*bêt*) for "B," the hand-like *kaf* for "K," wavy lines representing *mayim* ("water") or "M," the snake-like *naḥash* for "N," the eye for *'ayin* and the head (*rosh*) for "R."

During this early period (until the 13th–12th centuries) the script continued to be used in a very restricted way, mainly to record personal and divine names. No administration, institution or scribal school was involved. No official power-holders would have an interest in sustaining or developing this subversive fringe invention of the nomads. That is probably why individual re-creations of the signs differ so widely, even though they always preserved their fundamental iconicity.

During the 12th century B.C.E., the dominant civilizations that had cultivated the complex hieroglyphic and cuneiform scripts in Egypt and Mesopotamia fell out of power. New peoples—Israelites, Phoenicians, Moabites and Arameans—appeared in Canaan and the Levant. For these new people, emerging on the periphery of the old great cultures, it was only natural to write in the fringe-born system of writing that traveled in their own milieu. It suited their languages, their social needs and their newly established identities.

Sometime during this period of change, the new script must have become institutionalized, maybe even promulgated in schools. As a result, the script quickly underwent a process of linearization and abstraction.[12] More experienced writers could relinquish the pictorial link between the letter and its name. At this stage, the "script of the caravans" lost one of its greater assets: its mnemonic power. From this moment on (12th–11th centuries B.C.E.), the user of the script would have to learn a list of arbitrary signs. It would be difficult if not impossible to find the pictures of a bull, a head or a snake in the script.

During the ninth century B.C.E., the alphabet became the official script of the entire Near East. With its adoption—first for Greek, and later for Latin—the alphabetic script, invented in the milieu of Canaanite miners in the remote Sinai desert, became the script of Western civilization.

The alphabet was invented only once. All alphabetic scripts derive from this original one, which we may call the Serabit alphabetic script.

The invention of the alphabet altered, in the long run, the lives of millions of people for millennia. It was not invented by learned scribes in schools, however. It was the child of a few great minds—perhaps one—who lived among the Canaanites working in the turquoise mines of Sinai. Egyptian hieroglyphs, however, made this invention possible. Through the invention of the alphabet, the long-lost ancient Egyptian hieroglyphs secretively live within our own script to this day. ■

I would like to thank Professors Joseph Naveh and Benjamin Sass, both of whom contributed greatly to my understanding of various aspects of ancient epigraphy treated in this article. Thanks also to Dan Elharrar of the Hebrew University for his invaluable technical assistance in preparing images for this article.

[1] James B. Pritchard, ed., *Ancient Near Eastern Texts Relating to the Old Testament*, 2nd ed. (Princeton: Princeton Univ. Press, 1955), pp. 18–22.

[2] A few very short, similar inscriptions have turned up in Canaan—called Proto-Canaanite—but they are dated later, to the late Middle Kingdom and New Kingdom (17th–16th century B.C.E. at the earliest). See especially the examples of the Shechem plaque, the Gezer sherd and the Lachish dagger in Joseph Naveh, *Early History of the Alphabet: An Introduction to West Semitic Epigraphy and Palaeography*, reprint of 2nd rev. ed. (Jerusalem: Magness Press, 1997), pp. 26–27. See also the Tell Nagila sherd in Gordon J. Hamilton, *The Origins of the West Semitic Alphabet in Egyptian Scripts* (Washington, DC: Catholic Biblical Association of America, 2006), p. 392. Another small, two-line example comes from Wadi el-Hôl (near Thebes) from a wall with Egyptian inscriptions which date to the late Middle Kingdom (late Dynasty XII and Dynasty XIII) and Second Intermediate period. These inscriptions seem also to date a little later than the Sinai inscriptions.

[3] See Orly Goldwasser, "Canaanites Reading Hieroglyphs: Horus Is Hathor?—The Invention of the Alphabet in Sinai," *Egypt & Levant* 16 (2006), pp. 121–160 for a detailed table with all references.

[4] One example is known from an Egyptian inscription in Tell el-Daba and another from Wadi Gasus.

[5] Hamilton, *The Origins of the West Semitic Alphabet in Egyptian Scripts*, p. 84.

[6] See recently Anson F. Rainey, "Review of *The Origins of the West Semitic Alphabet in Egyptian Scripts*, by G.J. Hamilton," *Bulletin of the American Schools of Oriental Research* 354 (2009), p. 85.

[7] Hamilton, *The Origins of the West Semitic Alphabet in Egyptian Script*, p. 242 (after Huehnergard).

[8] Dated to year 13 of Amenemhet III.

[9] John C. Darnell, "Two Early Alphabetic Inscriptions from the Wadi el-Hôl. New Evidence for the Origin of the Alphabet from the Western Desert of Egypt" (together with: Meredith S. Chesson et al., "Results of the 2001 Kerak Plateau Early Bronze Age Survey"), *Annual of the American Schools of Oriental Research* 59 (Boston: American Schools of Oriental Research, 2005), p. 91.

[10] The god El is mentioned at least three times in the Proto-Sinaitic inscriptions in Serabit (Sinai 377, 378, 363), and once in Wadi el-Hôl. The god El plays a central role in the Book of Judges. See recently André Lemaire, *The Birth of Monotheism—The Rise and Disappearance of Yahwism* (Washington, DC: Biblical Archaeology Society, 2007), pp. 14–17.

[11] Seth L. Sanders, "What Was the Alphabet For? The Rise of Written Vernaculars and the Making of Israelite National Literature," *Maarav* 11 (2004), p. 44.

[12] From the 12th century B.C.E., see the Qubur el-Walaydah fragment (northwest Negev) and the Izbet Sartah ostracon in Naveh, *Early History of the Alphabet*, pp. 36–37. For a recently discovered mid-tenth century B.C.E. example, see the Tel Zayit abecedary in Ron Tappy et al., "An Abecedary of the Mid-Tenth Century from the Judaean Shephelah," *Bulletin of the American Schools of Oriental Research* 344 (2006), p. 27. A stratified ostracon carrying a text (probably a letter) dated to the tenth century B.C.E. was also found recently at Khirbet Qeiyafa near Beit Shemesh by Yossef Garfinkel. He identified the site as a Judean city from the time of King David. See "Newly Discovered: A Fortified City from King David's Time," BAR, January/February 2009 and "Prize Find: Oldest Hebrew Inscription Discovered in Israelite Fort on Philistine Border," on p. 51 of this issue. For a different, later dating of these inscriptions, see Benjamin Sass, "The Alphabet at the Turn of the Millennium," *The Journal of the Institute of Archaeology of Tel Aviv Univ*. Occasional Publications No. 4 (2005). However, the dates of these finds are still highly debated.

Anson Rainey, a master of ancient languages and leading historical geographer, responded to Goldwasser's article by engaging her in a lively debate about who really invented the alphabet. It was unfortunately brought to an abrupt end by Rainey's untimely death, but you can read their exchange on the BAS website at biblicalarchaeology.org/alphabet.

For more fascinating questions, responses and corrections that followed in the wake of Goldwasser's article, see the Queries and Comments section of the July/August 2010 and September/October 2010 issues of BAR.

2

In Formation

As gold is tested in fire, the Hebrews were tested in Egypt. Their confrontation with pharaohs and their escape from that land became a formative part of their history, as these articles reflect.

The Exodus from slavery in Egypt was the defining moment in Israel's memory. The time under pharaohs' domination and the subsequent escape to freedom in Canaan is recalled again and again in the Hebrew Bible. These articles shed new light on ancient Israel's relationship with Egypt and the storied journey to the Holy Land.

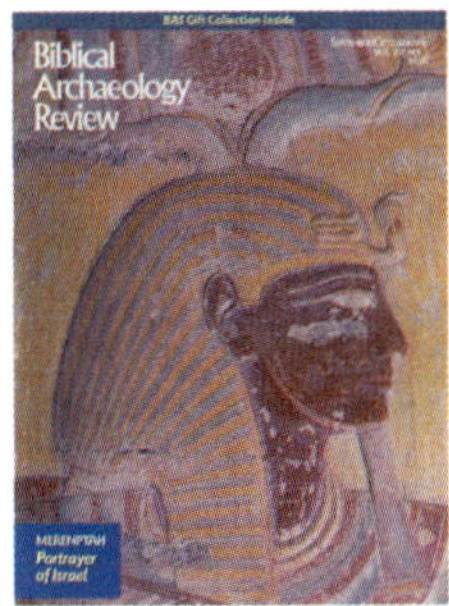

SEPTEMBER/OCTOBER 1990
3200-Year-Old Picture of Israelites Found in Egypt

Pharaoh Merneptah's famous hieroglyphic stele recounts his victories in Canaan against the cities of Ashkelon, Gezer and Yano'am—as well as the people of Israel at the end of the 13th century B.C.E. Slightly overstating the case, Merneptah claims that "Israel is laid waste; his seed is not." This is the earliest known written reference to Israel.

Frank Yurco, a Ph.D. candidate at the University of Chicago and a sometime lecturer at the university's Oriental Institute when he wrote this article, successfully identified reliefs depicting Merneptah's campaign in Canaan on the walls of Karnak's Cour de la Cachette. He described his detective work for BAR readers.

In a response to Yurco's article, Israeli scholar Anson Rainey, while acknowledging Yurco's "brilliant piece of detective work" and agreeing that Yurco had indeed found reliefs of Merneptah's campaign in Canaan, disagreed with Yurco as to which panel identified the Israelites. In a subsequent issue Rainey made the case for his choice of Israelites and Yurco responded, continuing to defend his choice of the panel portraying Israelites.

Yurco died young—in 2004 at 59.

JANUARY/FEBRUARY 1998
Let My People Go and Go and Go and Go

As the title suggests, Avraham Malamat argued that the Exodus was a "durative" event rather than a single "punctual" one: It may have extended over many, even hundreds of, years. Malamat drew on a number of Egyptian analogies to make his case.

JULY/AUGUST 1984
Red Sea or Reed Sea?—How the Mistake Was Made and What *Yam Sûp* Really Means

Just as Malamat gave us a new understanding of the Exodus event, American Bible scholar Bernard Batto gave us a new understanding of the "Red Sea." (If you think you already know it, you are wrong.) The Hebrew term is *yam sûp* (pronounced *yahm soof*). As Batto observes, in some Biblical passages it clearly does refer to the body of water we know as the Red Sea. But sometimes it doesn't, as scholars also recognize. In some modern Bible translations an alternative translation of *yam sûp* is used: the "Sea of Reeds." In instances where *yam sûp* does not refer to the Red Sea, Batto argued, it would more accurately be translated as the "Sea of the End." *Yam sûp* really refers to the end of the world in these instances. This translation significantly enriches our understanding of these passages.

3,200-Year-Old Picture of

JURGEN LIEPE

Israelites Found in Egypt

FRANK J. YURCO

WINTER OF 1976–1977. I WAS in Luxor, in Upper Egypt, site of the ancient city of Thebes. As a member of the University of Chicago's Epigraphic Survey, I was there studying the magnificent reliefs and recording the hieroglyphic inscriptions that almost cover the site.

In my spare time, I would work collecting whatever data I could find that might elucidate the late XIXth Dynasty (1293–1185 B.C.E.*), on which I was then writing my doctoral dissertation. It was in this connection that I found myself regularly studying a set of battle reliefs accompanied by extensive hieroglyphic inscriptions located in the famous Karnak temple.

This particular scene is on the outer western wall of the Cour de la Cachette.[1] The wall itself was originally about 158 feet long and 30 feet high and is composed of blocks about 50 to 63 inches long and 40 inches high. Time, unfortunately, has not been kind to the sculptors who created this monument. Except at the extreme left (north) end, the top of the wall is missing. Three scenes at the right (as one faces the wall) are no longer in place. The Romans took down the blocks forming these scenes, in order to widen the gateway to the right when they removed from Karnak the obelisk now in the Lateran Square in Rome. Sometime after the advent of Christianity, Egyptian Copts built their own structures against the wall and pulled out stones so that the holes thereby created in the wall would support sections of their buildings. Stones from the destroyed scenes of the wall are still strewn about in a field nearby. Fortunately, some of these blocks can be identified with particular locations in the wall.[2]

Near the left side of the wall, between two short engaged pillars that extend several inches from the wall, is a long hieroglyphic text

*B.C.E. (Before the Common Era) and C.E. (Common Era) are the scholarly alternate designations corresponding to B.C. and A.D.

KARNAK, THE GREAT TEMPLE of the god Amun-Re in Thebes, Egypt, appears here in the distance. Under construction for more than 2,000 years, the temple of Karnak is viewed through the hypostyle hall of the Akh-menu temple of Pharaoh Tuthmosis III (1504–1450 B.C.E.) in the foreground. An obelisk of Queen Hatshepsut, located beyond the Karnak sanctuary, is visible on a line with the center of the temple doorway. Flanking the doorway are engaged statues of Tuthmosis III.

According to author Frank J. Yurco, a wall adjoining Karnak's great Hypostyle Hall exhibits reliefs that illustrate the Canaanite campaign of Merenptah, pharaoh of Egypt from 1212 to 1202 B.C.E. Among the vivid portrayals is the oldest known depiction of Israelites, a discovery that may aid in solving the mystery of their origin.

(see photo on p. 44)—the text of the Peace Treaty that followed the great battle of Kadesh, on the Orontes in northern Syria in 1275 B.C.E., between Ramesses II and the Hittite army led by Muwatallis.

To the left of the Peace Treaty text are two battle scenes; to the right, two more. Then, farther to the right are—or were—six more scenes (two of the scenes at the far right are completely gone and must be entirely reconstructed, in part from blocks in the nearby field). The four battle scenes seem to frame the Peace Treaty, two on each side. To the right of these four battle scenes are other scenes that progress from left to right—the binding of prisoners, the collecting of prisoners, marching prisoners off to Egypt, presenting the prisoners to the god Amun, Amun presenting the sword of victory to the king (moving right to left) and finally a large-scale triumphal scene. The scenes stand in two registers, or rows, one above the other, except for the large triumphal scene at the right, which extended all the way from the top to the bottom of the wall. Each of the scenes also contains hieroglyphic inscriptions.

One of the things that especially interested me in the inscriptions was the cartouches—those oblong rings tied at the bottom that enclose the fourth and fifth names of the pharaoh. Both in the reliefs on the wall and on the loose blocks from these reliefs scattered about, all of the names in the cartouches had been usurped—that is, they had been partially erased and recarved with the names of a later king.

The names of the pharaoh that now appear in the cartouches belong to Sety II (1199–1193 B.C.E.). I wanted to look for the names of the earlier pharaoh under the names of Sety II. I should perhaps add that Egyptian pharaohs had five different royal names: The first four were given to him at his coronation: (1) The Horus name (so-called because it begins with a hieroglyph of the Horus falcon); (2) the Two-Ladies name (because it begins with a vulture and a cobra, both representing female goddesses); (3) the Golden-Horus name (because the Horus falcon stands on a symbol for gold); and (4) the prenomen (usually it is compounded with the name of the sun god). The fifth name is the king's personal name given to him at birth. All five names together are called his titulary. Only the fourth and fifth names are enclosed in cartouches. And it was these I especially wanted to examine.

My work with the Epigraphic Survey had provided me with the techniques, training and experience for just such a task. The principal tool in examining usurped cartouches is the mirror. With a mirror you rake the light across the cartouche to deepen the shadows. This makes the carving stand out more sharply. It is not difficult to use this technique on

Understanding the Wall of Reliefs

Now partially destroyed, the western wall of the Cour de la Cachette (right), in the Karnak temple, originally stood 30 feet high and about 158 feet long. Here we see a portion of it, along with a vertical drawing (middle, opposite) that locates the positions of its reliefs and gives page numbers for photos. The plan (bottom, opposite) shows the area as if looking down on it. The dashed lines in the drawings represent reconstructed portions of the wall based on the extant wall and on clues provided by the fallen blocks that lie in the field before the wall. Two rectangular areas from which blocks are missing can be seen in the middle of the wall, at right in the photo; these areas correspond to the first two gray rectangles from the left in the vertical drawing.

The wall adjoins the great Hypostyle Hall (below), partially represented at the left end of the plan. Karnak's great Hypostyle Hall, the largest such hall known from ancient Egypt, features 134 massive pillars. Hypostyle halls formed part of the standard architectural complex of Egyptian temples and symbolized the dense, papyrus-filled marsh, where according to myth, Isis reared young Horus after Seth slew his father Osiris.

At the center of the wall photo (opposite), inscribed between two engaged pillars (the slight projections from the wall's surface), is the Peace Treaty made by Ramesses II (1279–1212 B.C.E.) and the Hittite king Hattusilis III, after some two decades of hostilities over northern Syria. Four carved panels, two on each side of the Treaty, one above the other, depict battle scenes formerly attributed to Ramesses II but now identified as episodes from Merenptah's Canaanite campaign. Scene 4 gives us the oldest known visual portrayal of Israelites. Additional panels to the right of the battle scenes depict the fruits of Merenptah's successful campaign in Canaan.

JURGEN LIEPE

COURTESY OF LAWRENCE E. STAGER

FRANK J. YURCO

PEACE IN THEIR TIME. Filling the space between two engaged pillars—the slightly projecting blocks at left and upper right—this long hieroglyphic text established peace between Ramesses II and the Hittite king Hattusilis III after some two decades of hostilities that included the famous battle at Kadesh, in northern Syria, in 1275 B.C.E. Concluded in the 21st year of Ramesses II's reign (1258 B.C.E.), the Treaty misled earlier scholars into thinking that the four battle scenes, two on each side of the treaty, related to Ramesses II. Although reliefs depicting the battle of Kadesh once stood to the left of the Treaty, they were largely, though imperfectly, erased at some time before Merenptah's battle reliefs were carved. Who erased the Kadesh reliefs is not known, but it is possible that Ramesses II felt that the commemoration of the battle was inappropriate beside the Peace Treaty and therefore ordered his own relief erased.

a stone lying on the ground or even on one on the lower register of the reliefs. It is more difficult standing on a ladder 10 feet above the ground.

The technique employed by the usurping pharaohs—usurpation of cartouches was quite common all over ancient Egypt—was to hammer out and partly erase the original name. Then the surface was coated with plaster. But often the erased surface would first be scored to create a roughness that would better hold the plaster. Finally the new name would be incised in the plaster. Over the centuries, the concealing plaster tends to fall away, leaving visible traces of the carving beneath. In short, the very technique of usurpation often allows the traces to be unscrambled. In many cases, the traces are clearly visible.

This set of battle reliefs has dozens of usurped cartouches. But usurpation was not confined to the cartouches alone; it also appears on the full extended titulary of the pharaoh in the great triumphal scene, which originally was on the far right end of the wall.

The names of the latest versions in these cartouches and in the titulary belonged, as I said, to Sety II. Because of the statements of earlier scholars who had seen the wall, what I expected to see beneath the upper version were the names of Ramesses II. To my surprise, when I began examining these cartouches closely, I discovered they had been twice usurped. The original name had been partially erased; a second name had been incised on plaster that covered the original name; then that name on the plaster had been erased and replaced with the name of Sety II.

It gradually became clear that the name below Sety II was Amenmesse (1202–1199 B.C.E.), perhaps Sety's half-brother. But below the name of Amenmesse was not the expected Ramesses II (1279–1212 B.C.E.), but Merenptah (1212–1202 B.C.E.)!* This, as we shall see, had extraordinary consequences.

From a close examination of the cartouches on these reliefs, on the loose blocks and in the Cour de la Cachette, I could see that Pharaoh Amenmesse had the cartouches of Merenptah hammered out and partly erased. The surface was then coated with plaster, and the usurping names incised. Next, Sety II had the cartouches of Amenmesse partially erased by scraping away the surface of the plaster; he then had his own names incised into the plaster. The original names, those of Merenptah, were carved deepest and at a uniform depth. The first usurper, Amenmesse, carved his signs a little more shallowly. Moreover, these names were cut partially in the stone and partially in the plaster, and the depth varied. Sety II's erasure, by scraping away the name of Amenmesse, was quite thorough, leaving only scant traces of Amenmesse's name. But Sety did not remove Merenptah's name, which had been carved deepest. The net result is that the most visible

*This name is often written "Merneptah." The hieroglyphic signs do not indicate vowels, so either vocalization is possible. The name means Beloved of Ptah. The sign for "of" is the hieroglyphic equivalent of *n*. I believe it much more likely that it was read *en*, rather than *ne*.

Usurped Cartouches Key to Discovery

FRANK J. YURCO

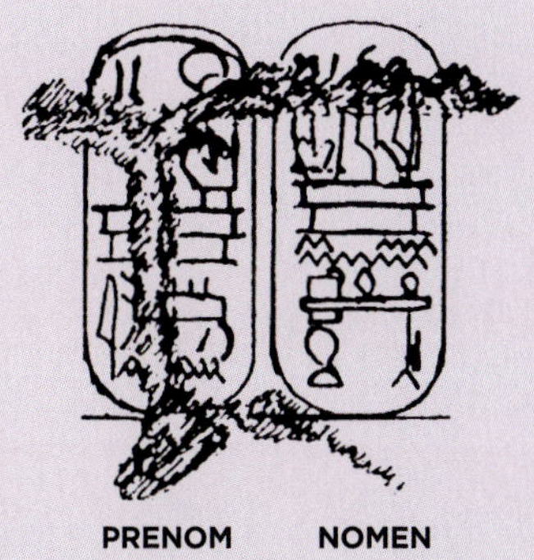

PRENOM NOMEN

SUPERIMPOSED CARTOUCHES

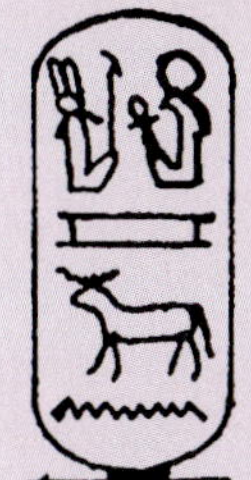
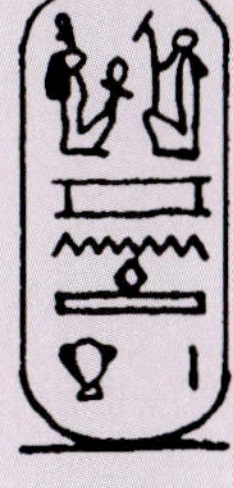

PRENOMEN NOMEN

MERENPTAH

NOMEN

AMENMESSE

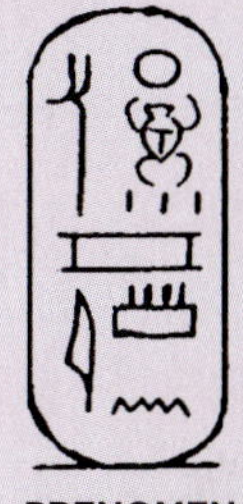
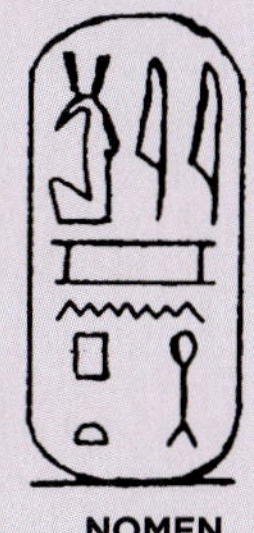

PRENOMEN NOMEN

SETY II

The inscriptions that accompany the reliefs on the Karnak wall actually tell us which pharaoh the scenes glorify, but the vital clues have been partially destroyed and hence long overlooked. The key lies in the inscriptions' cartouches—the oblong rings that enclose the pharaoh's fourth and fifth names (the prenomen and nomen)—which have been usurped, that is, partially erased and recarved with the name of a later pharaoh. Frank Yurco successfully identified the sequence of usurpation by discovering that the original cartouches of Merenptah (1212–1202 B.C.E.) had been usurped by Amenmesse (1202–1199 B.C.E.), whose cartouches were in turn usurped by Sety II (1199–1193 B.C.E.). The usurpation process consisted of shaving and then scoring the earlier cartouche to improve the hold of a coat of plaster, on which the new cartouche could be carved. Fortunately for history, this process failed to entirely obliterate the earlier cartouches, because the shaving did not reach the full depth of the original engraving and the plaster has fallen off in places.

Traces of Merenptah's and Amenmesse's usurped cartouches appear in the cartouches in this detail from scene 2 (upper row, left). The drawings show these cartouches as they appear today (upper row, right) as well as the cartouches of the three pharaohs (Amenmesse's prenomen is omitted because the traces of it are too difficult to read). By comparing the three pharaohs' cartouches to the extant cartouches on this exemplar, we can see that the latter is a composite of elements from the former. Slight remnants of the and of Amenmesse's nomen can be seen in the extant cartouche, the former just above the of Sety II's nomen, and the latter to the left of the of Merenptah's nomen.

Surviving signs from Merenptah's cartouches are more abundant and clear, because they were more deeply engraved than Amenmesse's cartouches. Almost the whole bottom half of Merenptah's nomen is still visible, as well as part of the from the upper portion of his nomen. From Merenptah's prenomen, the legs of the clearly remain below the from Sety II's prenomen.

names now to be seen are those of Merenptah beneath and those of Sety II above.[3]

A small confirming detail is found on a stray block that clearly once fit into scene 10, which depicts the spoils of the campaign being presented by the pharaoh (now almost completely missing from the scene) to the Theban deities (also now missing). The stray block I refer to is lying in the field nearby; it bears the visage of a pharaoh (see photo, p. 46). We have many depictions of Ramesses II, and some of Sety II also, but this visage does not resemble either of them. The closest parallels to this visage are found in the indisputably identified visages of Merenptah from his tomb in the Valley of the Kings, on the other side of the Nile from Thebes. Thus the evidence from the visages reinforces the epigraphic evidence.

What all this demonstrated was that the reliefs represent the military exploits of Merenptah rather than those of Ramesses II. As we will see, this makes a great difference. It will, among other things, allow us to identify the oldest pictures of Israelites ever discovered, engraved more than 3,200 years ago, at the very dawn of their emergence as a people.

Earlier scholars[4] who attributed the battle reliefs to Ramesses II were misled by the Peace Treaty text between Ramesses and the Hittite king Hattusilis III that alone occupied the panel between the pilasters and was framed by the four battle scenes. Moreover, a horizontal hieroglyphic inscription that runs just under the cornice at the top of the wall proclaims that the wall was built by Ramesses II. True, the wall *was* built by Ramesses II, but that does not necessarily mean that all the carvings on the wall are his!

When I carefully examined the two battle scenes to the left of the Peace Treaty text, I found that

FRANK J. YURCO

PORTRAIT OF MERENPTAH. Found at the site, a stray block broken off of the pharaoh's triumphal scene (scene 10) provides additional evidence that Merenptah, rather than Ramesses II, was the pharaoh whose victories the battle scenes portray. The pharaoh pictured on this block does not resemble the numerous depictions of Ramesses II that still exist, but it does closely resemble images of Merenptah from his tomb in the Valley of the Kings, including the painted wall relief from the tomb entrance. The men in both images have a very similar profile.

they were both carved over earlier reliefs, which the later engraver had attempted to erase. The erasure was not very thorough, however, and many traces of the earlier engraving were visible. Whoever had attempted the erasure then used plaster to cover the deeper strokes in the original engraving. By a careful examination, the earlier scene can be identified. It displays a concentration of horses moving to the left with water at the bottom. This combination is well known as the subject matter of the battle of Kadesh of Ramesses II. This material extends, however, only up to the Peace Treaty text, and in any event was covered by the later battle scenes. To the right of the Peace Treaty, the Merenptah reliefs were carved onto a blank, previously uninscribed, wall surface. The erased earlier material under the scenes to the left is clear evidence that Ramesses II had started the decoration of this wall,[5] but did not use the area to the right of the Peace Treaty text.

Accordingly, we can now quite securely date these four battle reliefs—two on each side of the Peace Treaty—to the reign of Merenptah.*

Having done this, the question naturally occurs to any Egyptologist as to whether Merenptah's battle reliefs, as we may now call them, can in any way be related to the famous Merenptah Stele (Cairo no. 34025), one of the major stars in the Cairo Museum. The reason for the extraordinary fame of this stele—even outside the coterie of Egyptologists—is that it contains the earliest known mention of Israel; for that reason it is also known as the Israel Stele.

The Merenptah Stele was discovered by Sir Flinders Petrie** in 1896 in the ruins of Merenptah's funerary temple in western Thebes. Interestingly, a fragmentary duplicate copy of the text, which contains part of the critical lines we will be discussing, was also found inside the Cour de la Cachette, beside the long inscription of Merenptah's victory over Sea Peoples and Libyans in his fifth year, and quite near the very battle reliefs we have just dated to the reign of Merenptah.

The stele in the Cairo Museum, which contains the complete text, stands 7.5 feet high and half that wide. It is made of black granite. Originally it was a stele of Amenhotep III, also known as Amenophis III (1386–1349 B.C.E.). By this time the reader should not be surprised that Merenptah, who demolished Amenhotep III's funerary temple to build his own, also appropriated and reused the reverse side of the stele. The text we are concerned with is carved on the verso, or back, of Amenhotep's stele. In the semicircular top (the lunette) of the verso is a depiction of Merenptah receiving the sword of victory from Amun (twice) with Mut in

*See Kenneth Kitchen, Pharaoh Triumphant (see endnote 5) pp. 215, 220 and fig. 70. In a recent article, Donald B. Redford ("The Ashkelon Relief at Karnak and the Israel Stele" [see endnote 14], pp. 188–200) tried to return to the older viewpoint by claiming that the usurped cartouches on this wall were unreadable, and that the pharaoh's chariot team names are the same as those used by Ramesses II. Both of these arguments and others he poses are based on inadequate study of the reliefs and Ramesside sources in general, and on a serious underestimate of epigraphic work; moreover, the usurpation sequence on this wall in some cartouches is unambiguous (for example, in scene 2; see box, p. 47). See further, my response to Redford, in Yurco "Once Again, Merenptah's Battle Reliefs at Karnak," *IEJ*, forthcoming.

**See Joseph A. Callaway, "Sir Flinders Petrie: Father of Palestinian Archaeology," BAR, November/December 1980.

THE MERENPTAH STELE, in the Cairo Museum, bears the oldest known written reference to Israel. Engraved with its current text in 1207 B.C.E., the 7.5-foot-high, black granite monolith was discovered in the ruins of Merenptah's funerary temple in western Thebes in 1896. Most of its hieroglyphic text celebrates Merenptah's defeat of the Libyans and their Sea Peoples allies in his fifth regnal year. The text's last two lines, however, briefly mention an earlier, successful campaign into Canaan, including four victories that seem to be depicted on the Karnak wall: "Ashkelon has been overcome. Gezer has been captured. Yano'am was made non-existent. Israel is laid waste, (and) his seed is not." The mention of Israel (see detail below) appears slightly to the left of center in the second line from the bottom. The glyphs include determinatives—signs indicating a word's category—that classify Ashkelon, Gezer and Yano'am as city-states; but the determinative attached to Israel identifies it as a people, apparently not yet possessing a distinct city. This classification corresponds to Merenptah's four battle scenes on the Karnak wall, the first three of which show besieged cities, while the fourth shows a people fighting in open country. Moreover, the first battle relief depicts Ashkelon, the first victory named in the stele. Further support for this correspondence comes from the location of a fragmentary duplicate of the stele text, including the description of the Canaanite campaign, discovered inside the Cour de la Cachette, near the battle reliefs.

FRANK J. YURCO

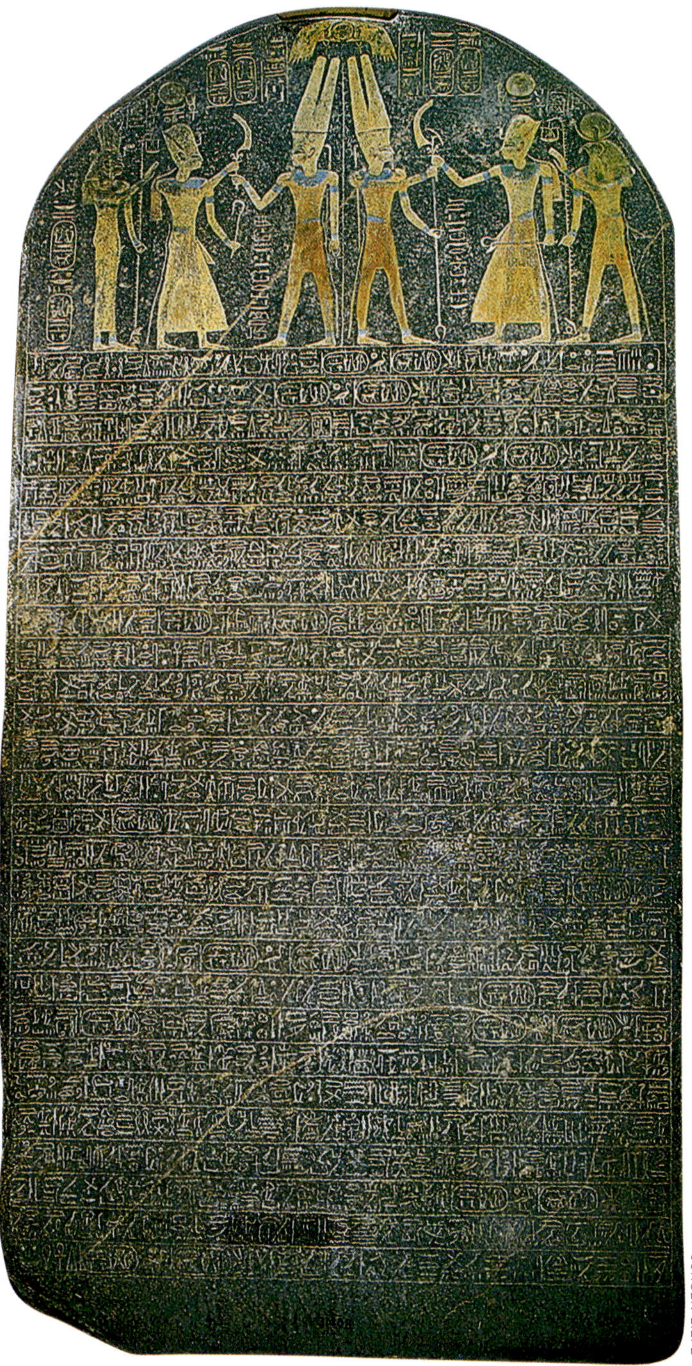

JURGEN LIEPE

attendance at the left and Khonsu at right. Carved in Merenptah's fifth regnal year, the text as a whole records Merenptah's overwhelming defeat of the Libyans and their Sea Peoples allies. But Merenptah also alludes retrospectively to an earlier campaign he conducted into Canaan.

This retrospective allusion, in the last two lines of the hieroglyphic text, reads as follows (the critical portions have been italicized):

"The princes, prostrated, say 'Shalom';
None raises his head among the Nine Bows.
Now that Tehenu has come to ruin, Hatti is pacified.
Canaan has been plundered into every sort of woe.
Ashkelon has been overcome.
Gezer has been captured.
Yano'am was made non-existent.
Israel is laid waste (and) his seed is not.
Hurru has become a widow because of Egypt.
All lands have united themselves in peace.
Anyone who was restless, he has been subdued by the King of Upper and Lower Egypt,
Ba-en-Re-mery-Amun, son of Re, *Mer-en-Ptah*
Hotep-her-Ma'at, granted life like Re, daily."†

This text was long dismissed by some scholars as simply a literary allusion with little basis in fact, a kind of poetic hyperbole.[6] Other scholars hesitantly granted it some historical value, especially because Merenptah took the title "Subduer of Gezer." He would be unlikely to adopt this title, obviously intended to reflect his achievements, if it were not soundly based on fact.[7]

The connections we are about to make strongly

† The poetical versification is my own, with the advice of Dr. Edward F. Wente of the University of Chicago.

buttress the conclusion that the description of Merenptah's campaign in Canaan was actually based on solid fact.

The first thing I noticed when I began to consider whether there is any connection between the battle reliefs in the Karnak temple and the campaign in Canaan described on the Merenptah Stele was that one of the four battle scenes (the one to the bottom right of the Peace Treaty, which I number scene 1) contains a hieroglyphic identification of the site of the battle: Ashkelon. Ashkelon is also mentioned in the Merenptah Stele: "Ashkelon has been overcome"! Was the appearance of a battle at Ashkelon on the wall of the Karnak temple and a reference to a battle at Ashkelon in the Merenptah Stele merely a coincidence? I searched the other three battle scenes for identification of the sites, but there is none—or at least none has been preserved.

But this brought to my attention another "coincidence." On the wall of the Karnak temple, Merenptah had four battle scenes carved (two on each side of the Peace Treaty); one of the battle scenes could be identified as Ashkelon. In the Merenptah Stele, four names appear to identify his victories in Canaan. One of them is identified as Ashkelon.

The other three victories mentioned in Merenptah's Stele are Gezer, Yano'am and Israel. Might it be possible to identify the other three battle scenes with these three designations?

Notice that I have not referred to the four designations in the Merenptah Stele as sites, or places or even geographical locations. Although I could characterize Ashkelon, Gezer and Yano'am in this way, that is not true in the same sense with respect to Israel.

Moreover, this difference is emphasized in the hieroglyphic text of Merenptah's Stele. Hieroglyphic writing consists not only of signs that have phonetic value—that is, are to be pronounced or vocalized—but it also includes other signs that have no phonetic value and are not intended to be vocalized. Their sole function is to indicate the category or kind of word to which they are attached. This kind of hieroglyphic sign is called a determinative.

The determinative used in the Merenptah Stele with the names of the three Canaanite city-states—Ashkelon, Gezer and Yano'am—is the familiar determinative regularly used for city-states that formed the Egyptian empire in Syria-Palestine during the New Kingdom period (1570–1070 B.C.E.). It is written like this: [hieroglyph] or [hieroglyph]. The name of Israel, however, is written on Merenptah's Stele using a different determinative [hieroglyph]—that is usually reserved for peoples without a fixed city-state area, or for nomadic groups.

This is especially noteworthy because Merenptah's scribes were very careful in their use of determinatives in their other inscriptions made during year five of his reign, which describe the defeated Libyans and Sea Peoples.[8]

As the case for a connection between Merenptah's battle reliefs in the Karnak temple and the victories described in Merenptah's Stele began to look stronger, I looked for further parallels between the battle scenes, on the one hand, and the description in the stele, on the other.

The next thing I noticed was that the relief of the battle of Ashkelon (scene 1; opposite) showed the siege of a fortified town. The pharaoh's horse and chariot team are at the far right, with the enemy fortress at the left in a balancing position. A siege ladder can be seen resting against the town wall, which has a crenelated top. The two battle reliefs to the left of the Peace Treaty also depict sieges of fortified towns, also with crenelated tops of walls (see photos, pp. 50–51).

The fourth battle scene, to the right of the Peace Treaty and above the siege of Ashkelon, is, unfortunately, only about half preserved (see photos, p. 52 The upper half is missing. Nevertheless, it is clear that it is a battle against an enemy without a fortified town. We can deduce this from the position of pharaoh's horse and chariot team. Egyptian battle scenes follow a standard compositional sequence, and this scene falls into the genre type of battle scene without an enemy fortress.[9] (Incidentally, the inscriptions, rather than the scenes, give the depictions their individual identity and historical context.)[10]

The fourth battle scene in the wall can be usefully contrasted with the relief of the siege of Ashkelon. In the latter, pharaoh's horse and chariot on the right are balanced by a carving of the fort of Ashkelon on the left, with a siege ladder resting against the wall

ASHKELON UNDER SIEGE. The first city to fall to Merenptah's onslaught, according to the Merenptah Stele, was Canaanite Ashkelon, which appears in scene 1 (photo and drawing opposite) on the lower right side of the Peace Treaty, on the Karnak wall. Men and women on top of the fortified city's crenelated walls—seen on the first complete block from the left on the second course from the top—seem to be appealing to heaven. Meanwhile, children are being lowered (or perhaps dropped as a sacrifice) from the tower on each side. Below them, an Egyptian soldier climbs the wall on a ladder as the battle rages before the city gate. Pharaoh and his chariot team, drawn on a larger scale to reflect pharaoh's importance, appear on the right side of the scene; this balance between the besieged city on the left and the large pharaoh on the right is an artistic convention that is also used in scenes 2 and 3 (see photos, pp. 50–51). The hieroglyphic text, to the right of the ramparts, identifies the city in this scene as Ashkelon. The two intact rectangular blocks in the top course bear the lower portion of the scene with the Israelites (see detail, pp. 52–53).

COURTESY OF LAWRENCE STAGER

FROM *ATLAS ZUR ALTAGYPTISCHEN KULTURGESCHICHTE* BY W. WRESZINSKI

FRANK J. YURCO

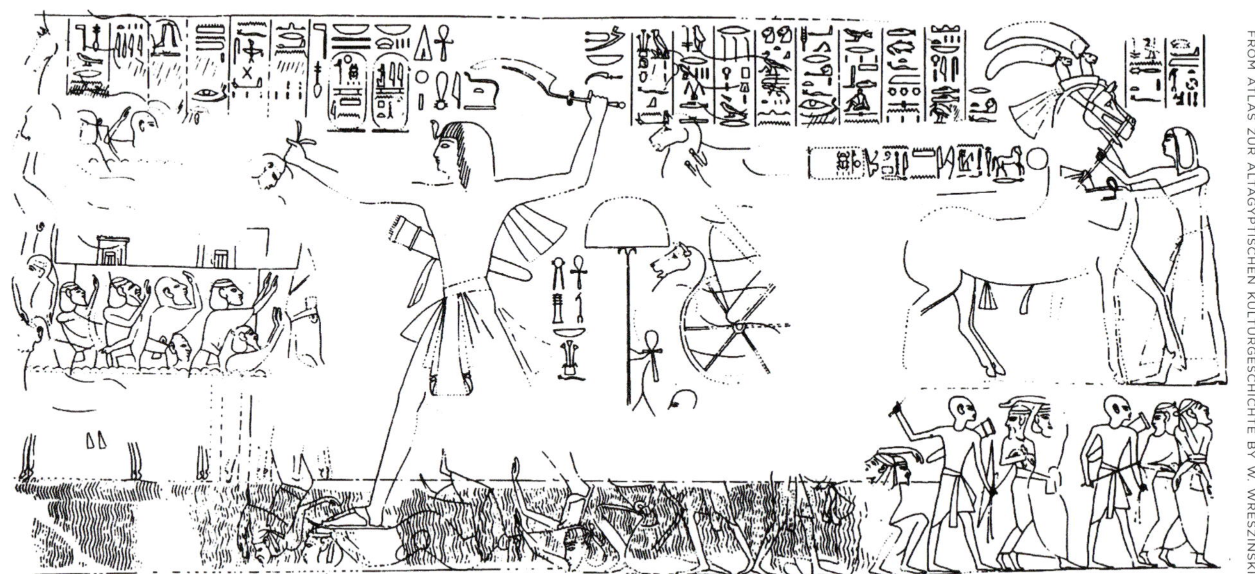

FROM ATLAS ZUR ALTAGYPTISCHEN KULTURGESCHICHTE BY W. WRESZINSKI

GEZER AND YANO'AM SUCCUMB. Although unnamed in the reliefs, the besieged cities in scene 2 (photo and drawing, above) and scene 3 (photo and drawing, opposite) are probably Gezer and Yano'am respectively. The Merenptah Stele (see photo, p. 47) lists these as the second and third of Merenptah's conquests during his Canaanite campaign.

In scene 2, a gigantic image of pharaoh tramples the enemy and threatens the defenders atop the walls of Gezer, at the left end of the two central courses. In scene 3, the Canaanites tumble like bowling pins beneath the enormous underbelly and legs of pharaoh's chariot team. The crenelated walls of Yano'am appear at upper left.

These scenes stand to the left of the Peace Treaty, on panels that formerly held reliefs of Ramesses II's battle at Kadesh. Someone, either Ramesses II's men or Merenptah's, imperfectly erased the Kadesh battle reliefs, leaving behind many traces, including water represented by the wavy lines at the bottom of scene 2. (Because scene 3 stands directly above scene 2 in the wall, the top portion of scene 2 is visible at the bottom of the photo of scene 3.)

Like the relief of the Ashkelon battle, these scenes depict besieged cities on the left side balanced by pharaoh and his forces on the right. This composition contrasts sharply with scene 4 (see photo, pp. 52-53), identified by the author as the battle with the Israelites, in which pharaoh and his men fight in the middle of the cityless enemy.

FRANK J. YURCO

FROM *ATLAS ZUR ALTAGYPTISCHEN KULTURGESCHICHTE* BY W. WRESZINSKI

FRANK J. YURCO

PAUL HOFFMAN/COURTESY OF LAWRENCE E. STAGER

FRANK J. YURCO

and two children being let down from the wall. In the fourth battle scene, by contrast, although only half of it is preserved, we see pharaoh's horse and chariot team directly in the center of the picture. There is no balancing enemy fortress at the left, nor could there be even in the missing upper half of the scene, for there would simply be no room for it before the front hooves of pharaoh's charging chariot team. In contrast to the other three battle scenes, this scene depicts a battle with an enemy in open country with low hills.

This battle scene matches the description of Israel in the Merenptah Stele text, where it is written [hieroglyphs] (*Ysr3l*), with the determinative [hieroglyphs] signifying a people without a city-state, as contrasted with the names for Ashkelon, Gezer and Yano'am, all three of which are written with the determinative [hieroglyph] or [hieroglyph], signifying a specific city-state. The other three battle reliefs on the Karnak temple all have fortresses that are besieged by the king, the first of which is specifically identified as the town of Ashkelon. So there is a perfect match between the text of Merenptah's Stele and Merenptah's reliefs. Ashkelon, Gezer, Yano'am and Israel, named in the stele, match three fortified towns and one battle in open country in the reliefs.

If you look at Ashkelon, Gezer and Yano'am on a map, you will see that they lie on a south-to-north progression from the coastal plain into the hill country, where the Israelites lived (although

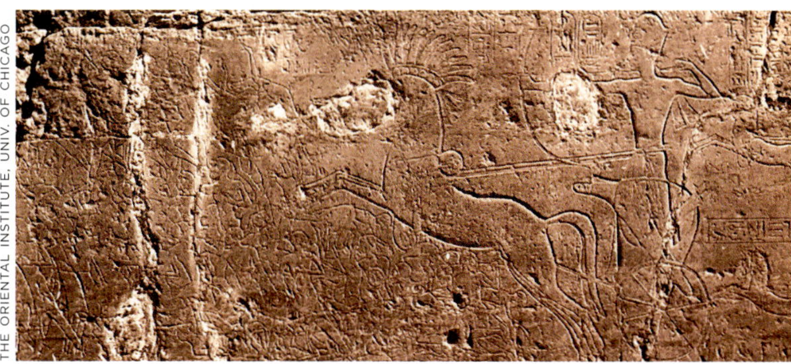

THE ORIENTAL INSTITUTE, UNIV. OF CHICAGO

"ISRAEL IS LAID WASTE," Merenptah boasted in his famous stele and also illustrated in scene 4 on the Karnak wall. Although more than half destroyed, this scene exhibits important differences from the other three battle reliefs of Merenptah's Canaanite campaign. The rear legs of pharaoh's chariot team, once again drawn on a larger scale, appear at right (above) in a rearing stance. If the scene were complete, pharaoh's horse would be seen looming over the confused jumble of Israelite soldiers, left, and the Israelite chariot, center, in a manner similar to a relief in the Beit el-Wali temple of Ramesses II (above, right). Unlike the other three battle reliefs on the Karnak wall, this scene contains no city; even if the relief were complete, there would be no room for a city. Instead, the battle takes place in the open in a somewhat hilly countryside, a setting that fits the non-urbanized Israelite tribes of the time.

Merenptah probably conducted his Canaanite campaign sometime between 1211 and 1209 B.C.E. If author Yurco's analysis is right, scene 4 gives us the oldest known visual portrayal of Israelites, more than 600 years earlier than the oldest previously known depictions (showing the conquest of Lachish in reliefs on the wall of the Assyrian king Sennacherib's palace at Nineveh), and only about 40 years after the time when the Israelites are thought to have emerged as a distinct group. The early date and the Israelites' manner of dress combine to provide an important clue to Israelite origins. The Israelites in the scene clearly wear ankle-length clothes, best seen in the half-destroyed standing figures on the left side of the drawing (opposite). This style of dress resembles that of the Canaanites in the other battle scenes, but differs substantially from the dress of the Shasu in some of the nonbattle scenes (see photo and caption, p. 55). This suggests that the Israelites may have derived, at least in part, from Canaanite society.

the site of Yano'am is a matter of some dispute). This parallels the whole narrative sequence of Merenptah's Karnak reliefs, for Ashkelon is shown in the first scene, two other cities in the next scenes (which I propose are Gezer and Yano'am) and an open battle in low hills in the last scene (which I propose is Israel). This same sequence of scenes—from right to left in the bottom register, followed by left to right in the top register—is attested elsewhere in New Kingdom narrative relief.[11]

It seems clear that Merenptah originally had these reliefs commissioned and carved to represent and commemorate his Canaanite campaign as described retrospectively in the Merenptah Stele!

If I am correct, then the enemy men depicted in the fourth battle scene are Israelites! These depictions are by far the earliest visual portrayals of Israelites ever discovered, dating to the late 13th century B.C.E. The next time we see Israelites in a visual depiction is over 600 years later, on the wall of Sennacherib's palace in Nineveh, where reliefs depict the siege and conquest of the Israelite city of Lachish, with the defeated Israelites being executed, or led to exile in Assyria.*

The most significant aspect of the depiction of the Israelites in the battle scene at Karnak is that they wear the same style of dress as Canaanites in the scenes of Ashkelon, Gezer and Yano'am. The Israelites are wearing ankle-length cloaks, just like the Canaanites. In short, the Israelites are identified pictorially as Canaanites in the Merenptah reliefs and textually as Israel in the Merenptah Stele. This may well have considerable historical significance, especially because the Canaanite—and therefore the Israelite—dress is distinctly different from the dress of the people known as Shasu, often associated with Israelite origins, who are also depicted in the Merenptah reliefs on the wall of the Karnak temple, but not in the battle scenes.

The Shasu are traditional Bedouin-type foes of Egypt. In one well-known papyrus, *Papyrus Anastasi* 1, Shasu are reported as being found all over Canaan, but particularly in the forested and wild hill-country.[12] In Merenptah's reign, as we know from another papyrus (*Papyrus Anastasi* VI), Shasu were found in southern Canaan and in Sinai. This papyrus is a frontier official's journal mentioning a peaceful migration of Shasu shepherds into the Delta for the purpose of watering their flocks.[13]

*See Hershel Shanks, "Destruction of Judean Fortress Portrayed in Dramatic Eighth-Century B.C. Pictures," BAR, March/April 1984.

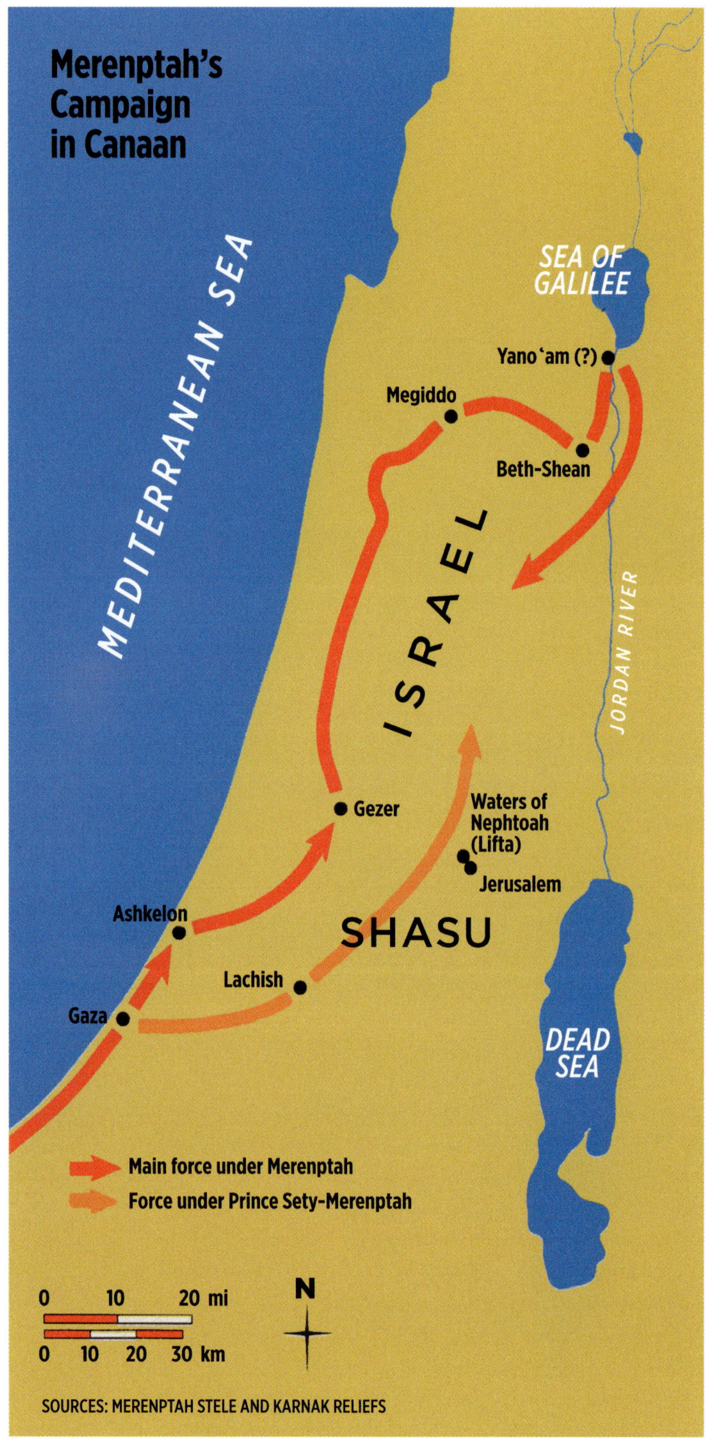

As they were wont to do, some others of these Shasu undoubtedly harried Merenptah's army as it was en route to subdue the Canaanite cities and Israel. They were defeated, of course, and some were captured, as we are told in the hieroglyphic text. In the carvings, we see Shasu prisoners in some of the reliefs to the right of the battle scenes on the Karnak temple wall. In scene 5 we see enemy Shasu being bound. Scene 7 depicts a file of Shasu prisoners being marched off to Egypt before and under pharaoh in his chariot. A vertical line of text separates scene 7 from scene 8 and translates in the surviving part, "rebels who had fallen to trespassing his boundary." In scene 8 another file of Shasu are depicted, above them a horizontal line of text reading "consisting of the Shasu whom his majesty had plundered." Above this text, just enough of the block remains to show that here was a file of Canaanite prisoners, readily distinguishable from the Shasu by their long, ankle-length cloaks. The Shasu, by contrast, wear short kilts and distinctive turban-style headdresses.

The Shasu were not the major focus of Merenptah's campaign in Canaan, and so they were given a secondary representation in the Karnak reliefs of the campaign, and they are not referred to at all in the Merenptah Stele.

According to some scholars, the Shasu formed the core of the people who became Israelites when they settled in the hill country of Canaan beginning in the late 13th to the 12th centuries B.C.E. The evidence from the Karnak reliefs contradicts the position taken by scholars who have tried to identify the Israelites with the Shasu.[14] The Karnak temple reliefs seem to suggest that at least some of the early Israelites coalesced out of Canaanite society, albeit Canaanites who did not live in the cities but who had withdrawn to the hill country, precisely where archaeological remains as well as Biblical texts place them.*

The attribution of these battle reliefs at Karnak to Merenptah puts Merenptah's campaign into Canaan on a firm historical footing. Moreover, the reliefs provide striking confirmation of accumulating archaeological evidence that the initial Israelite settlements were in the highlands and that they were in open, dispersed villages with no substantial fortified towns. Nonetheless the Israelites had already begun to disturb the settled towns under Egyptian suzerainty, and thus provoked a response from Merenptah. Whereas Egyptian control of the highlands was previously limited, this time Merenptah penetrated the hill country in force and there found the settlements of the Israelites. Judging by the name he recorded for them on the Merenptah Stele, they were already calling themselves Israel in about 1211 to 1209 B.C.E., the time frame of Merenptah's Canaanite campaign. This is the first extra-Biblical use of the name Israel.

A small detail suggests that the Israelites had been attacking the settled towns. In the scene representing the battle with the Israelites, there appears a chariot with wheels with six spokes that belongs to

*See "Israel's Emergence in Canaan—BR Interviews Norman Gottwald," *Bible Review*, October 1989.

FRANK J. YURCO

WERE SHASU ISRAELITES? A nomadic, Bedouin-type people of Canaan and Sinai, the Shasu traditionally opposed the Egyptians and probably harried Merenptah's army on its march. Merenptah took some Shasu prisoners who are shown in several scenes to the right of the battle scenes on the Karnak wall. Scene 5 (left) shows pharaoh, left, binding two Shasu prisoners, kneeling at lower right. (The gouges that deface this scene were caused by later Egyptians who, believing in the magical efficacy of the temple reliefs, scraped at the walls over the years, perhaps mixing scrapings in water and drinking them, a practice that has been observed at another site even in modern times.) In scene 7 (below), Shasu prisoners march off to Egypt; as enemies of Egypt, they are conventionally represented diminutively, dwarfed by the colossal legs of their captors' horses, center and right.

Some scholars have identified the Shasu with the Israelites, but the Merenptah reliefs at Karnak contradict that conclusion. The Israelites in scene 4 dress like the Canaanites, wearing ankle-length clothes, whereas the Shasu wear short kilts and turban-like headdresses, visible in the figures in scene 7.

FRANK J. YURCO

the pharaoh's enemy, that is, Israel! How could the early Israelites have gotten possession of chariots, once thought to be the exclusive possession of Israel's enemies such as the Canaanites? (In Judges 4–5, for example—which records a battle involving Jabin, king of Canaan; Sisera, his general; and the Israelite prophetess Deborah, who defeated the Canaanites—the Canaanites have all the chariots.) Perhaps the Israelites got chariots like the one depicted in their battle with Merenptah by raids on Canaanite towns. However, it is also possible they got them through an alliance with some of the Canaanite towns that Merenptah attacked or that feared such an attack.

These battle reliefs not only corroborate the historicity of Merenptah's campaign into Canaan, but they also shed some light on the precise date of that campaign. Scholars have of course considered these questions on the basis of the Merenptah Stele alone, and, as I have said, have raised some questions as to whether the campaign actually took place. The passage referring to Merenptah's campaign in Canaan is at the very end of the text, in the poetic conclusion of the stele. That this conclusion is so carefully laid out and very precisely arranged geographically also supports the conclusion that the text indeed has a historical basis. The outer verses refer to the broader international situation involving Libya (Tehenu) and the Hittite empire (Hatti). The inner verses balance a description of Canaan and Hurru, the two major components of Egypt's Syro-Palestinian realm.[15] The text for Canaan is further broken down into the three city-states and Israel. So, the breakdown neatly delimits the area of Merenptah's military activity—it is all within Canaan. Finally, Canaan and Hurru are poetically couched in terms of husband and wife. Such careful and neat geographical structure does not usually appear in fictional military campaigns.

The Merenptah Stele also contains a date for the inscription of the stele, the fifth year of Merenptah's reign. Merenptah ruled between 1212 and 1202 B.C.E., so his campaign into Canaan must have occurred between 1212 and 1207 B.C.E., the latter being the date of the Merenptah Stele.

Remember that the main subject of the Merenptah Stele is the Libyan campaign and his battle with the Sea Peoples. His Canaanite campaign is mentioned in the stele only retrospectively. This Libyan campaign too must have occurred by 1207 B.C.E. This campaign is also commemorated on a wall of the Karnak temple, but only with a long text and a triumphal scene,[16] and even these appear on an interior wall. War scenes generally occupied external walls of temples. The reason Merenptah's important Libyan campaign is depicted only with a triumphal scene and even this only on an interior wall, despite the fact that the Libyan campaign was a far more momentous victory than his Canaanite campaign, is that Merenptah had already used the last exterior space of the temple for the scenes of his Canaanite campaign. This confirms that the Canaanite campaign occurred before year five of his reign. In a lengthy, technical discussion based on a change in Merenptah's prenomen, I have excluded year one of Merenptah for this Canaanite campaign.[17] In another somewhat technical paper,[18] I concluded that the Canaanite campaign took place in year two, or early in year three. Briefly, no document of Merenptah dated year two or early year three demands his presence inside Egypt in that time span, so those are the narrowest limits within which the campaign may presently be dated. This corresponds to 1211–1209 B.C.E., and this therefore marks the first attested date for Israel outside the Biblical record.

To judge by his mummy, Merenptah was between 60 and 70 years old when he organized and led his Canaanite campaign and organized the defense of Egypt against the Libyans and the Sea Peoples in his fifth year.[19] Professor Donald Redford, of the University of Toronto, has belittled Merenptah's ability to lead a campaign of any importance into Canaan in his supposedly "decrepit"[20] condition. This argument is nothing short of ridiculous considering that Merenptah, even after his Canaanite campaign, organized Egypt's defense against Nubian, Libyan and Sea Peoples onslaughts in his fifth year. As to the age issue, General Douglas MacArthur was 70 years old when he led the attack on Inchon in Korea in 1950. Moreover, like MacArthur, Merenptah was a military man and a general.

It is true that Merenptah's mummy shows us an individual who was in poor physical condition at death. Yet that was five years after the Nubian, Libyan and Sea Peoples defensive operation, and seven to eight years after the Canaanite campaign.

After Merenptah's death, in 1202 B.C.E., competing branches of the royal family engaged in a bitter struggle for the throne. All the usurpation of cartouches and titularies in the reliefs is symptomatic of the struggle for the throne between different branches of the descendants of Ramesses II. This usurpation occurred not only in the reliefs we have been discussing, but also elsewhere in the Cour de la Cachette and in the entire temple of Karnak.[21]

Nevertheless, Egypt's control over Canaan, apparently solidified by Merenptah's campaign, seems, if anything, to have tightened rather than slackened between Merenptah's time and the reign of Ramesses III (1182–1151 B.C.E.) of the XXth Dynasty. Under Ramesses III, tax collection was instituted and substantial administrative centers were built at a number of locations.[22]

In addition, artifacts bearing the names of Merenptah or his successors in the XIXth Dynasty have been discovered in numerous excavations of Canaanite sites, providing further testimony of undisputed Egyptian control strengthened by Merenptah's campaign. Gezer[23] and possibly Lachish[24] have yielded objects naming Merenptah. At Gezer, a destruction level dated to Late Bronze II B (1300–1200 B.C.E.) probably is the work of Merenptah's campaign.[25] Sety II's name is attested at Tell el-Fara (South),[26] at Tell Beit Mirsim[27] and possibly at Tel Masos.[28] The names of other Egyptian rulers from this time are attested at Acco,[29] Beth Shemesh[30] and Deir 'Alla (Jordan).[31]

In addition, a papyrus (*Papyrus Anastasi* III) dated to Merenptah's third year[32] shows the Egyptians in possession of strategic places in the highlands of Canaan very shortly after the Canaanite campaign.

All of this suggests the following scenario: By this campaign, Merenptah reaffirmed Egyptian dominion over the Canaanite coastal towns and northern Canaan. His Transjordanian vassals, previously conquered by Ramesses II,[33] did not invite attack and so probably remained loyal. The chief trouble was found to be in the hill country west of the Jordan, where the Israelites had been settling in considerable numbers.[34] Very probably enboldened by the long period of quiet and absence of military activity that marked the last phase of Ramesses II's reign, some of these Israelites, now coalescing into a group identifying itself as Israel, attempted to penetrate into the lowlands held by Canaanite vassals of pharaoh.[35] Some of these vassals may have thrown their lot in with the Israelites, even enabling the Israelites to get some chariots. Pharaoh Merenptah, however, was not willing to let Canaan slip away, so that after he had dealt with the rebelling vassals on the coast and inland, he turned to the hill country and dealt a heavy blow to the Israelites.

The defeat must have been quite heavy to emerging Israel, for the Israelites could not take advantage of the struggle between Merenptah's successors. Ramesses III then imposed a tight Egyptian hold on Canaan, which was not broken until Sea Peoples (including Philistines) settling in Canaan weak ened the Egyptian hold sufficiently for the Israelites to begin to overcome the Canaanite strongholds. But this occurred only in the 12th century B.C.E., after the death of Ramesses III (1151 B.C.E.). Merenptah thus delayed Israel's emergence onto the lowland areas for at least a generation.

One final note: There may be a garbled reference to Merenptah's Canaanite campaign in the Bible itself. Joshua 15–19 records the allotment of the land to the various tribes. In Joshua 15:9, the border of Judah near Jerusalem is drawn from a hilltop at the northern end of the Valley of Rephaim to "the spring of the waters of Nephtoah" and then goes on to the cities of Ephraim. In Joshua 18:15, the southern boundary of Benjamin is drawn west from Kiriath-jearim "to the spring of the waters of Nephtoah." These Hebrew passages probably refer to a well, or spring, at Lifta near Jerusalem.

It is possible that Nephtoah in both of these Biblical references is actually a garbled version of Merenptah's name. *Papyrus Anastasi* III, which I mentioned above, dates from Merenptah's third year and describes the Egyptians as possessing strategic places in the highlands of Canaan; it also tells of the arrival of a military commander at Sile, coming from "the Wells of Merenptah-hotphima'e which are in the hills."[36]

The spring referred to in Joshua 15 and 19 is probably the same place: The Egyptian papyrus indicates there was a place in the highlands of Canaan that included the name Merenptah. Is the spring of Nephtoah, as referred to in Joshua, the same as the Well of Merenptah in the Egyptian papyrus? Remember, Merenptah is written in consonants, as is the Hebrew text. In the equivalent in Latin letters, Merenptah would be spelled *MRNPTH*; Nephtoah would be spelled *N(PH)TH*. The signs P and PH are identical in Hebrew. So the only difference in the two names is that the MR seemingly has dropped out of the Hebrew.[37] In the Hebrew Biblical text, "spring of the waters" is redundant. "Waters" in the Hebrew text is *MY*, but if this was originally *MR*, it would supply the missing letters of Merenptah's name and the Hebrew text would no longer be redundant; it would read simply the "Spring of Merenptah." Indeed, such naming of geographical features for the currently ruling pharaoh was a common practice in Ramesside Egypt.

If *MY* Nephtoah is indeed a garbled form of Merenptah, then we have further corroborating evidence from the Bible regarding the presence of Israelites in Canaan during Merenptah's reign.

Thus, in the last decade of the 13th century B.C.E., some of the Israelites in the highlands were already using the name Israel to designate their premonarchic tribal confederacy. This usage is its earliest occurrence and appears again only in the Song of Deborah (Judges 5), which scholars now date some three-quarters of a century after Merenptah.

[1]The reliefs I will be discussing are located on the transverse north-south axis of the Karnak temple on the outer western face of the court between the Hypostyle Hali and the Seventh Pylon, known as the Cour de la Cachette.

[2]Francoise Le Saout, "Reconstitution des Murs de la Cour de la Cachette," *Cahiers de Karnak* 7 (1978–1981), pp. 228–232, and pl. IV on p. 262.

[3]Adapted from Frank J. Yurco "Merenptah's Canaanite Campaign," *Journal of the American Research Center in Egypt (JARCE)* 23 (1986), p. 197 (fig. 10).

[4]See Yurco, "Merenptah's Canaanite Campaign," p. 196, n. 9.

[5]Another important element in the earlier attribution of all the reliefs on this wall to Ramesses II is the presence of a Prince Kha-em-Wast in one of the later battle reliefs to the left of the Peace Treaty text (scene 2)—for Ramesses II had a very famous son of that name. However, the Prince Kha-em-Wast shown in this scene is not the well-known son of Ramesses II, but a like-named son of Merenptah. Formerly Kenneth A. Kitchen took the Kha-em-Wast of these reliefs to be a son of Ramesses II ("Some New Light on the Asiatic Wars of Ramesses II," *Journal of Egyptian Archaeology* 50 [1964], p. 68, n. 9, and *Ramesside Inscriptions: Historical and Biographical* [Oxford: Blackwell, 1973-present] [hereafter *KRI*], vol. 2, p. 165, notes 4a-b); but since hearing my paper in Toronto in November 1977, he has accepted my position that Kha-em-Wast is indeed a son of Merenptah (see Kitchen: *KRI*, vol. 4, p. 82, no. 49 n. B, and *Pharaoh Triumphant: The Life and Times of Ramesses I* [Mississauga, Ont., Can.: Benben Publ., 1982], pp. 215–216 and fig. 17 on p. 220). Additional evidence supports this identification: in scene 2, Prince Kha-em-Wast is a military personage, while Ramesses II's like-named son was high priest of Ptah for much of his career. Further as shown by Eugene Cruz-Uribe ("On the Wife of Merenptah," *Göttinger Miszellen* 24 [1977], pp. 24–25), Merenptah's chief queen, Isis-nofret II, was a daughter of the high priest of Ptah, Kha-em-Wast I, and a granddaughter of Ramesses II. In the Ramesside royal family, it was very common practice to name grandchildren after their grandparents, and this is precisely what Merenptah seems to have done in the case of Kha-em-Wast II.

[6]For example, E.A. Wallis Budge, *A History of Egypt* (New York: Oxford Univ., Henry Frowde, 1902), vol. 5, pp. 103–108; John A. Wilson, *The Burden of Egypt* (Chicago: Univ. of Chicago Press, 1951), pp. 254–255, Wilson, "Hymn of Victory of Mer-ne-Ptah (The 'Israel Stele')," in *Ancient Near Eastern Texts Relating to the Old Testament (ANET)* with supplement, ed. James B. Pritchard (Princeton, NJ: Princeton Univ. Press, 3rd ed., 1969), pp. 376–378, esp. p. 376; Pierre Montet, *Lives of the Pharaohs* (London: Weidenfeld and Nicolson, 1968) pp. 198–200; and Montet, *Egypt and the Bible*, transl. Leslie R. Keylock (Philadelphia: Fortress, 1968), pp. 25–26.

[7]Kitchen, *KRI*, vol. 4, p. 1, line 9 *w'f K3d3r*. Scholars supporting the historicity of the texts include W.F. Flinders Petrie, *A History of Egypt* (London: Methuen, 1905), vol. 3, p. 114; Eduard Meyer, *Geschichte der Altertums* (Stuttgart and Berlin: J.G. Cotta'sche Buchhandlung Nachfolger, 1928), vol. 2, pp. 577–578; James Henry Breasted, *A History of Egypt* (New York: Charles Scribner's, 1912), pp. 465–466, and Sir Alan H. Gardiner, *Egypt of the Pharaohs* (Oxford: Oxford Univ. Press, 1961) p. 273.

[8]For the Libyan Victory texts, see Kitchen, *KRI*, vol. 4, pp. 2–12, esp. p. 8, lines 8–12.

[9]For a similar scene in complete form, see Herbert Ricke, George R. Hughes and Edward F. Wente, *The Beit el-Wali Temple of Ramesses I*, Oriental Institute Nubian Expedition, vol. I (Chicago: Univ. of Chicago Press, 1967), pls. 7–8.

[10]See Alexander Badawy, *A History of Egyptian Architecture: The Empire (the New Kingdom)* (Berkeley and Los Angeles: Univ. of California Press, 1968), pp. 448–474 for a discussion of fortress types found in Egyptian reliefs and their patterning on actual buildings.

[11]G.A. Gaballa, *Narrative in Egyptian Art* (Mainz am Rhein: Philipp von Zabern, 1976), pp. 100–104; applicable to battle reliefs and prisoner collecting scenes. But for Prince Kha-em-Wast II in scene 2, Kitchen would already have identified these battle reliefs with the texts on the Cairo stela no. 34025 and its fragmentary duplicate from Karnak, as he clearly had noted the usurped cartouches while collecting the texts of the scenes for his monumental *KRI* publications ("Some New Light on the Asiatic Wars," p. 48, n. 1, and p. 68, n. 9).

[12]Wilson, "An Egyptian Letter," *ANET*, pp. 475–479; from the place names within the text, it dates to the reign of Ramesses II. The Shasu are described on pp. 477–478.

[13]*Papyrus Anastasi* VI. See Ricardo A. Caminos, *Late Egyptian Miscellanies* (London: Oxford Univ. Press, 1954), p. 293; Wilson, "The Report of a Frontier Official," *ANET*, p. 259.

[14]For example, Raphael Giveon, *Les Bédouins Shosou des documents égyptiens Documenta et Monumenta Orientis Antiqui*, vol. 18 (Leiden: E.J. Brill, 1971), pp. 267–271, Manfred Weippert, "Canaan, Conquest and Settlement of," in *Interpreters Dictionary of the Bible* Supplement (Nashville, TN: Abingdon, 1976), p. 129; Weippert, "The Israelite 'Conquest' and the Evidence from Transjordan," in *Symposia Celebrating the Seventy-Fifth Anniversary of the American Schools of Oriental Research* (1900–1975), ed. Frank Moore Cross, (Cambridge, MA: American Schools of Oriental Research, 1979), pp. 32–34; Donald Redford, "The Ashkelon Relief at Karnak and the Israel Stele," *Israel Exploration Journal (IEJ)* 36 (1986), pp. 199–200; Redford's assumption that the Shasu in the Merenptah reliefs are the Israelites because Israel is not named elsewhere in the reliefs ignores the battle relief in scene 4, where the top is lost. His glib assertion that all the other names on the reliefs (except the Shasu) are also found on the Israel stele overlooks the plain evidence from the walls—only Ashkelon, in scene 4, is named; the fortresses in scenes 2 and 3 are unnamed, Yurco, "Merenptah's Palestinian Campaign," pp. 196 and 199–201; Kitchen, *KRI*, vol. 2, p. 165, lines 4–7. This position, again taken by Israel Finkelstein, "Searching for Israelite Origins," BAR, September/October 1988, uncritically following Redford, and without reference to either my paper ("Merenptah's Palestinian Campaign") or to that of Lawrence Stager, "Merenptah, Israel and Sea Peoples: New Light on an Old Relief," *Eretz Israel* 18 (1985), pp. 56–64. From *Papyrus Anastasi* I (Wilson, "An Egyptian Letter," *ANET*, p. 476), where the Shasu are described as uttering Semitic phrases as they furtively watch an Egyptian divisional camp, one may conclude that like other Canaanites the Shasu were Semitic peoples; it is not impossible that they were related to the Israelites, but Merenptah's reliefs, particularly scene 4 of the battle reliefs, make it quite clear that the Shasu were not Israelites.

[15]In Merenptah's reign, Gaza, capital of Canaan, was called *Gdt* (Gaza) and not Pa-Canaan, as in some other reigns. See Gardiner, *Ancient Egyptian Onomastica*, 2 vols. (Oxford: Oxford Univ. Press 1977), vol. I, p. 191, no. 624; and Caminos, *Late Egyptian Miscellanies*, pp. 108–110 (*Papyrus Anastasi* III, verso 6, 1 and 6, 6).

[16]Kitchen, *KRI*, vol. 4, pp. 2–12; and Kitchen and Gaballa, "Ramesside Varia II," *Zeitschrift für Agyptische Sprache* 96 (1969), pp. 23, 25, 27, and table 8, also, Kitchen, *KRI*, vol. 4, pp. 23–24.

[17]Yurco, "Merenptah's Canaanite Campaign," p. 213 and n. 55.

[18]Yurco, "Once Again, Merenptah's Battle Reliefs at Karnak," *IEJ*, forthcoming.

[19]Under Merenptah, the Sea Peoples attacked from the west, and did not settle in Canaan. See Kitchen, *Pharaoh Triumphant*, p. 215; see also Itamar Singer, "The Beginning of Philistine Settlement in Canaan and the Northern Boundary of Philistia," *Tel Aviv* 12 (1985), pp. 111–114.

[20]Redford, "The Ashkelon Relief at Karnak," p. 199.

[21]See Yurco, "Amenmesse: Six Statues at Karnak," pp. 15–31; and Cardon, "An Egypt-Royal Head of the Nineteenth Dynasty in the Metropolitan Museum," pp. 5–14.

[22]Eliezer D. Oren, "'Governors' Residences' in Canann under the New Kingdom: A Case Study of Egyptian Administration," *Journal of the Society for the Study of Egyptian Antiquities (JSSEA)* 14, no. 2 (March, 1984), pp. 37–56.

[23]Ivory sundial, see Kitchen, *KRI*, vol. 4, p. 24, no. 7B; R.A.S. MacAlister, *The Excavation at Gezer* (London: John Murray, 1912), vol. I, p. 15 and vol. 2, p. 331, fig. 456 (described as a pectoral). First identified as a sundial by E.J. Pilcher, "Portable Sundial from Gezer," *Palestine Exploration Fund Quarterly Statement* (1923), pp. 85–89. See also Singer, "An Egyptian 'Governor's Residency' at Gezer," *Tel Aviv* 13 (1986), pp. 26–31.

[24]Kitchen, *KRI*, vol. 4, p. 37, no. 17 (bowl), dated year 4, king unnamed. Merenptah has been proposed as the pharaoh under whom this bowl was inscribed partly based upon another similar bowl dated year 10 (or higher?), Mordechai Gilula "An Inscription in Egyptian Hieratic from Lachish," *Tel Aviv* 3 (1916), pp. 107–108, also Redford, "Egypt & Asia in the New Kingdom: Some Historical Notes," *JSSEA* 10, no. I (December, 1978), pp. 66–67. This dating, however, has been challenged by Orly Goldwasser ("The Lachish Hieratic Bowl Once Again," *Tel Aviv* 9 [1982] pp. 137–138), who would read the texts in a different order and date them to Ramesses III. As the bowl's texts concern tax collection, Ramesses III seems the probable date. Regardless of this problem with the dating of the bowls, Lachish remained firmly in Egyptian control at least into Ramesses III's reign; see also David Ussishkin, "Lachish—Key to the Israelite Conquest of Canaan," BAR, January/February 1987, pp. 34–39.

[25]Stager, "Merenptah, Israel, and Sea Peoples," p. 62, n. 2; William G. Dever et al., "Gezer II: Report of the 1967–70 Seasons in Fields I and II," *Annual of the Hebrew Union College Nelson Glueck School of Biblical Archaeology* (Jerusalem: Keter, 1974), p. 52 and n. 26. See also, Singer, "An Egyptian 'Governor's Residency' at Gezer," pp. 26–27.

[26]Kitchen, *KRI*, vol. 4, p. 242, no. 1, inscribed jar fragments, see Eann MacDonald, J. L. Starkey and G.L. Harding, *Beth Pelet II*, British School of Archaeology, vol. 52 (London: British School of Archaeology and Bernard Quaritch, 1932), pp. 28–29, and pls. 61, no. 3, and 64, no. 74.

[27]Trude Dothan, *The Philistines and Their Material Culture* (Jerusalem: Israel Exploration Society, 1982), p. 43 and n. 109.

[28]Scarab: Giveon, "A Monogram Scarab from Tel Masos," *Tel Aviv* I (1974), pp. 75–76; another from Tel Taanach, now in the Dayan Collection, p. 76 and n. 3; also Giveon, "The Impact of Egypt on Canaan," *Orbis Biblicus et Orientalis*, vol. 20 (Freiburg: Universitäts Verlag, 1978), pp. 107–109, and fig. 58b.

[29]Moshe Dayan, "Akko, 1980," *IEJ* 31 (1981), p. 111.

[30]Scarab: Kitchen *KRI*, vol. 4, p. 341 no. 1; Alan Rowe, *Catalogue of Scarabs, Scaraboids, and Amulets in the Palestine Archaeological Museum* (Cairo: Institut francais d'archéologie orientale, 1936), p. 164, no. 690, and pl. 18.

[31]Kitchen, *KRI*, vol. 4, p. 341 no. I, and p. 351, no. 17 (faience vessel naming Tawosret, misidentified as Ramesses II), in H.J. Franken "The Excavations at Deir 'Alla in Jordan," *Vetus Testamentum* (*VT*) 11 (1961), p. 385, and pls. 4–5. Correctly read as Tawosret by Jean Yoyotte, "Un Souvenir du 'Pharaon' Taousert en Jordanie," *VT* 12 (1962), pp. 464–469.

[32]*Papyrus Anastasi* III, verso 6, 4 to 6, 6. Caminos, *Late Epyptian Miscellanies*, p. 108; and Wilson, "Journal of a Frontier Official," *ANET*, p. 258 and n. 6.

[33]Kitchen, *Pharaoh Triumphant*, pp. 67–68.

[34]Stager, "Merenptah, Israel and Sea Peoples," pp. 60–62; Stager, "The Archaeology of the Family in Ancient Israel," *Bulletin of American Schools of Oriental Research* 260 (1985), pp. 1–24.

[35]Yohanan Aharoni, *The Land of the Bible: A Historical Geography* (Philadelphia, Westminster, 2nd ed., 1979) pp. 183–184, 195 and 218–220. Contra Aharoni, the Israelites did not conquer Lachish at the end of the XIXth Dynasty, see note 24 above.

[36]Caminos, *Late Egyptian Miscellanies*, p. 108, and Wilson, "Journal of a Frontier Official," *ANET*, p. 258 and n. 6.

[37]That the Hebrew is a garbled version of Merenptah was already suggested by Franz Prh. von Calice, "König Menephthes im Buche Josua?" *Orientalistische Litteratur-Zeitung* (May 1903), p. 224.

Related Reading

Anson F. Rainey, "Rainey's Challenge," BAR, November/December 1991.

Frank J. Yurco, "Yurco's Response," BAR, November/December 1991.

Manfred Bietak, "Israelites Found in Egypt," BAR, September/October 2003.

Anson F. Rainey, "Inside, Outside: Where Did the Early Israelites Come From?" BAR, November/December 2008.

Anson F. Rainey, "Shasu or Habiru: Who Were the Early Israelites?" BAR, November/December 2008.

Hershel Shanks, "When Did Ancient Israel Begin?" BAR, January/February 2012.

For a number of other responses to Yurco's original article, see Queries and Comments in the January/February 1991 issue of BAR.

Let My People Go and Go

EGYPTIAN RECORDS SUPPORT

ABRAHAM MALAMAT

Nothing in the archaeological record of Egypt directly substantiates the Biblical story of the Exodus. Yet a considerable body of Egyptian material provides such close analogies to the Biblical account that it may, in part, serve as indirect proof for the Israelite episode.

No other event figures so prominently in the Biblical tradition as one of the foundations of Israelite faith. The Bible refers to the Exodus from Egypt more often than it does to any other event in Israel's past—in the historical narratives, in the prophets and even in the psalms.

Is the Exodus story merely the product of later, primarily theological, contemplation, or was it a historic event? To decide, we must first recognize that the Exodus story is a folktale. This does not automatically deprive it of all historicity, but it does require us to focus not on the elements of folklore and artifice in the account, but on what Goethe called *die grossen Züge*, "the broad sweep of affairs." Does the Israelites' sojourn in Egypt, their enslavement there in what the Bible terms *beth avadim*, the house of bondage (a very apt coinage characterizing totalitarian regimes throughout history), their exit and flight from Egypt into the Sinai desert and, finally, their takeover of Canaan hold a kernel of historical truth, or are these events merely figments of the imagination of later scribes?

The lack of direct Egyptian evidence for any of these events does not prove that they didn't happen. Egyptian sources could have been indifferent to the Exodus and the takeover of Canaan merely because these events did not shake the foundations of the political and military scene of the day. The events were central, however, to Israel's turbulent history.

In the past, the debate over the Exodus often focused on when it could have happened. Much of this debate, unfortunately, ignored what I call the "telescoping process"—the compression of a chain of historical events into a simplified and brief account of Biblical historiography—especially of Israel's proto-history. Complex events were compressed into a severely curtailed time span by later editors viewing the events in retrospect. The Bible presents

A CENTURIES-LONG EXODUS

a relatively brief, streamlined account of the Exodus, a "punctual" event, as opposed to a "durative" event, which could conceivably involve two or more exoduses or even a steady flow of Israelites from Egypt over hundreds of years.

If the Exodus was a durative event, as seems likely, the search for a specific date for it is futile, since it might have happened anywhere from the 15th to the 12th centuries B.C. Even so, there must have been a peak period when the most Israelites left Egypt—we will call this the Moses movement—that can be dated more exactly. To identify when this punctual peak, the climactic stage within the durative event, happened, we must survey the history of Egypt in the context of the contemporaneous regional history.

In the 13th century B.C., the Egyptians fought the famous battle of Kadesh against the Hittites, the other superpower of the day. The battle site, Kadesh-on-the-Orontes (to be distinguished from Kadesh-Barnea, where the Israelites camped in the Sinai), lies about 70 miles north of Damascus, in modern Lebanon. Descriptions of this battle have survived in both Egyptian and Hittite records. The Hittite account explicitly states that the battle was a fiasco for the Egyptians, although this is not as clear in the Egyptian records. Even before the battle, which we can now date rather securely to 1273 B.C., give or take a few years, Egyptian hegemony was suffering a decline, especially in Canaan, where local rulers had erupted in revolt. In the wake of the battle of Kadesh, such a situation could well have facilitated, in a broad manner of speaking, an Israelite exodus. For some time I set the punctual peak, the Moses movement, at this time, as did other scholars.

Now, however, I am inclined to lower the date of the Moses movement to the early 12th century B.C. During this time both the Egyptian and Hittite empires suffered breakdowns. In modern terminology, the political systems of two opposing superpowers collapsed. This simultaneous decline of previously dominating empires provided a rare historical opportunity, the *occasione*, in Machiavellian terms, for the oppressed—the small peoples and ethnic minorities from Anatolia to lower Egypt.

ERICH LESSING

This fluid time may be the true setting for the Israelite escape from Egypt into Canaan.

Significant *indirect* Egyptian sources provide a sort of circumstantial evidence for this dating of the Moses movement and thereby lend greater authority to the Biblical account. Let us look at some of this evidence.

The Leiden Papyrus 348 and Pi-Ramesses. According to Egyptian records, Ramesses II (1279-1212 B.C.) built a new capital called Pi-Ramesses, the House of Ramesses, on the eastern delta (where the Israelites had apparently settled). Exodus 1:11 records that the store cities of Pithom and Ramesses were built by enslaved Israelites. Are these sources referring to the same place?

SEMITES IN EGYPT (preceding pages). Bearing the title Hyksos, a figure named Abisha (leaning over an ibex just to the right of center) leads his Semitic clansmen into Egypt to conduct trade. This scene dates to about 1890 B.C. and is preserved at Beni Hasan, halfway between Cairo and Luxor. The Hyksos (a Greek term meaning "ruler of foreign lands" or "shepherd kings") were Canaanites who ruled Egypt for roughly two and a half centuries, starting in about 1800 B.C. Foreign groups often sojourned in Egypt for business reasons or, at times, to escape from drought—a fact echoed in the Bible's account of Abraham and Jacob.

While we have Egyptian evidence for Semites entering Egypt, what proof is there for Semites—specifically the ancient Israelites—escaping Egypt? Author Abraham Malamat shows in the accompanying article that while there is little direct corroboration for the Exodus, there is much indirect evidence—not for a sudden Exodus, but for a gradual one that reached a climax about 1200 B.C. Photo by Erich Lessing.

Leiden Papyrus 348, a decree by an official of Ramesses II concerning construction work at his new capital, Pi-Ramesses, declares: "Distribute grain rations to the soldiers and to the *'Apiru* who transport stones to the great pylon of Ramesses." Although the matter is still debated, some scholars connect the *'Apiru* (and *Habiru*) referred to in this and other Egyptian documents with the Hebrews (*'Ibri*), both linguistically and ethnically. From the context of the *'Apiru* references, they were apparently a renegade population or displaced persons, possibly outlaws or mercenaries.[1] If the *'Apiru* were indeed connected to the Hebrews,[2] it would seem that the Hebrews were forced to build the capital city of Ramesses. This evidence is circumstantial at best, but it is as much as a historian can argue.

The Merneptah Stele. Although it has no direct connection with the Exodus, the famous Merneptah Stele, now dated to 1208 B.C., does mention a people called Israel living in Canaan.

The Egyptian Military Road in Northern Sinai. Exodus 13:17 states:

PHARAOH'S MIGHTY STEEDS rear menacingly at left in this depiction of the Battle of Kadesh, preserved on the walls of the Ramesseum at Luxor, Egypt. The battle occurred in about 1273 B.C. on the banks of the Orontes, in modern Lebanon, and pitted the two great superpowers of the day—the Egyptians and the Hittites—against each other. Ramesses II (1279-1212 B.C.) tried to put the best face on the outcome with heroic battle scenes such as this, but the Hittite account states that the pharaoh's forces were routed. In the wake of the battle, Egyptian hegemony over Canaan went into eclipse and numerous local rulers broke away in revolt. Some scholars have suggested that this period of Egyptian decline would have been a likely time for the Israelite Exodus.

> When Pharaoh let the people go, God did not lead them by way of the land of the Philistines, although that was near; for God said: "Lest the people repent when they see war and return to Egypt."

Early in the 13th century B.C., Pharaoh Seti I built the tight network of strongholds along the coast of northern Sinai referred to as the "way of the Philistines" in Exodus 13:17. This military road remained under the strict control of the Egyptians throughout that century.[3] It might easily have become a trap for the wandering Israelites; hence, the command attributed to God to avoid this route.

Also, Moses tells the Israelites to encamp at a site that will mislead the pharaoh: Once camped here, the pharaoh will say (according to Moses) that the Israelites "are entangled in the land [that is, Sinai]; the wilderness has closed in on them" (Exodus 14:3). This passage reflects a distinctly Egyptian viewpoint that must have been common at the time: In view of the fortresses on the northern coast, anyone seeking to flee Egypt would necessarily make a detour south into the desert, where they might well perish.

Papyri Anastasi. The reports of Egyptian frontier officials stationed in the border zone between Egypt and Sinai, known as the Papyri Anastasi, are especially significant. They reveal the tight control exercised by Egyptian authorities over their eastern frontier in the last decades of the 13th century B.C. Some of these papyri, which surfaced as early as 1839, show that neither Egyptians nor foreigners could enter or leave Egypt without a special permit from the Egyptian authorities.

Papyrus Anastasi III[4] records the daily border crossings of Egyptian-approved individuals during the reign of Pharaoh Merneptah (at the end of the 13th century B.C.). Papyrus Anastasi VI[5] records the passage of an entire tribe from Edom into Egypt during a drought. The papyrus records that for some travelers, passage into Egypt was necessary "to keep them alive and to keep their cattle alive." This report is reminiscent of several Biblical episodes

NEWS FROM THE EGYPTIAN OFFICIALS kept careful watch over the frontier between Egypt and Sinai in the late 13th century B.C. Papyrus Anastasi III (right), a remnant of an Egyptian historical archive known as the Papyri Anastasi, provides a daily account of movement across the border. Although no one was permitted to cross without a permit, Papyrus Anastasi V tells of the escape of two slaves (or servants) from the palace at Pi-Ramesses. According to the report prepared by the border official assigned to capture them, the slaves fled into the Sinai. The nighttime flight of the slaves, with Egyptian authorities close at their heels, roughly parallels that of the Biblical Exodus.

BRITISH MUSEUM

PELIZAEUS-MUSEUM, HILDESHEIM

PELIZAEUS-MUSEUM, HILDESHEIM

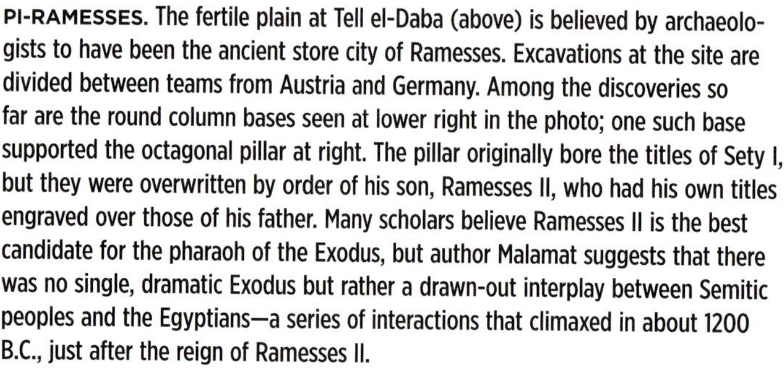

PI-RAMESSES. The fertile plain at Tell el-Daba (above) is believed by archaeologists to have been the ancient store city of Ramesses. Excavations at the site are divided between teams from Austria and Germany. Among the discoveries so far are the round column bases seen at lower right in the photo; one such base supported the octagonal pillar at right. The pillar originally bore the titles of Sety I, but they were overwritten by order of his son, Ramesses II, who had his own titles engraved over those of his father. Many scholars believe Ramesses II is the best candidate for the pharaoh of the Exodus, but author Malamat suggests that there was no single, dramatic Exodus but rather a drawn-out interplay between Semitic peoples and the Egyptians—a series of interactions that climaxed in about 1200 B.C., just after the reign of Ramesses II.

involving Abraham and Jacob, who are also said to have descended into Egypt to escape a drought.

Without this strict border control, minorities as well as entire groups of Egyptians could have escaped from the Nile delta into Sinai and Palestine. No wonder Moses and Aaron had to repeatedly plead with Pharaoh to "Let my people go!"

Indeed, Papyrus Anastasi V (also from the end of the 13th century B.C.) refers to the escape of two slaves, or servants, from the royal residence at Pi-Ramesses. The fugitives fled across the fortified border into the Sinai wilderness. The high-ranking Egyptian military commander who wrote the papyrus had been ordered by the Egyptian authorities to ensure the capture of the runaways and their return to Egypt. He writes to the Chief of Bowmen of Tjeku, Ka-Kem-wer, the Chief of Bowmen Ani and the Chief of Bowmen Bak-en-Ptah:

> In life, prosperity, health! In the favor of Amon-Re, King of the Gods, and of the *ka* of the King of Upper and Lower Egypt:...Another matter: I was sent forth...at the time of evening, following after these two slaves...[Now] when [I] reached the fortress, they told me that the scout had come from

> the desert [saying that] they had passed the walled place north of the Migdol of Seti Mer-ne-Ptah...[W]hen my letter reaches you, write to me about all that has happened to [them]. Who found their tracks? Which watch found their tracks? What people are after them? Write to me about all that has happened to them and how many people you send out after them. [May your health] be good![6]

This story shares at least four parallels with the Exodus story: (1) Slaves, or semi-slaves, escape from the area near the city of Ramesses in search of freedom; (2) an Egyptian military force pursues them with the intention of returning them to Egypt; (3) the runaways follow an escape route into Sinai roughly identical with the Biblical route; and (4) the flight takes place at night, as hinted at by the pursuing Egyptian official, who mentions leaving a short time after the escapees, "at the time of evening." Similarly, the Exodus of the Israelites started "toward midnight" (Exodus 11:4).

The Elephantine Stele. Our final indirect proof comes from a stele found on the island of Elephantine near the First Cataract of the Nile. Published for the first time in 1972, this stele still receives intense study. It dates to the second year of Pharaoh Sethnakht's rule (or Setnakht), in the second decade of the 12th century B.C.[7] According to the stele, one Egyptian faction was apparently rebelling against the pharaoh and battling a faction that remained loyal. The revolutionaries bribed some Asiatics in Egypt to assist them in their plot against the crown. They bribe them with silver, gold and copper—"the possession of Egypt." The pharaoh foiled the plot and drove the Asiatics out of Egypt, most likely forcing them on an exodus of sorts toward southern Canaan.

An enigmatic episode in the Exodus story[8] resembles this stele story. Exodus records that the Israelites, according to the usual translations, "borrow" from or "ask" (*sha'al*) the Egyptians for "silver and gold, and clothing," which the Israelites then take with them on their flight (Exodus 3:21-22, 11:2, 12:35-36; Psalm 105:37). In this context the word *sha'al* really means "appropriate" or "steal" rather than "borrow" or "ask."

In both cases, Asiatics take the same objects from the Egyptians. This may simply be an example of parallel literary motifs. But Exodus 1:10 reveals the pharaoh saying, "Come let us deal shrewdly with [the Israelites]...[lest] if war befall us, they join our enemies and fight against us and escape from the land." The Egyptians are explicitly fearful that these Asiatics, the Israelites, might join the Egyptians' enemies in a revolt. That is precisely what happened in the episode recorded in the Elephantine stele.

In sum, although an Israelite exodus is not mentioned in Egyptian sources, a number of important analogs are apparent. These may date back to the time of the Hyksos, an Asiatic people who conquered Egypt in the 17th to 16th centuries B.C., during the 15th and 16th Egyptian dynasties. These analogs are more concentrated, however, in the late 13th century, around 1200 B.C., supporting that date for the climax of the Israelite Exodus.[9] ■

For a more extensive version of this paper, and an expanded bibliography, see Abraham Malamat, "The Exodus: Egyptian Analogies," in Exodus: The Egyptian Evidence, *ed. Ernest S. Frerichs and Leonard H. Lesko (Winona Lake, IN: Eisenbrauns, 1997).*

1 If the *'Apiru* are, as I suggest, connected with the Hebrews, this would rule out the suggested connection with the *Shasu*, another group sometimes alleged to be connected with the emerging Hebrews/Israelites.

2 Although every Israelite is a Hebrew and likely an 'Apiru, not every Hebrew or 'Apiru is necessarily an Israelite.

3 Alan H. Gardiner, "The Ancient Military Road Between Egypt and Palestine," *Journal of Egyptian Archaeology* 6 (1920), pp. 99-116; Eliezer D. Oren, "'Ways of Horus' in North Sinai," in *Egypt, Israel, Sinai*, ed. Anson F. Rainey (Tel Aviv: Dayan Institute, Tel Aviv Univ., 1987), pp. 69-119.

4 John A. Wilson in James B. Pritchard, ed., *Ancient Near Eastern Texts Relating to the Old Testament*, 3rd ed. (Princeton, NJ: Princeton Univ. Press, 1969), p. 258.

5 Wilson, *Texts*, p. 259.

6 Wilson, *Texts*, p. 259.

7 See R. Drenkhahn, *Die Elephantine Stele des Sethnakht* (Wiesbaden, 1980).

8 Hinted at by M. Görg, *Kairos* 20 (1978), p. 279f. and n. 28.

9 For an even later dating in the 12th century B.C., see M.B. Rowton, "The Problem of the Exodus," *Palestine Exploration Quarterly* 85 (1953), pp. 46-60; and Gary A. Rendsberg, "The Date of the Exodus," *Vetus Testamentum* 42 (1992), pp. 510-527.

Related Reading

Alan R. Millard, "How Reliable Is Exodus?" BAR, July/August 2000.

Baruch Halpern, "Eyewitness Testimony," BAR, September/October 2003.

James K. Hoffmeier, "Out of Egypt," BAR, January/February 2007.

Red Sea or Reed Sea?

How the mistake was made and what yam sûp *really means*

BERNARD F. BATTO

A TRIANGLE OF SAND AND GRANITE, limestone and sandstone, the Sinai Peninsula appears as a rugged wasteland in this view to the north from a NASA satellite miles out in space.

Two fingers of the Red Sea separate the peninsula from the land on the west and east—the 180-mile-long Gulf of Suez on the west and the 112-mile-long Gulf of Eilat or Aqaba on the east. Clearly visible are the coastal plains, the barren interior Tih Plateau, and the mountainous southern region that constitutes one third of the total area of the peninsula.

IF THERE IS ANYTHING THAT sophisticated students of the Bible know, it is that *yam sûp*, although traditionally translated Red Sea, really means Reed Sea, and that it was in fact the Reed Sea that the Israelites crossed on their way out of Egypt.

Well, it doesn't and it wasn't and they're wrong!

Yam sûp (pronounced yahm soof) appears many times in the Bible. In a number of these instances, it clearly refers to the body of water we know as the Red Sea (including its two northern fingers, the Gulf of Suez and the Gulf of Eilat or Aqaba).

Note that I do not say that *yam sûp* literally means Red Sea. What *yam sûp* literally means is part of the problem. *Yam* indeed means sea; that much is clear and agreed. But the word for red is *adam* (pronounced a-dahm), not *sûp*. Literally, Red Sea should be *Yam Adam*, not *Yam Sûp*. Yet from the context, we know that in a number of Biblical references, *yam sûp* refers to the body of water that we know as the Red Sea.

Look, for example, at 1 Kings 9:26, where we are told that "King Solomon built a fleet of ships at Ezion-Geber near Elath [or Eilat] on the shore of the *yam sûp* in the la nd of Edom." From the other geographical references, it is absolutely clear that *yam sûp* refers to the northeastern finger of the Red Sea, known today as the Gulf of Eilat or the Gulf of Aqaba.

Or consider Jeremiah 49:21. Jeremiah prophesies that the dying babies of Edom will be crying, and "the sound of screaming shall be heard at the *yam sûp*." A glance at a map indicates that the *yam*, or sea, referred to is again the northeastern finger of what we call the Red Sea. *Yam sûp* again refers to the body of water we call the Red Sea. (For other examples, see Numbers 21:4 and, with less certainty, Numbers 14:25; Deuteronomy 1:40; 2:1; and Judges 11:16.)

One especially important reference, to which we shall return later in this article because it describes the Israelites' journey out of Egypt, is found in Numbers 33. Numbers 33 contains the ancient list of camping stations of the exodus, all the way from Rameses and Succoth in Egypt to Kadesh and the land of Edom. In verse 8, we are told that the Israelites "passed through the sea [*yam*] into the wilderness." Which "sea," we are not told. Then the Israelites travel for three days and camp at Marah. Then they leave Marah and go to Elim. Then they leave Elim and camp by the *yam sûp*. It is obvious that they have reached the northwestern finger of the Red Sea, which we call the Gulf of Suez. *Yam sûp* here again refers to the body of water we call the Red Sea. It is at minimum five days' travel from the sea the Israelites miraculously passed through.

Based on these clear geographical referents, it is easy to understand how the traditional translation of *yam sûp* came to be Red Sea.

In the earliest known translation of the Bible—from Hebrew to Greek—*yam sûp* is consistently translated as *Erythra Thalassa*, which means "Red Sea." This Greek Bible, known as the Septuagint, was translated in about 300 B.C. In St. Jerome's Latin translation, known as the Vulgate (from about 400 A.D.), *yam sûp* is translated *Mare Rubrum*—Red Sea. Because of the Vulgate translation, "Red Sea" became firmly entrenched in western tradition, appearing for example, in the King James Version.

The Red Sea/Reed Sea problem arises because *yam sûp* is also used in the Bible as the name of the body of water that parted to allow the Israelites to pass through and then came together to drown the Egyptians. The most important of these Biblical passages is found in Exodus 15, which scholars consider to be one of the oldest, if not the oldest and most archaic poems in the entire Bible. Known as The Song of the Sea,* Exodus 15 celebrates the miracle of the sea by which the Israelites were saved from Pharaoh's pursuing horsemen:

> I will sing to the Lord, for he has triumphed gloriously;
> Horse and driver he has hurled into the sea [*yam*].
> ...
> Pharaoh's chariots and his army he has cast into the sea [*yam*];
> And the pick of his officers are sunk in the *yam sûp*. (Exodus 15:1, 4)

*It is also referred to as the Song of Moses or the Song of Miriam by some scholars.

In later Biblical books, the sea that parted for the Israelites to pass through is consistently referred to as the *yam sûp*. In Joshua 2:10, for example, Rahab the harlot who let the Israelite spies into Jericho tells them, "We have heard how the Lord dried up the water of the *yam sûp* before you when you came out of Egypt."

When the Lord parted the Jordan River to allow the Israelites to cross, Joshua told his people that this was just "as the Lord your God did to the *yam sûp* which he dried up for us until we passed over," (Joshua 4:23). (See also Joshua 24:6; Deuteronomy 11:4; Psalms 106:7,9,22; Psalms 136:13–15; and Nehemiah 9:9.)

Traditionally, *yam sûp* is translated as Red Sea in these passages too. Yet something seems to be wrong with this translation. It doesn't seem to fit the geography of the Israelites' trek out of Egypt, quite apart from the fact that the Gulf of Suez is over 20 miles wide. Moreover, there is absolutely no philological reason to think that *sûp* means "red" or anything like it.

Thus was born the translation "Reed Sea."

Translating *yam sûp* as Reed Sea arguably solves all these problems. It allegedly fits the geography, it involves a body of water that could dry up under the force of a heavy wind, and *sûp* has an arguable basis for an Egyptian etymology meaning "reed."

We don't know who first suggested the translation Reed Sea. The 11th-century medieval French Jewish commentator known as Rashi accepted a connection between *yam sûp* and a marsh overgrown with reeds.[1] Ibn Ezra, a Spanish Jewish commentator of the 12th century, commenting on the meaning of *yam sûp* in Exodus 13:18, notes that "Some say that it is so called because reeds grow round about it." Martin Luther may have been acquainted with such opinions; he translated *yam sûp* as *Schilfmeer* (meaning Reed Sea).

Among modern scholars, Heinrich Brugsch in 1858 was apparently the first to develop a comprehensive, coherent theory of the "Reed Sea," including the alleged connection between Biblical *yam sûp* and *p3-twf(y)* (pronounced approximately pi thoof) of the Egyptian texts.[2]

These Egyptian texts form the principal pillar of the Reed Sea hypothesis. According to this argument, these texts establish that *yam sûp* literally means "Sea of Papyrus" or "Sea of Reeds." Etymologically, we are told, Hebrew *sûp* is a loan-word from Egyptian *twf* which means "papyrus (reeds)." This etymology is supposed to be proved from those Biblical passages where *sûp* refers to vegetation growing along the banks of the Nile. For example, in Exodus 2:3, 5, the baby Moses is hidden from Pharaoh who has threatened to kill all newborn Hebrew males; he is hidden among the suph (reeds) by the bank of the Nile (see also Isaiah 19:6).

One Egyptian text, known as Papyrus Anastasi III, supposedly even speaks of a "Papyrus Marsh" or "Papyrus Lake" not far from the city of Rameses (=Tanis?), the very place from which the Biblical narrative says the Israelites began their journey out of Egypt (Exodus 12:37).

The "Reed Sea" hypothesis has now become so widely accepted that one can scarcely pick up a handbook or treatise on the Bible, regardless of the author's theological affiliation or scholarly bent,[3] that does not espouse the theory that *yam sûp* means Reed Sea when used in connection with the body of water the Israelites passed through on their way out of Egypt. The ubiquity of the hypothesis is even reflected in modern critical translations of the Bible. Although English versions normally adhere to the traditional rendering as "Red Sea," practically every respected translation of the Book of Exodus now includes at minimum an annotation that *yam sûp* actually means "Reed Sea" when used with reference to the body of water the Israelites passed through and in which the Egyptians drowned.**

This Reed Sea solution is not so simple as it seems, however. Right off the bat, we have the problem of how to translate those passages where *yam sûp* has nothing to do with the exodus (such as 1 Kings 9:26 cited above) and where the body of water referred to is clearly the Red Sea. Here there is no choice but to translate *yam sûp* as the Red Sea. And that is what is regularly done when *yam sûp* obviously refers to the Red Sea or when Reed Sea is a problem in itself because the referent is not clear to the translator. The results are not consistent from Bible to Bible. But in any event, we regularly find *yam sûp* translated two ways—in the same Bible translation! Check your own Bible translation, for example, at Exodus 15:4 and 1 Kings 9:26.

There is another problem with translating *yam sûp* as Sea of Reeds based on a supposed etymological connection between *sûp* and reeds. There are absolutely no reeds in the Red Sea (or in the Gulf of Suez). The ancients would surely not apply *yam sûp* to what we call the Red Sea if *yam sûp* were intended to refer to reeds. In short, a translation such as "Sea of Papyrus Reeds" is inappropriate when applied to the Red Sea because papyrus does not grow in those salty waters!

Finally, the connection between *yam sûp* and Egyptian *p3-ṯwf* will not stand up under scrutiny. There can be no doubt that the Egyptian word for papyrus, *ṯwf*, passed into Hebrew as a loanword, *sûp*, with only a slight modification in pronunciation as required by Hebrew phonology. Hebrew *sûp* has this meaning of papyrus in Exodus 2:3, 5 and Isaiah 19:6. Nevertheless, Egyptian *p3-ṯwf* has nothing to do with Biblical *yam sûp*.

Let us look more closely at the evidence. The hieroglyphic signs in question are written in Latin letters as *p3-ṯwf. P3* is the definite article, and *ṯwf* means "papyrus." The phrase appears a number of times in Egyptian texts. It refers, however, to a papyrus marsh *area* or *district*, not to a lake or body of water.[4] In some texts *p3-ṯwf* is used to designate a district or area not only where papyrus grows but also where animals are pastured and agricultural enterprises undertaken.

In hieroglyphic writing an unpronounced sign, called a determinative, is often included in the spelling to indicate the class of noun the word falls into. Thus the determinative for god is added to the phonetic signs for gods, so we know which names refer to gods. *p3-ṯwf* is always written with the determinative for plant. Occasionally it is written with the determinative for town, but never is it written with the determinative for lake or water.

Moreover, the term *p3-ṯwf* does not indicate a specific area. Several places in the eastern delta of the Nile are referred to as *p3-ṯwf*.†

The text most often cited in support of the connection between *p3-ṯwf* and *yam sûp* is, as I noted earlier, Papyrus Anastasi III, which describes the residence of Pharaoh Rameses II (often identified as the Pharaoh of the Exodus): "The papyrus marshes *p3-ṯwf* come to it [the Pharaoh's residence] with papyrus reeds, and the Waters-of-Horus with rushes."[5] This text hardly indicates a single lake or body of water called the Reed Sea.

Indeed, the identification of *p3-ṯwf* as a body of water owes more to the desire to find confirmation for the hypothetical Reed Sea of the Bible than to the internal evidence of the Egyptian texts. Egyptian *p3-ṯwf* would scarcely ever have been understood as referring to a body of water apart from the Biblical term *yam sûp*. In Roland de Vaux's recent classic *The Early History of Israel* (Westminster Press:

**The Revised Standard Version and the New American Bible are examples of Bibles containing this annotation. The New English Bible gives Sea of Reeds as an alternative translation. The editors of the New International Version append a corrective note at each occurrence: "Hebrew *Yam Suph*; that is, Sea of Reeds." The New Jewish Publication Society translation and The Jerusalem Bible both translate *yam sûp* as "the Sea of Reeds."

†Much of this evidence comes from the preeminent authority on hieroglyphics, Sir Alan Gardiner; he thus refutes his own conclusion that the connection between *p3-ṯwf(y)* and Biblical *yam sûp* is "beyond dispute." A. Gardiner, *Ancient Egyptian Onomastica* (Oxford University, 1947) 2, pp. 201–202.

Philadelphia, 1978, p. 377), he translates *p3-ṯwf* as "the land of the papyrus."

I believe there is another, wholly satisfactory way out of the dilemma. *Yam sûp* for the ancients had a symbolic as well as a historical meaning. Indeed, its symbolic meaning preceded its historical meaning. Symbolically, it means Sea of the End, the sea at the end of the world. Historically, it came to mean the Red Sea and what lay beyond.

Sûp should be connected not with Egyptian *p3-ṯwf* but with the Semitic root *sûp*, meaning "to come to an end," "to cease to exist." The Hebrew word *sôp* means simply "end." *Yam sûp* is the equivalent of *yam sôp*. This association has been suggested by Norman Snaith, who correctly argues that *yam sûp* thus refers to "that distant scarcely known sea away to the south, of which no man knew the boundary. It was the sea at the end of the land."*

What we call the Red Sea came to be known as the *yam sûp* because it was regarded by the ancients as the sea at the end of the world. Interestingly enough, the Greeks applied the name Red Sea (*Erythra Thalassa*) not only to our Red Sea but also to the Indian Ocean[6] and, later when they discovered it, even to the Persian Gulf.[7] The phrase "Red Sea" could even be vaguely used to designate faraway, remote places.[8] Likewise in Jewish intertestamental literature the designation "Red Sea" included the Persian Gulf and everything to the south. Thus, both the fragmentary Aramaic text from the Dead Sea Scrolls known as the *Genesis Apocryphon* (21.17–18) and the famous first-century A.D. Jewish historian Josephus (*Antiquities* 1.1.3) state that the Tigris and the Euphrates empty into the Red Sea. The book of *Jubilees* (third or second century B.C.) says that Eden and the lands of India and Elam (Persia) all border on the Red Sea (8.21, 9.2). It is thus very clear that these ancients thought of the Red Sea as a continuous body of water that extended from the Red Sea through the Indian Ocean to the Persian Gulf and that included all connecting oceans to the south. Presumably the earlier Israelites likewise included in the designation *yam sûp* all those connecting oceans to the south.

* "ים-סוף: The Sea of Reeds: The Red Sea," *Vetus Testamentum* 15 (1965), pp. 395–98, esp. 397, 398. See also J. A. Montgomery, "Hebraica (2) *yam sûp* ('The Red Sea') = Ultimum Mare?" *Journal of the American Oriental Society* 58 (1938), pp. 131–132. It has been objected that *sôp* is an Aramaic word which was introduced into Hebrew at a late date (M. Wagner, *Die lexikalischen und grammatikalischen Aramaismen in Alttestamentlichen Hebräisch* [Beihefte zur Zeitschrift für die alttestamentliche Wissenschaft 96; Alfred Töpelmann: Berlin, 1966], p. 87). However, the occurrence of verbal forms of this root in Amos 3:15; Psalm 73:19; Jeremiah 8:13 and Zephaniah 1:2, 3 indicates that *sôp* need not be considered a late Aramaism in Hebrew; see G. Ahlström, "Joel and the Temple Cult in Jerusalem," *Supplements to Vetus Testamentum* 21 (1971), pp. 2–3.

The designation *yam sûp* thus had both a geographical and a symbolic meaning. The "Sea of the End" means not just the sea at the physical end of the world but also the "place" where non-Creation or nonexistence begins.

In the ancient Near East the idea of "the sea" carried with it many mythological connotations. A common theme in cosmogonic myths from Mesopotamia to Egypt was the creation of the cosmos through some kind of primeval battle against the force of chaos. Chaos, variously named Leviathan, Rahab, and the dragon, was most commonly known simply as "Sea" (Akkadian *Tiamat*, Canaanite *Yamm*). "Creation" meant that which was most solidly formed, the dry land, out of the chaos of the sea. At the center of the cosmos stood the cosmic mountain, the home of the creator deity. At the opposite pole lay the realm of chaos, uncreated and unformed, the most graphic symbol of which was "the sea." To these ancients' way of thinking, this feared and apparently limitless abyss really was the "end of the world." This was what the Hebrews called *yam sûp*.

These mythic cosmic elements are surely embedded in the term *yam sûp* as it is used in the Bible. Indeed these elements unlock new meaning in °the Biblical text. Moreover, the "fit" is so good that it provides corroboration for the theory. Consider, for example, the Song of the Sea, Exodus 15, one of the most ancient passages in the entire Bible. This justly famous poem in archaic Hebrew celebrates the deliverance of the Israelites:

Then Moses and the Israelites sang this song to the LORD.
They said:
I will sing to the LORD, for He has triumphed gloriously;
Horse and driver He has hurled into the sea.
The LORD is my strength and might;
He is become my salvation.
This is my God and I will enshrine Him;
The God of my father, and I will exalt Him.
The LORD, the Warrior—
LORD is His name!
Pharaoh's chariots and his army
He has cast into the sea;
And the pick of his officers
Are sunk in the yam sûp.
The deeps covered them;
They went down into the depths like a stone.
Your right hand, O LORD glorious in power,
Your right hand, O LORD, shatters the foe!
In Your great triumph You break Your opponents;
You send forth Your fury, it consumes them like straw.

The floods stood straight like a wall;
The deeps froze in the heart of the sea.
The foe said,
"I will pursue, I will overtake,
I will divide the spoil;
My desire shall have its fill of them.
I will bare my sword—
My hand shall subdue them."
You made Your wind blow, the sea covered them;
They sank like lead in the majestic waters.
Who is like You, O LORD, among the gods;
Who is like You, majestic in holiness,
Awesome in splendor, working wonders!
You put out Your right hand,
The underworld swallowed them.
In Your love You lead the people You redeemed;
In Your strength You guide them to Your holy abode.
The peoples hear, they tremble;
Agony grips the dwellers in Philistia.
Now are the clans of Edom dismayed;
The tribes of Moab—trembling grips them;
All the dwellers in Canaan are aghast.
Terror and dread descend upon them;
Through the might of Your arm they are still as stone—
Till Your people cross over, O LORD,
Till Your people cross whom You have created.[9]
You will bring them and plant them in Your own mountain,
The place You made to dwell in, O LORD,
The sanctuary, O LORD, which Your hands established.
The LORD will reign for ever and ever!

Modern source critics have identified four different textual strands in the Pentateuch. These four strands are labeled J (for Yahwist in its Germanic form), E (for Elohist), P (for Priestly writer) and D (for Deuteronomist). The Song of the Sea, however, is recognized as independent of all these textual strands that have been interwoven to form the Biblical text as we know it. Moreover, the Song of the Sea is also recognized to be older than even the earliest of these textual strands (J).

The Song of the Sea follows the basic pattern of ancient mythological cycles such as Enuma Elish, the Mesopotamian epic about the god Marduk, and the Ugaritic cycle concerning the god Baal. In these mythological texts the creator god overcomes his watery foe of chaos, bringing order out of this chaos and creating a people in the process. The creator god then retires to his mountain sanctuary where as king he rules his newly ordered cosmos.[10] As has often been observed, the Biblical description in Exodus 15 is heavily dependent on this mythological language. The defeat of the historical Pharaoh plays only a minor role in the poem. The struggle against Pharaoh is portrayed as part of the larger battle of the deity against the powers of chaos; Pharaoh is identified with those chaotic powers and is destroyed with them. For this reason Pharaoh is submerged into the sea and defeated along with the sea.

In this Biblical poem, the *yam* in verse 4a is the equivalent of the sea dragon in ancient Near Eastern mythologies. In the second half of verse 4, *yam* is paired with *yam sûp* which here means literally "Sea of End/Annihilation." The *yam sûp* was the sea at the end of the earth, a sea which in the ancient mind was fraught with connotations of primeval chaos.**

These mythical associations explain the presence of *yam sûp* in the Song of the Sea. Traditional mythical language is used to express the belief that the emergence of Israel as a people during the exodus was due to a creative act by Yahweh equal to that of the original creation of the cosmos itself. The Egyptians, the evil force which threatens the existence of this new creation, are appropriately cast into the sea to perish. A more powerful symbol for nonexistence can scarcely be found than submergence into the Sea of End/Annihilation.

Specific philological confirmation of these connotations emanating from the word *sûp* may be found in a passage from Jonah. The word *sûp* is used there in a prayer of thanksgiving Jonah delivers from the belly of the whale, at a time when he has just been rescued from watery chaos:

I called out in my distress to Yahweh
and he answered me;
From the belly of Sheol I cried
and you heard my voice.
You had cast me into the deep,
in the midst of Sea
and River surrounded me.
All your breakers and your billows
passed over me.
Then I said, "I am driven
away from your presence.
How can I continue to look
to your holy temple?"
The waters engulfed me up to the neck;
the Abyss surrounded me;

** One is reminded that in the Israelite conception, the earth was an island of dry land surrounded on all sides by, and floating in, the primeval waters of chaos (Psalms 24:1–2; 104:5–7; 136:6). E. Levine (*The Aramaic Version of Jonah* [Jerusalem: Jerusalem Academic Press, 1975], pp. 75–77) relates that in later midrashic tradition Jonah while in the belly of the fish was shown the path of the Israelites through the Red Sea (*b. Sota 45b*; Midrash Jonah, *h.l.*; *Yal.* 551: Rashi, Comm. *ad h.l.*); this was possible, according to Ibn Ezra and Kimchi *ad h.l.*, because "the Red Sea extends to, and mingles with the waters of Jaffa."

sûp was bound to my head.
To the foundations of the mountains I
descended;[11]
the underworld and its bars closed after me
forever.
But you brought my life up from the Pit,
O Yahweh, my God.
When my soul went faint within me,
I remembered Yahweh;
And my prayer came unto you,
into your holy temple.
Those who worship vain idols
forsake their true loyalty.
But I with acclamations of thanksgiving
will sacrifice to you.
What I have vowed I will pay;
deliverance is from Yahweh.

Sûp is usually translated in this passage as seaweed, weeds, or the like. Seaweed doesn't grow, however, in the depths of the sea. And there is surely no philological basis for a translation like seaweed. What it really means is the "End/Annihilation." *Sûp* here is parallel to the abyss that surrounded the prophet and the waters that engulfed him up to his neck. In the same way the End/Annihilation was bound to his head. All the images in the psalm concern the realm of the primeval chaos: Sheol, the Pit, and the underworld as the abode of Death; the Sea-Dragon under its twin names of Sea and River; the primeval Abyss (*tehôm*) and its associated terms, "the deep," "breakers," "billows," "waters"; the foundations of the mountains in the underworld. Clearly, context requires *sûp* to have something to do with the cosmic battle against chaos.

In Jonah, as in the Song of the Sea in Exodus 15, God rules from his holy temple or mountain. This rule is a continuation of his primordial battle against the nihilistic forces of chaos. God's holy mountain, where his temple is located, is the center of the cosmos, or orderly creation. To the ancient mind, the further away from the center of the cosmos one goes, the more one moves into the realm of chaos or noncreation. The spatial image is both vertical and horizontal. Vertically, the heavens are the source of existence and creation; the underworld and the abyss are the place of death and nonexistence. Horizontally, the land around the mountain of one's god is known and understood and therefore thought of as the most "created." The sea, which lies beyond the limits of the land, is unsolid, nonformed—in other words, "uncreated." Thus, the sea and the abyss are simultaneously symbolic and real to the ancient mind.

In the same way *yam sûp* had both a symbolic meaning and a real meaning. When it refers to the body of water that engulfed the Egyptians after the Israelites passed through, it has a symbolic meaning. Elsewhere it refers to a particular body of water, the Red Sea, which for the ancients was really the Sea at the End of the World. But *yam sûp* never refers to the Reed Sea.

Yam sûp came to refer to the Red Sea because like other ancient peoples, the Israelites did not distinguish the Red Sea from oceans further to the south. To their way of thinking, the Red Sea—the *yam sûp*—was the sea at the end of the earth. It was a real place, but it also extended to the end of the world and thus carried an enormous symbolic and mythic freight.

It is interesting to note how the sea figures in each of the textual strands that make up the narrative account found in Exodus 13:17 through Exodus 14:30. While there may be some minor disagreements among scholars about how to divide the text, text critics generally agree on the division among the three strands represented in this passage. These three strands are J and E (which were combined into JE by a so-called redactor or editor at an early stage) and P. I have set forth the division among the three strands in a footnote.*

In the J narrative the sea is not identified; it is called simply *ha-yam*, "the sea" (Exodus 14:21b).** The sea bed is bared by a strong east wind blowing all night. Towards morning God somehow panics the Egyptian army so that it flees headlong into the dried sea bed. At the same time the waters flow back to their normal place and the Egyptians are drowned and the Israelites are free to continue on their way. Of the three textual strands, J is accepted as the oldest (probably about 10th–9th century B.C.), and in this version "the sea" clearly connotes a symbolic significance. The Egyptians are drowned in primeval chaos.

The textual strand known as E is scarcely represented in the sea narrative. There are no clear references to any miracle at the sea in this strand. The only possible reference to the sea is in 14:25a, which talks about chariot wheels clogging. This allusion to God's clogging the chariot wheels so that the Egyptians could not drive may stem from a setting in a dried sea bed, but it is equally appropriate to a "flight" story. What the original E account contained, we cannot be sure. Not much of it has been left by the redactor.

The P narrative presents the familiar story. Trapped between the sea and the pursuing

*To J, I assign the following verses 13:21–22; 14:5b–6, 9a, 10b, 11–14, 19b, 20, 21b, 24, 25b, 27b, 30–31. To E, I assign the following 13:17–19; 14–5a, 7, 19a, 25a. To P, I assign the following: 13:20; 14:1–4, 8, 9b–10a, 10c, 15–18, 21a, 21c–23, 26–27a, 28–29.

**The small b indicates the second half of the verse. Scholars divide Biblical verses into colons or parts, designated a and b, and sometimes a third colon designated c.

Egyptians, the Israelites cry to Yahweh for help. Yahweh commands Moses to stretch his staff over the sea, and the sea is split in twain. The Israelites march dry-shod through the middle of the sea, between walls of water to the right and to the left, with the Egyptians in pursuit. After the Israelites have crossed, Moses raises his staff and the waters return; the trapped Egyptian army perishes in the midst of the sea. Here too the place of the miracle is designated simply as "the sea." Accordingly, some scholars have argued that P, like J, did not connect the miracle with *yam sûp*. It is more likely, however, that P did identify the sea of the miracle with *yam sûp*. As I have shown elsewhere,† P is responsible for editing the exodus narrative and the wilderness journey so that it conforms to the list of camping stations listed in Numbers 33. But there is one very important exception. In Numbers 33 the station at the sea of the crossing (verse 8) is quite distinct from *yam sûp* (verses 10–11), since the Israelites arrive at the latter some three camping stations later. In the exodus narrative, however, P has deliberately suppressed the latter station at *yam sûp* and changed the setting of the miraculous crossing from an unnamed sea to *yam sûp*. You can easily observe this for yourself. Compare the stations given in Exodus 13:20; 14:2; 15:22–23; 15:27–16:1 with the parallel list in Numbers 33:5–11. By telescoping the stations at "the sea" and at *yam sûp* into one, P surely wanted the reader to understand the defeat of Pharaoh as happening in *yam sûp*.

On the one hand, P clearly intended to historicize his account by providing concrete chronological and geographical referents. It must be assumed, then, that P intended *yam sûp* as a specific, identifiable body of water.

On the other hand, P also wished to play upon the cosmic and mythic elements connoted by the *yam sûp*. In P's retelling of the exodus, the *yam sûp* is split, and the Israelites—freed from the slavery of Pharaoh—emerge out of its midst as God's new creation (even as Marduk cleaved Tiamat in twain and out of her carcass created the cosmos). The "splitting" of the sea is clearly reminiscent of the West Semitic myth of the creator god overcoming his watery foe of chaos. Various commentators have noted that P's account of creation (Genesis 1) contains various allusions to the common Semitic creation myth, including the reference to the "darkness upon the face of the abyss" (Hebrew *tehôm*, which is a cognate of the Akkadian *Tiamat*). P describes the universal flood as the irruption of the abyss into creation (Genesis 7:11; 8:2). In P's flood story, the Creator once again has to defeat the nihilistic power of evil (the waters) encroaching upon the kingdom of God. In P's version of the exodus story, the Israelites' deliverance from Egypt is another instance of the Creator's continuing battle against contemporary manifestations of chaos represented by the Sea. In "splitting" the sea so "that the people of Israel might go through the midst of the sea on dry land" (Exodus 14:16), God once more displayed his creative power over chaos. As in the creation and the flood accounts, the Creator caused dry land to appear in the midst of the abyss, in effect making the realm of chaos recede before a superior, positive power. The people of God of course walked in the realm of creation (dry land), while the Egyptians were submerged into the realm of non-creation (sea).

P was not the only Biblical author to portray Egypt as the embodiment of chaos. In Isaiah 30:7, Egypt, again in the role of opponent to Yahweh, is called "Rahab the quelled." Rahab is one of the names of the primeval sea-dragon. Also, in Ezekiel 29:3, Pharaoh, together with all Egypt, is depicted as "the great sea-dragon" (*tannim*), an epithet of Leviathan (see Isaiah 27:1; 51:9–11). Thus P, in portraying the exodus from Egypt as an extension of the creative will of God, stood solidly within Israel's theological traditions.

The cosmological and mythological conceptions embodied in the Biblical account of the miracle of the Sea are foreign to us post-Enlightenment readers, but they were an important source for creative theologizing by Biblical writers, both in Exodus and elsewhere.

The Exodus narrative should not be read as a historical account of what actually transpired in those days. Biblical writers were less interested in reporting historical data than in symbolizing for their contemporaries the salvational significance of their traditions. The significance of those original symbols, so meaningful when first written, has been lost in our modern scientific and technological world. Nevertheless, if we are to understand the exodus as the ancient Israelites did, we must also learn to understand the meaning of their symbols.

†"The Reed Sea: *Requiescat in Pace*," *Journal of Biblical Literature* 102 (1983), pp. 27–35.

[1] A. M. Silberman, ed., *Pentateuch with Rashi's Commentary Translated into English: Exodus* (London: Shapiro, Valentine & Co., 1930), p. 67.

[2] H. Brugsch, *L'Exode et les monuments égyptiens* (Leipzig, 1875); see H. Cazelles, "Les localisations de l'Exode et la critique littéraire," *Revue Biblique* 62 (1955), p. 323. The identification of *p3-twf* with Biblical *yam sûp* is also espoused by R. Caminos (*Late Egyptian Miscellanies* [London, 1954], p. 79) and R. Montet (*Egypt and the Bible* [Fortress: Philadelphia, 1968], p. 64).

[3] Representative examples include the following: Y. Aharoni and M. Avi-Yonah, *The Macmillan Bible Atlas* (Macmillan: New York, 1968), p. 40; B. W. Anderson, *Understanding the Old Testament*, 3d

ed. (Prentice-Hall: Englewood Cliffs, N.J., 1975), p. 68; J. Bright, *A History of Israel*, 2d ed. (Westminster: Philadelphia, 1972), pp. 120–21; H. Cazelles, "Les localisations de l'Exode et la critique littéraire," *Revue Biblique* 62 (1955), pp. 321–64, esp. 340–43; B. S. Childs, *The Book of Exodus*, Old Testament Library (Westminster: Philadelphia, 1974), p. 223 *et passim*; F. M. Cross, *Canaanite Myth and Hebrew Epic* (Harvard University: Cambridge, Mass., 1973), p. 128; J. Finegan, *Let My People Go* (Harper & Row: New York, 1963), pp. 17–89; S. Herrmann, *A History of Israel in Old Testament Times* (Fortress: Philadelphia, 1975), pp. 62–64; J. E. Huesman, "Exodus from Egypt," *New Catholic Encyclopedia* 5, pp. 741–48, esp. 745–46; N. Lohfink, *Das Siegeslied am Schilfmeer* (Joseph Knecht: Frankfurt, 1965), pp. 102–28; J. L. McKenzie, *Dictionary of the Bible* (Bruce: Milwaukee, 1965), p. 723; J. L. Mihelic, "Red Sea," *Interpreter's Dictionary of the Bible* 4, pp. 19–21; M. Noth, *Exodus*, Old Testament Library (Westminster: Philadelphia, 1962), pp. 107–11; J. C. Rylaarsdam, "Exodus: Introduction and Exegesis," *Interpreter's Bible* 1, pp. 930–31; G. E. Wright, *Biblical Archaeology*, rev. ed. (Westminster: Philadelphia, 1962), pp. 60–62; "Exodus, Route of," *Interpreter's Dictionary of the Bible* 2, pp. 197–99. The Reed Sea hypothesis is given as a possibility, without endorsement, by M. Brawer and M. Avi-Yonah, "Red Sea," *Encyclopedia Judaica* 14, pp. 14–16; G. Cornfeld, ed., *Pictorial Biblical Encyclopedia* (Macmillan: New York, 1964), pp. 302–303; B. Oded, "Exodus," *Encyclopedia Judaica* 6, pp. 1042–50, esp. 1048–50.

[4]The eight certain references in Egyptian texts have been carefully collated and annotated by A. Gardiner, *Ancient Egyptian Onomastica* (Oxford University, 1947), 2, pp. 201–202.

[5]Translated by R. Caminos, *Late Egyptian Miscellanies* (London, 1954), p. 74.

[6]Herodotus, 1, 180, and Pindar, *Pythian Odes* 4, 448 in the fifth century B.C.

[7]Xenophon, *Cyropaedia* 8.6.10, fourth century B.C.

[8]See Liddell and Scott, *Greek-English Lexicon*, under the word *erythros* II.

[9]*Am zû qanîta* means "the people whom you have created," not "the people whom you have purchased" (Revised Standard Version) or "ransomed" (New Jewish Publication Society). Although *qanâ* normally does mean "to acquire," a second meaning of "to create" is now established from extra-Biblical texts wherein one of the titles of the god El is "Creator of heaven and earth"; see F. M. Cross and D. N. Freedman, "The Song of Miriam," *Journal of Near Eastern Studies* 14 (1955), p. 249. The reluctance of P. Humbert ("Qana en hébreu biblique," in *Opuscles d'un hébraïsant* [Université de Neuchatel, 1958], pp. 166–174), to accept this meaning because of the parallel to *'am zû ga'al ta* "the people whom you have redeemed" (verse 13) is unwarranted; *ga'al* (to redeem) is elsewhere paralleled by verbs of "creation" (Deuteronomy 32:6 and Isaiah 43:1; Isaiah 44:24; Isaiah 54:4). The concept of God creating Israel as a people is present elsewhere in Malachi 2:10 and frequently in Second Isaiah; for the latter see C. Stuhlmueller, "Creative Redemption in Deutero-Isaiah," *Analecta Biblica* 43 (Rome: Biblical Institute Press, 1970), pp. 193–229.

[10]See Cross, *Canaanite Myth and Hebrew Epic*, pp. 138–44; P. Miller, *The Divine Warrior in Early Israel* (Harvard University: Cambridge, 1973), pp. 113–117; S. Norin, "Er Spaltete das Meer: Die Auszugsüberlieferung in Psalmen und Kult des Alten Israel," *Coniectanea Biblica*, Old Testament Series 9 (C.W.K. Gleerup: Lund, 1977), pp. 77–107.

[11]The punctuation of the Masoretic Text followed here yields better sense than the common modern practice of editing the text according to strictly metrical considerations (*Biblia Hebraica* [Kittel], *Biblia Hebraica Stuttgartensia*, etc.).

BAR received a number of letters in response to Batto's article. To read a selection of them, see the Queries and Comments section of the November/December 1984 issue.

Batto recently republished the scholarly article that inspired this BAR feature and then reviewed the most important rejoinders, both critical and favorable, and concluded that none of them necessitated alterations to his original thesis. This can be found in "The Reed Sea: *Requiescat in Pace*: Postscript," pp. 166–174 in Bernard F. Batto, *In the Beginning: Essays on Creation Motifs in the Ancient Near East and the Bible* (Winona Lake, IN: Eisenbrauns, 2013).

Related Reading

James K. Hoffmeier, "Out of Egypt," BAR, January/February 2007.

3

Israel Emerging

How did the Israelites come to live in Canaan—by conquest, peaceful settlement or class revolution? These articles demonstrate why this period is one of the most hotly debated in Israel's history.

How did the Israelites come to settle and live in the Promised Land? Few questions have been more controversial—and absorbing—in the Biblical and archaeological world. We have reached out to worldwide authorities to explore what their excavations tell us.

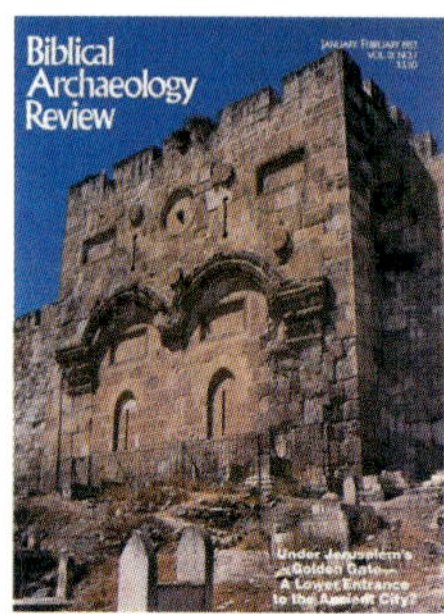

JANUARY/FEBRUARY 1983
BAR Interviews Yigael Yadin

An interview with Israel's most exciting, even legendary archaeological hero, Yigael Yadin, opens this chapter. The son of a prominent leading archaeologist, Yadin led the Jewish forces in Israel's War of Independence in 1948, excavated Herod's dramatic mountain fortress and palace at Masada, published a major Dead Sea Scroll (in three volumes), served as Israel's Deputy Prime Minister and then settled down to a life of scholarship. Here he talked about the historicity of the Bible, the role of archaeology in Biblical interpretation, whether there really is a scholarly discipline of Biblical archaeology, and what he was looking for in his excavation of the Canaanite city of Hazor. The latter subject is taken up anew in the next article—by Yadin's successor at the Hazor expedition, Amnon Ben-Tor. Yadin died in 1984 at 67.

Did the Israelites conquer Hazor? Whether or not the emergence of Israel in Canaan involved military victories has been much debated. If there is any site that seems to support the position that there were military confrontations in which Israel prevailed, Hazor is it.

Ben-Tor became director of the Hazor excavations following Yigael Yadin's death. In this BAR cover story, Ben-Tor defended the Israelites as the military might that destroyed Hazor—the "head of all those kingdoms," as Joshua 11:10 describes the city—by eliminating all of the other possible destroyers. He nevertheless recognized that his codirector and probable successor (Sharon Zuckerman) does not agree with him on this matter. She thinks it was an inside job of local Canaanites.

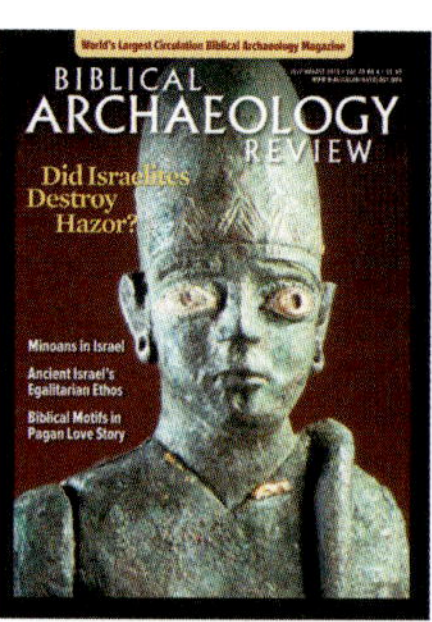

JULY/AUGUST 2013
Who Destroyed Canaanite Hazor?

Early Israel—An Egalitarian Society

Incidentally, Ben-Tor still has not found the cuneiform archive that everyone who studies the matter concludes must be hidden somewhere on the site.

The next article just appeared in 2013 and brought a new perspective to Biblical archaeology. It connects sociology to archaeology. Through a sociological analysis of archaeological finds, Israeli archaeologist Avraham (Avi) Faust was able to characterize early Israelite society as having an "egalitarian ethos."

In this area subtle distinctions are important, however. In popular magazines like BAR, the magazine gives the title to each article. And in this case we goofed. This article is titled: "Early Israel—An Egalitarian Society." Not quite. We got it right on the cover, however, as Faust explained to me after the issue came out. On the cover, we noted that on the inside was a story on "Ancient Israel's Egalitarian Ethos." That is, ancient Israel had an egalitarian ethos, but it was not an egalitarian society. Read the article and understand the important difference.

SEPTEMBER/OCTOBER 1978
An Israelite Village from the Days of the Judges
An Alphabet from the Days of the Judges

This next article is really a double-header. The site is Izbet Sarteh, probably Biblical Ebenezer, where the Israelites mustered for the fateful battle in which the Philistines captured the Ark of the Covenant (1 Samuel 4). For the BAR articles, two senior Israeli scholars teamed up—one, the archaeologist (Moshe Kochavi) who led the excavation of the site, the other the epigrapher (Aaron Demsky) who studied the prize find of the excavation, an ancient alphabet, or abecedary, perhaps penned by a scribe or scribes in training and evidencing literacy early in Israel's history.

The excavation at the site also exposed one of the finest examples of the so-called four-room house, the signal architectural structure of the early Israelites. The authors of the first article are Kochavi and Demsky. For the article on the abecedary, the authors are reversed, Demsky and Kochavi.

The last article in this chapter may perhaps be the most controversial in this book. The author Adam Zertal is a *kibbutznik* who was severely wounded in the 1973 Yom Kippur War. After a year in Hadassah Hospital, he was able to walk, but only with crutches. Among his hospital visitors was another veteran of Israel's wars who would also walk with crutches for the rest of his life. Yoram Tsafrir,

JANUARY/FEBRUARY 1985
Has Joshua's Altar Been Found on Mt. Ebal?

however, was a leading archaeologist who made a practice of visiting soldiers like himself who had been severely injured and were struggling to return to a normal life. Under Tsafrir's influence, Zertal decided to become an archaeologist. For his doctoral dissertation, Zertal chose to do an archaeological survey *on foot* of the territory of Biblical Manasseh.

Zertal soon became an active archaeologist and a member of the faculty of Haifa University. Among his discoveries was a structure on Mt. Ebal that he identified as the altar built by Joshua, as described in Joshua 8:30–35. It is no ordinary altar. It stands even today to a height of nearly 9 feet. Huge quantities of animal bones were associated with the altar.

Some scholars deny that it is an altar. For example, Israeli archaeologist Aharon Kempinski believes it is a watchtower. Others acknowledge that it is a cultic site, but question whether it is the altar referred to in the Bible. A review in BAR of a recent book (Ralph K. Hawkins, *The Iron I Structure on Mt. Ebal: Excavation and Interpretation* [Winona Lake, IN: Eisenbrauns, 2012]) recounts reactions to Zertal's thesis as running the gamut "from full acceptance ... to full denial, and everywhere in between". Both the BAR reviewer (Israeli archaeologist Aren Maeir of Bar Ilan University) and the book's author (American Bible scholar Ralph Hawkins of Averett University) agreed that Zertal found an early Israelite cult site of considerable importance. Whether or not it is Joshua's altar is less certain.

BAR Interviews **Yigael Yadin**

On July 22, 1982, BAR editor Hershel Shanks visited Yigael Yadin in his home in Jerusalem. Shanks spoke for several hours with Yadin, who had recently returned to full time archaeology after one of the many discursions that have marked his amazing life. Yadin has had a number of careers—soldier, scholar and politician among them. In 1948, he commanded the Haganah, Israel's pre-state army, in that country's War of Independence. Most recently, he served for four years as Israel's Deputy Prime Minister. Before and since, he has lived a life of the mind as an archaeologist, Biblical scholar and historian. But he also gets his hands dirty as a field archaeologist, having led a number of important expeditions—including one to Masada, Herod's wilderness palace—fortress where Jewish fighters made their last stand in the First Revolt against Rome, and another to Hazor, a site Yadin believes was captured by Joshua. Yadin also figured prominently in the acquisition by Israel of the Dead Sea Scrolls. He has recently published a three-volume edition of the Temple Scroll, the latest to be found and the longest of the Dead Sea Scrolls. (A BAR article by Yadin on the Temple Scroll is scheduled for a future issue.) Yadin often writes for BAR; his most recent contribution was "Is the Biblical Account of the Israelite Conquest of Canaan Historically Reliable?" BAR, March/April 1982.

YIGAEL YADIN

HERSHEL SHANKS: **Professor Yadin, one of the things that we hear about most frequently from our readers, and which is somewhat puzzling to them, involves the relationship of archaeology to the historical accuracy of the Bible. We know that archaeology is not supposed to prove the truth of the Bible. Most of our readers are more sophisticated than that. But sometimes they get the feeling that archaeologists are too quick to accept archaeological evidence and find that it contradicts the Bible, too quick to conclude that therefore the Bible is inaccurate. Our readers often point out how uncertain archaeological evidence really is; how often archaeologists argue from silence, from the absence of evidence; and how often there are explanations other than that the Bible is wrong. After all, we know very little of the full archaeological picture. Most of it still lies underground. And even if it were all uncovered, there would still be enormous gaps in our knowledge of the ancient world. I wonder if you feel that archaeologists are sometimes too quick to reject the Bible in favor of limited archaeological evidence?**

YIGAEL YADIN: I think your question is really a basic one. Our knowledge of the Bible as a historical document is not yet complete. It's limited. And with all the advances in the archaeological discipline, including field archaeology with all that goes with it, it is far from providing 100% answers to many questions people would like to know about the Bible.

My definition of archaeology sounds a bit sophisticated—and incidentally I didn't invent it. It was written by someone a hundred years ago. I don't remember who wrote it, but I follow it, and that is that archaeology is the science that examines the mind of man to the extent it is reflected in material or has been expressed in material.

If the thoughts of Jeremiah or Isaiah were not written down, let's say they were known only orally, or if the writings were lost, archaeology can never recover what was in their minds. It's beyond archaeology's realm.

On the other hand, if Jeremiah says that as a result of the onslaught of the Babylonians, only Lachish and Azekah remained undestroyed until the time that he was uttering his words [Jeremiah 34:7], here of course is a field day (double meaning) for archaeology. Because here I think archaeology can say, "Yes, Lachish and Azekah really were destroyed in 586 [B.C.]." We can say, "Yes, they were in the end destroyed by the Babylonians." And if we excavate, as we have, an adjacent fort, let's say 50 miles from there, we are in trouble again. Although it may seem very easy, we cannot prove that some fort, say Eglon, was destroyed five years before the other two sites. We cannot determine things so closely. If we didn't have the Bible, an archaeologist who excavated Lachish, Azekah, and, let's say, Tel Ira, would have come to the conclusion that they were *all* destroyed at the beginning of the sixth century. Does that disprove or prove what Jeremiah said? Jeremiah is saying that on the day that he was uttering his thoughts, only Lachish and Azekah remained [undestroyed], which means that a month before, five years before, twenty years before, the other sites had already fallen into the hands of the Edomites or Babylonians. We archaeologists cannot be so precise as to say that. But we can say for sure that these cities were destroyed at the beginning of the sixth century.

So to sum up: I think that there are certain questions that the archaeologist can answer. Sometimes if the answer contradicts what the Bible says, then we have to accept it because, after all, the Bible itself was not composed as a historical book. Some of those historians who wrote it, or compiled it, perhaps didn't know exactly what the historical facts were. But in many, many cases—and there are more of those cases than the others—archaeology, at the moment, cannot give a positive answer as to whether a historical statement in the Bible is true or not.

If there is a contradiction between a Biblical assertion and the archaeological evidence, I would be extremely reluctant to say that archaeology proved that the Bible was wrong. There are some cases like that, but they are fewer than most people think.

The most well-known supposed contradiction concerns Jericho. At the time most scholars date the conquest of Canaan, there was no settlement at Jericho, according to Kathleen Kenyon, who excavated the city.

Or take Jerusalem, the City of David. Only yesterday, at the City of David excavations, Yigal Shiloh showed me the evidence he found in a very, very limited area for a 10th- and 11th-century occupation of Jerusalem. Now, if Shiloh had not dug in this particular area, there would not be archaeological evidence for the existence of Jerusalem in the 10th–11th century. But now Shiloh has the evidence.

Kathleen Kenyon's Jericho excavations also involved opening only a very limited area, so can we really be sure that there was no city at Jericho at the time of the Israelite conquest?

I think there is enough evidence, even in Kenyon's excavations—and also in the earlier excavations of Garstang—to show that at Jericho there is no necessary contradiction to the Bible. We shouldn't forget that there were Jericho tombs to show that there must have been a Late Bronze 14th–13th century settlement in Jericho, even if we haven't found the settlement itself. How large it was, unfortunately, we cannot say. I think the site has been absolutely mutilated, both by nature and by earlier archaeologists. But there is evidence that there was something there [in the late Bronze Age]. Now whether the walls fell the way the Bible describes it, that is another story.

That's beyond the realm of archaeology, isn't it?

That's beyond the realm of archaeology, and I think it's beyond the realm of history as well. It's a matter of faith. The ancient people believed that this was the cause. Now if you want to believe it, you believe it; if you don't believe it, don't. But the fact is that there was a city there, in my opinion, and it was conquered. There can be no doubt. Maybe it was a small city. Maybe tradition then magnified it until it became larger than it was, but there must have been a core of history there.

I belong to a school of thought that thinks tradition must be used as a source for history, of course with caution. People don't invent certain things. For example, you can't deny that the Israelites were once in Egypt. What nation would invent such a crazy story, that they were slaves in Egypt and they left that country and came to this country, and then make that the kernel of all their history? There is a historical core. Even if you want to minimize it, there is a core of truth there. Maybe it did not happen exactly as it is recorded, down to the last detail. But there is a historical core.

So, what I'm trying to say is, in the case of Jericho, for example, I entirely agree that one has to be very careful. They didn't find a Late Bronze Age wall. But when Kathleen Kenyon excavated Jericho, in fact even when the Germans excavated there, and then later, Garstang excavated, they found a Middle Bronze wall absolutely intact. Now, if the Middle Bronze wall was intact when the archaeologists found it in the 20th century, then it was surely intact in the Late Bronze Age. We archaeologists sometimes make a terrible mistake. We think that when a new king begins to reign, then a new level must be found in the city; when he dies, the city must die as well. When a new period comes, there must be a new city wall. But this isn't true. Look, today, even today, you can see old city walls that have survived for 300, 400, 500 years. And I believe that the Middle Bronze city wall at Jericho was used in the Late Bronze Age.

I would go further, in fact I believe that most of the Canaanite cities in Canaan at the time of the conquest were rather weakly fortified. Not only in Jericho—in other cities too that the Bible claims were conquered, and in other cities that [Pharaoh] Ramesses II claims he conquered, and that [Pharaoh] Seti I claims he conquered. We acknowledge these Pharaonic conquests of Ramesses II and Seti I as accurately reported because there are reliefs and there are inscriptions as proof. Some scholars do not rely on the Bible [as you know, there is so much skepticism regarding its historical accuracy]. When we come to these cities conquered by the Egyptians, however, and we excavate, we don't find any formidable new walls that Ramesses destroyed and that supposedly were built by the people of the 14th–13th century. We find walls that were built in an earlier period.

One of the reasons scholars are reluctant to believe that there is a kernel of truth in the Jericho story is that they say that there is no evidence from the Late Bronze Age at Jericho. But this is not true. There is evidence, even according to Kenyon. She had to admit that in one spot she did find one house. All right, if you find one house, there may be more. Secondly, that they didn't find a city wall from the Late Bronze Age is not evidence. The Middle Bronze Age city wall could easily have been re-used in the Late Bronze Age.

You mentioned that there are some cases in which archaeology does contradict the Bible. Now you say Jericho isn't one

of them. What is one of them?

Well, I'll tell you what. When I say contradict, I still qualify it a little bit, and I'll tell you why. Apparently there is a contradiction. But even this may not be true. Take the story of the second city occupied by the Israelites, the one after Jericho; that is Ai. Ai was excavated rather thoroughly by the late Judith Marquet-Krause and by Joseph Callaway. Neither found any evidence for a Late Bronze Age city. Of course there still can be room for doubt. It's a huge site, and it's still possible that in one quarter, evidence of a Late Bronze Age city will be found. If I were in court, I would say it's still possible that in one area there may be a Late Bronze Age city. But from the evidence we have today, and there has been quite an extensive excavation, no Late Bronze Age city, not one Late Bronze Age sherd has been found at Ai. Now, if we believe that Joshua conquered Jericho in the 13th century, in the Late Bronze Age—and we do have evidence for this—and Ai was the second city occupied a few weeks or months after Jericho, and we can't find evidence of a city at Ai, then there is here an apparent contradiction.

Are there no other possibilities? For example, that we've incorrectly identified the city that Joshua conquered.

That's why I qualified my statement a bit. We identify this tel, et-Tel as it is in fact named which means literally the ruin—Ai also means the ruin—we identify this site as the Biblical Ai. There have been many surveys in this area and no other candidate for Biblical Ai has been found. But still I do qualify my finding of an apparent contradiction. Maybe we were looking all the time for a huge mound strongly fortified, as it is described in the Bible. The Bible has crystallized in writing what the Biblical writer imagined the city to be. But it may have been a much smaller place. That's why I do qualify my statement.

Let's sum it up. If we take the Biblical stories concerning the two cities you mentioned, Jericho and Ai, if we take these stories literally, and if people would like to know whether archaeology can say whether the trumpets caused the walls to fall or not, I say it is beyond archaeology anyhow. This is a matter of belief. I don't believe it was the trumpets that caused it, but some people may believe it. This is not a matter of argument for us now—it has nothing to do with archaeology. But as a historical question, I think we have a problem. In the case of Jericho, I would say most probably archaeology does not contradict the Biblical story. In the case of Ai, I would say that at present our knowledge, our archaeological knowledge, does contradict the Bible. But still I qualify it as I indicated.

You said that you don't believe the trumpets mentioned in the Bible caused the walls to fall down. Does that reflect your view of the Bible, your personal relationship to it as a matter of fact?

Well, I think the Bible is composed of many, many elements, absolutely different from one another. For example, let's take the first few chapters of Genesis. You cannot put the first few chapters of Genesis in the same category as the books of Kings. The books of Kings are based on the annals of the kings in which, more or less yearly, a scribe recorded the main events. If you believe that God created the world in seven days, or six days rather, to be more accurate, then you believe in that; if you don't believe, you don't believe. I, as a man who knows enough about geology, about the history of this planet, think that the way it is described there—I leave God out of the story for the moment—is contradicted by science.

The early Genesis stories are more in the nature of mythology. They crystallized perhaps a certain knowledge. I think basically the stages of creation are perhaps correct as they are described in Genesis, stages that were telescoped in the tradition, in the faith, into short periods rather than much longer. Of course, people can say that the days referred to in the Bible meant actually millions of years and the years were billions of years. I don't want to go into that. But I can't put the first few chapters of Genesis in the same category as the books of Samuel or Kings. And therefore I cannot speak of the Bible as a whole, as it relates to archaeology or faith or belief.

But even in the historical sections the Bible reflects a presence of God, a God acting in history. And even if you accept the historicity of the conquest of Jericho, you've indicated that you don't accept the miraculous aspects of the trumpets causing the walls to fall down.

When we study history, I think it's very important not to project what we think onto what people thought at the time. Today there are millions of people who believe that events happened exactly as described in the Bible and I'm sure that in those days when the Israelites managed to conquer cities, and when their grandchildren saw that they, a desert people, were able to become masters of a land that had been owned by giants and had been fortified, the Israelites were absolutely convinced that it was not only their act of valor but it was mainly God's wish and with God's help that they were able to do this. Therefore, whatever they wrote is not a bluff. They really believed it. Now you can say that this doesn't prove that God actually helped them, but it does prove one thing: it proves what motivated them, what moved them to do what they did; it was that belief.

We have to understand that; otherwise we can't understand why they built these temples and in fact why they behaved as they did. Whatever I think today is my own private view which I am free to believe. I don't even have to tell anybody what I believe. It is not important. If, however, as a scholar, I have evidence that shows that something didn't happen the way the Bible says, then it is my duty of course to present it. I gave you one example in which there are difficulties. There are also other difficulties that the editors and the compilers of the Bible knew about. They themselves knew that there were contradictions within the Bible.

But it is absolutely untrue that archaeology disproves the Bible. On the contrary, I think archaeology proves it, that is, that the great events—for example the conquest of Canaan by the children of Israel, which was a major event in the history of the people—cannot be thrown away and be explained by all sorts of sociological theories, as is sometimes attempted. First, archaeology proves that there was a conquest at that period, and second, the tradition is so strongly imbedded in the Bible, I don't believe that it was invented.

I am reminded of the story about whether it was Joshua who conquered Canaan. Who would invent Joshua? It's like the discussion about whether there was a Shakespeare; whether it was Shakespeare or somebody else by the name of Shakespeare. Was it Joshua or somebody else who was called Joshua? Why suddenly invent a Joshua? Now maybe he did less than is ascribed to him. But to deny completely the fact that there was a hero by the name of Joshua who led the tribes at a certain period and that they managed to conquer the land is, I think, to deny archaeology and the Bible at the same time.

You mentioned that you would leave God out for the moment.
Well, I don't think God has anything to do with archaeology.

You've been an archaeologist almost all your life.
That's true.

Has that affected the way you think about God or feel about God?
No, it hasn't. Incidentally, I didn't tell you what I believed before I was an archaeologist.

And you haven't told me what you believe now.
I say it did not affect my beliefs. It did not affect my thinking about whether there is a God or not. This has nothing to do with archaeology.

Has your career in archaeology affected your appreciation of the Bible?
Oh, yes.

Has it deepened your respect or made it more questionable?
Well, let's put it this way. My reaction to the Bible is very, very complex and subjective. I must be very, very careful to answer your questions as an archaeologist. After all, as a Jew, as an Israeli, I was brought up from childhood on the Bible as the history of my people, as the mandate for my being in this particular country. I still believe the Bible really records the main, the salient events in the history of my ancestors. If someone attacks the Bible, saying that it is not historical (I'm not talking about the early part of Genesis but the historical books), that it is nonsense and fiction, then I say that archaeology has increased my belief that basically the historical parts of the Bible are true. No doubt of that. But if I say, okay, I'm not a Jew at the moment, I'm not an Israeli, I am only an archaeologist, I would still say yes, on the whole, archaeology has increased my belief in the historical parts of the Bible. In fact, I am amazed. I am amazed because the more we discover, the more we dig, we see—how shall we put it?—there is always a grain of truth and I minimize it, in any event the Bible actually describes. It is true that if you understand the Bible literally, there are apparent contradictions. But if you look at the more general sweep, it is accurate. I think archaeology has actually given me, if you ask me subjectively, a greater respect for the Bible.

You know the same kinds of questions are involved in other ancient documents. I wouldn't put the Bible in the same category, but the same kinds of questions are involved. Take Josephus, for example [a first-century A.D. Jewish historian]. Before archaeological excavations, it was the vogue among historians—very serious historians—to argue that Josephus in many places relates sheer nonsense, that he is not historical, that he exaggerates, and so forth. But the more we dig in Jerusalem and at Masada and at Herodium and in [Herodian] Jericho, the greater respect we—both archaeologists and historians—have for the accuracy of Josephus. He is one of the greatest historians. Of course he had his own prejudices. But show me any historian without them. Josephus is accurate not only for his own period but for previous periods as well, for example, the Hellenistic period. Josephus had theories; of course he made mistakes in his theories—so we think—but basically as historian, he is much, much more respected as a result of archaeology.

Take Homer as another example. He was always considered and still is, but less so, like the Bible, as a kind of fiction writer recording myths and legends of a heroic period that is not really history. A whole feud went on in classical studies exactly as we have in Biblical studies between those who said that whatever is in Homer is nonsense and fiction that has no historical validity and the others who said the opposite. Slowly but surely, archaeology showed that basically the whole idea—the destruction of Troy and the Mycenaean might, and so on and so forth—was true.

Of course Homer is a later recording of events that took place several hundred years before they were written down. I have a book here by Professor [Hilda Lockhart] Lorimer, which I cherish, *Homer and the Monuments*. Lorimer is one of the most serious classical scholars, and what she does is to show that all the excavations at Greek sites have proved that Homer actually was right, even in details, when he described the detail of a shield of Ajax, or the shape of an arch, or an arrow, or whatever.

To sum up, tradition is a very powerful historical instrument, provided we know how to understand it. We must not simply swallow it lock, stock and barrel, on the one hand, and we must not throw the baby out with the bath by saying the whole thing is nonsense. If we can sharpen our tools for understanding the recorded tradition, then, together with archaeology and other sources, we can understand much better what is described in the Bible.

Is there a subject, an academic discipline of Biblical archaeology? As you know, some scholars believe that it's not a real academic discipline, but simply a historical description of what certain scholars in the past have done and they believe that the term should be abandoned.

Well, of course, as the editor of *Biblical Archaeology Review*, you are touching on something very important to your readers. You're touching a very vexing problem. I know, of course, about the views you refer to.

I think those who object to the term Biblical archaeology have absolutely misused it and therefore created confusion. You put in the mouths of those who object to the term a very mild description of their objections. Some of those who object say that Biblical archaeology is "coffee table archaeology," for example. The truth of the matter is that unfortunately we are working in a country—let's say Palestine, it's the land of the Bible we're talking about—which for a 2,000-year period [3000 B.C. to 1000 B.C.] left no substantial inscriptions or writings to enable us to understand what we excavate, unlike Egypt and Babylon which have left substantial inscriptions on monuments and written documents.

Now I wouldn't like to be an archaeologist who is only a technician in dissections. Of course it's important to know how to excavate, just as it is vital for a pathologist to know how to make a dissection. But if this is all he knows, then he'll never be a doctor; he'll never contribute to the understanding of the human body. So what are we to do. From 3000 B.C. to at least 1000 B.C., we have so little written material because our forefathers [unlike Babylonians] did not write much on clay; and papyrus, because of the humidity, did not stay well-preserved. We don't have Egypt's dry weather which preserved not only the pyramids but also papyrus. So our forefathers are silent in this respect. So today we can dig. We can know exactly the pottery, the fortifications, and stratification and relative chronology of sites and so on. And we shall be able to reconstruct a fair picture of the culture. But this is not enough. In order to understand the human mind, we have to know more. And we do have sources. We have the Bible, if we understand it correctly. We have Egyptian archaeology. We have Mesopotamian archaeology. We have philology. There are written documents from Mesopotamia and from Anatolia. Some of them are related to what happened here. Now why should we, as archaeologists who want to understand what happened in the minds of the people who lived here and built these skeletons of cities that we find, the ruins, why should we deprive ourselves of all these other sources of knowledge that I just listed.

This is Biblical archaeology. I wouldn't say Biblical archaeology is a discipline as you put it. I think it is a multi-discipline. Or, if you like, an art.

It is necessary to control certain disciplines in order to achieve certain knowledge. Today it is true that you cannot be a master of all the many disciplines I mentioned. But if somebody's studying archaeology today with the aim of understanding the minds of the ancient people in this part of the world and he's being taught only pottery and the technique of digging, and typology, and fortifications, I would say that he is not going to be an archaeologist unless he also studies at least one or two other disciplines that will help him to understand what he is going to find, either the Bible or philology or Assyriology or history.

I really don't understand why this objection to the term Biblical archaeology has arisen. Can you show me one archaeologist in Greece who has not pursued classical studies as a *sine qua non* of his education?

That's an interesting observation. I recently discussed this subject with a prominent scholar in Israel who noted that some scholars wanted to substitute Syro-Palestinian archaeology for

Biblical archaeology as a technical term. This scholar asked me, would the same people want to substitute Balko-Aegean archaeology for Greek archaeology.

I would like to comment afterwards about Syro-Palestinian archaeology, where we delineate the supposed geographical limits of our branch of archaeology. But I still want to finish the point I was making. If someone wants to excavate Knossos [on the island of Crete] and uncover materials from the beginning of the second millennium, or Mycenae [in Greece] from the third millennium, he would never be given a license, he would not even dare to go to Crete or Mycenae unless he first mastered classical studies, unless he knew Homer, unless he understood the literary sources. Similarly, no one would think of excavating in Mesopotamia who has not been trained in Assyriology. Perhaps one or two have not been trained, but they are the exception to the rule. Because in Mesopotamia, too, you cannot interpret bricks and pottery unless you understand and study a little about the history of the area from the written documents. This is also true about Egypt. All the great Egyptian archaeologists are Egyptologists too. In other words, it is a discipline which is more than just the technique of digging to discern the artifacts, to be able to reconstruct history based on typology. Impossible. This is only a skeleton without a soul. Biblical archaeology really is the complete thing. It's like a human being. You have a skeleton; you have flesh; and you have a soul, so to say. For the periods, let's say, from the Bronze Age to the Second Jewish Commonwealth [70 A.D.], it must be *Biblical* archaeology.

What used to be called in the good old days field archaeology, some people now would like to call archaeology, period. For them, archaeology is identical with field archaeology. It's a technique, they say. But the real job of the archaeologist is to understand the human mind as expressed in the material, as I said before. And that's why I think that Biblical archaeology should not be discussed, vis-a-vis archaeology itself, as something different.

Of course, the prehistoric periods are different. I wouldn't call that Biblical archaeology in the same sense because unfortunately the prehistorical archaeologist hasn't got the Bible to provide the background. But even there, if he studies the Paleolithic period of Palestine, of the Holy Land, I would still call him a Biblical archaeologist in that sense, as I would the Greek scholar, the Greek archaeologist who studies the Paleolithic period of Greece. After all, this is the land of the Bible. True, there is very little difference between the hand-axes that we find here [in Israel] and those that are found in France. But there is a difference. The difference is that they are found here. Therefore they add to the understanding of the history of the human being, of man and his history in the land of the Bible. So this is another aspect of Biblical archaeology. But it's not the same as Biblical archaeology in the periods in which the Bible as such is a source of information.

I would make two circles. The inner circle of Biblical archaeology is the period in which the Biblical historical books are sources of information. We supplement this and enrich it with all the cognate studies I mentioned before. The outer circle is the history of the land of the Bible.

Now we come to your question, "What is the land of the Bible?" I don't criticize those who use the term Syro-Palestinian. I think we should let it stand if they wish. It is a political term. But it has nothing to do with our discipline of archaeology. You can show that it is true that Syria and Palestine had a lot in common in certain periods of history. But today the term Syro-Palestinian is used by certain archaeologists in such a way that they will be able to roam about in Jordan, to roam about in Syria. You know Biblical archaeology has already become taboo there. The Bible is already not to be mentioned in certain areas. In Syria, for example, I'm sure Biblical archaeology is becoming a dirty word. But Syro-Palestinian is acceptable, particularly if you put Syro before Palestine, as it was phrased by the Roman conquerors and even before them. The Romans always saw Palestine as an offshoot of Syria. Well, that is wrong. It is not an offshoot.

Now where do we fix the geographical border of Biblical archaeology? That is a very difficult question.

I had an argument with a gentleman who always used the term Syro-Palestinian. I told him that I cannot teach the archaeology of Palestine unless I also teach at the same time the archaeology of Anatolia, of Mesopotamia, and of Egypt in certain periods. You cannot understand the archaeology of this country—particularly because it was a bridge country between these other countries and was always being conquered—unless you understand what happened there as well. I called my book on warfare *The Art of Warfare in Biblical Lands*. War is something between two parties. Normally, it is between one party and another who comes from the outside. How can we understand what happened here unless we know exactly how the Hittites or the Egyptians or the Mesopotamians fought. So the whole book tried to present the way the Assyrians fought, the way the Egyptians fought, and so on, because how can I understand fortifications in this country unless I know what it was fortified against. This is clear.

We should project this same idea onto culture trade, all sorts of things, which are reactions and counter-reactions to things that happen around us. Syro-Palestine is definitely not a meaningful archaeological term in my opinion. For the ninth century, the eighth century, and the seventh century B.C., it is more vital to know what happened in Mesopotamia than in Syria. How can we understand the fortifications, the culture, the artifacts we find here unless we know Assyrian archaeology?

Therefore, if we're talking about Biblical archaeology, obviously the land of the Bible is the center. If we're talking about Homeric archaeology or Greek archaeology, then obviously Greece is the center. You have to draw circles around the center. Some giants, like [W. F.] Albright, managed to control many disciplines. Of course in those days we knew less. Today, when knowledge is accumulating, each of us is able to control fewer disciplines. But this is only because of our shortcomings, not because the discipline doesn't need it. Therefore, we have to cooperate. I would say that a good Biblical archaeologist today is composed of at least five people. Albright could do it by himself. We can't; so we are five.

For example, yesterday you and I attended a panel discussion about a statue found at Tell Fakhariyah in Syria, inscribed in both Aramaic and Assyrian. In that discussion there were two epigraphers, one Assyriologist, one specialist in Semitic languages, and one historian. Even this was not enough because archaeology proper was not represented. Neither was the history of art, the history of statues and so forth. So these five people yesterday were together, in a way, one Biblical archaeologist, if you like.

Because of the accumulation of knowledge, we cannot master everything. Because of that, I wouldn't like to define Biblical archaeology in a limited way.

You mentioned that there is very little extant written material in Palestine. This leads me to a personal question. Are you yourself going to go back into the field?

Well, I will go back to Hazor and I think that I will find an archive there.

Why?

Well, we have some very simple evidence to begin with. For example, in famous archive from el-Amarna [in Egypt] from the beginning of the 14th century B.C., we have letters written by kings, or rather mayors we would call them today, of cities of Palestine. These letters [written in cuneiform on clay tablets] were written here [and sent to Egypt]. From these letters we know that there were archives here. I mean those people here must have kept copies of their letters. After all, there was a correspondence. And they had a bureaucracy in those days. So if we find letters in Egypt from the king of Hazor, there must have been an archive of that particular king in Hazor. This applies similarly to quite a number of Biblical cities. In Mari [in Mesopotamia], we found a letter written three hundred years, if not four or five hundred years earlier, saying that they are sending an ambassador to Hazor. And ambassadors from Hazor go to Mari. Some letters found at Mari concern shipments of precious metals to Hazor and vice versa, and so on and so forth. At Hazor, a young boy, not an archaeologist found a little broken piece of a tablet which contained a dictionary, a Sumero-Akkadian dictionary; this find shows there was a scribe at Hazor. This dictionary must have been made by a scribe for other scribes. So I think up to now we have simply been unlucky in many of the cities where we have dug in Israel. You know we excavate on a huge mound, and if you don't hit the archive, you don't even know it's there. Even in Ebla [in Syria where a fabulous third-millennium archive was recently found] they had fantastic luck. They could have dug for another 50 years and not hit that one particular spot.

Personally, I still hope that I will be able to contribute to negating the statement I made at the beginning, that Palestine has no inscribed writings for two millennia. I still want to go back to Hazor. I worked there for five years, in the biggest excavation up to that time. That excavation was in fact the cradle and the school of Israeli archaeologists. It shaped the whole method of those Israeli archaeologists who were with us at the time. Now they are archaeologists in their own right.

I believe I know at least where the palace of Hazor was. That much I am sure of. I will bet that I know where the king's palace was, just as I bet when I last dug there that I knew where the water tunnel was. [And I found the water tunnel.]

It is not just that I am a soothsayer. My belief about the palace is based on deductions, observations there at the site. We found a corner of a huge building, of such proportions that it could only be a palace. And these tablets I mentioned, the two fragments of tablets that were found by visitors, came from the debris not far from that spot.

Unfortunately, we hit only the corner. We went down 14 or 13 strata from the top, working our way for four years. And then we came to the corner. What I want to do now is to go down systematically, because every layer above it is important, although I only want to find the archive. I want to go down in the area between the two arms of the corner. And I know where it is.

I have two difficulties, which I would like to share with your readers. One is very simple. I have to go down first through a great many other layers. Nothing would deter me from doing that carefully and systematically, stratum by stratum. Each stratum might bring surprises of its own. I don't know what might be uncovered. I have to go through Ahab's period again, then Solomon's period and so on.

The second difficulty is a real dilemma. In the area where I think the palace is I have already found very important monuments which I left on the site as they were excavated. These include the famous pillared building of Hazor from the time of King Ahab. There is also a very beautiful private house or mansion or villa, named in my book Yael's House after the woman student who served as the area supervisor there. I left these buildings standing at that time because they were so rare. In order to go now to the palace where I believe the archive is, I would have to remove all this, to dig beneath. If I undertake this project, I think the Department of Antiquities will give me permission to remove the existing monuments. I may perhaps go first around the exposed buildings a little bit. But if I have to remove them, I would like to rebuild them exactly as they are a hundred yards away. It will not be a fake. Every visitor will know they are the exact buildings with their original stones, but they will stand 50 or 100 yards away. For example, in London when they found within the city a temple of Mithras where they intended to build a bank or a post office, they rebuilt the whole temple nearby.

Anyway, this is a problem for me. It is even possible that under the presently exposed buildings I will find something else I wouldn't like to remove before I reach the palace. But that's the risk.

It might take a good year, one season, just to reach the palace. I think we have a very good chance of finding the archive of Hazor—from the late Bronze period (more or less the time of Joshua), from the Amarna period [14th century B.C.], and the earlier one from the Mari period [18th to 17th centuries B.C.]. The archive from the Mari period might be as important as the Ebla archive and perhaps even more important because Hazor covered as big an area as Ebla and was definitely as important as Ebla. In all the Mari correspondence, Ebla is not mentioned but Hazor is. Ebla was perhaps in decline at this time. Perhaps Ebla was off the beaten track of the Mari correspondence that we have found so far.

I would like to come back to what I said earlier. Daily written material from our area, such as transactions and letters and even what the prophets wrote, has unfortunately been lost because most of it was written on papyrus. Even the Dead Sea Scrolls would have been lost were it not for the fact that they were, so to say, buried or hidden in caves in the Dead Sea area which is so dry. Otherwise, they would have been lost as most other scrolls either on papyrus or on leather have been lost everywhere else in the country. But I think there's good chance that one day we shall have a surprise either from Hazor or from Aphek or from Lachish or from somewhere else in the country. And we will find these clay tablets from the Amarna period, even up to the eve of the conquest of Canaan.

When are you going to start at Hazor?

I don't know yet. I have to finish preparation of the English translation of my Temple Scroll book. I must get that out. And I have other work. But I think at the moment it might be in the autumn of '83. I can't give you a firm date yet. I have to think about it very carefully. I do not want to start this dig before I push some other publications. You are one of those who are always harassing us for not publishing, and I think you are right. And I still have on my desk some publications that I must finish before I start with a new dig.

Let me mention just one of them. The publication of Hazor.

Well, Hazor, I can tell you that it's not [being ignored]. First of all, I've already published three huge volumes; very few excavations even today have been that well reported. The fourth volume of Hazor, which is the complementary text to the plates in Volume III, is being worked on. I have an assistant, and I think it is in a very advanced stage now. In the future, I can't say when, but in the near future, I hope to see light. It is already on the right track.

So that will be it for the publication of Hazor?

Hazor, yes. But I still have the Masada material. The technical work hasn't been finished, the mending and cleaning of the material. We have so much of it. But I also want to accelerate this. This doesn't mean that I will have to wait until it is finished to go to the [new] dig, but before I go to a new dig I want to set up the apparatus and staff to prepare these publications. As you know, this [delay] is not only because of the scientific reasons. Maybe it's my fault. But for five years I was out of circulation, trying to do something else which maybe archaeologists in 2,000 years or 3,000 years from now will discover. [Professor Yadin served as Deputy Prime Minister of Israel from 1977 to 1981]. This of course slowed down my archaeological work a bit.

Would you tell me a little about the difference in the way of life and what it's like to be an archaeologist as compared to a politician who's a leader of his country and second in command, so to speak.

It was quite a change from an archaeologist's way of life. There is really a difference between a scholarly way of life and, as I learned, a political way of life. I always remembered, when I was being attacked and my life was not very happy, the answer your President Wilson gave when he was in trouble and being attacked and people asked him how did he find life in the White House compared to life as President of Princeton. He said, "It's nothing compared to Princeton."

My own personal view—and my political colleagues will, I am sure, try to discredit this—is that a scholar is raised to tell the truth. And not only the scholar. Every American is told the story about Washington and the cherry tree and is told to tell the truth. But for the scholar, it is in his blood. I mean he cannot present data, he cannot present material, unless he is sure that he is presenting it to the best of his knowledge. In politics, unfortunately, I discovered what I should have known before, that to tell a lie, some people want to euphemize it by calling them "white lies," is considered all right. (When a treasurer cheats on the budget, that is a black lie. That is a sheer lie.) But I found that very difficult. I couldn't play the game, by the rules of the game of the politician. That was, I think, my greatest weakness. I suddenly found myself in a jungle, if you like. And in the jungle, there are the rules of the jungle. If you can't play by the rules of the jungle, then you are prey for other animals.

On the other hand, I don't regret those five years. I thought the social programs of the country were in trouble, and they still are, and I managed to establish something that I think is the greatest social enterprise ever undertaken by the country and the fruits of which will be shown in the coming years.

You're referring to Project Renewal?

I'm talking about Project Renewal, which is a giant enterprise of Jewry throughout the world working with the people of Israel to really change the social structure of the slums, not only the physical structure of the slums.

I was a part of the government that signed the peace treaty with Egypt. I really had great moments and hours of sitting with Sadat and in negotiation with his government.

So all told, I am very glad. After five years as a politician, I have something to go back to. And it's good that it is in archaeology. All the things have not been discovered. They are just five years older than they were.

Do you have any advice for a student interested in archaeology as to how he or she should pursue a career in archaeology?

Yes, I think every student should do it the difficult way, the hard way and not the easy way. First of all, really master the techniques of archaeology. As everyone who starts to study medicine has to know anatomy, so a student of archaeology has to study the pottery and the stratigraphy and the technique of excavation and the typology and so on. But I would advise the student who wants to study the archaeology of this part of the world also to take a course in the history or in the literature or the philology of the country or the adjacent countries. Don't limit yourself to becoming only a technician/archaeologist. My advice would be to do both. And remember it takes seven years, at least, to really become a qualified archaeologist. That is not a short time. Of course field experience is very important. It is like any practice. But don't neglect the theoretical, the historical, the philological, the background of the area in which you want to dig. I think it's vital to do this. ■

To read a selection of letters BAR received in response to our interview with Yadin, see the Queries and Comments section of the May/June 1983 issue.

Related Reading

Yohanan Aharoni, "The Israelite Occupation of Canaan: An Account of the Archaeological Evidence," BAR, May/June 1982.

Amnon Ben-Tor, "Excavating Hazor, Part One: Solomon's City Rises from the Ashes," BAR, March/April 1999.

Sharon Zuckerman, "Where Is the Hazor Archive Buried?" BAR, March/April 2006.

Strata: "On the Trail of Hazor's Royal Archive," BAR, November/December 2010.

Amnon Ben-Tor, "Who Destroyed Canaanite Hazor?" BAR, July/August 2013 (see p. 90 of this book).

Who Destroyed Canaanite Hazor?

AMNON BEN-TOR

Joshua turned back at that time and took Hazor, and struck its king with the sword, for Hazor was formerly the head of all those kingdoms. And they struck all the people who were in it with the edge of the sword, utterly destroying them… Then he burnt Hazor with fire.

JOSHUA 11:10–11

FACT OR FICTION? HISTORY OR THEOLOGY? It is commonly recognized that interest in the Biblical account of the Israelite settlement in Canaan was, to a large extent, responsible for the rise of "Biblical archaeology." It is no wonder, then, that one of the first sites to be investigated archaeologically was Jericho (in 1868 and 1907–1909). The main aim of the excavation was to uncover the walls of the city that "came tumbling down," which, in due course, were indeed "found." These controversial walls were later dated to the Middle Bronze Age (c. 1550 B.C.E.), centuries before the Israelites entered the land.

This "discovery" finds a nice parallel in another excavation motivated by a desire to prove a story. Homer's account of the Trojan War and the settlement of the Greeks in Asia Minor brought German amateur archaeologist Heinrich Schliemann to Troy in 1871, where he discovered "the treasures of Priam." In fact these treasures belonged to a city more than a millennium earlier than Homer's Troy.

In the early days of archaeology in the Land of Israel, excavations at other

DUBY TAL/ALBATROSS

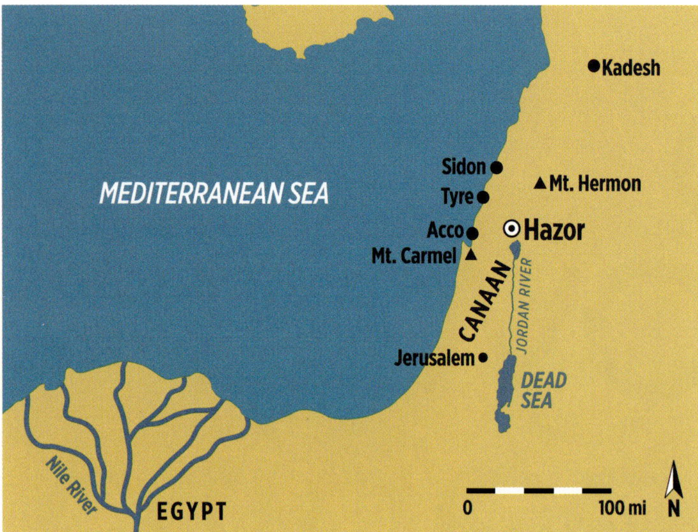

PREVIOUS PAGES: "THE HEAD OF ALL THOSE KINGDOMS." As reflected in the Book of Joshua (11:10), Hazor was one of the mightiest of the Canaanite city-states in the period before the Israelite settlement. Located north of the Sea of Galilee, the site boasted an impressive upper city on the oblong tell and a lower city spread out below (not shown in the opening photo). Is it possible that the Israelites conquered Hazor and burned this large city?

sites connected with the Biblical account of Joshua's conquests soon followed the excavation of Jericho—among them Tell el-Hesi (in 1890, then identified with Lachish), 'Ai (in 1933), Bethel (in 1934) and others.

However, of all the sites mentioned in the Book of Joshua as having been conquered by the Israelites, none is as important, with a destruction as significant, as Hazor, a large Canaanite site north of the Sea of Galilee. The culmination of the conquest and the final blow to the Canaanites was the Israelite victory over the coalition of Canaanite kings led by Jabin, king of Hazor (Joshua 11:1–4), which was followed by the slaying of Jabin and the burning of his city. As a result of this victory, "Joshua took all this land... the mountains of Israel and its lowlands from Mt. Halak and the ascent to Seir, even as far as Baal Gad in the Valley of Lebanon below Mt. Hermon" (Joshua 11:16–17).

Hazor was first investigated by British archaeologist John Garstang in 1928. Large-scale excavations were undertaken by Israel's then-leading archaeologist Yigael Yadin in 1955–1958 and 1968. It is certainly no accident that Yadin appointed Yohanan Aharoni as a key member of the excavation team, since he and Aharoni held opposing views regarding the process of the Israelite conquest and settlement. Yadin was an ardent supporter of the so-called Albright school (named for its founder, the great American Biblical scholar William Foxwell Albright), which tallies more or less with the conquest account reflected in the Book of Joshua. Aharoni was a keen supporter of the Alt school (later known as the Alt-Noth school after German scholar Albrecht Alt and his student Martin Noth), which saw the process basically as the one reflected in the Book of Judges: a slow, peaceful infiltration first, followed by a second stage in which the Israelites expanded into more fruitful plains and valleys that were still occupied by the Canaanite cities.

At the outset of the excavation, the two protagonists, Yadin and Aharoni, agreed that Hazor should be a testing ground, both historically and archaeologically, for the opposing theories. When the excavations were concluded, the stratigraphic picture was straightforward: The last Canaanite city (Stratum XIII) was violently destroyed and, after a short occupational hiatus, a new settlement (Stratum XII), confined to Hazor's acropolis, was discovered. This new settlement was poor in nature and was most probably of a seminomadic character. The many pits, which are a common feature of this new settlement, were clearly dug into the destruction layer of the last Canaanite city. The pottery found in these pits, as well as the pottery associated with the flimsy architectural remnants of this new settlement, was identical to the ceramic repertoire of the tiny Iron Age settlements Aharoni had found in his archaeological survey in the Upper Galilee.[1] Aharoni had attributed these settlements to the *early, peaceful* phase of the Israelite settlement, which, as a follower of the Alt school, he saw as belonging to a period *preceding* the downfall of Hazor. Yet the results of Yadin's excavations (just like those of the renewed excavations under my direction) clearly showed that this new (Israelite) settlement, poor in nature, *followed* the fall of Canaanite Hazor.

Bear in mind, however, that the sequence of Stratum XIII (the last Canaanite occupation level) followed by Stratum XII (the first Israelite settlement) can be observed only on Hazor's acropolis, since the earliest Israelite occupation of Hazor was confined to that part of the site. Moreover, even on the acropolis, this sequence could be tested only on a very limited scale: Yadin's excavations barely reached remnants of Stratum XIII on the acropolis, as they underlie the thick accumulation of six Iron Age strata (X–V). These Iron Age strata, spanning some 200 years, were dated by Yadin to the period between King Solomon (c. 970–930 B.C.E.), who rebuilt Hazor after the last Canaanite city was destroyed, and Pekah, king of Israel, during whose reign Hazor was finally destroyed by the Assyrians (in 732 B.C.E.). The remains of the Iron Age strata include fortifications, a citadel, storage facilities, dwellings and a water system, all of which were the focus of Yadin's excavations on Hazor's acropolis (in Areas A, B, G and L).

Yadin's investigation of the last Canaanite city at Hazor (Stratum XIII on the acropolis) revealed a temple (most of which underlies the tenth-century six-chamber city gate) and a corner of a huge building Yadin termed "the palace." In addition, a test trench ("Trench 500") exposed what Yadin identified as a Middle Bronze Age city wall. All three major finds (the temple, the "palace" and the "city wall") are located in the center of the acropolis (Area A). A stretch of fortifications some 100 feet long, which Yadin dated to the Middle Bronze Age, was exposed on the eastern flank of the acropolis (Area G).

Neither Yadin nor Aharoni considered their conclusions final; both expressed hope that future excavations would help to clarify the picture. "With all the problems still outstanding," Yadin wrote, "we can sum up with the encouraging note that the excavations [carried out in the 1950s and also in 1968] have cleared away many apparent obstacles created by earlier wrong data and have opened new avenues to a fresh examination of these vital and important problems from archaeological, historical and biblical aspects."[2]

ISRAEL GOVERNMENT PRESS OFFICE

G. LARON

OPPOSING VIEWS. YIGAEL Yadin (right) directed excavations at Tel Hazor in 1955–1958 and 1968 with the assistance of senior staff member Yohanan Aharoni (left). The two great archaeologists belonged to different schools of thought when it came to the Israelite settlement in Canaan. Yadin, a follower of the Albright school, believed the Israelites conquered Canaan as recorded in the Book of Joshua. Aharoni, however, followed the Alt-Noth school in seeing the settlement as a slow, peaceful process reflected in the Book of Judges. The men saw Hazor as a testing ground for their theories. Iron Age I (Early Israelite) pottery from the excavation, such as this decorated storage vessel (left), proved that the early phase of Israelite settlement followed the destruction of Hazor, supporting Yadin's argument.

The excavation of Hazor was resumed in 1990 under my direction, recently joined by fellow Hebrew University archaeologist Sharon Zuckerman as codirector.*

With the conclusion of the 23rd season of the renewed excavations in August 2012, it is perhaps time to consider new data we have uncovered and re-address the question formulated in the title of this article: Who was responsible for the massive destruction of Canaanite Hazor?

The renewed excavations drastically changed the analysis that had been based on Yadin's limited exposure of remnants from the last Canaanite city (Stratum XIII) on Hazor's acropolis. In the middle of the acropolis, a large building, which we named the "Ceremonial Palace," was exposed. Its walls, made of mudbricks placed on stone foundations, are 6–10 feet thick and are preserved to a height of approximately 6.5 feet. A large pebble-paved courtyard, measuring close to 10,700 square feet, extends to the east of the building. The rich assemblage of finds—including two unique bronze statues, one of a deity, the other of a king; a basalt statue of a deity, the largest ever found in the country; a decorated jewelry box; an assortment of weapons; a faience ceremonial rhyton

*The excavations, named The Selz Foundation Hazor Excavations in Memory of Yigael Yadin, are sponsored by the Institute of Archaeology of the Hebrew University and the Israel Exploration Society and take place within the Hazor National Park.

SKY-BALLOON

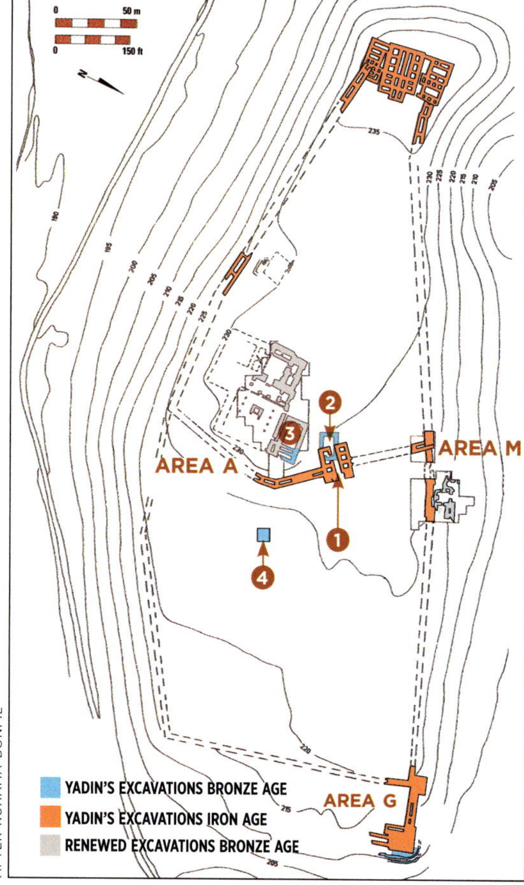

THE CANAANITE CITY. Yadin's excavations on the bottle-shaped acropolis of Tel Hazor only scratched the surface of the last Canaanite city in the Late Bronze Age (Stratum XIII) because he spent much of his time digging through the thick Iron Age layers of the later Israelite city (Strata X–V). The Iron Age six-chamber gate (1) can be seen prominently at the center of the recent aerial photo above and on the plan at left. He did, however, uncover remains of a Canaanite temple (2 in the photo), most of which underlies the six-chamber gate. He also uncovered the northeastern corner of a structure (3)—that he identified as a palace but the renewed excavations identified as a temple—and remnants of a city wall (4), all in Area A of the upper city (see plan). In Area G at the northeast corner of the tell, Yadin also exposed 100 feet of fortifications, including a thick stone wall and a deep fosse (a ditch or moat), which he dated to the Middle Bronze Age.

(drinking cup) in the shape of a lion's head—recovered on the palace floors attests to the importance of this palace and the violent fire that destroyed it sometime in the 13th century B.C.E. The fire that consumed the palace was extremely intense: It melted clay vessels and vitrified the mudbricks, indicating that the temperature of the fire was around 1,300 degrees Celsius (2,372 degrees Fahrenheit), twice the temperature of a regular fire. The combination of three factors explains this extraordinary phenomenon: a very large amount of wood used to construct the roof and the floor of the building; close to 1,000 gallons of olive oil stored in several huge *pithoi* (storage jars) found in two of the building's rooms; and the strong winds prevailing in the region, especially in the afternoon. Such an unusual fire is certainly something to be remembered for generations and could explain the reference to Hazor as the only site set on fire by the Israelites (Joshua 11:13).

We also discovered a fragment of what was probably an Egyptian offering table associated with a cultic installation on the northern slope of Hazor (in Area M). It was covered by the rubble of a mudbrick wall that fell during the destruction of the last Canaanite city. Unfortunately only a small part of the original inscription carved on the object remains, but even the few preserved hieroglyphic signs are enough to tell us that the object was most probably dedicated by the high priest Rahotep, who served under Pharaoh Ramesses II, and should probably be dated "to as late as the third decade of Ramesses II's reign [c. 1250 B.C.E.]," to quote the scholar who studied it.[3] Since there would be no point for anyone to set up an offering table in a city that is already in ruins, it follows that Hazor was still a thriving city during the first half of the 13th century B.C.E., worthy of a visit by such a distinguished Egyptian. The date of the city's destruction must therefore be no earlier than the middle of the 13th century B.C.E.

Having settled the issue of the date of Canaanite Hazor's final destruction as accurately as possible at the present time, let us turn to the identity of its destroyers.

Hazor was not destroyed by an accidental fire, an earthquake or any other natural catastrophe. The destruction was clearly the result of human activity, as indicated by the large number of statues of deities and rulers that were intentionally disfigured by cutting off their heads and hands.[4]

Since we have no record mentioning the destruction other than the Book of Joshua, the only way to go about answering the question of who destroyed Hazor is to consider all those peoples who were around at the time, examining whether any of them can be regarded as a possible candidate for the city's destroyer.

The Babylonians were too far away and too weak at the time, so we can eliminate them immediately. Egyptians returning from the Battle of Kadesh are often considered a prime candidate.[5] This well-documented battle on the banks of the Orontes River in southern Syria was an indecisive struggle between the army of Pharaoh Ramesses II (Ramesses the Great) and the Hittite forces led by Muwatallis. The two sides ultimately agreed to a truce, leaving

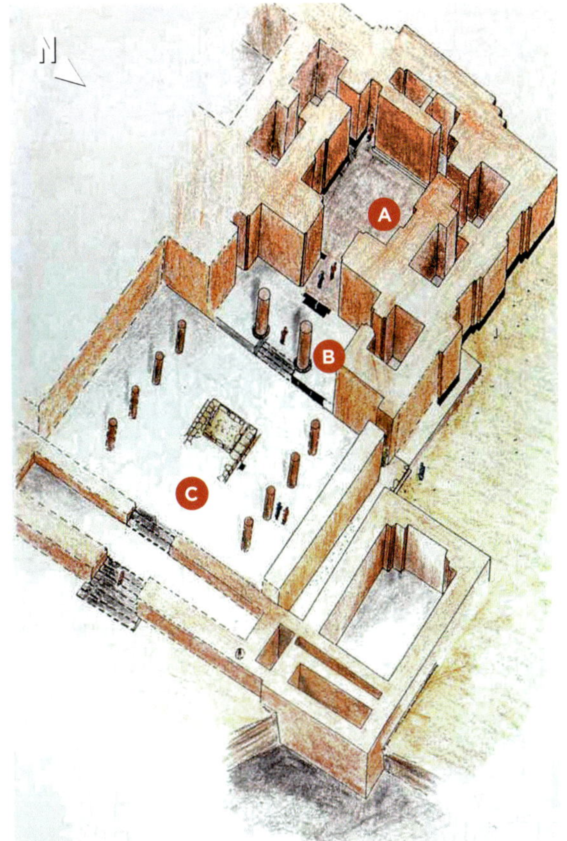

M.T. RUBIATO

SKY-BALLOON

SEAT OF POWER. Under the direction of Amnon Ben-Tor since 1990, the renewed excavations of Hazor have revealed much more of the Canaanite city in both the upper and lower cities. In the middle of the acropolis, excavators uncovered a large building that they termed the "Ceremonial Palace" (see A and B in photo at right and reconstruction drawing above it). The mudbrick walls on stone foundations were 6–10 feet thick and still stood about 6.5 feet tall. Extending east of the palace is a 10,700-square-foot pebble-paved courtyard (C).

G. LARON

G. LARON

PALACE TREASURES. A rich assemblage of finds discovered in the ceremonial palace hints at the importance of the structure. The objects included luxury items such as a decorated jewelry box with bone inlay (above) that held various beads, faience seals and gold jewelry (above right), unique bronze statues such as the one of a Canaanite ruler at left, and a faience lion-head rhyton (drinking cup; far right).

Kadesh under Hittite control, but Ramesses boastfully considered it a great Egyptian victory, setting up numerous (exaggerated) celebratory reliefs. In fact, the battle was a costly draw.

Could Ramesses II have destroyed Hazor? Not only is the destruction of Hazor completely absent from the many inscriptions of Ramesses II but the Egyptian troops would not have gone anywhere near Hazor on their march back from Kadesh to Egypt. Egyptologist Kenneth A. Kitchen has convincingly shown that the Egyptian army returned home along the Lebanese coast (see map on p. 92), via Sidon, Tyre and Acco before bypassing Mt. Carmel, traveling on to the Jezreel Valley, and from there along the southern part of the Via Maris (the "Way of the Sea"), all the way back to Egypt.[6] The Egyptians can therefore be dismissed from the list of candidates responsible for Hazor's destruction.

Next on the list of possibles are the Sea Peoples, seafaring warriors from the Aegean that included the Philistines.[7] Hazor is situated too far inland,

M. GRAYEVSKI

however, to be a site of interest to the Sea Peoples, whose activity was restricted mainly to coastal areas. Furthermore, among the millions of potsherds uncovered at Hazor during the many years of excavation in various areas of the site, not one sherd typical of the Sea Peoples has ever been found.

We can also reject the other Canaanite city-states as having been responsible for Hazor's destruction, for not one of them could challenge Hazor, "the head of all those kingdoms." Even if Hazor was in decline at the time of the city's destruction (see below), so were all other neighboring Canaanite cities.

Finally, another candidate has recently been added to the list of possible agents responsible for the violent end of Canaanite Hazor. This new suggestion is that it was not an outsider but an enemy from within the city.[8] Based on her observation that the only structures violently destroyed at Hazor were those of a public nature—temples and palaces—while private dwellings show no sign of having been destroyed, my codirector Sharon Zuckerman has concluded that Hazor's destruction resulted from an uprising of the local population against the ruling classes. In her words, the fall of Hazor came "as a result of social, political, cultural and ideological circumstances ... stressing the role of internal socio-economic and ideological factors rather than external agents."[9] This theory seems to be a revival of George E. Mendenhall's approach, according to which the entire process of the settlement of the Israelites in Canaan was actually the result of an egalitarian revolution within the Canaanite society.[10]

As for Hazor, the following arguments refute this theory:

(1) The archaeological data from Hazor does not unequivocally support Zuckerman. Her basic observation is based almost entirely on a single (!) dwelling uncovered in her excavation of Area A-210, located in the Lower City of Hazor.[11] As a matter of fact, the number of private dwellings thus far uncovered from the last Canaanite city at Hazor is extremely small. These include a few remnants in Areas C and F in the Lower City, but they suffered severely from erosion and repeated modern agricultural plowing due to their proximity to the surface of the site. It is impossible to conclude whether they ended in fire or not.[12] Basing the entire scenario of Hazor's destruction on a single dwelling exposed by Zuckerman in Area A-210 seems a bit far-fetched.

(2) Furthermore, the main targets for destruction of any city—whether by locals or by an external agent—are always the symbols of religion, power and government. Private houses are usually left intact; if destroyed, these are isolated cases. For instance, nobody doubts that Israelite Hazor was conquered by an external agent (the Assyrians in 732 B.C.E.), yet evidence for a violent destruction of the last phase of the city is only sporadically

H. SHAFIR

H. SHAFIR

A BRUTAL BLAZE brought an end to the ceremonial palace (above) and much of Canaanite Hazor. The fire was so violent that it reached 2,370 degrees Fahrenheit, melting clay vessels (see photo at left) and heating mudbricks into glass. Three factors contributed to the inferno's intensity: the large amount of wood construction, especially in the palace roof and floor; nearly 1,000 gallons of highly combustible olive oil stored in ***pithoi*** (storage jars) in the building; and the high winds common in the region. Such an immense conflagration may explain why Hazor is the only site remembered in the Book of Joshua as having been set on fire. The photo above shows the ashy remains of the ceremonial palace as well as some broken pithoi (in the foreground) that may have contributed to the blaze.

found. A good example is the situation in Yadin's Area B, where the citadel (Stratum V) was indeed destroyed by fire, but only one of the six private dwellings in the immediate vicinity was destroyed by fire. The others were left untouched.[13] The same phenomenon was also observed in the renewed excavations by our expedition.[14]

(3) If the city was destroyed by its local inhabitants, how does one explain the fact that Hazor was deserted and remained uninhabited for a period of approximately 200 years after its destruction? The local population still had houses (which stood

HIGH PRIEST OF PHARAOH. Beneath the collapsed rubble of a mudbrick wall that fell during the destruction of the last Canaanite city, Hazor's excavators uncovered this small fragment of a likely offering table. The few preserved Egyptian hieroglyphs suggest that the table was dedicated by Rahotep, high priest of Pharaoh Ramesses II, as late as 1250 B.C.E. Hazor must have still been thriving at that time, so the city could not have been destroyed before the mid-13th century B.C.E.

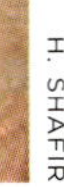

H. SHAFIR

undestroyed), land and families to support. If they won the battle, why leave town?[15]

(4) Clashes within the city, sometimes resulting in the overthrow of the local ruler, are well known in antiquity. But these clashes were always confined to the upper classes, either within a royal family or among the military elite. The very idea that the masses could have instigated a revolt against the ruling class of Hazor is an anachronism. No similar revolt is known anywhere in the ancient Near East; such an act would have been considered almost sacrilege by the people. The king was regarded by his subjects as ruling by the grace of God. Any questioning—let alone considering his overthrow—was unthinkable.

If we can eliminate the Egyptians, the Sea Peoples, rival Canaanite city-states and even the local population of the city as being responsible for the fall of Hazor, who then are we left with?

The differences between the Alt and Albright schools with regard to the process of the early Israelites' settlement in Canaan (outlined above) were discussed with much passion at the time but are of little consequence for the issue at hand. Both sides eventually agreed that Hazor was indeed destroyed by the early Israelites.[16] Even Martin Noth, the greatest exponent of Alt's school of thought, admits to a link between the capture of Hazor and Joshua 11:10.[17] Both sides thus agree on the "who"—the early Israelites—but still differ with regard to the "how"—the nature of the process by which the early Israelites took possession of, and eventually settled in, the Land of Canaan.

An array of publications by various scholars over the years, trying to determine who was responsible for the downfall of Hazor, indicates a tendency to attribute the site's destruction to anyone except the ones specifically mentioned in the Bible as having done so.[18]

As clearly shown by the famous Merneptah

G. LARON

DISFIGURED DEITIES and mutilated rulers leave no doubt that Canaanite Hazor was destroyed intentionally rather than by a natural disaster or accidental fire. Cutting the heads and hands off of almost all statues sent a clear message that the old rulers and their gods were now powerless and obsolete. This locally made ivory head of an Egyptian king (blackened by the fire that destroyed the palace) was among the casualties of the city's destruction, making it unlikely that Egyptians destroyed Hazor.

SKY-BALLOON

REBEL DWELLING? Hazor excavation codirector Sharon Zuckerman believes that the enemy came from within the Canaanite city. Based on this undestroyed private dwelling in the lower city and the contrasting devastation wrought in the upper city, Zuckerman concludes that the local population revolted against the ruling class, damaging all signs of their power and elite status. Excavator Amnon Ben-Tor disagrees, however, pointing out that elite symbols and structures were always the targets of outside conquerors as well, and that there isn't enough evidence to support Zuckerman's claim about the lower city's private dwellings. He also notes that in antiquity the lower classes would have considered it unthinkable to challenge a ruler's authority. Finally, he asks, if the locals took control of the city, why were their homes left abandoned for the next two centuries?

Stele,*[19] dated to the last decade of the 13th century B.C.E., the Israelites were present in Canaan at this time. They must have arrived some time before their encounter with Merneptah, the Egyptian pharaoh. Some prefer to call this group "proto-Israelites," but there is no reason for this. If the term "Israel" was good enough for Pharaoh Merneptah to designate this particular group of people, it should be good enough for us. Indeed, those Israelites were still largely a seminomadic society, and their national identity was not exactly the same as that of Israel in the ninth century B.C.E. A lot of changes occurred during the three centuries separating their presence in the region in the 13th century B.C.E. from the foundation of the Kingdom of Israel. Certain groups from among the local population must have been absorbed into Israel, while others left. The same is true for other national groups: The Americans of today are certainly different from those two centuries ago, and even more so the Israelis of today are very different from those who were in the country just 65 years ago when the State of Israel was founded. Such changes do not justify considering the Israelites of Merneptah and the inhabitants of the Kingdom of Israel as two different peoples.

Biblical historiography, in particular the books of Joshua–Kings, cannot be considered a completely accurate account of the events described in them, because they are motivated by a theological and—to some extent—a political agenda. They do contain a considerable number of true historical nuclei, however, and the account of the downfall of the last Canaanite city of Hazor is very probably one of them. Left with the early Israelites as the only viable agent responsible for the destruction of Hazor, one may wonder how it was possible for such a ragtag group of people to bring down a mighty city like Hazor. We need only look at analogous instances of ancient states, and even empires, being overwhelmed by "uncivilized" tribes—for example, the destruction of the Roman Empire by Germanic tribes and the Arab conquest of Byzantine Palestine.**[20]

*See Hershel Shanks, "When Did Ancient Israel Begin?" BAR, January/February 2012; "Part II: The Development of Israelite Religion," *Bible Review*, October 1992; Anson F. Rainey, "Rainey's Challenge," BAR, November/December 1991.

**See Yigael Yadin, "Is the Biblical Account of the Israelite Conquest of Canaan Historically Reliable?" BAR, March/April 1982.

As for Canaan, after some 300 years under oppressive Egyptian rule, it was drained of most of its resources. Egyptian documents tell us about constant military raids, during which the pharaoh's army lived off the land; what was not consumed or taken as tax was burned. Huge numbers of sheep, cattle and slaves were taken to Egypt as well. The various Canaanite cities were divided and poor. Most of them were not fortified, and even Canaanite Hazor's fortifications probably went partially out of use.[21] The constant disputes among the Canaanite city-states are clearly reflected in the 14th-century Amarna letters,† which also inform us of the meager number of warriors kept by the Canaanite rulers: Requests for military assistance from neighbors often mention no more than 10 to 50 men. The decline in the 13th–12th centuries B.C.E. of all the major powers that had previously ruled the region has been documented and discussed thoroughly.[22]

Seizing the opportunity—while the cat was away, the mice filled the power vacuum and settled all over the region at the end of the Late Bronze Age (c. 1200 B.C.E.): the Greeks in western Asia Minor, the Sea Peoples in the eastern Mediterranean, the Arameans in Syria, the Arabs in the Arabian peninsula—and the Israelites in Canaan.

Canaan of the 13th–12th centuries B.C.E. was "ripe for the taking," and the early Israelites were in the right place at the right time. None of the other potential destroyers of Hazor can be held responsible. The early Israelites were in the region at the time, and they are the only ones who have a record of doing the deed. They should therefore be credited with having brought down Canaanite Hazor. ■

†See Nadav Na'aman, "The Trowel and the Text," BAR, January/February 2009; Carolyn R. Higginbotham, "The Egyptianizing of Canaan," BAR, May/June 1998.

[1] Yohanan Aharoni, *The Settlement of the Israelite Tribes in Upper Galilee* (Hebrew) (Jerusalem: Magnes Press, 1957).

[2] Yigael Yadin, *Hazor, The Schweich Lecture Series 1970* (London: Oxford Univ. Press, 1972), p. 109.

[3] J. Allen, "A Hieroglyphic Fragment from Hazor," *Bulletin of the Egyptological Seminar* (2001), p. 15. See also Kenneth A. Kitchen, "An Egyptian inscribed Fragment from Late Bronze Age Hazor," *Israel Exploration Journal* 53 (2003), p. 24.

[4] Amnon Ben-Tor, "The Sad Fate of Statues of Hazor," in Seymour Gitin, George E. Wright and J.P. Desel, eds., *Confronting the Past: Archaeological and Historical Essays on Ancient Israel in Honor of William, G. Dever* (Winona Lake, IN: Eisenbrauns, 2006), pp. 3–16.

[5] Chr. Schäfer-Lichtenberger, "Hazor—A City Between the Major Powers," *Scandinavian Journal of Old Testament* 16 (2001), pp. 104–122.

[6] Kenneth A. Kitchen, *Ramesside Inscriptions Translated & Annotated,* vol. II (London: Blackwell, 1996), pp. 13–14, 20–21, map 11. The same description of the route usually taken by the Egyptians has also been defined by H. Jacob Katzenstein, *The History of Tyre from the Beginning of the Second Millennium B.C.E. Until the Fall of the Neo-Babylonian Empire in 538 B.C.E.* (Jerusalem: Shocken Institute, 1973), p. 53.

[7] Volkmar Fritz, "Das Ende der Spätbronzezeitlische Stadt Hazor Stratum XIII und die Biblische Überlieferung in Josua 11 und Ricter 4," *Ugarit Forschungen*, vol. 5 (1973), pp. 123–139.

[8] Sharon Zuckerman, "Anatomy of a Destruction: Crisis Architecture, Termination Rituals and the Fall of Canaanite Hazor," *Journal of Mediterranean Archaeology* 20 (2007) pp. 3–32.

[9] Sharon Zuckerman, "Anatomy of a Destruction," p. 3.

[10] George E. Mendenhall, *The Tenth Generation, the Origins of the Biblical Tradition* (Baltimore: Johns Hopkins, 1973).

[11] Sharon Zuckerman, "The Lower City of Hazor (Notes and News)," *Israel Exploration Journal* 58 (2008), pp. 234–236.

[12] Yadin's conclusion that "the end of stratum IA [in Areas C and F] came about as a result of fire, as indicated by the ashes found in the less exposed areas excavated in Areas H and K," speaks for itself. Yadin, *Hazor, The Schweich Series*, p. 37.

[13] Yigael Yadin et al., *Hazor* vol. II (Jerusalem, 1960), pp. 49–50, 58, 63; Yadin et al. (Amnon Ben-Tor and S. Geva, eds.), *Hazor*, vol. III–IV, 1957–1958, Text (Jerusalem: IES, 1989), pp. 105–111.

[14] Amnon Ben-Tor, Doron Ben-Ami, D. Sandhaus, *Hazor: 1990–2009*, vol. VI (Jerusalem: IES, Hebrew Univ., 2012), pp. 306–344.

[15] Nadav Na'aman, "Hazor in the Fourteenth-Thirteenth Centuries B.C.E., in the Light of Historical and Archaeological Research," *Eretz Israel* vol. 30 (Jerusalem 2011), p. 337.

[16] Yohanan Aharoni, *The Archaeology of the Land of Israel* (Philadelphia: Westminster Press, 1982), p. 178; M. Weippert, *The Settlement of the Israelite Tribes in Palestine* (London: Allenson-Breckinridge, 1971), p. 135; Yigael Yadin, "The Transition from a Semi-Nomadic to a Sedentary Society in the Twelfth Century B.C.E.," in Frank M. Cross, ed., *Symposia, Celebrating the Seventy-Fifth Anniversary of the Founding of the American Schools of Oriental Research, 1900–1975* (Cambridge, MA: ASOR, 1979), pp. 57–68.

[17] "In short, in the case of Jericho and 'Ai one may speak of aetiological traditions, while in the case of Hazor one may not." Martin Noth, "Der Beitrag der Archäologie zur Geschichte Israels," *Supplements to the Vetus Testamentum* vol. 7 (1959), p. 275.

[18] Yadin, "The Transition from a Semi-Nomadic to a Sedentary Society in the Twelfth Century B.C.E.," p. 66. As Frank Cross has observed: "I find it bemusing that given the widespread evidence of destruction in Canaan at the end of the Late Bronze Age and the beginning of the Iron Age, some scholars are inclined to attribute the violence to various peoples, to almost anyone—except Israel." As Cross also notes: "Nomads are not merely pastoralists but also warriors." (Frank Moore Cross, *From Epic to Canon* [Baltimore: Johns Hopkins Univ. Press, 1998], p. 70.)

[19] J. Pritchard, ed., *Ancient Near Eastern Texts Relating to the Old Testament* (Princeton: Princeton Univ. Press, 1955), pp. 376–378; M.G. Hasel, "*Israel* in the Merneptah Stela," *Bulletin of the American Schools of Oriental Research* 206 (1994), pp. 45–61.

[20] Abraham Malamat, "Israelite Conduct of War in the Conquest of Canaan According to the Biblical Tradition," in Cross, ed., *Symposia*, pp. 35–55.

[21] Yigael Yadin et al., *Hazor* vol. III–IV, pp. 170, 264, 297; Amnon Ben-Tor, R. Bonfil and Alan Paris, eds., *Hazor, 1968*, vol. V (Jerusalem: IES, Hebrew Univ., 1997), p. 382.

[22] A. Ward and M. Sharp-Joukowsky, eds., *The Crisis Years: The 12th Century B.C.* (Dubuque: Kendall/Hunt, 1992).

For more on the excavations of Hazor, see BAR's interview with Yigael Yadin (on p. 80 of this book) and the Related Reading (p. 89).

EARLY ISRAEL

An Egalitarian Society

AVRAHAM FAUST

MISSING: Early Iron Age tombs (1200–780 B.C.E.) in the highlands of ancient Israel.

This is going to be a difficult article to illustrate, I thought to myself as I started to write this article for BAR. How do you illustrate something that isn't there?

This is an article about burials—or perhaps tombs would be more accurate. But they aren't there![1]

At least not at this time and place. The time is Iron Age I and Iron Age IIA—and even early Iron Age IIB. This is essentially the Biblical period. Iron I is usually denominated the period of the Judges, from about 1200 to the first half of the tenth century B.C.E. Iron Age IIA and the beginning of the Iron Age IIB cover the rest of the tenth century (the time of the United Monarchy) as well as the ninth and even the first part of the eighth century B.C.E. So we're really talking about 1200 B.C.E. to the beginning of the eighth century B.C.E., a period of about 450 years.

The place is (mainly) the highlands of ancient Israel, which includes the area from northern Samaria all the way south through Benjamin and Judah to the southern slopes of the Hebron hill country (but the phenomenon expands even somewhat beyond that).

At this time and in this region, archaeologists have rarely discovered a tomb. While briefly mentioned by many scholars, this phenomenon has received only scant attention.[2] Yet the contrast is stark. In the very same region in other periods, including the Late Bronze Age (1550–1200 B.C.E.) and later phases of the Iron Age (eighth–seventh centuries B.C.E.), burials are common.[3] And contemporaneous Iron Age I burials have been found in other parts of the Land of Israel.[4]

The rarity of Iron Age I–IIA burials in the highlands cannot, therefore, be attributed to a differentiation between highlands and lowlands, on the one hand, nor to the time frame on the other. The "lack of burials phenomenon" is unique for the early Iron Age in the highlands. This glaring characteristic of the Iron Age highland society requires a systematic explanation.

Theoretically there are a number of possible explanations. This Iron Age highland population could have left dead bodies unattended or even intentionally exposed. This was inferred, for example, in Iron Age Britain, where burials are lacking.[5] But in that case human bones were found scattered all over excavation areas at many sites. Not so in Israel's Iron I–IIA. Moreover, historically, such treatment is alien to the ancient Near East in general, and to ancient Israel in particular. Other theoretical possibilities, like cremation, are also inappropriate in our case.

Israeli archaeologist Raz Kletter was the first to address the phenomenon systematically,[6] and he clearly came up with the right answer: The Iron Age dead in this area were buried in simple inhumations located outside settlements, in open fields with no grave goods. And, by the way, archaeological excavations are not usually conducted in these areas.

Although this explanation provides an explanation as to *how* these ancient Israelites were buried, the more difficult question is: Why? Why did the Israelite population[7] during the period of the settlement and most of the period of the monarchy bury their dead so simply?

Kletter himself has suggested some possibilities: This was, in his words, "a relatively poor society, without a developed class structure and consolidation of wealthy, upper classes. It does not mean complete lack of classes, only that distances between ranks were not large. Most of the people had little or no surplus to afford for grave goods, hence there are no burials with large assemblages of artifacts, nor burials of an aristocracy."[8]

While clearly pointing in the right direction, this remains only a partial (and brief) explanation at best and cannot fully account for the phenomenon.

Kletter discusses only Iron Age I society, but the rarity of burials continues into the time of the kingdoms of Israel and Judah down to the eighth century B.C.E. (in the case of the northern kingdom of Israel, until its destruction by the Assyrians).[9] Society in these kingdoms was not poor. Kletter's explanation falls short of accounting for the rarity of burials in the Iron Age IIA and much of the Iron Age IIB (980–750 B.C.E.).

Moreover, grave goods, including pottery of all types, were not expensive. Even "poor" or "simple" societies (e.g., in the Neolithic) could afford them, let alone the Iron I society, which clearly possessed material surpluses.

Finally, multiple cave burials, which were typical during the Late Bronze Age, could have been carried out during the Iron Age I (even in new caves) without any surplus being "wasted" and with even less work than digging graves in the ground. Such burials would easily fit a "classless" society as depicted by Kletter.

Any of the above arguments, let alone the combination of all of them, is enough to show that the lack of surplus—or the "poor" situation in the highlands—does not account for the observed phenomenon. The poverty of this society cannot, therefore, explain the phenomenon. So if "poor" burials (simple inhumations) do not reflect "poor" society, what do they reflect?

The above explanation is based on an assumed direct connection between social reality and the archaeological record, similar to ideas that were prevalent in the 1960s and 1970s, during the heyday of the "New (Processual) Archaeology." According to this view, burials reflect social reality, and an analysis of burials will expose all segments of society. However, more recent studies have shown that this equation of behavior and social structure is not necessarily correct. While there are many instances in which burials can be used as an index of ranking, there are also many instances in which this is not the case. Archaeology does preserve a record of past behavior, but there are elements that stand between the record left by behavior and the actual social structure of the society that produced the archaeological record—and these are *ideas* and *beliefs*. In short, ideology can influence behavior, resulting in a pattern that is different from social reality.

Examples that highlight the possible difference between social reality and its supposed material representations are multiple. For example, among the Sakalawa of Madagascar, social hierarchy is expressed in burials, but due to complex symbolism, kings are buried in the "poorest" tombs.[10] Hence, an analysis of Sakalawa burials will not expose their social structure.

UNDECORATED POTTERY reflects an ethos of simplicity, as seen in this assemblage of unadorned collar-rimmed jars, kraters and bowls from Shiloh, typical of Iron Age I and early Iron Age II Israelite hill-country settlements.

ISRAEL FINKELSTEIN

An example closer to Israel comes from Saudi Arabia. It is described in a classic study by Peter Metcalf and Richard Huntington[11]: "[T]he Kings of Saudi Arabia are buried with Spartan simplicity, their only monuments being rough piles of stones." This was a result of the fact that "in some of the stricter sects of Islam a conscious effort is made to stress the 'leveling' aspect of death." In short, "simple" burial does not correspond to social reality. Here the simplicity of the tomb reflects an ideology or ethos, rather than "social reality."

In the case of Israel in the Iron Age, it is also true that simple burials do not reflect "social reality." The society in much of this period was not poor. Nor was it unstratified. We must look elsewhere for an explanation. In short, there must have been an ideology of some sort that influenced the way the Israelites disposed of their dead. What was this ideology or belief system that led the Israelites to use simple inhumations, and to avoid more permanent types of tombs so typical in other regions and in other periods?

I believe the answer lies in an ideology of egalitarianism and simplicity. The simplest type of burial is simply a reflection of this ideology or ethos.

The best way to test this interpretation is to see whether a similar pattern is reflected in other aspects of the life of that society. Is the same ideology mirrored in other archaeological remains? I think it is.

As is well known, Israelite pottery of the Iron Age is undecorated.*[12] This is in contrast to the situation in the Late Bronze Age and in the adjacent lowlands during the Iron Age. It is commonly recognized that pottery decoration conveys messages of various aspects of the society that produced it and that a lack of any decoration is an appropriate channel to convey a message of egalitarianism and simplicity. An illuminating parallel to such behavior, although in a completely different time and place, can be seen in James Deetz's discussion of early American life. Deetz concludes that "Puritan attitudes toward decoration of everyday objects might have had an effect on the delftware industry in the London area in the form of reduction of the amount of decorated pottery before the restoration."[13] Deetz applied the same type of reasoning to explain the lack of decoration on various other Anglo-American artifacts: It was a reflection of Puritan attitudes. What we

*See also Avraham Faust, "How Did Israel Become a People? The Genesis of Israelite Identity," BAR, November/December 2009.

THE HAZOR EXCAVATIONS

witness in Iron Age Israel is a similar situation, where an ethos is responsible for the "simple" pottery and for the extreme rarity of decoration.

Turning from the decoration on the pottery to the extent of the pottery repertoire, we find a similar situation. Much has been written recently about the continuity of pottery forms from the Late Bronze Age to the Iron Age. This is true as far as forms are concerned, but the ceramic repertoire—that is, the pottery forms that are used—is extremely limited when compared to both Iron Age I lowlands and the Late Bronze Age throughout

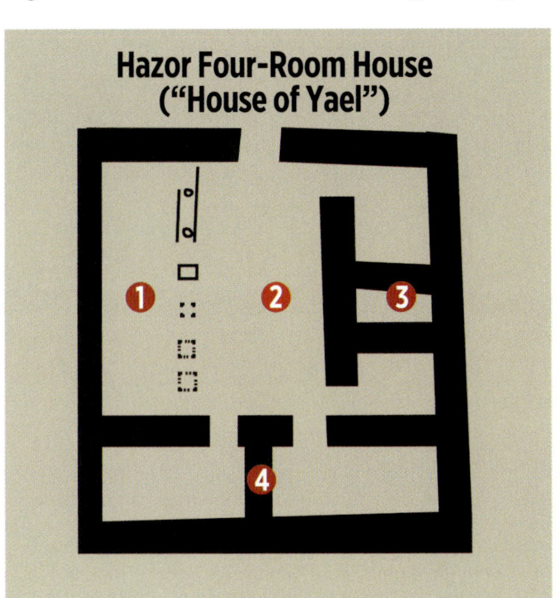

EQUAL ACCESS. A typical Iron Age Israelite dwelling, this "four-room house" was excavated at Hazor. Walls and pillars divide the house into three long rooms that join a broad room at one end of the structure (outlined in yellow in photo above; see plan at left). These four rooms were sometimes subdivided into smaller spaces, as at Hazor. This design offers easy access to all rooms, lacks any hierarchical arrangement and reflects an egalitarian lifestyle.

the region. My colleagues Shlomo Bunimovitz and Assaf Yasur-Landau have suggested that the "poverty and isolation reflected in the Israelite [pottery] assemblage" might "hint at *ideological* behavior" (emphasis in original).[14] Clearly, a limited pottery repertoire can also convey a message of simplicity and egalitarianism.[15]

Still another indication of these characteristics is the extreme rarity of imported pottery. The rarity of imported pottery to Israelite sites reflects this same ethos of simplicity.[16]

The almost-total absence of temples in the Iron Age I highland villages and in the kingdoms of Israel and Judah is also very indicative. While temples are abundant all over during the Late Bronze Age, they disappear from the archaeological record in Iron Age I and II in the highlands.[17] The extreme rarity of temples (probably also temple personnel, although it is likely that there were local priests) might also be a result of an egalitarian ideology that rejected overt signs of hierarchy.

The common Israelite domestic structure of this period is known as the four-room house. Although a few examples can be found in adjacent areas, the vast majority are within Israel. An egalitarian ideology is clearly reflected in the plan of the four-room house, as can be seen in an analysis of the movement within this house.* Each room is easily accessible; there is no hierarchy in the structuring of the rooms. Once in the central room, a person could go directly to the desired space. If a "better" space was reserved for a superior person, this is not reflected in the spatial arrangements.

Finally, we note a phenomenon that has been little discussed: the lack of royal inscriptions in the kingdoms of Israel and Judah. Israel and Judah have been excavated to a much greater extent than any other polity in the region. And, as might be expected, they yield more finds of almost any type, including inscriptions, than any other state in the region. But when one examines the quantity of *royal* inscriptions, the situation changes dramatically. Although not abundant anywhere, every state in the region has yielded some royal inscriptions—except Israel and Judah.[18] This is not likely to be simply an accident of archaeological preservation—the luck of the spade—and the large number of excavations suggests that this is a representative sample. It is likely that a few royal inscriptions will be found in the future, but their relative quantity (in comparison with the area exposed) will always be minimal when compared with other states (unless many dozens are suddenly found in Israel and Judah). The absence of royal inscriptions is also an indication that Israel and Judah did not generally approve of this genre, thus limiting the king's ability to "show off," in line with the above-mentioned ideology.

All these factors point in the same direction. The Israelite population had an ideology of egalitarianism and simplicity. It is this ideology that is probably responsible for the fact that burials are so rare at this time and in this place.

This same ethos of simplicity and egalitarianism—what some have characterized as a primitive democracy—was noticed by a number of scholars from various schools of thought, in works written generations ago up to the present day, and by scholars as prominent as William Foxwell Albright, Frank Moore Cross and William Dever.[19] As Dever has put it:

"[T]here does appear to be a kind of primitive democracy reflected in the settlements and the remains of their material culture."[20]

This is an echo of a sentiment earlier articulated by Cross:

"[T]here is a strong...patriarchal-egalitarian anti-feudal polemic in early Israel, which appears to be authentic, grounded in history."[21]

Similar views have been expressed by Ephraim Speiser, Norman Gottwald, George E. Mendenhall, Robert Gordis, James L. Kelso, Gerhard Lenski and many others.[22] While many of these studies—especially the earlier ones—were naïve and simplistic, it is clear that something in the data drove all these scholars to the same conclusion—that ancient Israel had an egalitarian ethos. I must stress that ancient Israel was not an egalitarian society—no society is truly egalitarian, and Iron II Israel was quite hierarchical—but, like some other societies, it had an egalitarian *ideology*. Keep in mind the above example from Saudi Arabia, which shows how ideology comes between human behavior (and the archaeologcal record) and "real" social structure.

The rarity of Israelite burials is a unique phenomenon of *that* society, as burials are identified in other regions at that time and in the very same region in other periods. This is not simply a representation of social reality but seems to have resulted from an ideology of simplicity and egalitarianism. A similar ideology seems to explain additional facets of Israelite material culture, as discussed above. It is likely that when facing societies in which burials had an immense social meaning, the Israelites chose not to use such burials.[23] In this way the particular trait (burial practice) seems to converge with the general (egalitarian ideology), both of which were used to differentiate the new settlers in the highlands from their contemporaneous "others," forming part of Israel's self-definition in the Iron Age.

In the Iron Age IIB–C, the Judahite tomb—a typical burial cave that was used by extended families over generations—became dominant. The reasons behind the adoption of this new type of burial by large segments of Judahite society will be discussed in a future article.[24]

*Shlomo Bunimovitz and Avraham Faust, "Ideology in Stone: Understanding the Four Room House," BAR, July/August 2002.

[1] This article is a shorter and updated version of Avraham Faust, "'Mortuary Practices, Society and Ideology': The Lack of Iron Age I Burials in Highlands in Context," *Israel Exploration Journal (IEJ)* 54 (2004), pp. 174–190.

[2] Although many observed the phenomenon, one of the only detailed treatments was by R. Kletter, "People Without Burials? The Lack of Iron I Burials in the Central Highlands of Palestine," *IEJ* 52 (2002), pp. 28–48. (See more below.)

[3] See Rivka Gonen, *Burial Patterns and Cultural Diversity in Late Bronze Age Canaan* (Winona Lake, IN: Eisenbrauns, 1992); Gabriel Barkay, "Burial Caves and Burial Practices in Judah in the Iron Age," in I. Singer, ed., *Graves and Burial Practices in Israel in the Ancient Period* (Jerusalem, 1994), pp. 96–164 (Hebrew).

[4] See list in Kletter, "People Without Burials?" pp. 28–48; see also Faust, "'Mortuary Practices, Society and Ideology,'" pp. 174–190.

[5] See Ann Ellison and Peter Drewett, "Pits and Post-Holes in the British Early Iron Age: Some Alternative Explanations," *Proceedings of the Prehistoric Society* 37 (1971), pp. 190–192; Peter Ucko, "Ethnography and Archaeological Interpretation of Funerary Remains," *World Archaeology* 1 (1969), pp. 262–280; Ian Morris,

Burial and Ancient Society: The Rise of the Greek City-State (Cambridge, 1987), p. 105.

[6] Kletter, "People Without Burials?" pp. 28–48.

[7] I am referring to the Israelite population, not to all the population within the kingdom of Israel.

[8] Kletter, "People Without Burials?" p. 39.

[9] For a few exceptions, see Irit Yezerski, "Iron Age Burial Customs in the Samaria Highlands," *Tel Aviv* 40 (2013), pp. 72–98; note that the few reported tombs (many of which represent precisely the phenomenon discussed here, i.e., simple burials) do not change the overall pattern. If burials were as common in the Kingdom of Israel as in the Late Bronze Age, for example, hundreds of tombs would be expected to be found.

[10] Maurice Bloch, "Tombs and States," in S.C. Humphreys and Helen King, eds., *Mortality and Immortality: The Anthropology and Archaeology of Death* (London, 1981), p. 144.

[11] Peter Metcalf and Richard Huntington, *Celebrations of Death, the Anthropology of Mortuary Ritual* (Cambridge, 1991), p. 134.

[12] Avraham Faust, *Israel's Ethnogenesis: Settlement, Interaction, Expansion and Resistance* (London: Equinox, 2006), and many references.

[13] James Deetz, *In Small Things Forgotten: An Archaeology of Early American Life* (New York: Anchor Books, 1996), p. 81.

[14] Shlomo Bunimovitz and Assaf Yasur-Landau, "Philistine and Israelite Pottery: A Comparative Approach to the Question of Pots and People," *Tel-Aviv* 23 (1996), p. 96.

[15] Note that the limited repertoire is relevant only for the Iron I, and disappears in the transition to the Iron II.

[16] Faust, *Israel's Ethnogenesis* and many references.

[17] Avraham Faust, "The Archaeology of the Israelite Cult: Questioning the Consensus," *Bulletin of the American Schools of Oriental Research* 360 (2010), pp. 23–35 and bibliography.

[18] Faust, *Israel's Ethnogenesis* and references.

[19] See C. Umhau Wolf, "Traces of Primitive Democracy in Ancient Israel," *Journal of Near Eastern Studies* 6 (1947), pp. 98–108; Joshua Berman, *Created Equal: How the Bible Broke with Ancient Political Thought* (Oxford: Oxford Univ. Press, 2008); William F. Albright, *The Archaeology of Palestine* (Harmondsworth, 1961); Frank M. Cross, "Reuben, First-Born of Jacob," *Zeitschrift fur die Alttestamentliche Wissenschaft* 100, Supplement (1988), pp. 46–65.

[20] William G. Dever, "How to Tell a Canaanite from an Israelite?" in Hershel Shanks, ed., *The Rise of Ancient Israel* (Washington, DC: Biblical Archaeology Society, 1992), p. 54.

[21] Cross, "Reuben, First-Born of Jacob," p. 62.

[22] G. Mendenhall, "The Hebrew Conquest of Palestine," *Biblical Archaeologist* 25 (1962), pp. 66–87; Robert Gordis, "Primitive Democracy in Ancient Israel," in Gordis, *Poets, Prophets and Sages* (Bloomington: Indiana Univ., 1971), pp. 45–60; James L. Kelso, *The Excavation at Bethel* (Cambridge MA: ASOR, 1968); Gerhard Lenski, review of Norman K. Gottwald, *The Tribes of Yahweh* in *Religious Studies Review* 6 (1980), pp. 275–278.

[23] It is likely that this is the reason the Israelites did not use even the multiple-burial natural caves.

[24] See Avraham Faust and Shlomo Bunimovitz, "The Judahite Rock-Cut Tomb: Family Response at a Time of Change," *IEJ* 58 (2008), pp. 150–170.

An Israelite Village from the Days of the Judges

MOSHE KOCHAVI AND **AARON DEMSKY**

ONE OF THE MOST CRITICAL battles in early Israelite history was fought about 1050 B.C. between the Israelites and the Philistines. At that time, the Bible tells us, the twelve tribes had settled the land and the Ark of the Covenant had been installed at Shiloh under the authority of Eli the High Priest. The people were ruled by tribal elders, by priests, by charismatic leaders called Judges who arose in times of crisis, and ultimately by the God of Israel.

The Book of Judges makes clear that not all the land allotted by God to the Israelites had been occupied by them. Various Canaanite enclaves remained. The principal problem for the Israelites in the 11th century, however, was the encroaching power of the Philistines, one of the Sea Peoples who settled and occupied the Mediterranean coastal region from Gaza to the Yarkon River, north of the modern city of Tel Aviv. On the border between the coastal plain, occupied by the Philistines, and the rising hills of Samaria, occupied by the Israelites, and the two principal powers of the country—the Philistines and the Israelites—clashed in battle.

THE PHILISTINE STAGING area for the battle with the Israelites described in 1 Samuel 4 was at Aphek. Here we see Tell Aphek from the south. Aphek guards a narrow pass between the springs of the Yarkon River to the west and the mountains of Samaria to the east. The fortress was built by the Turks in the 17th century, the latest structure on a site first occupied in 3000 B.C. The square grids in the left foreground and within the fortress walls are the areas currently being excavated. The Israelite staging area for the battle was at Ebenezer, probably the modern site of Izbet Sartah.

The battle itself is described in 1 Samuel 4.

The Philistines camped at Aphek; the Israelites at Ebenezer. In the initial skirmish, the Philistines defeated the Israelites, killing 4000 men. The Israelites in desperation sent to Shiloh to have the Ark of the Covenant brought to lead them in battle. Eli's sons Hophni and Phineas came with the Ark.

In the subsequent battle, the Israelites were again defeated. Thirty thousand Israelite soldiers were killed. The Ark was captured by the Philistines. Hophni and Phineas were killed. Upon hearing the news, Eli himself died. Archaeological evidence from Shiloh as well as literary evidence from the Bible (Jeremiah 7:12,14, 26:6,9; Psalms 78:60) suggests that the Philistines followed up their battlefield victory with a lightning march on Shiloh and destroyed the city along with the building or tent that had housed the Ark.

Israel and its ruling structure were in disarray. Israel was in danger of being overrun by the Philistines. A fair reading of the Biblical text indicates that it was probably the Philistine threat that required the formation of a centralized government ruled over by an earthly king. And so Samuel, the priest and prophet of the Lord, anointed Saul as king of Israel.

Recent excavations can fill in some of the background to this critical battle and of the way the Israelites lived in the 11th and 12th centuries B.C.—the days of the Judges.

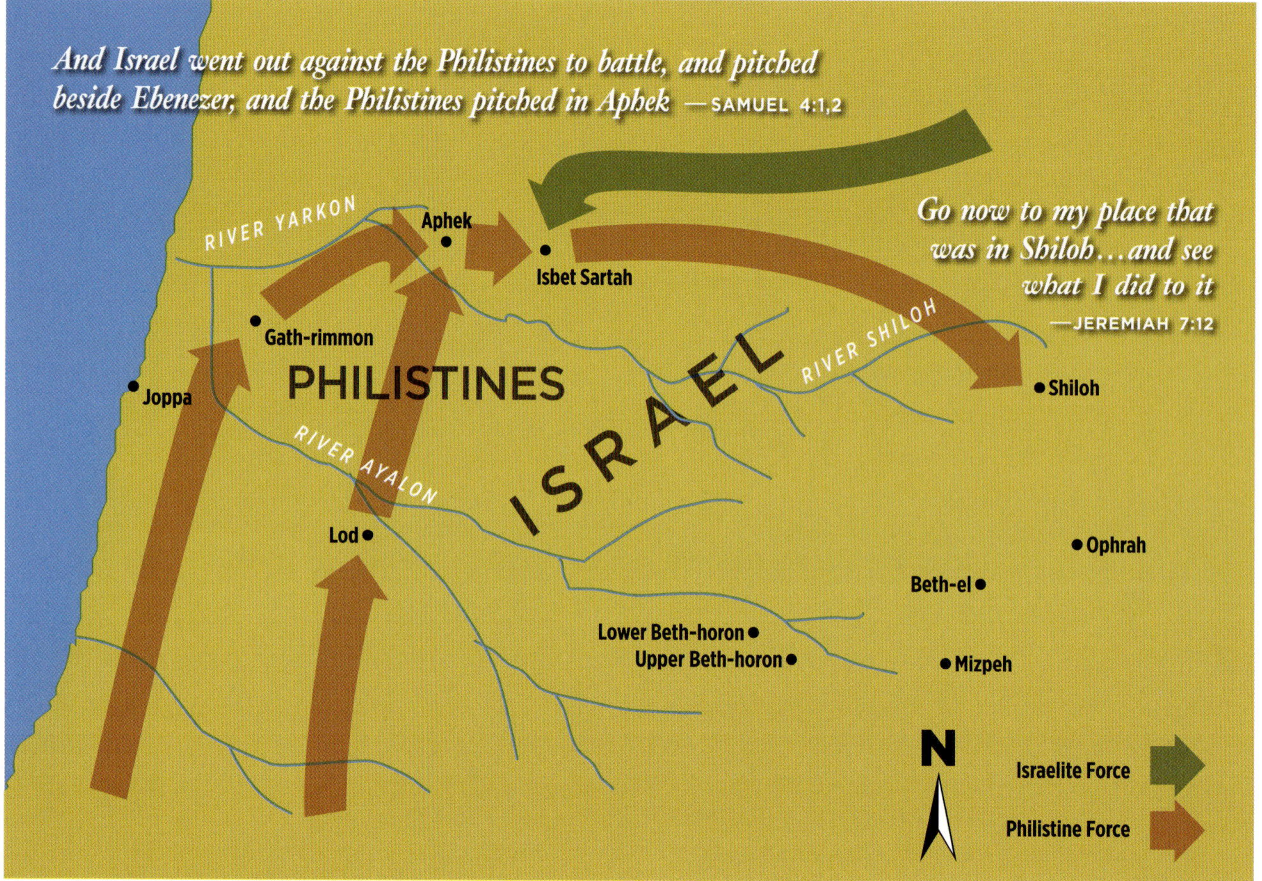

THE BATTLE OF EBENEZER showing location of Aphek, the Philistine base, and Izbet Sartah, probably Biblical Ebenezer, the Israelite encampment.

Aphek, the site of the Philistine encampment for the battle, has long been known. It is an important crossroad on the Via Maris, the ancient international route from Egypt to Mesopotamia and is well supplied with water from the springs of the Yarkon River. Although the Bible refers to the site as Aphek, Herod built a city on the same site which he named Antipatris. The Arabs today call it Ras el-Ein. In the 19th century, the Turks built an Ottoman fort on the site.

Since 1972, a team of archaeologists from Tel Aviv University Institute of Archaeology in collaboration with various American universities has been excavating at Aphek. Remains from 3000 B.C. to our day were found, including inscriptions in the Canaanite, Hittite, Sumerian, Accadian and Egyptian languages.

While the identification of Aphek is clear (it is mentioned as being between Ono on the south and Socho on the north in Pharaoh Tutmosis' III list of towns on the Via Maris), the location of the Israelite encampment at Ebenezer has never been found. As part of our regional survey of the area, we came across a small settlement across the plain from Aphek, called by modern Arabs Izbet Sartah, which may well be Israelite Ebenezer. As the nearest Israelite settlement on the fringe of the hill country facing Philistine Aphek in the Sharon plain, it is the best candidate for the Israelite staging area for the decisive battle with the Philistines.

Izbet Sartah offers a striking contrast to Aphek. Canaanite Aphek had palaces and temples and inscriptions in all the major languages of the Ancient Near East. Philistine pottery with its beautiful forms and multi-colored decorations was found in abundance at Aphek, above the debris of the Canaanite town.

Izbet Sartah, by contrast, is a rather rude village. It stretches over less than one acre. There is only one substantial building—a typical "Israelite four room house" located in the middle; poorer farm buildings surround it to form a protective belt. Stone-lined silos fill the area in between the buildings, and here and there a crude rock-cut cistern shows that the ancient Israelites had to rely on "stored" rain water because the only nearby living source of water, the rich Yarkon River springs, was controlled by Canaanite, and later Philistine Aphek.

Perhaps the most striking contrast between Aphek and Izbet Sartah is a geographical one. Although the two sites are only about 2 miles apart, Tell Aphek rises on the central plain and is watered by the Yarkon River, while Izbet Sartah is in the rocky hill country of Samaria. The one is green, the other brown. The one is fertile, the other stony. The one is on a major crossroads, the other is in the midst of nothing. That is why Aphek has been settled in every archaeological period from the Early Bronze Age (3000 B.C.) to our day, while Izbet Sartah was occupied only for about 200 years during the period that archaeologists call Iron Age I (1200 B.C.–1000 B.C.).

In short, Izbet Sartah was apparently an Israelite outpost in the days of the Judges—when Israel was able to occupy only the hill country. When King David finally subdued the Philistines (ca. 990 B.C.), and Israel occupied both the Yarkon River basin and the Mediterranean coastal plain, no one needed or wanted to live in Izbet Sartah any longer. The site was simply abandoned and never again occupied.

A number of factors suggest that Izbet Sartah may be Israelite Ebenezer referred to in the First Book of Samuel. It is in the hill country opposite the site of Philistine Aphek. Indeed, it is the nearest settlement to Aphek in any direction. Between the two is the border between the Samarian hills and the coastal plain which marked the border between Israelite and Philistine occupation in the days of the Judges.

Finally, Izbet Sartah is directly on the road from Aphek to Shiloh. Down this road, the Ark of the Covenant was carried so it could lead the Israelites in battle. Up this road, the Philistines marched on Shiloh after they had defeated the Israelites and captured the Ark.

Certainty is usually beyond the grasp of archaeologists—as it is here—, but the available evidence does indicate that Izbet Sartah is probably Israelite Ebenezer. And we have no alternative candidate which has anything like this support.

The material culture of the Philistines at Aphek was far superior to the Israelite material culture at Izbet Sartah. But the most important single find of our expedition was at Israelite Izbet Sartah—a small sherd inscribed with a 22 letter proto-Canaanite alphabet indicating that even in this outpost the Israelites used an alphabetic script during the early Iron Age. Not a single inscription in anything like a Philistine language has been found.

For further details, see Moshe Kochavi, "An Ostracon of the Period of the Judges from 'Izbet Sartah'" Tel Aviv *Vol. IV, pp. 1–13 (1977).*

THE IZBET SARTAH SHERD containing the longest proto-Canaanite inscription and the oldest Hebrew abecedary ever discovered. The first four lines (counting the short line on the far left as line three) cannot be read as words. They are probably a schoolchild's exercise. From the shape of the letters, however, we can tell they were written left to right. The fifth line is the Hebrew alphabet, also written left to right (rather than right to left as in modern Hebrew). Proto-Canaanite is the name of the earliest alphabet ever discovered: it was used to write many Semitic languages, including Hebrew. Two letters are missing: ***mem*** which should have been where the small line similar to an apostrophe appears, and ***resh***, which seems to have been overlooked. A second ***qof*** is written in its place (see third and fourth letters from the right). The ***kaf***, similar to the earliest Greek ***kappa***, is the first letter on line two and the 12th letter in the abecedary, reading from left to right.

An Alphabet from the Days of the Judges

AARON DEMSKY AND **MOSHE KOCHAVI**

AT A SITE CALLED IZBET SARTAH, now believed by some scholars, to be Biblical Ebenezer, a recent excavation by Tel Aviv and Bar-Ilan Universities has uncovered a small clay potsherd—unrelated to the Biblical story—which, however, is the most important single find of the excavation. The sherd contains the longest proto-Canaanite inscription ever discovered.*

The unimpressive looking sherd measures only 3 1/2 by 6 inches, but it contains a dramatic addition to the study of ancient Hebrew epigraphy and to the early history of the alphabet.

Inscribed on the sherd are five lines of letters. Most of the letters on the first four lines have been identified, but make no sense as words. We suspect that they are random exercises in writing letters by a student scribe.

The fifth line is, with minor deviations, the Hebrew alphabet, consisting of 22 letters! Unlike modern Hebrew, which is written from right to left, this alphabet was written from left to right (like English). At the time it was written, the writing direction had not yet been fixed.

Two kinds of evidence ordinarily enable scholars to date ancient writings, and both are involved in dating the Izbet Sartah sherd: first, the archaeological evidence; that is, what is the date of the archaeological stratum in which the inscription was found? Second, the evidence of the letters themselves—their shape, direction and form. The first type of evidence entails a stratigraphic analysis; the second, a palaeographic analysis.

*Proto-Canaanite is the name scholars give to the oldest known alphabet. Presumably many Semitic languages, including Hebrew, were written in this alphabet.

In the case of the Izbet Sartah sherd, the archaeological evidence tells us in general that the inscription comes from the time of the Judges, between 1200–1000 B.C.** But because of the context in which this sherd was found, it is difficult to be certain of a more exact date on the basis of archaeological evidence. Let us explain why. A typical, even ubiquitous, feature of early Israelite settlements are round storage silos or pits. Grain, jars of olive oil, and other foods were stored in these pits. Sometimes these storage pits are as much as 20 feet deep. At Izbet Sartah, the storage pits are quite shallow because of the thin soil layer: a few inches below the surface, rock is reached. As a result, there are many more storage pits at Izbet Sartah than we customarily find at early Israelite settlements. In the field drawing of the plan of a four-room house, each of the circles represents one of these shallow storage pits. In the vicinity of this house, we found 21 storage pits.

Some of the storage pits are attached to the house. These pits can be related to the various strata of the house; that is, these pits are stratigraphically related to the house and can therefore be dated more exactly.

Unfortunately, the Izbet Sartah sherd was found in Pit 605, which is unattached to the house. Therefore, we cannot be sure in which phase of the house the silo was used, and its contents cannot be dated stratigraphically.

**Three occupational strata were found at Izbet Sartah. The earliest, Stratum III, dates from the 12th century. Stratum II from later in the 12th century revealed the most important occupation. The Stratum II village was abandoned after the battle of Aphek-Ebenezer in about 1050 B.C. The site was unoccupied until about 1000 B.C. when it was very briefly resettled, as revealed in Stratum I. Then Izbet Sartah was abandoned forever.

However, based on the shape and form of the letters—by comparing them with other letters on other inscriptions which have been reliably dated and by fitting the letters into a developmental sequence—we can date the Izbet Sartah sherd more precisely—to about 1200 B.C., the beginning of the period of the Judges, shortly after the Israelite settlement in Canaan. This dating is confirmed by the fact that the writing is horizontal and in the left-right direction. (Later, the left-right direction disappeared both in Israel and in Phoenicia, but it reappeared in Greece and the West. Thus, we who use the Latin alphabet, write from left to right today.)

Evidence for Israelites

Another question which arises is how we know the Izbet Sartah sherd is an Israelite, and therefore Hebrew, inscription. We believe that Izbet Sartah is an Israelite settlement. Geographically, the settlement is in the area settled by the Israelites (see "An Israelite Village from the Days of the Judges" on p. 108 of this book). A comparison of the rather rude material culture of Izbet Sartah with the sophisticated Philistine material culture at Aphek also suggests that the former was Israelite. In addition, we found typical Israelite storage pits in abundance. Finally, the four-room house which we excavated is a unique architectural contribution of early Israelite settlements. In the house in the plan we find a broad (but relatively narrow) room and three long (but relatively narrow) rooms extending from the broad room, so that the house forms a rectangle like this:

The middle long room was probably an unroofed court in which the cooking was done. This architecture also suggests that the village was Israelite. Together, all these factors leave little doubt that Izbet Sartah was an Israelite town. A peculiar letter order in the alphabetic inscription also indicates that the sherd was written by an Israelite.

The Izbet Sartah sherd was almost missed. It was saved from the discard heap by an alert Tel Aviv University student named Aryeh Bornstein, who thought he saw writing on the sherd. But it was so faint that others refused to believe him. The letters became clearly visible, however, when (following the suggestion of Professor David Owen of Cornell University, an Assyriologist who has worked with ancient cuneiform texts) we applied an ammonia solution to the sherd. To appreciate how faint the writing was—to the point even now of being semi-illegible—consider that the width and depth of the incisions *do not exceed* 1/10 of a millimeter.

However, by careful study we have been able to discern at least 85 letters on the sherd. The importance of this contribution to early epigraphy is emphasized by the fact that this sherd is the longest inscription in the so-called proto-Canaanite script available from the 12th century.

The first four lines of the Izbet Sartah inscription are much shallower than the fifth line, which suggests that one scribe wrote the first four lines and another the fifth. Probably the first four lines were added after the fifth by a student who was less artful than the one who wrote the fifth line. However, the first four lines, like the fifth, are written from left to right, as we know from the fact that the letters face right.

The alphabet in the fifth line is known to scholars as an abecedary. Although partial abecedaries have been found in a number of excavations, complete abecedaries in Phoenician, Hebrew and Aramaic are very rare. The Izbet Sartah sherd's 12th century date makes it the oldest Hebrew abecedary yet discovered from the Iron Age. It is also the most complete; it is missing only the letter *mem* (m), though a line or two of the letter may be discerned. It is 400 years older than the next oldest Hebrew abecedary, a five letter graffito found about 1935 by J. L. Starkey incised on the step of the palace at Lachish. The Izbet Sartah abecedary is about 200 years older than the famous Gezer calendar, a 10th century school child's mnemonic ditty about the agricultural seasons, which, prior to the discovery of the Izbet Sartah inscription, was considered the earliest Hebrew inscription of any significant length.*

Literacy in the Bible

The Bible contains a number of tantalizing references to early writing and Israelite literacy. Naturally, the question arises as to whether these references are anachronistic—written at a later time and describing a later practice which was incorrectly projected backward to an earlier time—or whether these Biblical passages accurately reflect contemporaneous conditions.

For example, after the conquest and settlement of five of the tribes, Joshua gathered representatives of the remaining seven at Shiloh and commanded

*The text of the Gezer Calendar is as follows: (as translated by W. F. Albright *Ancient Near Eastern Texts Relating to the Old Testament* [*ANET*], p. 320)

His two months are (olive) harvest,
His two months are planting (grain),
His two months are late planting;
His month is howing up of flax,
His month is harvest of barley,
His month is harvest and feasting;
His two months are vine-tending,
His month is summer fruit.

It was found by R.A.S. Macalister during his extensive Gezer excavations between 1902 and 1909.

them: "And you shall *describe* the land in seven divisions and bring the *description* here to me..." (Joshua 18:6). These tribal officials wrote lists of the cities (Joshua 18:9) which were to become part of their territories. Whatever the period of the final redaction of the chapters of Joshua describing the division of the land (Joshua 15–19) and their incorporation into the Book of Joshua, it is now quite clear from the discovery of the Izbet Sartah sherd that there was some degree of literacy among the ancient Israelites.

The Song of Deborah (Judges 5) is almost universally attributed to the period it describes (12th century B.C.). This ancient poem states that some of the tribal leaders were literate. Deborah describes the mustering of her forces: "...from Machir the commanders marched down and from Zebulun the bearers of the scribes'** staff [marched down]" (Judges 5:14).

The most frequently quoted passage used as evidence for widespread popular literacy is Judges 8:14: "And [Gideon] caught a young man [*na'ar*] of Succoth, and questioned him; and [the young man] wrote down for [Gideon] the officials and elders of Succoth, seventy-seven men."

This verse has often been taken to imply popular literacy, as if the young man Gideon questioned was just an ordinary student who happened to be passing by. In fact, the *na'ar* is not an ordinary boy returning from his lessons who could, upon request, recall the names of the many town elders; he is an official of the local municipality whose duties demanded a familiarity with lists of the local aristocracy who were taxpayers and members of municipal oligarchy. Translating *na'ar* as young man is misleading in this passage. Recently discovered seals indicate that a *na'ar* was also an official position, a kind of attendant or steward of a large estate, royal, municipal, or (possibly) private. In a military context, *na'ar* may be translated as attendant, squire or armour-bearer (see N. Avigad, "New Light on Na'ar Seals" in Frank Cross, et al, ed. *Magnalia Dei*, 1976). Moreover, Succoth was probably a Canaanite enclave, which means that this official was not an Israelite at all. However, the Israelites probably learned from the Canaanites and developed their own scribal schools for administrative purposes. The scribes at Izbet Sartah may have been part of this tribal administration.

Thus, although the Izbet Sartah sherd does not indicate how widespread popular literacy was in the day of the Judges, it does substantiate the fact that writing was a medium already adopted by the Israelite tribes for administrative purposes.

** The Hebrew word here translated "scribe" is *sopher*, the first time it appears in the Bible. Some scholars have deleted it from their reconstruction of the original poem, others have translated it "official."

Earliest Alphabets

There is, however, another reason to believe that the ability to read and write was more widespread in Palestine than elsewhere in the Middle East. That is because it is so much easier to read and write with the use of an alphabet than with the extraordinarily complex, multi-sign system commonly used for writing in Egyptian hieroglyphs

THE GEZER CALENDAR, 10th century B.C., discovered in 1908 by Irish archaeologist R. A. S. Macalister. The verse inscribed on soft limestone is a ditty which lists the months by their agricultural tasks. It seems to have been a schoolchild's exercise tablet. Before the discovery of the Izbet Sartah sherd the Gezer calendar was considered the oldest Hebrew inscription of any length.

The Four-Room House Found at Izbet Sartah

A typical Israelite dwelling from about the 12th century B.C.

MOSHE WEINBERG

THE FOUR-ROOM ISRAELITE house at Izbet Sartah. Two people sit on the long walls dividing the main space of the house into three rooms which are perpendicular to the fourth, foreground room. The straight earthen walls overlying the house are not architectural; they are unexcavated balks or catwalks used by archaeologists to divide their digging space into five meter squares. The balks contain a vertical record of the various archaeological levels or strata.

The drawing at right corresponds to the photograph, above, of the four-room house. The numbers distinguish the rooms.

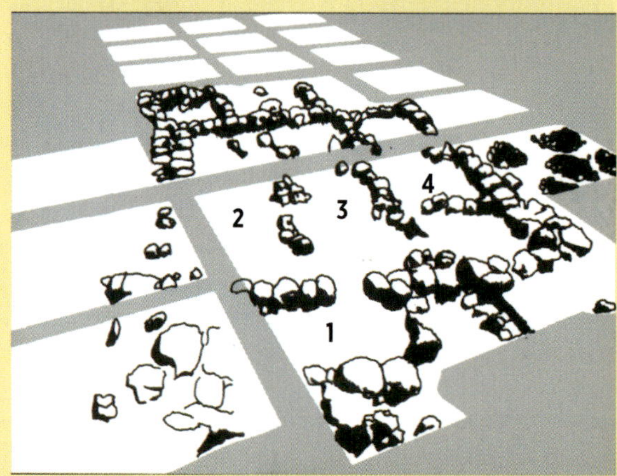

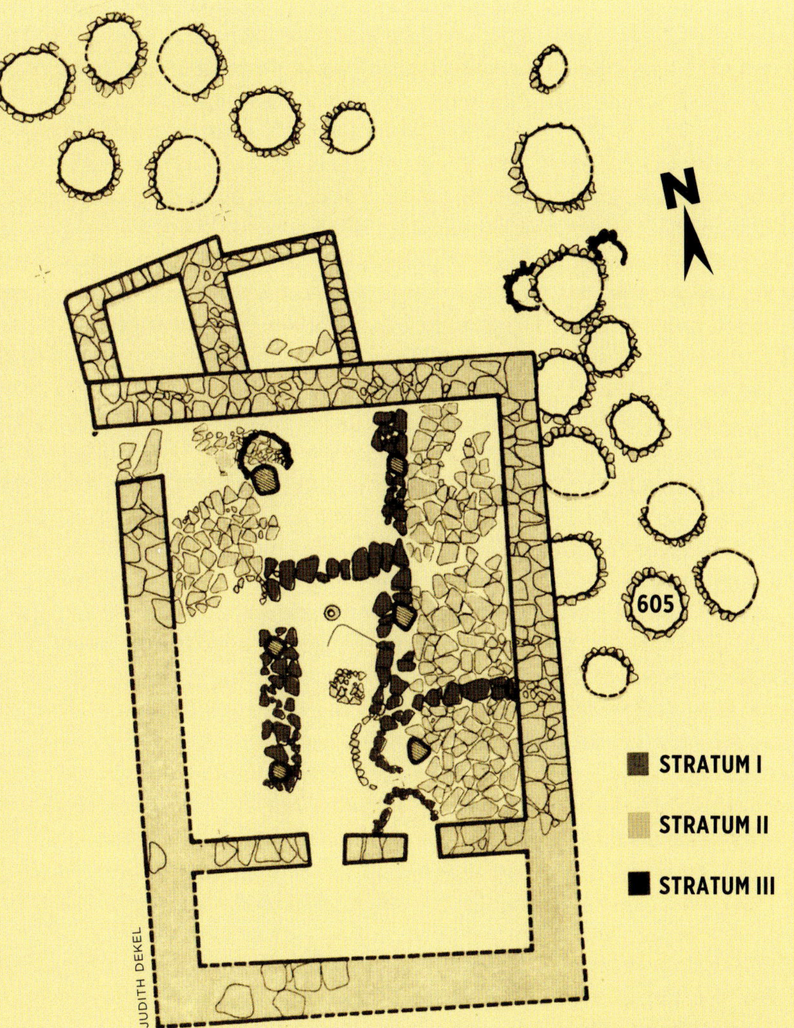

THIS PLAN SHOWS the three periods of settlement at Izbet Sartah. Stratum III—the earliest occupation level from about the 12th century B.C.—is represented only by a few storage silos. In Stratum II, from later in the 12th century B.C., the four-room house is found. Most of the silos were also constructed at this time. The village was abandoned in about 1050 B.C. following the defeat of the Israelites by the Philistines. The remains in Stratum I are from a short period of rebuilding and resettlement about 1000 B.C. The site was never again occupied. Dotted lines mark structures assumed but not found. The storage silo in which the abecedary or alphabet was found is marked 605.

OSTRACON SILO. The silo in the center with a meter stick on the bottom is No. 605, the one in which the abecedary sherd was discovered. On the far left is the outer wall of the 4-room Israelite house. The horizontal earth wall behind the man is a balk wall, part of the archaeologists' excavation square and not an architectural feature.

and Mesopotamian cuneiform. Frank Moore Cross Jr. has said that "The invention of the alphabetic principle put literacy in the reach of every man, permitting the democratization of higher culture." (*Eretz-Israel*, Vol. 8:8–24 (1967))

The hieroglyphic system has hundreds of different signs. Similarly, cuneiform systems commonly require the use of hundreds of signs representing a variety of syllables and non-phonetic elements.* With the exception of the cuneiform system developed in Ugarit, in the 14th century, no cuneiform system of writing ever developed into an alphabet (the Ugaritic exception very probably occurred when the Ugaritic people adapted their cuneiform signs to the alphabetic concept already developed in Canaan).

The alphabet—originally consisting of 22–30 signs—appears to have been invented by Semites in Canaan sometime between the 18th and 16th centuries B.C. At least these are the earliest examples of alphabetic signs which have been uncovered thus far.

The Izbet Sartah sherd is evidence of the presence of Israelite alphabetic exercises even in this small outpost on the Philistine border at a time when the Israelites were just beginning to settle the land.

Ultimately, the Canaanite alphabet spread throughout the world. The Greeks adapted that alphabet to their own language and from there it spread to the West.

The Izbet Sartah inscription also sheds unexpected light on the vexed question of how old the Greek alphabet is. The Greeks devised the letters of their alphabet from a Semitic prototype. The question is when?

Most modern scholars of ancient Greek scripts have followed Rhys Carpenter who in the 1930's argued that the Greeks developed their alphabet during the 8th century B.C. His argument was based on the similarity of Greek and Semitic letters in the 8th century and also on the absence of any earlier Greek texts.

Recently, however, Joseph Naveh of the Hebrew University has argued that the Greek borrowing of the alphabet occurred as early as 1100 B.C., despite the absence of Greek epigraphic evidence at such an early period. Naveh bases his argument on two points. First, 8th century Greek inscriptions are written left-to-right, right-to-left, and boustrophedon (back and forth, as the ox plows). This is also true of proto-Canaanite inscriptions from the Late Bronze Age, 17th–12th centuries B.C., but is not true of later Phoenician inscriptions which were once thought to provide the example for the Greek adoption of the Semitic alphabet. These later Phoenician inscriptions (10th to 8th centuries B.C.) are all written from right to left. Therefore, argues Naveh, if the Greeks had borrowed the Semitic alphabet from later Phoenician inscriptions, the Greek inscription would have been written right-to-left, not in the variety of directions characteristic of earlier Semitic inscriptions.

Naveh's principal argument, however, is based on the shape of the Greek letters. He convincingly argues that the Greek letter shapes of the 8th century far more closely resemble the proto-Canaanite letters of the Late Bronze Age than letter shapes (including Phoenician letters) as they had developed by the 8th century. Thus, he concludes that the Greek borrowing occurred during the earlier period.

The major stumbling block to Naveh's argument has been the absence of a long-legged *kaf* in the proto-Canaanite alphabet which could serve as an example for the Greek *kappa*. If there was no long-legged Semitic *kaf* at this early period (when Naveh contends the borrowing took place), the Greeks could not have borrowed their *kappa* at this early period. And if not *kappa*, perhaps not the rest of the letters. The 12th century Izbet Sartah sherd, however, contains welcome confirmation for Naveh's thesis. The Izbet Sartah sherd contains two forms of the *kaf*. Each has a long leg, a suitable prototype for the Greek *kappa*! Thus the Izbet Sartah sherd provides important evidence for the very early diffusion of the alphabet and significantly strengthens Naveh's thesis that the Greeks borrowed the Semitic alphabet in about 1100 B.C.

In addition, the earliest Greek letters from the 8th century are closer to other letters in the 12th century Izbet Sartah sherd (*alef*, *dalet*, *he*, *het*, *yod*, *nun*, *ayin* and *shin*) than the early Greek letters are to Phoenician letters of the 10th–8th century B.C. This too suggests that the Greek borrowing occurred earlier—from Canaan rather than from Phoenicia as so long supposed.

These are exciting developments in the history of the alphabet. This modest sherd from an Israelite village has made an unusual contribution to our understanding of this history.

Acrostic Puzzle Solved

The Izbet Sartah Sherd helps solve one final alphabetic puzzle. The alphabet is frequently used in the Bible as a poetic guide. The Bible contains numerous alphabetic acrostics: The first letter of each line of these poems forms the alphabet. Many psalms are alphabetic acrostics (Psalms 9, 10 [Psalm 9 contains the first half of the alphabet and the reconstructed Psalm 10, the second half], Psalms 25, 34, 37, 111,

*Cuneiform denotes writing systems which use wedge-shaped signs made by pressing a stylus into soft clay tablets.

112, 119, 145). The Book of Proverbs ends with a famous acrostic poem, a paeon to the "Woman of Valor", which is frequently recited in Jewish homes by the husband to his wife on Sabbath evening (Proverbs 31:10–31). The prophet Nahum opens his book with a partial alphabetic acrostic.

The first four chapters of Lamentations are alphabetic acrostics, the third chapter repeating each letter three times. There is a peculiarity in the letter order, however, in Chapters 2, 3 and 4 of Lamentations. Instead of the usual order of the letters, two letters are reversed. Instead of the order *ayin-pe*, we find *pe-ayin***. This reversal has long puzzled scholars.

A peculiarity of the Izbet Sartah abecedary is that it too contains the *pe-ayin* letter order. It thus verifies a local scribal tradition in which this was once the order of the letters. Another Hebrew abecedary recently found by Ze'er Meshel at Kuntillat Ajrud, an Israelite fortress in the Sinai dating from the late 9th or early 8th century B.C., also contains the *pe-ayin* sequence. Hence it appears that this local Israelite variation in letter order was used from the time of the Judges at least through the Israelite monarchy and probably through the Exilic Period when the Book of Lamentations was written.

**The sequence *pe-ayin* is also found in the Septuagint version of Proverbs 31:25–26. At least two Psalms (Psalms 10 and Psalms 34) have been reconstructed by scholars who suggest that the original form of the poem included an acrostic with a *pe-ayin* sequence.

For further details, see A. Demsky, "A Proto-Canaanite Abecedary Dating from the Period of the Judges and Its Implications for the History of the Alphabet," Tel Aviv, *Vol. IV, p. 14 (1977).*

Related Reading

"BAR Readers to Restore Israelite Village from the Days of the Judges," BAR, January/February 1979.

Orly Goldwasser, "How the Alphabet Was Born from Hieroglyphs," BAR, March/April 2010 (see p. 20 of this book).

Christopher A. Rollston, "What's the Oldest Hebrew Inscription?" BAR, May/June 2012.

Has Joshua's Altar Been Found on Mt. Ebal?

ADAM ZERTAL

M. WEINBERG

THE HILLS AND FIELDS OF ISRAEL are dotted with stone piles created by farmers clearing their land. When the author explored this mound, only telltale pottery sherds scattered on the surface distinguished it from dozens of other stone-strewn mounds. But the sherds were enough to warrant archaeological investigation at the site.

Digging beneath this particular pile of stones revealed a nine-foot-high structure dating to the early Iron Age, 1220–1000 B.C., the time archaeologists assign to the settlement of the Israelites in Canaan. In Biblical terms, this was the period when the Israelites under Joshua entered the Promised Land. According to the Bible, Joshua built an altar on Mt. Ebal, where all Israel gathered and worshipped. Could the nine-foot-high structure be Joshua's altar?

As the view of Mt. Ebal shows (opposite), even those people who stood not next to the altar, but on the hillside beneath it, would have had a clear view of the altar and of the ritual performed on it.

M. WEINBERG

TO APPRECIATE FULLY THE SIGNIFICANCE of the unique altar and cult center we are excavating on Mt. Ebal, one must first understand the archaeological context in which these discoveries were made.

We found the altar and cult center, not in the course of excavating a tell, but in the course of conducting an archaeological survey. The recent history of archaeology in Israel and in adjacent lands has seen a slow movement away from the excavation of large, well-known tells in favor of surveys of larger geographic areas. A survey not only provides a comprehensive background of an area, but it also gives the archaeologist a broader understanding of individual sites discovered during the survey.

It would be difficult to find a better example to illustrate this than Mt. Ebal and the altar and cult

center we found on it. To understand what we found, we must understand not only the site itself, but the mountain on which it was discovered and, indeed, how this mountain relates to the surrounding area in a particular time period.

An archaeological survey is conducted by surveyors who systematically walk over a defined area, so that trained eyes examine the surface of every square meter of land, slope after slope, ridge after ridge, field after field, searching for evidence of human occupation. All such evidence is carefully examined, recorded, mapped, and in the case of our survey, programmed into a computer. Sometimes limited excavation is undertaken at key sites. A survey is thus a slow, tedious process; paradoxically, it is at the same time exciting.

Our survey, which began in 1978, intends to cover the area allotted to the Israelite tribe of Manasseh. We expect to complete the survey by 1990.

Incidentally, the altar and cult center on Mt. Ebal have not been our only important discoveries. Another was Khirbet el Hammam, which has now been conclusively identified as ancient Narbata, where the First Jewish Revolt against Rome started in 66 A.D. And the city in the stratum just beneath Narbata has been identified as Arubboth, the third district capital of King Solomon (1 Kings 4:10). But this site will be the subject of another article. Let us return to Mt. Ebal.

Our survey of Mt. Ebal itself began in February 1980, nearly two years after we began our survey of Manasseh. Ebal is a huge mountain—about six and a half square miles (18 square kilometers)—in the southern part of Manasseh. It is also the highest mountain in northern Samaria, rising over 3,000 feet (940 meters) above sea level. From its peak, on a clear day, we could see the snows of Mt. Hermon in the north, the mountains of Gilead across the Jordan to the east, the Mediterranean Sea to the west, and the hills surrounding Jerusalem to the south. Our survey of this mountain alone took nearly two months to complete.

Mt. Ebal, known from Deuteronomy, chapters 27 and 28, as the mountain where the curses were pronounced, is separated on the south from Mt. Gerizim, the mountain of the blessings, by the deep narrow valley of Shechem.

On a cool spring afternoon in April—April 6, 1980, to be exact—when we had nearly completed our survey of the mountain, we came upon a large

HERSHEL SHANKS

ON THE SLOPE of Mt. Ebal, the Israelite altar overlooks terraced rows of olive trees to the east. In the distance, the settlement of Elon Moreh, center, interrupts the ridge line rising toward the summit of Jebel Kebir.

heap of stones that was not very different from the thousands of stone heaps we had already found, collected by farmers as they cleared their fields for planting. True, this stone heap was somewhat larger than the typical one, but what really distinguished it was the great quantity of pottery sherds lying around it.

We were immediately able to date these sherds to the early part of the period archaeologists call Iron Age I (1220–1000 B.C.), the period during which the Israelites entered Canaan and settled there. Iron Age I also includes the period of the Judges.

Our survey of the territory of Manasseh proved very rich in the number of sites from Iron Age I. To date, we have discovered approximately 160 sites from this period. This was hardly surprising. The Bible tells us that Israel was really born here—in the central hill country and especially near the ancient city of Shechem (Genesis 11:31, 12:6; Joshua 24).

But Mt. Ebal itself was different. Except for the heap of stones mentioned above, there was not a single site from Iron Age I on Mt. Ebal. Here, amidst evidence of dense Iron I occupation in the hill country of Manasseh, in an area identified in the Bible with the new Israelite settlements, was a prominent mountain devoid of any Iron Age sites, except one—our heap of stones. We discovered more than ten other sites on Mt. Ebal, but none of these was occupied in the Iron Age.

It took us two years to raise funds to excavate the heap of stones, and to organize our expedition. But I must confess we did not rush, for we never dreamed that the site would prove to be the earliest and most complete Israelite cultic center ever discovered and the prototype of all later ones. It took us another two years and three seasons of digging to find out what we were really excavating.

The heap of stones was called *El Burnat* by the local fellahin. It means "the hat" in Arabic. It is located on the northeastern side of Mt. Ebal on a low, stony ridge, on the so-called second step of the mountain. The site is enclosed on three sides by beautiful little valleys, producing an amphitheater-like setting. Here, we began to dig with eight volunteers in September 1982.

We have completed four seasons of excavation; one in October 1982, two in 1983, and the last in the summer of 1984, and we now have a reasonably complete picture of the site.

The central feature of the site, found under the heap of stones, is a rectangular, nearly square

M. WEINBERG

structure. Today it stands to a height of almost nine feet. Since it is so beautifully preserved, we conclude that this is probably close to its original height. It is constructed of large, unhewn field stones. The outside measurements are 24.5 feet by 29.5 feet. Its walls are 5 feet (1.4 meters) thick.

Our first season, in October 1982, concentrated on this central structure. Our initial thought was that this was a farmhouse or perhaps a watchtower. But it was different in almost every respect from the farmhouse's watchtowers we know from examples all over the country. When we reached the bottom of the structure, we immediately noticed that there was neither a floor nor an entrance. The walls were laid directly upon bedrock. Obviously, we were not dealing with a building that had been regularly lived in.

To explain the structure as a watchtower is even less satisfactory, because there is no reason for a watchtower to be here. Mt. Ebal has always been an obstacle to transportation. All transportation routes have avoided it. There is, thus, no road for a watchtower to observe. And there were no Iron Age settlements nearby.

The strangest feature of the structure was the filling, which, together with the structure, formed a kind of stage. When we excavated the fill within the structure, we found that it consisted of deliberately laid strata or layers of field stones, earth and ashes, one layer on top of the other. The earth and ashes contained pieces of pottery, all from Iron Age I, and animal bones. The ash was of different kinds of burnt wood, principally evergreen oak (*Quercus Calliprinos*).

Getting a little ahead of my story, I will tell you that the bones, which were found in such large quantities in the filling, were sent for analysis to

THE RECTANGULAR ALTAR on Mt. Ebal was once filled with alternating layers of earth, ash and fieldstones. Here, inside the altar's exterior wall, bordering the edges of the photo, we see the excavation of the fill in progress.

When archaeologists removed that fill, they discovered an interior dividing wall, center, extending part of the way across the altar. As the archaeologists continued to excavate, they came to an ash layer (to the left of the dividing wall), which they preserved for a time. To the right of the dividing wall, they continued excavating and reached bedrock. The walls of the altar had been built directly on bedrock.

Sometime after this photo was taken, the area in front of the dividing wall was excavated, and a circular structure on bedrock was revealed (opposite).

the zoology department of the Hebrew University in Jerusalem. The bones proved to be from young male bulls, sheep, goats and fallow deer. Most of the bones had been burnt in open-flame fires of low temperature (200–600 degrees C.). Some of the bones were cut near the joints. The first chapter of Leviticus describes the animals that may be offered as sacrifices. A burnt offering must be a male without blemish (Leviticus 1:3). It may be a bull (Leviticus 1:5) or a sheep or a goat (Leviticus 1:10). The close match of the bones we found in the fill with this description in Leviticus 1 was a strong hint as to the nature of the structure we were excavating. Although fallow deer were not included in the Biblical description, they are a kosher animal that may be slaughtered and eaten, so it is possible that during the early stages of the Israelite religion, a fallow deer could also have served as an acceptable sacrifice.

But all this analysis of the bones actually occurred much later. At the end of our first season, when the winter rains began, and it turned cold on Mt. Ebal, we still had no idea what this mysterious structure was.

When we excavated under the fill, we found some curious stone-built installations. One installation consisted of a circle made of medium-sized field stones laid on bedrock and located at the exact geometric center of the structure. The outside diameter of the circle of stones was 6.5 feet. The circle of stones was filled with a thin, yellowish material that we have not yet identified. On top of this yellowish layer was a thin layer of ash and animal bones.

This installation as well as the others inside the structure were clearly used in some fire-related activity before the structure was built. It is quite obvious, now, that the installations at the bottom of the structure represent an earlier phase, and the large structure itself represents a later phase—both from the same Iron I period.

Two cross-walls divide the structure. If these cross-walls extended further, they would meet and divide the structure in two. They are too short to meet, however. One of these short walls was built over the circle installation at the center of the structure.

Another curious discovery: two corners of the structure point precisely (within an error of less than one degree) to the north and the south; since the structure is rectangular, the other two corners point nearly but not exactly east and west.

Attached to the structure on the southwestern side were two adjacent, stone-paved courtyards. In each courtyard were stone-built installations, three in one and four in the other. Some of

HERSHEL SHANKS

HERSHEL SHANKS

CIRCULAR STRUCTURES of small fieldstones. Constructed on bedrock at the exact center of the rectangular structure at Mt. Ebal, the circle (top) was filled with a layer of ash and animal bones. Its location and filling tell archaeologists that it was built sometime before the rectangular structure was erected and was probably used for animal sacrifice.

In the courtyards of the altar, seven other variously shaped stone installations were uncovered, such as the one just to the man's right. Inside these installations, excavators found either complete pottery vessels, which originally probably contained offerings, or animal bones and ashes.

Behind the installation, both the higher level and the slightly lower level ramps are visible, sloping downwards from the top left to the middle right of the photo.

M. WEINBERG

THE EXCAVATED ALTAR is situated on the northeastern slope of Mt. Ebal in the Biblical territory of Manasseh. At this stage of the excavations, the structure in the center of the photo appears as a large rectangle to which a square is attached on its left. The lower horizontal "wall" of the square on the left is, in fact, a ramp leading up to the rectangular altar platform. On either side of the ramp are courtyards. These structures can be easily distinguished in the drawings on pp. 130–131.

In this view from the southeast, a thin wall of fieldstones is barely visible to the left of the courtyards. A thicker retaining wall appears as a line separating the dark area to the right of the altar and the light-colored stone slope. Both the thin wall and the earlier, thicker wall originally looped entirely around the excavated structures to form a sacred area archaeologists call a temenos.

Although the territory of Manasseh is dotted with sites that date to Iron Age I, the period when the Israelites settled here, this structure is the only Iron Age I site on Mt. Ebal.

these installations were paved with crushed chalk. They contained either ashes and animal bones, or complete pottery vessels (jars, jugs, juglets and pyxides)—one or the other, but not both.

What at first glance appears to be a wall separating the two courtyards outside the rectangular structure actually rises from the far side up to the main structure at an incline of 22 degrees. This is in fact a ramp leading up to the stage on top of the main structure. This ramp is a bit over 3 feet wide and 23 feet long. It is made of medium-sized field stones. The highest point of the ramp indicates that the main structure was one layer of stones higher than its present elevation, rising to a height of approximately 10 feet. So both the ramp and the excellent state of preservation of the structure indicate it has been preserved to nearly its full original height.

This structure, together with its ramp and courtyards and adjacent area, is surrounded by a thin elliptical wall enclosing about 37,650 square feet (3,500 square meters). We refer to this wall as the temenos wall. (*Temenos* is a Greek word meaning "an enclosed sacred place.") The temenos wall stands to a height of about one and a half feet and is made of small field stones. This wall is built on the edge of the slope. About seven feet west and down the slope from this wall is a retaining or revetment wall, which we now assume to be an earlier temenos wall, made of very large boulders. The space between the two walls is filled with field stones that support the later temenos wall.

During the last excavation season, we located the gateway through the temenos wall. It consists of two parallel walls perpendicular to the temenos wall, 23 feet apart. Three wide steps lead up the slope and through the gateway. The entrance is beautifully

paved with large, flat stones, creating a very wide and precisely detailed processional entrance. No parallel to this entranceway has been found in Iron Age Israel. This beautiful entrance emphasizes the significance of Mt. Ebal as a sacred cultic center.

Within the temenos or sacred precinct but outside the main structure, we found different stone installations, in addition to those already described. They are mostly built of small flat stones and are arranged in three groups. In some we found pottery vessels but no ashes or trace of fire. Originally, the vessels probably contained some kind of offering. In other installations, we found ash and animal bones but no pottery.

A word about the pottery. In the past few years our knowledge of the pottery of this period in the area of Manasseh has increased greatly. We can now say with considerable confidence that the site on Mt. Ebal consists of two distinct levels, to which two very similar groups of pottery are related. The earlier level is from the second half of the 13th century B.C., and the later from the first half of the 12th century B.C. Much of the later pottery is uniquely adorned on its handles with a reed-hole decoration and a "man's face" decoration. Both were discovered and studied during our survey in Manasseh, and now we consider these handles to be the clearest indication that the particular stratum in which they are found dates to the Israelite settlement period—especially in the territory of Manasseh.

About 70 percent of the pottery vessels are large collar-rim storage jars, which are known to have been the principal storage vessels of the newly settled Israelites. About 20 percent of the pottery vessels are jugs and chalices. The balance are small vessels, mostly votive, specially made by hand for ritual use. We found only a small quantity of common

A RAMP THREE feet wide, flanked on its left side by a slightly lower ramp, or ledge, makes a gradual ascent to the top of the Mt. Ebal altar. The ledge turns left, or north, when it meets the altar top and gradually widens on the altar's north side. In this view from the west, we see the 23-foot-long ramp and two courtyards, one on either side of the ramp.

An artist's reconstruction of the Ebal altar (opposite) shows the ramp with its ledge, the two courtyards and other features: the retaining wall around the sacred precinct and the temenos wall with its wide three-step processional entrance.

JUDITH DEKEL

domestic pottery, such as cooking pots.

In retrospect it seems strange, but the truth is that the finds I have just described did not suggest to us that the structure itself was an altar. That insight came only toward the end of the third season. Up to that time we remained in the dark as to what our mysterious structure was. We looked for parallels by which to interpret it, but could find none; it seemed our structure was unique. Then the light dawned—in a flash.

I remember it vividly. It was a Thursday, the morning of October 13, 1983. A friend of mine, a young archaeologist named David Etam, visited the site, and I gave him a tour. I was explaining the site to him, especially the difficulty we were having understanding the function of the strange central structure that had been filled. David interrupted me: "Why don't you think the opposite? Why don't you think that the filling is the important part, rather than the building?"

For months we had been trying to understand the structure by thinking of the filling as secondary. We were concentrating on the outside structure. David's insight stunned me. I grabbed a Bible and opened it to Exodus 27:8, which describes the portable Tabernacle altar the Israelites were commanded to build in the wilderness: "Make it hollow, with boards. As you were shown on the mountain, so shall it be made."

Then I went to a Biblical encyclopedia and looked under "altar" and read as follows: "The Tabernacle altar is described as having four walls; it was filled with earth and stones to its full height. On this filling the fire was burned. This construction method is well-known from Assyrian altars. That is why the altar is described [in the Bible] as being 'hollow with boards' (Biblical Encyclopedia, Vol. 4, p. 773 [Hebrew]).

Suddenly it all became clear: the filling and the structure were together one complete unit—an altar!

That evening, after a long day of excavating and washing pottery, I took a piece of paper and pencil and drew a rough sketch of what I thought the structure would have looked like, assuming it was an altar. I showed my sketch to one of the staff. He was dumbstruck. He ran from the room and soon returned with a Mishnah.* He opened the Mishnah to a passage in tractate *Middot* that minutely describes the Second Temple and surrounding structures. The particular edition he was using contained a drawing of the Second Temple altar as it was described in *Middot*. The drawing in the book was almost identical to the sketch I had drawn. Now it was I who was dumbstruck.

Beyond question, our site is a cultic center. The more than 50 installations containing either animal bones and ashes (the remains of sacrifices) or pottery vessels (which must have once contained offerings) seem irrefutable evidence of the cultic nature of the site. The special nature of the bones further supports this conclusion. The isolated location of

***Mishnah*: (from the Hebrew, to "repeat") The body of Jewish oral law, specifically the collection of oral laws compiled by Rabbi Judah the Prince in the second century.

Mt. Ebal Altar Part of a 2,000-Year-Old Architectural Tradition

Huge stepped structures called ziggurats are well-known from the third and second millennia B.C. in Mesopotamia. One of the most famous examples is the ziggurat of Ur, built about 2100 B.C. Originally, this ziggurat had four stages or steps; each of the upper three was smaller than the one below. A stepped ramp ascended to all the stages. The first, tallest stage and its steep ramp, seen here, have been restored by the Iraqi authorities to their original size. Author Zertal suggests that the stepped ledges and ramp of the Mt. Ebal altar reflect architectural traditions of Mesopotamian ziggurats. The altars of Solomon and Ezekiel described in the Bible also resemble Mesopotamian ziggurats. However, the design of the distinctive Mesopotamian ramp was modified in the later Israelite versions. The Israelite ramps were less steep than those of the Ur ziggurat and, as described in Exodus, they did not have steps: "Neither shalt thou go up by steps unto mine altar…" (Exodus 20:26).

The persistence for more than 2,000 years of this architectural tradition of ledges and a ramp is suggested by a drawing (right) based on a description in tractate *Middot* of the Mishnah, a collection of oral Jewish laws compiled in the second century A.D. The drawing shows the first-century B.C. altar from the Jerusalem Temple. The similarity of this drawing to the artist's reconstruction of the Mt. Ebal altar (below) is dramatically evident. A plan (lower right) showing an overhead view of the Mt. Ebal altar also indicates the ramp and ledges. In all three renderings, a lower ledge colored blue surrounds three sides of the top of the altar and continues as a narrower, lower ramp along the side of the broad, main ramp. The rectangular structure and the main ramp leading up to it are colored yellow. In the plan and the reconstruction of the Mt. Ebal altar the circular installations are colored green.

JUDITH DEKEL

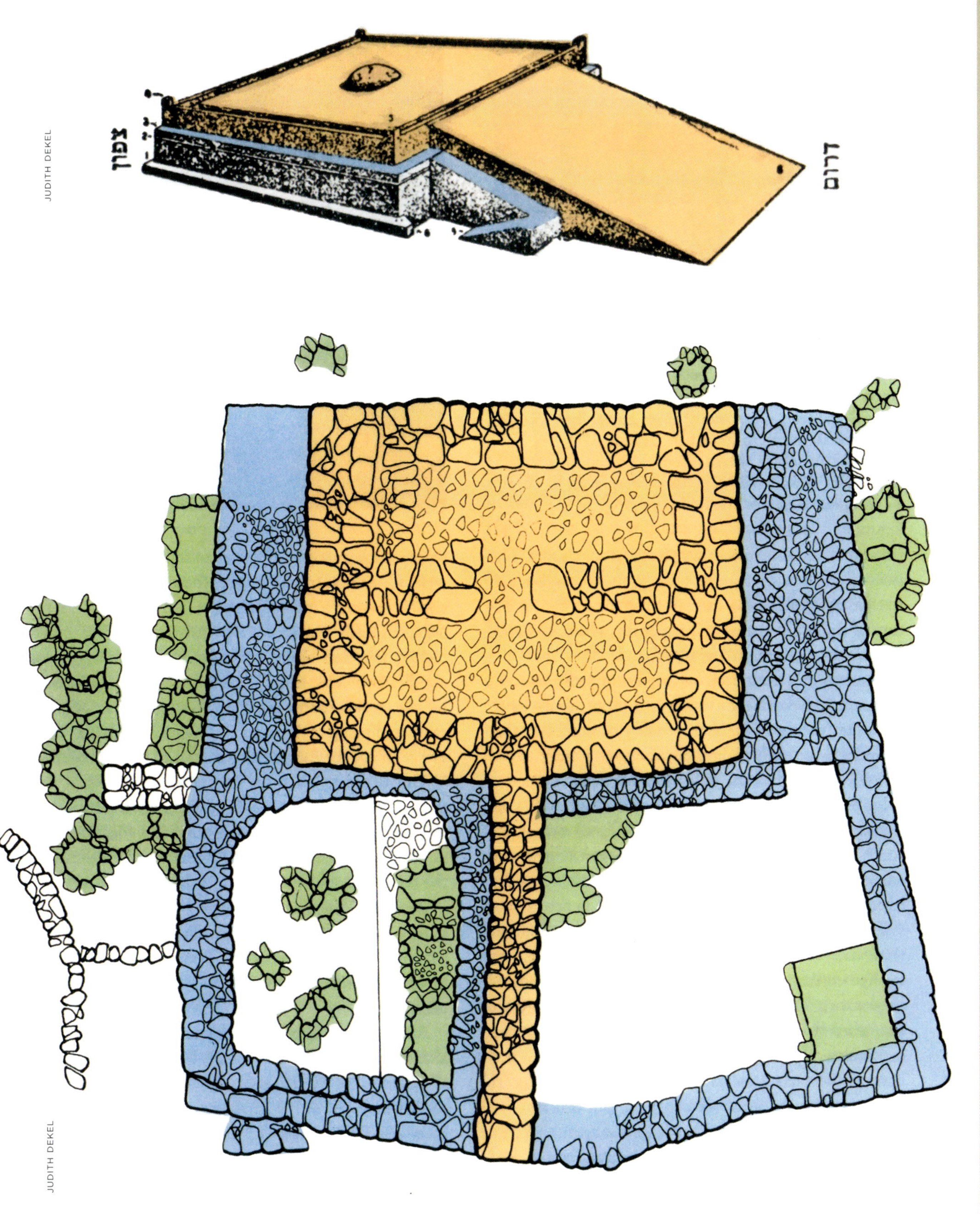

JUDITH DEKEL

JUDITH DEKEL

DAN COLE

© ERICH LESSING

ANIMAL SACRIFICES were made on this Israelite altar from Beer-Sheva (above) and incense was burned on a much smaller altar from Israelite Megiddo (right). Unlike the Mt. Ebal altar, both of these altars have horns at their corners.

The Beer-Sheva altar stands three cubits high (5 1/4 feet), like the altar described in Exodus 27:1, on which the Israelites offered sacrifices when they were camped in Sinai. The Megiddo incense altar is only 27 1/2 inches high and 16 inches square.

the site on a prominent mountain further strengthens the case. But the most striking feature of the site is the central structure, which, it seems, must now be interpreted as an altar.

One curious feature of our structure provides well-nigh conclusive evidence that it is an altar. About three feet below the top of the altar is the top of a thin wall that encircles three sides of the altar, in effect creating a kind of ledge attached to the outer wall of the altar. As this ledge goes from the northwest side to the southwest side, it gradually widens from about two feet until it reaches a width of 7.5 feet. This ledge also curves around the corner formed by the intersection of the altar and the ramp and continues down one side of the ramp.

There is absolutely no functional explanation for this thin wall or ledge. Obviously it was not built to strengthen the main structure, whose walls are made of large stones. These walls of large stones were certainly not supported by a thin wall on the outside. Moreover, the archaeological evidence indicates that the thin wall was built at the same time as the thick inner wall against which it leans; the thin wall was not a later addition.

The puzzle of this thin wall or ledge was again solved by reference to the description of the Second Temple altar in tractate *Middot* of the Mishnah. According to this description, the square Second Temple altar had two ledges surrounding it. The base of the altar was 32 cubits wide. One cubit from the base, the altar narrowed to 30 cubits, leaving a two-cubit ledge around it, or as the Mishnah calls this ledge, a "surround." Five cubits higher, the altar again narrowed to 28 cubits, leaving another two-cubit ledge or surround. The ledge created by the second narrowing curved around and down the ramp leading up to the altar. The Mishnah calls it a "small ramp," made for the priest to ascend to the "surround."

This is exactly what we have at our site, except that there is only one ledge or step instead of two. The step or ledge of our altar even curves around and goes down the ramp, thus creating a beautiful "small ramp" attached to the main one.

Of course, the Second Temple altar was built a thousand years or more after our altar, but it now seems beyond doubt that the Second Temple altar, as described in *Middot*, preserved ancient traditions of Israelite altar construction.

Although the Biblical description of the Tabernacle altar built by the Israelites in the wilderness is not absolutely clear on this point, there is a hint that it, too, was constructed with a narrower block set upon a wider base. The Bible speaks of this altar's having a "ledge" (Exodus 27:5). Ezekiel's description of the future Temple's altar is clearer. It will have a number of ledges, creating a stepped tower (Ezekiel 43:14).

As early as 1920, the great American archaeologist William F. Albright suggested that the Israelite altar had a Mesopotamian origin, ultimately based on the well-known ziggurat, a huge multi-stepped temple that some have suggested is the model for the Tower of Babel. The Bible tells us that the Judean king Ahaz, in the latter part of the eighth century B.C., ordered a new altar to be built for the Jerusalem Temple, based on the plan of an altar he had seen in Damascus, where he had met the Assyrian king Tiglath-Pileser III (2 Kings 16:10–16). This, too, suggests Mesopotamian influence on the Israelite altar.

Sacred traditions tend to endure. The two ledges on the Second Temple altar as described in the Mishnah may well preserve a very ancient tradition. And the ledge surrounding much of our altar on Mt. Ebal may also reflect this tradition of the Mesopotamian altar built up with ledges.

Yet another detail of our altar suggests its Mesopotamian roots. The four corners of our altar point north, south, east and west. In Mesopotamia, all sacred structures were oriented so that each corner was directed to a point on the compass. By contrast, the Second Temple was oriented so that its sides, not its corners, faced the four directions of the compass. The Temple altar had this same orientation. We are not told the orientation of the First Temple—Solomon's Temple—but it, too, probably faced east. The altar associated with Solomon's Temple doubtless followed the same orientation as the Temple itself. Why this difference in orientation between our Mt. Ebal altar and the Temple altars? Perhaps altars associated with temples were oriented differently from open-air altars not associated with temples. Other explanations, however, are also possible.

At this point, it may be instructive to consider what we know about altars from the Bible and how our altar illuminates or is illuminated by these passages.

Altars are frequently mentioned in the Bible. There are two principal types: the small incense altar and the large altar for burnt offerings. Archaeologists have uncovered many incense altars. Each is square, carved from a single stone and small—never measuring more than about a foot and a half in any direction. A depression on the top held the burning incense presumably used in the temple. Some incense altars have horns at the upper corners; others do not.

The burnt offering altar was much larger and was used for animal sacrifices. Animal sacrifice was at the core of Israelite cultic activity. Comparatively few burnt offering altars have been found in archaeological excavations in Israel, however. As we shall see, our Mt. Ebal altar is one of only three Israelite burnt offering altars ever discovered, and of these ours is both the oldest and the most complete.

There seem to have been two kinds of burnt offering altars—one associated with a temple where, in the Near Eastern religious purview, God dwelled. The other might be called an independent burnt offering altar, because it was not associated with a temple.

Although the subject is not free from controversy, it appears that the independent altar is part of what the Bible describes as a *bamah* or high place, probably an open-air cultic center where sacrifices were offered. For example, in 1 Kings 3:4, we learn that King Solomon went to Gibeon to sacrifice there, for that was the great high place (*bamah*); on that altar Solomon presented a thousand burnt offerings. There God appeared to Solomon in a dream.

If this analysis is correct, our Mt. Ebal altar is an independent altar (not associated with a temple), the central structure in a *bamah*.

It might be helpful briefly to place our altar in a general context of ancient Near Eastern altars that have been found throughout the region—in ancient Mesopotamia, Syria, Egypt, Anatolia, Greece, Cyprus and the Aegean Islands. In Israel, altars have been found from the Early Bronze Age (3150–2200 B.C.) to the late Iron Age (800–586 B.C.). From the Bronze Age, altars have been found at Megiddo, Shechem, Hazor and Nahariya. From the Iron Age, a Philistine altar was found at Tel Qasile, and Israelite altars were discovered at Tel Arad and Beer-Sheva.

From this very considerable archaeological material, we get some idea of what ancient altars were like, but only a partial idea as to the form of an Israelite altar. In general, Near Eastern burnt offering altars, like our Mt. Ebal altar, are square or rectangular structures of considerable size. They are built of worked and squared ashlar blocks. Sometimes they have horns at the upper corners (as at Beer-Sheva and Kition in Cyprus), and sometimes they do not (as at Arad).

Altars were ascended by stairs—at least this is true in cases where the means of ascent have been preserved. Unfortunately, until now, no ascent to an Israelite altar has been discovered in a preserved state, but the ramp on our Mt. Ebal altar indicates a strict adherence to the law in Exodus 20:26, which requires a ramp rather than steps.

In many cases, Near Eastern altars are stepped; that is, they are built in square or rectangular layers, each one higher and smaller than the one beneath. This is especially the case in Mesopotamia, Anatolia and Syria.

Some altars, like ours, have outer stone frames and

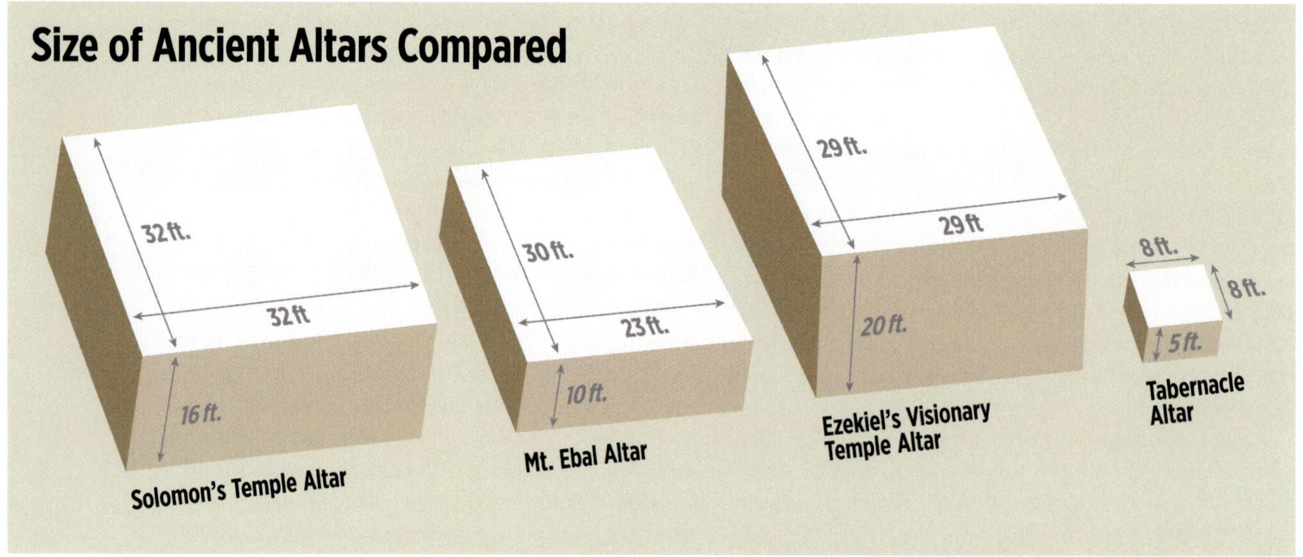

are filled on the inside with earth or pebbles. This is true of altars in Greece and Assyria, and it may also be true of the Israelite altar at Arad. We cannot be sure about the Arad altar because a section has never been cut through it that would reveal what lies inside the outer stone frame.

The size of ancient Near Eastern altars varies from about 3 feet on a side (Alalakh) to about 20 feet on a side (temple 2A at Shechem). It is difficult to tell their original heights because they are not usually well preserved. Before our altar was discovered, the height of the highest preserved altar was about five feet.

Our altar fits well within the pattern established by these other altars, although it is the best preserved and stands almost to its original height (ten feet). Our altar apparently did not have horns, or they were not preserved.

Every other ancient altar that has been discovered thus far, however, was connected with a temple, or as at Beer-Sheva, was in a city where we may suppose a temple existed in connection with the altar (2 Kings 23:8). With the possible exception noted below,* our altar alone seems to have been an independent altar in the countryside, not associated with a temple or a settlement. This is probably because the Mt. Ebal altar and its associated cult site were built at a very early period in the development of Israelite cult and religion; at that time, there was no temple.

*The possible exception is an open-air cult center also from the period of the Judges. This site was found very recently. It was investigated by Amihai Mazar, who has already written a report for BAR readers ("Bronze Bull Found in Israelite 'High Place' from the Time of the Judges," BAR, September/October 1983). This cult center was built on a mountain, as was our site. It was surrounded by an elliptical wall, as was our site. But if it had an altar, it was preserved only in a single stone about four feet long, three feet high and about one and three-fourths feet thick.

Moreover, the Mt. Ebal cult center lasted for only a relatively short time. It is unlikely that a temple could develop in such a short time. Even at Shiloh, which was the site of the successor to the Mt. Ebal cult center, no temple was built.

It may be interesting to compare the size of our altar to other altars mentioned in the Bible—the Tabernacle altar in the wilderness, the altar in Solomon's Temple, and the altar associated with Ezekiel's future Temple. As the table (above) shows, the Tabernacle altar was much smaller than the other two; the Mt. Ebal altar is closer to the larger ones.

While the Biblical altars are all square, ours is slightly rectangular. Many other Near Eastern altars are rectangular, and it may be that independent Israelite altars not associated with temples were rectangular rather than square.

The Bible makes it clear that there were many independent Israelite altars. During the religious reforms of King Hezekiah (eighth century B.C.) and King Josiah (seventh century B.C.), these outlying ritual centers were suppressed and destroyed, in order to centralize the cult in Jerusalem.

In terms of height, and in terms of width and length, our altar is closer to the altar in Solomon's Temple and in Ezekiel's visionary Temple than to the Tabernacle altar.

Incidentally, the Second Temple altar was much larger than all these altars. Although slightly different figures are given for the Second Temple altar in the various sources—the Mishnah, Josephus, and the newly published Temple Scroll from the Dead Sea caves—all agree that it was much larger than the altars described in the Bible.

After discussing all these technical data, important as they are, and proving that we are dealing here with a burnt offering altar in an Israelite cult center, we come now to the most intriguing question: Is this altar related to the Biblical traditions which describe Joshua's building of an altar on Mt. Ebal?

The building of an altar on Mt. Ebal is described in two places in the Bible, once in Deuteronomy, when the Israelites are commanded to build the altar after they pass into the Promised Land, and again in the book of Joshua, when the altar is actually built.

In Deuteronomy 27:1–10, Moses, in some of the most dramatic and awe-inspiring words in the Bible, commands the people to build the altar:

> Now Moses and the elders of Israel commanded the people, saying, "Keep all the commandments which I command you this day. And on the day you pass over the Jordan to the land which the Lord your God gives you, you shall set up large stones, and plaster them with plaster; and you shall write upon them all the words of this law, when you pass over to enter the land which the Lord your God gives you, a land flowing with milk and honey, as the Lord, the God of your fathers, has promised you. And when you have passed over the Jordan, you shall set up these stones, concerning which I command you this day, on Mount Ebal, and you shall plaster them with plaster. And there you shall build an altar to the Lord your God, an altar of stones; you shall lift up no iron tool upon them. You shall build an altar to the Lord your God of unhewn stones; and you shall offer burnt offerings on it to the Lord your God; and you shall sacrifice peace offerings, and shall eat there; and you shall rejoice before the Lord your God. And you shall write upon the stones all the words of this law very plainly." And Moses and the Levitical priests said to all Israel, "Keep silence and hear, O Israel: this day you have become the nation of the Lord your God. You shall therefore obey the voice of the Lord your God, keeping his commandments and his statutes, which I command you this day."

With this commandment, Israel has become the people of the Lord.

The ceremony on Mt. Ebal is described in Joshua 8:30–35:

> Then Joshua built an altar in Mount Ebal to the Lord, the God of Israel, as Moses the servant of the Lord had commanded the people of Israel, as it is written in the book of the law of Moses, "an altar of unhewn stones, upon which no man has lifted an iron tool"; and they offered on it burnt offerings to the Lord, and sacrificed peace offerings. And there, in the presence of the people of Israel, he wrote upon the stones a copy of the law of Moses, which he had written. And all Israel, sojourner as well as homeborn, with their elders and officers and their judges, stood on opposite sides of the ark before the Levitical priests who carried the ark of the covenant of the Lord, half of them in front of Mount Gerizim and half of them in front of Mount Ebal, as Moses the servant of the Lord had commanded at the first, that they should bless the people of Israel. And afterward he read all the words of the law, the blessing and the curse, according to all that is written in the book of the law. There was not a word of all that Moses commanded which Joshua did not read before all the assembly of Israel, and the women, and the little ones, and the sojourners who lived among them.

In Deuteronomy 27:11–13, we are told that half the tribes are to stand on Mt. Gerizim for the blessing of the people, and half on Mt. Ebal for the curses. The curses are recited in Deuteronomy 27:14–26; then in Deuteronomy 28:1–14 come the blessings, followed by additional curses in Deuteronomy 28:15–68.

If the people follow the Lord's commandments, they will be blessed; if not, they will be cursed. As foretold in Deuteronomy 11:22–29,

> If you diligently keep all these commandments that I now charge you to observe, by loving the Lord your God, by conforming to his ways and by holding fast to him, the Lord will drive out all these nations before you and you shall occupy the territory of nations greater and more powerful than you. Every place where you set the soles of your feet shall be yours. Your borders shall run from the wilderness to the Lebanon and from the River, the river Euphrates, to the western sea. No man will be able to withstand you; the Lord your God will put the fear and dread of you upon the whole land on which you set foot, as he promised you. Understand that this day I offer you the choice of a blessing and a curse. The blessing will come if you listen to the commandments of the Lord your God which I give you this day and the curse if you do not listen to the commandments of the Lord your God but turn aside from the way that I command you this day and follow other gods whom you do not know. When the Lord your God brings you into the land which you are entering to occupy, there on Mount Gerizim you shall pronounce the blessing and on Mount Ebal the curse.

PHOTOS BY M. WEINBERG

Evidence for Dating the Mt. Ebal Altar

In the fill of the Mt. Ebal altar, along with bones and pottery sherds, we found an Egyptian-style scarab (above). Within an oval frame, the scarab displays a geometrical pattern consisting of a four-petal rosette and, between the petals, four branches. From each branch comes a uraeus (an Egyptian cobra).

This scarab is very rare; only five known parallels exist—one from Egypt, three from Israel and one from Cyprus. All these parallels date this special find to the period between the reigns of Ramses II (19th dynasty; 13th century B.C.) and Ramses III (20th dynasty; beginning of 12th century B.C.).

This scarab fixes the earliest date for the construction of the Mt. Ebal altar; it could not have been built before the 13th century B.C. Moreover, because this scarab comes from a stratigraphically sealed locus, together with a well-dated pottery sequence, it has even greater chronological significance—it gives us an approximate date for the original erection of the altar and cultic center.

Other distinctive pottery forms buttress the argument for a 13th–12th century B.C. date for the Ebal altar. Collar-rim jars were commonly used storage vessels during the settlement period and are dated by archaeologists to the 13th through the 11th centuries B.C.

Excavators discovered a collar-rim jar in a circular stone installation in the altar's courtyard. Since they found no ashes in the vessel, they assume that it once contained a non-burnt offering.

Pottery handles decorated with designs of reedholes (top left) and a "man's face" (center left) were discovered during the survey of the territory of Manasseh. The clearly recognizable handles are now used as indicators that the strata in which they appear date from the Israelite settlement period. **—A.Z.**

After these references to Mt. Ebal, the name Ebal is never mentioned again in the entire Bible.

A question may arise concerning the identification of our Mt. Ebal altar with the one described in the Bible because our altar is not on the very peak of Mt. Ebal. Mt. Ebal descends in what may be described as four very wide terraces or steps. Our altar is on the second step from the top. Moreover, Mt. Gerizim cannot be seen from our site.

On the other hand, the Bible itself hints that Joshua's altar was not built at the top of the mountain. In Joshua 8:30, we read that Joshua built the altar *b*-Mt. Ebal. The Hebrew letter *beth* (pronounced "b") usually means "in" rather than "on top of." This might suggest that the altar was not built on the top of Mt. Ebal. In Deuteronomy 27:4, where the instructions are given to build the Mt. Ebal altar, we find the same verbal construction, with a *beth*.

By contrast, in Deuteronomy 11:29, where the instructions for pronouncing the curses are given, we are told that they are to be pronounced *al* Mt. Ebal, that is, on Mt. Ebal.

For a Biblical archaeologist, a comparison between the Bible and archaeological finds is always inspiring, but like a mine field as well. Is the cultic center altar unearthed by us on Mt. Ebal the one mentioned in the Bible? How can one judge such a fundamental issue? What criteria should we use for such a judgment?

The main problem, I suppose, is that archaeology has not always corroborated the Biblical stories of Joshua's time. At Jericho, Ai, Arad, and other sites, archaeology does not corroborate what the Bible tells us. No evidence from the period of Joshua has been found at these sites.

With respect to the Mt. Ebal altar, however, all the scientific evidence fits very well with the Biblical description. The three main factors that correlate precisely are the period, the nature of the site, and the location. True, no inscriptions have been found as yet. But apart from that one point, it may be said with all scientific restraint that there must be a connection between the strong, important and authentic Biblical tradition that identifies Mt. Ebal as a central Israelite cultic center and the gathering place of the Israelite tribes, on the one hand, and the site unearthed by us, on the other. There are still debates about most of the issues: Who was Joshua? When did the Israelite tribes enter the Land? Did they enter from the east, as the Bible states?

But this rare case, where Biblical tradition and concrete archaeological evidence coincide, cannot be ignored. We have on Mt. Ebal not only the complete prototype of an Israelite altar, but moreover, a site that might prove to be directly related to the Biblical traditions concerning Joshua's building of an altar on Mt. Ebal.

We have a few more seasons of work at least before any further conclusions can be drawn. Certainty as yet eludes us; all the evidence has still not been analyzed. For the moment, we leave the reader to reach his or her own conclusion. As scientists, we must say that the case has not yet been proven.

Related Reading

Aharon Kempinski, "Joshua's Altar—An Iron Age I Watchtower," BAR, January/February 1986. See also Zertal's response: "Different Interpretations—How Can Kempinski Be So Wrong?" BAR, January/February 1986.

Aren M. Maeir, ReViews: "The 'Joshua's Altar' Debate," BAR, July/August 2013, reviewing Ralph K. Hawkins, *The Iron I Structure on Mt. Ebal: Excavation and Interpretation* (Winona Lake, IN: Eisenbrauns, 2012).

For an article about the excavations on Mt. Ebal's twin peak, Mt. Gerizim, see Yitzhak Magen, "Bells, Pendants, Snakes and Stones," BAR, November/December 2010.

4

Israel's Rivals

Much of the Hebrew Bible describes the Israelites' interactions with hostile neighbors who surrounded them. This group of articles helped shed light on two of these oft-misunderstood enemies of Israel: the Philistines and the Edomites.

Every good story needs a villain, and the Bible is no exception. For ancient Israel, there was no shortage of hostile neighbors—Edomites, Moabites, Ammonites, Canaanites and others. But the Moriarty to their Sherlock Holmes, so to speak, was undoubtedly the Philistines. In BAR we let the archaeology speak on their behalf in order to gain a better understanding of those peoples and their conflicts with ancient Israel.

JULY/AUGUST 1982
What We Know About the Philistines

If there is one archaeologist who has refuted the Philistines' reputation as, well, philistine, it is Israeli archaeologist Trude Dothan, often referred to as the "Queen of the Philistines." In BAR she surveyed their rich culture as revealed at sites both in modern Israel and elsewhere.

This article also includes three sidebars by American scholar Robert R. Stieglitz: "Philistines in the Patriarchal Age," "Did the Philistines Write?" and "Philistines After David."

MARCH/APRIL 1991
When Canaanites and Philistines Ruled Ashkelon

The largest and longest-running American excavation in Israel is directed by Harvard's Lawrence E. Stager (and recently joined by his former student Daniel Master as codirector) at Ashkelon on the Mediterranean coast. In this general survey article, Stager reported on the discovery of a silver calf, which the press widely compared to the golden calf that faithless Israelites crafted at the foot of Mt. Sinai. Ashkelon's silver calf was housed in a unique miniature shrine. No less significant, however, are the city's massive fortification wall, the decorative pottery and the puzzling cylinders of unbaked clay.

NOVEMBER/DECEMBER 1982
How Iron Technology Changed the Ancient World

The title tells it all in James D. Muhly's "How Iron Technology Changed the Ancient World—And Gave the Philistines a Military Edge." This has proved to be one of the most widely cited articles that BAR has ever published.

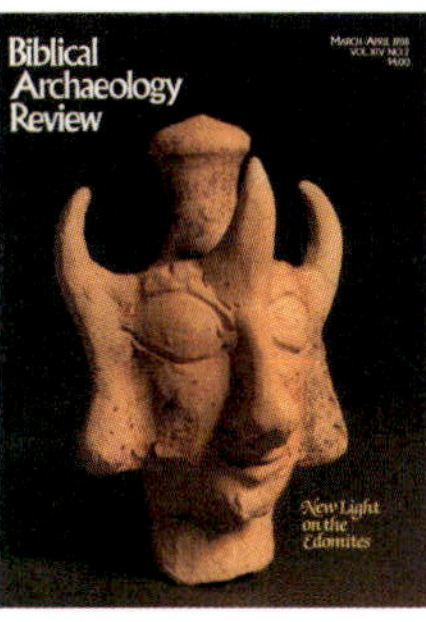

MARCH/APRIL 1988
New Light on the Edomites

Israeli archaeologist Itzhaq Beit-Arieh reported on discoveries relating to those implacable, but little-known, enemies of the Israelites, the Edomites. The remains of an Edomite shrine indicate that they penetrated into the Negev desert of Judah, where Beit-Arieh found some of the most intriguing and unusual human figurines ever discovered.

The stunning Edomite figurine that graced the cover of this issue was described by ancient art and ceramics expert Pirhiya Beck of Tel Aviv University in a box titled "Head of a Goddess" (see p. 207 of this book). Professor Beck died suddenly in 1998 at age 67.

WHAT WE KNOW ABOUT THE PHILISTINES

TRUDE DOTHAN

The Bible is understandably hostile to the Philistines, describing them as a pleasure-loving, warlike society of pagans ruled by "tyrants" who threatened ancient Israel's existence. An unscrupulous enemy, the Philistines deployed Delilah and her deceitful charm to rob Samson of his power. In a later period, they slew King Saul and his sons in battle, then cruelly hung the king's headless body from the walls of Beth Shean. And for three millennia now, the rousing story of David's victory over the awesome Goliath has been told and retold, creating an indelibly negative image of the Philistines in the imagination of each new generation.

Today, the negative image is entrenched. The dictionary defines a "Philistine" as "...a crass, prosaic, often priggish individual, guided by material rather than intellectual values;...belonging to a despised class; one deficient in originality or aesthetic sensitivity." But is this image, in fact, deserved? In order to uncover an accurate picture of the Philistines and the cultural milieu in which they lived, we must clear away many strata of archaeological debris, along with the many layers of misunderstanding and misconceptions that have accumulated over the centuries. In the past 2,000 years, many books have been written about the Philistines, but the "research" on which these books were based was limited primarily to speculation on the Biblical sources. Then in 1821 Jean Francois Champollion deciphered ancient Egyptian hieroglyphics and an intriguing new resource for the study of the Philistines appeared. The war reliefs of Ramesses III at Medinet Habu, which could now be read, told a story in words and pictures about the arrival and subsequent defeat of the "Sea Peoples." Among these invaders were the *prst*, the Philistines.

Still later, in the 20th century, archaeology began to reveal a picture of the Philistine settlement in Palestine. (Long after the Philistines had disappeared from the stage of history, Herodotus called their descendants *Palastinoi*, a name subsequently given to the geographic area called Palestine.) The early pioneering efforts of archaeologists like R. A. S. Macalister at Gezer, Sir William Flinders Petrie at Tell el-Far'ah (South), and William Foxwell Albright at Tell Beit Mirsim were followed by the more recent and more dramatic discoveries of Philistine towns by Moshe Dothan at Ashdod and by Benjamin Mazar and later by Amihai Mazar at Tell Qasile.

The Sea Peoples, including the Philistines, first

PHILISTINE WARRIORS. A detail from a Medinet Habu relief shows the characteristic feathered Philistine headdress. The headband to which the feathers are attached was probably made of metal. The headband has a zigzag pattern; a headband of similar design decorated an anthropoid coffin lid found at Beth Shean.

appeared in the eastern Mediterranean in the second half of the 13th century B.C. At the time, the Egyptians and the Hittites were in power in the Levant (the Hittite empire centered in Anatolia), but both were weak, politically and militarily. The Sea Peoples exploited this power vacuum by invading areas previously subject to Egyptian and Hittite control. In wave after wave of land and sea assaults they attacked Syria, Palestine, and even Egypt itself. In the last and mightiest wave, the Sea Peoples, including the Philistines, stormed south from Canaan in a land and sea assault on the Egyptian Delta. According to Egyptian sources, including the hieroglyphic account at Medinet Habu, Rameses III (c. 1198–1166 B.C.) soundly defeated them in the eighth year of his reign. He then permitted them to settle on the southern coastal plain of Palestine. There they developed into an independent political power and a threat both to the disunited Canaanite city-states and to the newly settled Israelites. Philistine culture and military power thrived, principally from the middle of the 12th to the end of the 11th century B.C., exerting a major influence on the history and culture of Canaan. From the end of the 11th century, Philistine influence and cultural

MANACLED PHILISTINE PRISONERS. In this wall relief (opposite) from Ramesses III's mortuary palace at Medinet Habu, Philistines, whom Rameses has just defeated, are shown being led into captivity. This relief clearly depicts the distinctive Philistine dress—a short paneled kilt with wide hem and tassels. The battle headdress is also a Philistine trademark. Since these prisoners have been stripped of their armor, we do not see the ribbed corselets visible in the naval battle reliefs.

The hieroglyphic inscription over the prisoners' heads reads: "The vanquished Peleset [Philistines] say: 'Give us the breath of our nostrils, O King, Son of Amon.'" Other inscriptions at Medinet Habu relate that Ramesses III defeated the Sea People invaders in the eighth year of his reign, c. 1190 B.C. "Those who entered the river mouths were like birds ensnared in the net." Ramesses eventually allowed the Sea Peoples, including the Philistines, to settle on the southern coastal plain of Palestine.

THE MORTUARY TEMPLE of Ramesses III at Medinet Habu in Thebes (below). To scholars studying the Sea Peoples, the Medinet Habu temple, erected in the first half of the 12th century B.C., offers a treasure of detailed wall reliefs from which we learn how the Sea Peoples looked and how they fought. In this view of the east face of the massive second pylon, Ramesses is depicted presenting captives to the gods. Not seen in this view are reliefs of a group of captured Sea Peoples and Ramesses III's naval battle with the Sea Peoples.

JEHON GRIST

YIGAEL YADIN, *THE ART OF WARFARE IN BIBLICAL LANDS*, VOLUME II

NAVAL BATTLE between Ramesses III and the Sea Peoples. This artist's reconstruction of the wall relief from Medinet Habu (see photograph below) shows the fierce battle, probably fought in the Nile Delta, between the Sea Peoples and the victorious Egyptians. Elaborate details of naval weaponry, vessels and tactics, as well as the dress of the Sea Peoples may be seen.

The drawing shows major portions of six vessels—three Egyptian vessels (left) and three Sea Peoples' vessels (right). In the relief the Sea Peoples' vessels seen in the drawing are in the center; half of the two Egyptian vessels are visible on the left edge. Several features distinguish the ships and men of the Egyptians from those of the Sea Peoples. The Egyptian vessels have lion headed prows and undecorated sterns while the vessels of the Sea Peoples have a bird head at either end. The oars of the Egyptian vessels are fully arrayed, those of the Sea Peoples' ships are stowed. (The artist of the relief may have wanted to show that the Sea Peoples were caught by surprise and had no chance to run out their oars.) The Egyptian shields are rectangular; the Sea Peoples' shields are round. Two distinctive Sea Peoples' headdresses are present: the horned helmets of the Sherden whose ship is center right in the drawing and the familiar "feather" headgear of the Philistines and other Sea Peoples seen top and bottom right.

In addition to the Egyptians' bows and the Sea Peoples' long spears, the drawing of the relief shows clearly another weapon—the grappling hook. An Egyptian seaman attempts to snare the Philistine ship to his right by flinging the long line of his hook into the rigging.

JEHON GRIST

distinctiveness waned. Ultimately, it was eclipsed by the rising star of the united Israelite monarchy.

According to inscriptions of Pharaoh Merneptah (c. 1236–1223 B.C.), the Sea Peoples had also attempted to invade Egypt in that monarch's fifth regnal year, this time from the direction of Libya. The attack was led by Libyans, but joining them were "foreigners from the Sea"—the Sherden, Sheklesh, Tursha (Teresh), and Akawasha. This list of Sea Peoples does not, however, mention the Philistines and the Tjekker. They are mentioned as invaders only later, during the reign of Ramesses III where, as I have said, they are mentioned and pictured in the texts and reliefs of the mortuary temple at Medinet Habu in Thebes.

The vivid battle scenes depicted on the walls of this temple (pp. 146–147) are our most precious and most graphic representation of the Sea Peoples' dress, weaponry, chariotry, naval equipment, and battle tactics. The accompanying inscriptions are invaluable records of attacks on the Egyptian frontier by foreigners:

> "The foreign countries made a conspiracy in their islands. All at once the lands were removed and scattered in the fray. No land could stand before their arms, from Hatti, Kode, Carchemish, Arzawa, and Alashiya on, being cut off at [one time]....Their confederation was the Philistines, Tjekker, Shekelesh, Denye[n], and Weshesh, land united. They laid their hands upon the lands as far as the circuit of the earth, their hearts confident and trusting 'Our plans will succeed.'"

After describing his preparations for the great battle with Sea Peoples in the Nile delta, Ramesses relates the results of the conflict:

> "Those who came forward together on the sea...were dragged in, enclosed, and prostrated on the beach, killed and made into heaps from tail to head. Their ships and their goods were as if fallen into the water....The northern countries quivered in their bodies, the Philistines, Tjekk[er, and...]....They were teher [chariot] warriors on land; another [group] was on the sea. Those who came on [land were overthrown and killed]....Those who entered the river-mouths were like birds ensnared in the net.

According to the inscription under the land battle scene, the Egyptian army fought the Sea Peoples in the land of Djahi, the Egyptian term for the Phoenician coast and hinterland down to Palestine.

The Philistine camp was composed of three

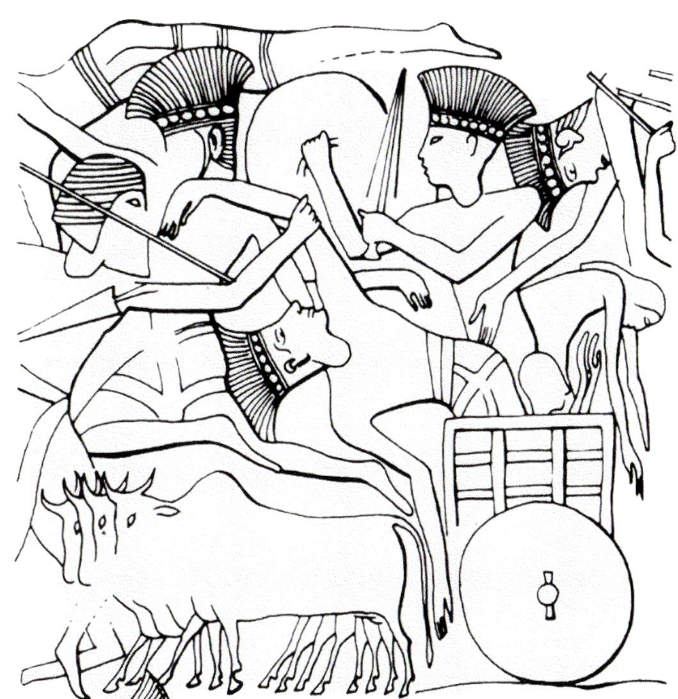

THE WAGON OF THE SEA PEOPLES. Slowly drawn by four oxen, two wheeled wagons carried women and children to settle in territories conquered by the Sea People warriors.

separate units: noncombatant civilians, chariotry, and infantry. The noncombatants, shown in the center of the upper register, included men, women and children riding in slow-moving, two-wheeled carts, each harnessed to a team of four oxen. These carts were very similar to transport wagons still in use today in some parts of Turkey. This picture of the Sea Peoples, invading both by land and sea, reflects their purpose—to occupy and settle the lands they overrun. They were not merely staging a large-scale raid.

The military chariots of the Philistines are similar to those of the Egyptians (see illustrations to "How Inferior Israelite Forces Conquered Fortified Canaanite Cities," BAR, March/April 1982). Both have six-spoked wheels and are drawn by two horses. The Philistine chariots functioned as mobile infantry units; the charioteers engaged in hand-to-hand combat after the initial chariot charge had stunned the enemy.

The Philistine infantry is shown fighting in small phalanges of four men each; three men are each armed with a long, straight sword and a pair of spears, the fourth with only a sword. All carry round shields and wear plain upper garments—possibly plain breastplates.

The Sea Peoples and the Egyptians fought not only in a land battle but also in a great naval battle which took place at the entrance to Egypt itself, possibly in the Nile Delta. The few ships depicted in the Medinet Habu reliefs are no doubt meant to represent a larger fleet. Four Egyptian warships engage five of the Sea Peoples' vessels. The sea battle is another version of the land battle to the extent that grappling hooks were used to pull enemy ships together so that hand-to-hand fighting could ensue on deck.

The Philistine and Egyptian ships have many features in common: furled sails, a single mast with a crow's nest, and identical rigging. The main difference between the ships of the Egyptians and the Philistines is that the latter are shown without oars (except for oars used as rudders). The figureheads are also different. The Philistine ships have birds' heads at prow and stern; each Egyptian ship has a lioness's head with a figure symbolizing Asia in her jaw at the prow and a plain, undecorated stern.

The battle headdress of the Sea Peoples clearly distinguishes the different groups. The Sherden wear horned helmets, the Teresh and Shekelesh have fillet headbands. The Philistines, the Tjekker, and the Denyen wear the so-called "feather" headdress, a leather cap and an ornamental headband from which a row of slightly curving strips stands upright to form a kind of diadem (see opening photo). Regardless of whether the strips are feathers, reeds, leather strips, horsehair, or some bizarre hairdo, this headgear is the distinguishing mark of the group dominated by the Philistines. We shall encounter it again in archaeological finds from Canaan.

The Philistines are also distinguishable by their dress. Each wears a short paneled kilt with wide hem and tassles. Above the waist is a ribbed corselet over a shirt. The thin strips of the corselet (made of leather or metal) are jointed in the middle of the chest and curve up. (On Sherden warriors, these strips curve down.) Perhaps these strips are meant to simulate human ribs. Similar corselets are known from Cyprus during this period and somewhat earlier; they indicate the Aegean background of the Sea Peoples. The corseleted Sea Peoples carry small round shields, easily distinguishable from the rectangular Egyptian shields.

Despite the massive forces of the Sea Peoples and their two-pronged land and naval approach, Ramesses successfully thwarted their attempt to overwhelm Palestine and the Egyptian Delta, as this passage from the Harris Papyrus* demonstrates:

"I [Ramesses III] extended all the frontiers of Egypt and overthrew those who had attacked them from their lands.... I settled them in strongholds, bound in my name. Their military classes were as numerous as hundred thousands. I assigned portions for them all with clothing and provisions from the treasuries and granaries every year."

The resettlement program of Ramesses III is confirmed by the Onomasticon of Amenope,** (end of the 12th or beginning of the 11th century B.C.) which mentions those areas settled by the Sea Peoples in Canaan that were within the sphere of Egyptian influence. The three Sea Peoples included are the Philistines, the Tjekker and the Sherden. Ashkelon, Ashdod, and Gaza are listed as cities situated in the territory controlled by the Philistines. The emphasis Amenope gives to these three Philistine cities suggests that this territory still served as an Egyptian line of defense, and that the Philistines at this time were still, at least nominally, under Egyptian rule.

The famous Wenamun tale,† (middle of the 11th century B.C.) contains the sole reference to the area occupied by the Sea People known as the Tjekker. From this surviving story, we know the Tjekker occupied Dor. Wenamun, the author of the story, was a priest of the temple of Amun at Karnak who was sent to Byblos to buy cedar logs for the construction of Amun's ceremonial barge. Wenamun's misadventures and occasional humiliations by such characters as Beder, prince of the Tjekker town of Dor, indicate that Egypt's hold on its Asian empire was already seriously weakened.

The Biblical references to Philistine origins are few and sometimes unclear. The earliest appears in the Table of Nations or "Generations of the Sons of Noah" in Genesis 10:14. The probable meaning of this verse, insofar as it relates to the Philistines, is "and the Caphtorim, out of whom came the Philistines." According to this passage,

*The Harris Papyrus, now located in the British Museum, comes from Thebes and dates from the end of the reign of Ramesses III. It is an important source for the history of the early Twentieth Dynasty.

**The Onomasticon of Amenope is a collection of nine different manuscripts, attributed to Amenope, son of Amenope. These manuscripts, now scattered in various museums throughout the world, were found and purchased in different localities in Egypt during the last two centuries. Their attribution to Amenope is supported by five of the nine sources. Virtually nothing is known concerning Amenope except that he was a "scribe of sacred books in the House of Life." These manuscripts have been dated to the end of the reign of Ramesses IX. Both the Tjekker and Philistines are mentioned.

†The Wenamun papyrus, now in the Moscow Museum, was found at el-Hibeh in Middle Egypt and dates to the Twenty-first Dynasty (11th century B.C.), shortly after the events in the story. It presents a picture of a disintegrating Egyptian Empire which left a vacuum in the region, allowing Asiatics and others to challenge its dominance over the area of Canaan.

Troy
Athens
Mycenae
Perati
Pylos
Miletus
CILICIA
Tarsus
Ialysos
CRETE
RHODES
Knossos
Ugarit
CYPRUS
Kition
Sinda
Enkomi
Kouklia
MEDITERRANEAN SEA
Byblos
Sidon
Tyre
Dor
Beth Shean
Ashdod
Ashkelon
Gaza
Tanis
Tell Nebesheh
Tell el-Yahudiyeh
N
SINAI
0 100 mi
0 100 km
EGYPT
Tell el-Amarna
RED SEA
Medinet Habu
Thebes
The Ancient Near East at the Time of the Philistines
Aniba
Tel Dan
Hazor
SEA OF GALILEE
Tel Keisan
Tell Qiri
Dor
Afula
Megiddo
JORDAN RIVER
Tel Zeror
Beth Shean
Tell Deir Alla
Tel Qasile
Tel Aphek
Izbet Sartah
Tel Jerishe
Jaffa
Azor
Bethel
Tell en-Nasbeh
Gezer
Tel Mor
Tell el-Ful
Khirbet Muqanna
Tell el-Batashi
Jerusalem
Ashdod
Beth Shemesh
Tell es-Safi
Ashkelon
Tel Sippor
Sheikh el-Areini
Beth Zur
Principal Sites with Philistine Remains
Lachish
Tell el-Hesi
Tell Aitun
Gaza
DEAD SEA
Tel el-'Ajjul
Tell Beit Mirsim
Tell esh-Sharia
Deir el-Balah
Tell Jemmeh
Tell Ma'aravim
NAHAL GERAR
Tel el-Far'ah
NAHAL BEERSHEBA
Tell ez-Zuweyid
Tel Beersheba
Tel Masos
0 5 10 mi
0 5 10 15 km
N

Philistines in the Patriarchal Age

Most of the references to the Philistines in the Bible relate to events between about 1200 B.C. and 950 B.C. This period began with the Israelite settlement in Canaan, when the Philistines too were occupying the area, and continued through the period of King David, who finally suppressed what was for the Israelites the Philistine scourge.

There are other Biblical references to the Philistines, however, from the Patriarchal period. Abraham, we are told, lived in the land of the Philistines at Beer-sheba, and made a treaty with Abimelech, a Philistine king who ruled nearby in Gerar (Genesis 21:22–34). One of the three versions of a Patriarch passing off his wife as his sister concerns Isaac's disguising his marriage to Rebecca before the same Philistine king Abimelech (Genesis 26). A similar episode also involves Abraham and King Abimelech at Gerar (Genesis 20).

These Biblical references to the Philistines during the Patriarchal age are a special problem. Archaeologists have learned a great deal about the Philistines, including the fact that they came to Canaan in about 1200 B.C., shortly after the Israelite settlement of the land. But there is no archaeological evidence for a Philistine presence earlier than this. Moreover the Biblical Philistines from the Patriarchal age did not inhabit the land assigned both by archaeology and later Biblical references to the Philistines (the Mediterranean coastal area), but an area further inland centering in their capital Gerar and extending westward through the Sinai peninsula to the border with Egypt.

Most scholars regard the Biblical references to Philistines during the Patriarchal Period as anachronistic—that is, an identification inserted by a later writer or editor despite the fact that the events themselves occurred in a period hundreds of years before the arrival of the Philistines. Perhaps the reference is to another group that did inhabit the designated area during the patriarchal Period, a group whose identity is now unknown. —ROBERT R. STIEGLITZ

the Caphtorim (and thus the Philistines) came from Egypt (Genesis 10:13). This may reflect the fact that the Philistines and other Sea Peoples were first settled in Egypt after their defeat by Ramesses III and then served as mercenaries in the Egyptian army. The homeland of the Philistines, Caphtor (Amos 9:7), is generally recognized by scholars as Crete (although some believe Caphtor to be located in Cilicia in Asia Minor).

In other Biblical references, the Philistines are synonymous with the Cherethites; that is, Cretans (see Zephaniah 2:5 and Ezekiel 25:16). Various Biblical traditions suggest that the Caphtorim (or at least some of them) are to be identified with the Cherethites. Thus the Biblical sources seem to link the Philistines with a previous home in Crete.

The Bible also gives us historical references to the Philistine settlement in Canaan, beginning with the book of Judges. These references are far more explicit than those in Genesis, Zephaniah and Ezekiel previously mentioned. The well-known Samson cycle (Judges 13–16) must be understood against the background of a territorial conflict between the Philistines and the Israelite tribes of Dan and Judah. Samson's tribe, Dan, was fighting for its very existence in the territory allotted to it on the eastern border of Philistia. Ultimately, the tribe of Dan was unsuccessful in this struggle, and by the end of the period of the Judges, was forced to abandon its inheritance and move to the Northern Galilee. The major conflict at this time was not between Dan and the Philistines but between the Philistines and the tribe of Judah. Judah was forced by Philistine pressure to occupy an area much smaller than that allotted to it. Open warfare between the Philistines and Judah began with the battle of Ebenezer (1 Samuel 4). The Israelites were thoroughly routed. The Philistines even captured the Ark of the Lord which the Israelites had brought to the battlefield in a vain effort to stave off defeat. The Philistines followed up on their victory by advancing all the way to Shiloh, where the ark had been kept in a tent-shrine. The Philistines apparently destroyed Shiloh (see Jeremiah 7:12–14; Psalms 78:60), and then continued northward on the Via Maris to capture Megiddo and Beth Shean. This gave them control of most of the territory west of the Jordan River; With these victories and with their monopoly on metalworking in the area (see Yohanan Aharoni, "The Israelite Occupation of Canaan," BAR, May/June 1982), the Philistines were able to keep the Israelites in a position of economic as well as political dependence.

Philistine dominance lasted for several generations, reaching its zenith during the second half of the 11th century. Despite their victories in the Jezreel Valley and at Beth Shean, the Philistines never enjoyed complete control over this territory for any extended period of time. For the most part, the Philistines occupied the territory in southern Palestine described in Joshua 13 as belonging to them at the death of Joshua, plus the coastal region extending north to the Yarkon River (near Tel Aviv) and east to the slopes of the Judean Hills.

The decisive clash between Israel and the Philistines took place soon after Saul was anointed king of Israel. Indeed, the primary motive for the creation of the Israelite kingdom was the Israelites' desire to free themselves from Philistine domination. For this purpose, Saul organized a regular army. With this army, Jonathan assaulted the Philistines at Michmas (1 Samuel 13–14). The tide had turned in favor of the Israelites.

One of the best-known encounters between the Israelites and the Philistines was the contest between the respective champions David and Goliath. After David slew Goliath in the Elah Valley, the Philistines were pursued "even unto Gath and unto Ekron" (1 Samuel 17:52).

The successful advances of Israelite forces under King Saul soon ended, however. On the slopes of Mt. Gilboa, in a battle with Philistines forces, Saul and three of his sons were killed (1 Samuel 31). When the Philistines found Saul lying among the dead, they cut off his head and hung his body, stripped of its armor, from the walls of Beth Shean.

Following up on their victory, the Philistines captured and briefly held Canaanite cities in the Jezreel Valley including Megiddo.

After David's victory over Goliath, he fled from Saul to escape Saul's jealous wrath. David actually entered the service of the Philistine king of Gath, one Achish. David served Achish as a mercenary commander and later served as the vassal king of Judah (1 Samuel 21). About ten years later, David established his rule over the United Monarchy, and he "...smote the Philistines, and subdued them, and took Gath and her towns out of the hand of the Philistines" (1 Chronicles 18:1). Consolidating his victories, David conquered the northern Shephelah and the coastal plain (formerly the tribal portion of Dan), including Dor, the Jezreel Valley, and finally the Beth Shean Valley. Thus, he greatly reduced Philistine territory; he may even have turned some Philistine cities into Israelite vassal states.

The famous Philistine Pentapolis consisted of the following major cities: Gaza, Ashkelon, Ashdod, Gath, and Ekron. Gaza appears in the Samson cycle (Judges 16) as the principal Philistine center, where the *seranim* (Philistine lords) gathered for festivals and sacrifices in the Temple of Dagon.

Ashkelon was also an important city-state and was known for its seaport. It is mentioned in the Samson cycle (for example, Judges 14:19), although less often than Gaza. A later reference to the "markets of Ashkelon" (2 Samuel 1:20) attests to that city's status as an important mercantile center.

Ashkelon's neighbor to the north was Ashdod, mentioned in the Bible chiefly in the account of the capture of the Ark of the Lord at the battle of Ebenezer. The Philistines took the Ark all the way to Ashdod, evidence that by about 1050 B.C. Ashdod was a major Philistine city-state. According to 1 Samuel 5, one of the two temples of Dagon was at Ashdod.

Considerably less is known about Gath, which may be located at Tell es-Sag. Gath's strength and importance are attested by David's vassalage to Achish, the king of Gath. Ekron was the northernmost of the Philistine cities, and controlled the territory allotted to the tribe of Dan. New excavations, begun at Tel Miqneh in 1981, already suggest that this may have been the site of Ekron. An interesting detail about Ekron is preserved in 1 Samuel 17:52; the men of Israel and Judah pursued the fleeing Philistines "to the gates of Ekron."

In addition to the Pentapolis, two lesser Philistine cities, Ziklag and Timna, are mentioned in the Bible (1 Samuel 27:5). Like the smaller settlements of the Israelite tribes, these smaller Philistine cities are called *haserim* (villages) or *banoth* (daughters) in the Bible.

The government of the Philistine Pentapolis is, at best, adumbrated in the Bible. At the head of each Philistine kingdom (city-state) stood the *seren* (1 Samuel 5:8; 6:4, 16) a word that seems to be linguistically related to the Greek, *tyrannos* (tyrant).

NATIONAL MUSEUM, ATHENS

WARRIORS' VASE. Soldiers in full battle dress decorate an early 12th century B.C. vase from Mycenae. Their bronze helmets and leg guards, coats of mail and spears are all similar to Goliath's armor and weaponry as described in the Bible. These well-known elements of Aegean warfare, shared by the Mycenaean warriors and Goliath, show the transfer of Aegean tradition to Philistia.

The passage in 1 Samuel 17:5–7 compares Goliath's spear to "a weaver's beam" because this type of weapon had not been seen in Israel before and had no Hebrew name. The Warriors' Vase shows the earliest representation of this javelin-type spear with loop.

The Philistine ruler may also have borne the title "king," as did King Achish of Gath (1 Samuel 21:11; 27:2). The limitation on the *seren's* power is reflected in a disagreement between the Philistine princes (*sarim*) and Achish: Could David (who was then fighting for Achish) take part in the battle against Saul at Gilboa? (1 Samuel 29:4–10) Because of the princes' objection to Oavid's participation in the battle, Achish, despite his own judgment to the contrary, ordered David to remain behind while the Philistines went off to battle. The Philistine rulers obviously did not have absolute power over major political or military decisions.

The *seranim* led the armies that were vital to control the large civilian population. Each *seren* commanded his own army, assisted by *sarim* who undoubtedly held positions of high military rank. These armies included infantry, archers (see 1 Samuel 31:3), chariotry, and horsemen (1 Samuel 13).

The detailed Biblical account of Goliath's armor and weaponry is a vivid description of a Philistine warrior in full battle dress:

> "And he had a helmet of brass upon his head, and he was armed with a coat of mail.... And he had greaves of brass upon his legs, and a target of brass between his shoulders. And the staff of his spear was like a weaver's beam, and his spear's head weighed six hundred shekels of iron; and one bearing a shield went before him." (1 Samuel 17:5–7)

Goliath's dress and armour (bronze helmet, coat of mail, bronze greaves [leg guards], and javelin) as well as the duel between champions are all well-known features of Aegean arms and warfare. They clearly indicate Aegean traditions carried on by the Philistines. The 12th century Warriors' Vase from Mycenae shows Mycenaean warriors very similarly equipped.

Philistine religious organization and beliefs, as reflected in the Bible, suggest that by the 11th century the Philistines had already assimilated the main elements of Semitic Canaanite beliefs into their own religion. Biblical evidence gives no trace of a non-Semitic tradition, except the absence of circumcision. Apparently, the Philistines, alone among the peoples in Palestine during this period, did not practice circumcision (see 1 Samuel 18:25; Judges 14:3; and 1 Samuel 17:26, 36). The term "uncircumcised" by itself was sometimes used to refer to the Philistines (Judges 15:18; 1 Samuel 14:6; 31:4), indicating that all other peoples in the area (e.g., Israelites, Canaanites) must have been circumcised.

The head of the Philistine pantheon appears to have been the Canaanite god, Dagon (or Dagan) (1 Chronicles 10:10), to whom the temples of Gaza and Ashdod, and possibly one at Beth Shean, were dedicated. Another god, Baal-zebub (Baal-Zebul), had his oracular temple in Ekron. The goddess Ashtoreth, or Ashtaroth, apparently also had a temple at Beth Shean (1 Samuel 31:8–13). Philistine priests are mentioned only once in the Bible, when the Ark of the Lord is placed in the Temple of Dagon at Ashdod (1 Samuel 5). One of the few specifically Philistine religious beliefs in the Bible is the guilt offering (*asham*) sent to the Lord when the Ark was returned. The guilt offering was golden mice and golden tumors or boils (1 Samuel 6:4).

There is both agreement and discrepancy between the Biblical references to the Philistines and the archaeological evidence. The Aegean background of Philistine religion (which is not disclosed in the Bible) is especially evident in the earliest examples of cult objects from Ashdod (from the 12th century B.C.) which emphasize the worship of the Mycenaean "Great Mother" or "Great Goddess." Archaeological evidence from the Aegean has revealed that in that area, female, not male, deities were predominantly worshipped. Apparently by the 11th century this pantheon was replaced by a male Canaanite pantheon reflecting the Philistines' more recent cultural milieu.

The sites containing Philistine cultural remains are found principally in the Shephelah and the southern coastal plain, but there is also evidence that Philistine culture spread to a variety of sites in other areas of the country. Major excavations have established a clear stratigraphic sequence through which we can trace the initial appearance, then the flourishing, and finally the subsequent assimilation of Philistine material culture, a process which spanned the period from about 1200 B.C. to 1000 B.C. (When I refer to Philistine material culture I include all Sea Peoples whose cultural backgrounds were similar.)

Of the five Pentapolis sites, only three—Gaza, Ashkelon, Ashdod—have been definitely located, and only one, Ashdod, has been thoroughly excavated. At Gaza, only the slightest evidence attesting a late Philistine occupation has been uncovered. The limited archaeological work at Ashkelon has revealed that the last Canaanite stratum suffered a violent destruction and was followed by a Philistine settlement. Khirbet Muqanna (Tel Miqneh) may be the site of Ekron, an identification that has been strengthened by our recent excavations there. The location of Gath is still an open question: the most likely site is Tell es-Sefi. The most extensive evidence of Philistine material culture has come from recent excavations at Tell Ashdod and from a site on the

Did the Philistines Write?

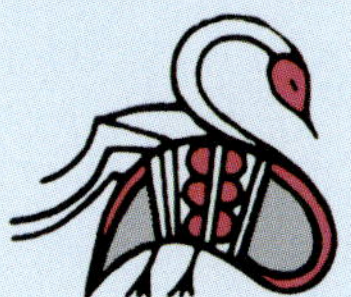

Could the Philistines write? Of course they could. They must have been able to write. The question arises because we can't produce a single specimen that can be identified positively as Philistine writing. We don't even know what language the Philistines spoke.

We know the Philistines could write because writing was well-known in the ancient world and the Philistines were a great ancient civilization.

Many large caches of ancient texts have been found by archaeologists, and occasional inscriptions are continually uncovered in excavations. Scholars have identified and translated texts in Sumerian, Akkadian, Babylonian, Egyptian, Ugaritic, Hittite, Hebrew, Moabite, Aramaic and Greek, just to name some of the best known Near Eastern languages—but not Philistine.

The absence of Philistine inscriptions is especially anomalous because we know so much about the Philistines, not only from the Bible, but from innumerable excavations where they left their remains and from the walls of Egyptian temples where they are depicted.

In 1964 some clay tablets inscribed in a linear script were found by Professor H. J. Franken at Deir Alla in the Transjordan. Some scholars have suggested that the script is Philistine. The tablets were found in association with Philistine pottery. In 1968–1969, Professor Moshe Dothan, digging at Ashdod, uncovered two inscribed seals from strata XIII–XII, again associated with the Philistines, which he dated to 1700–1150 B.C. This script is otherwise unknown, but it resembles the Deir Alla script. It may well be written in the Philistine script, but it, like the Deir Alla tablets, is still undeciphered. Both the Deir Alla and the Ashdod scripts are apparently related to the linear scripts utilized in the Aegean Basin throughout the Late Bronze Age, i.e., Linear A and B and the Cypro-Minoan syllabary, and as such add still another independent source pointing to the Aegean as the Philistine homeland. —ROBERT R. STIEGLITZ

northern border of Philistia whose ancient name we do not know—Tell Qasile within the city limits of modern Tel Aviv. These two sites, Tell Ashdod and Tell Qasile provide complementary data on the nature of Philistine urban settlement, facets of their material culture, and cultic structures and practices.

Strata XIII through X at Ashdod tell the story of the Philistines' occupation there. The first sign of the new population's arrival is dramatic: the Egyptian-Canaanite fortress (stratum XIV, Area G) was partially destroyed and an open-air cult installation was built over it (stratum XIII). Adjacent to this installation was a potter's workshop housing a rich collection of locally made Mycenaean III C:1 pottery. This pottery, originally Aegean in style, seems to be a precursor of the earliest Philistine ware. These monochrome Mycenaean III C:1 pottery sherds appeared just before the colorful Philistine ware and continued to be produced along with the Philistine pottery, indicating perhaps that an earlier wave of Sea Peoples had preceded the great invasion described in the Medinet Habu inscription in the first half of the 12th century B.C. Mycenaean III C:1 ware has very recently been found in large quantities at Tel Miqneh (Ekron) and indicates that the same settlement pattern is evident in this Philistine city.

ISRAEL DEPARTMENT OF ANTIQUITIES AND MUSEUMS

STAMP SEAL FROM ASHDOD. Used in the late 13th or early 12th century B.C. to imprint a lump of clay affixed to a letter, the stamp bears signs that may be related to the Cypro-Minoan script. When pressed into clay, the writing on the seal may be read in its correct orientation. This find emphasizes the affinities between Philistine Ashdod and the Aegean world. Ashdod, a major Philistine city-state, stood on the main military and commercial road between Egypt and Canaan. Both Egyptian and Aegean influence are exhibited in Ashdod but Aegean elements, like this seal, predominate.

ISRAEL DEPARTMENT OF ANTIQUITIES AND MUSEUMS

GOLD DISC FROM ASHDOD. Aegean in style, this gold disc was made by a Philistine craftsman in the 12th century B.C.

THE APSIDAL PHILISTINE STRUCTURE FROM ASHDOD. This curved apsidal structure was found in stratum XII (mid-12th century B.C.) along with impressive quantities of Philistine pottery, jewelry, metal objects and ivory. One discovery from this area is a stamp seal bearing signs related to the Cypro-Minoan script. The local cult centered around the worship of a female deity, familiarly referred to by modern archaeologists as "Ashdoda." A representation of "Ashdoda" (see p. 162) was discovered nearby.

After stratum XIII, a thriving fortified Philistine city was found at Ashdod in strata XII through XI. The small finds include a gold disc and seals inscribed in a still undeciphered script. These may be our only examples of Philistine language and writing. Until more samples of this script are found, however, we must be cautious about its identification, but it may have Aegean affiliations.

The Philistine city at Ashdod was well-planned; the archaeologists uncovered two building complexes carefully divided by a street. The northern complex consisted of an apsidal structure with a courtyard and adjacent rooms. Here the earliest known Philistine cult deity, nicknamed "Ashdoda," was found. It is a figurine whose prototypes seem to be the figurines of the Mycenaean "Great Mother." Elsewhere at Ashdod, excavators uncovered a cultic stand decorated with musicians. A similar cultic stand was found at Tell Qasile.

Stratum X (c. 1050 B.C.) represents the last, largest and most prosperous Philistine city at Ashdod. At that time a Lower City outside the acropolis area was occupied for the first time. Massive brick walls and a very strong gate were built to protect this enlarged city. Ironically enough, although the Philistine population had grown and flourished, its culture, as evidenced by its pottery, had not. The pottery reflects assimilation into the local pottery repertoire and some types disappear altogether. New hybrid forms are created. For example, at Ashdod, black on red decoration shows affiliations with the Phoenician culture, while at Tell Qasile, a new krater form was created through the fusion of old and new, local and foreign features coming together. Ceramic features which usher in the ceramic style of the Iron Age are its red slip and burnishing. Eventually pottery and all other evidence of Philistines totally disappeared from higher strata at the site.

The city at Tell Qasile was founded by the Philistines in the first half of the 12th century B.C. on the northern bank of the Yarkon River. The site was obviously chosen because it was a perfect inland

Philistines After David

What happened to the Philistines after David? Although their military superiority was shattered, and their distinctive material culture disappeared from the archaeological record soon afterwards, the Philistine people and culture did not vanish. They are referred to in the Assyrian Annals and the Books of Kings and Chronicles as well as by the later Biblical prophets. There is also literary and numismatic evidence that their descendants continued to perpetuate some native Philistine traditions right into the Roman and Byzantine periods.

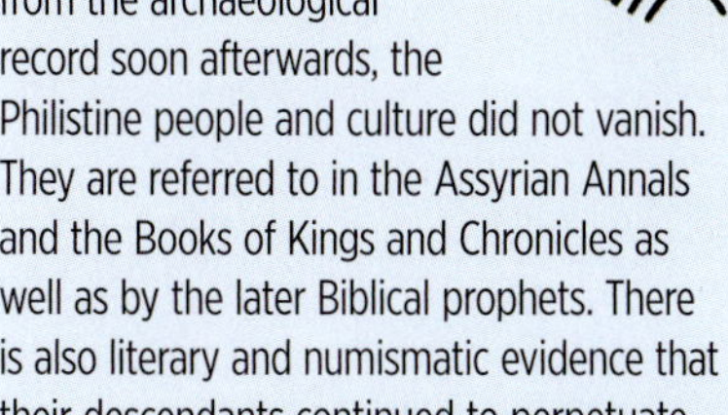

The Assyrian Annals are the official historical records of the Assyrian kings written in cuneiform script on clay and stone. They date from c. 900–600 B.C. Mentioned in the Annals are several major Philistine cities. The Annals also refer to payments made by Philistine cities to the Assyrian kings.

In the Biblical sources we read of continued tension between the Philistines and Israel and Judah:

"Some of the Philistines brought Jehoshaphat [King of Judah, 871–849 B.C.] presents and silver for tribute." (2 Chronicles 17:11)

"And the Lord stirred up against Jehoram [King of Judah, 849–841 B.C.] the anger of the Philistines...and they came up against Judah and invaded it." (2 Chronicles 21:16, 17)

"He [Hezekiah, King of Judah, 715–687 B.C.] smote the Philistines as far as Gaza and its territory, from watchtower to fortified city." (2 Kings 18:8)

"He [Uzziah, king of Judah, 780–741 B.C.] went out and made war against the Philistines, and broke down the wall of Gath and the wall of Jabneh and the wall of Ashdod; and he built cities in the territory of Ashdod and elsewhere among the Philistines." (2 Chronicles 26:6)

"And the Philistines had made raids on the cities in the Shephelah and the Negev of Judah." (2 Chronicles 28:18)

References to Philistines in the books of the late prophets Amos and Isaiah indicates that even at that time the Philistines had an independent existence.

"Thus says the Lord: For three transgressions of Gaza, and for four, I will not revoke the punishment, because they carried into exile a whole people to deliver them up to Edom. So I will send a fire upon the wall of Gaza, and it shall devour her strongholds. I will cut off the inhabitants from Ashdod, and him that holds the scepter from Ashkelon; I will turn my hand against Ekron; and the remnant of the Philistines shall perish, Says the Lord God." (Amos 1:6–8)

"The Syrians on the east and the Philistines on the west devour Israel with open mouth." (Isaiah 9:12)

An administrative tablet found at Babylon, dating from the reign of Nebuchadnezzer II (early sixth century B.C.), speaks about the Kings of Ashdod and Gaza as well as the inhabitants of Ashkelon.

Subsequently, in the fifth century B.C., the Greek historian Herodotus (2.157) describes the capture of the city of *Azotus* (Ashdod) after a 29 year siege by an Egyptian king, Psammitichus. Moreover, Judah the Maccabee (second century B.C.) destroyed the pagan temples at Azotus (1 Maccabees 5:68).

At Gaza in the Roman period there was a temple and local cult of a god called Mama. The coins of Gaza minted under the Roman Emperors show both this deity and a figure labelled MEINO—apparently referring to Minos the ancient ruler of Crete. Gaza also bore the epithet MINOA, like other cities in the Mediterranean which tradition connected with Minos of Crete. The tradition of Caphtor/Crete as the homeland of the Philistines was, therefore, still perpetuated in Gaza some 1,500 years after their settlement in Canaan.

—ROBERT R. STIEGLITZ

port site. Tell Qasile was established on virgin soil to suit particular socio-economic needs. The town was well-planned, with separate residential, industrial, and sacred quarters.

Three superimposed temples were uncovered in the northeast part of the tell, the first well-defined Philistine temples ever discovered (see next page). This area was evidently the cultic center of the Philistine city. In each of the three strata, XII through X, a new temple was constructed, each larger than the last. The earliest temple (stratum XIIa) was a one-room mud-brick structure.

The stratum XI temple was larger than its predecessor, but still consisted of a single room, the *cella*. The stratum XI temple had a plastered floor and brick benches along the wall. The stratum X temple was evidently merely an enlargement and rebuilding of the stratum XI temple on a different plan. The stratum X temple (the latest) consisted of two main rooms—the main hall and an antechamber.

The altar was located directly opposite the central opening of the main hall so that the visitor had an unobstructed view from the entrance. No exact parallels have been found in Canaan. Many features continue the Canaanite tradition but other features incorporate Aegean characteristics. The Tell Qasile temple is similar to the 13th–12th century temples at Kition, Cyprus, and to recently discovered shrines at Mycenae, mainland Greece, and Phylakopy on the island of Melos. This again indicates the clear connection between the Aegean and Philistine cultures.

In the open courtyard west of the Tell Qasile temple, excavators found a pit, or *favissa*, containing a buried cache of cult vessels used in the stratum XI temple. Among the finds were a lion-head *rhyton* and a female figure vessel. Perhaps this female figure was the goddess of the temple.

In other quarters of the city at Tell Qasile, residential and industrial structures were uncovered. The flourishing city in stratum X had well-planned houses with courtyards. The furnishings found in these houses are illuminating clues to the daily life

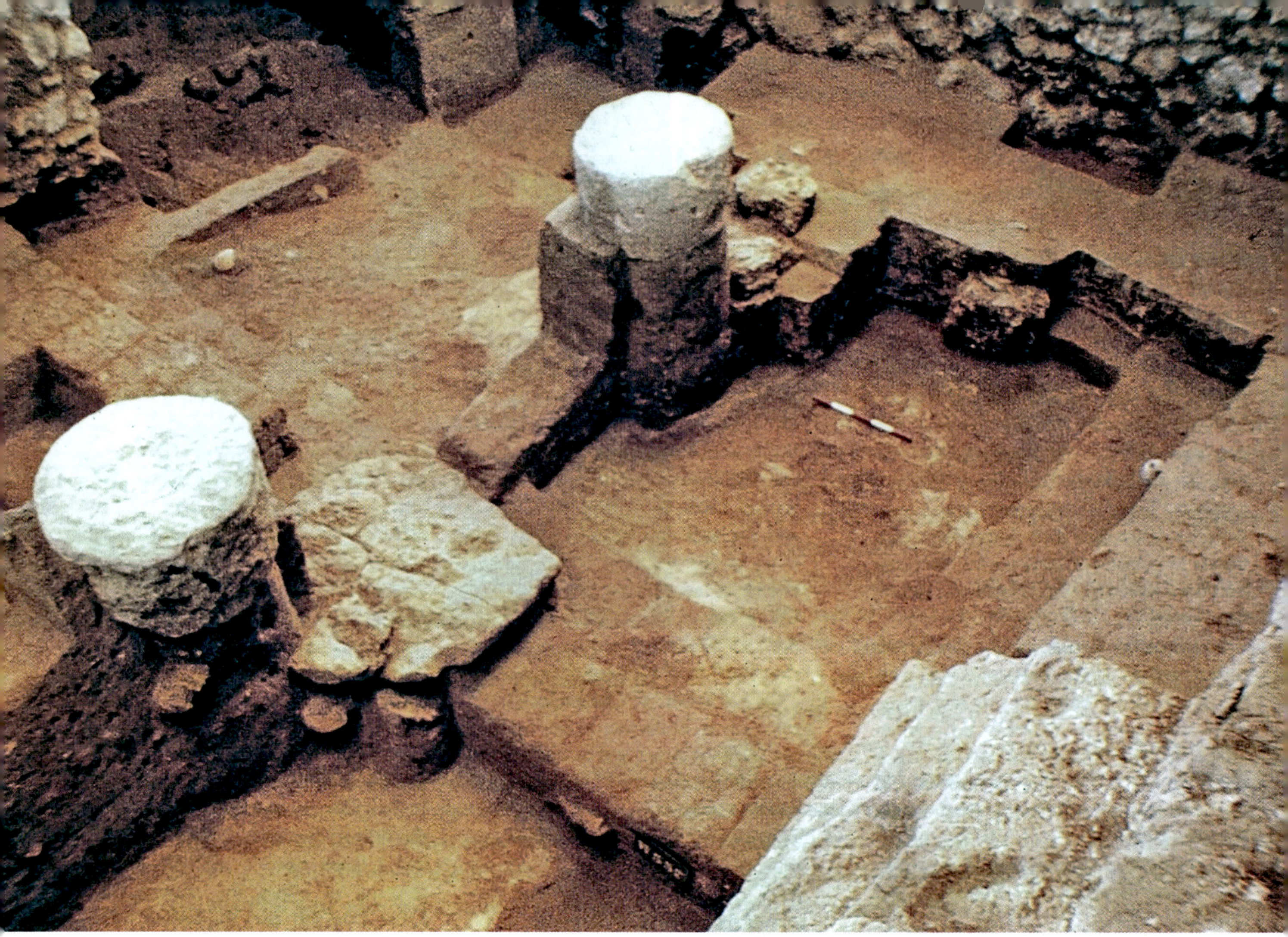

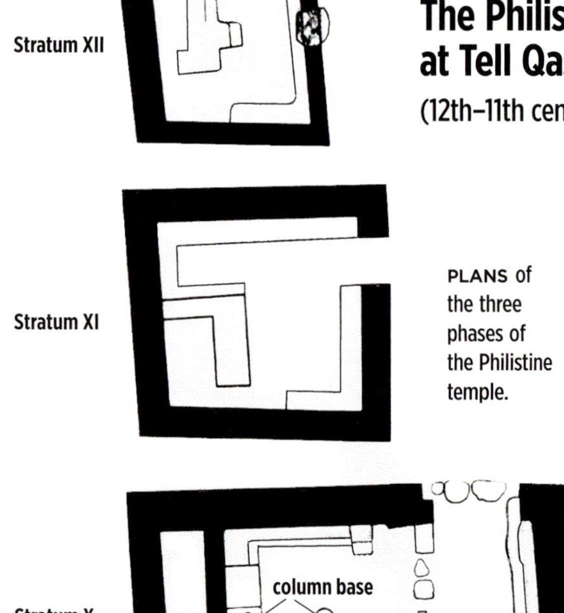

The Philistine temple at Tell Qasile

(12th–11th centuries B.C.)

Stratum XII

Stratum XI

Stratum X

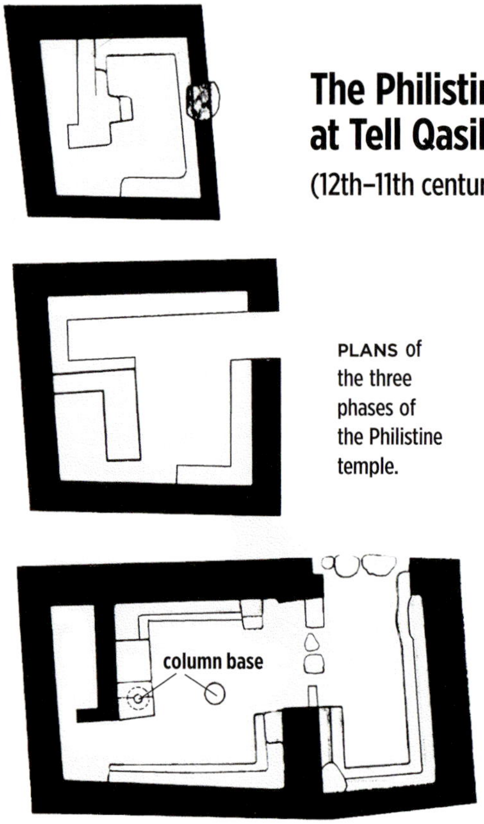

PLANS of the three phases of the Philistine temple.

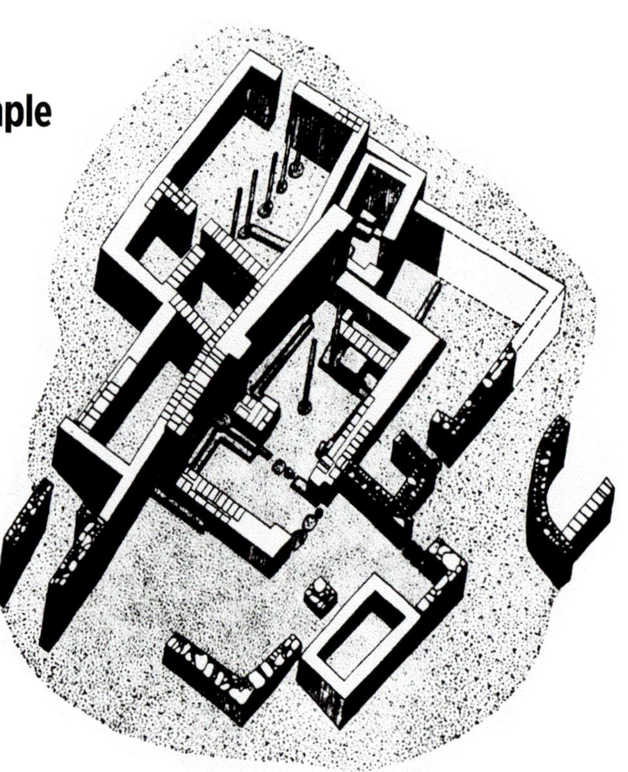

AN ARTIST'S RECONSTRUCTION shows stratum X at Tell Qasile, with the temple at the center.

PHILISTINE TEMPLE AT TELL QASILE. The first Philistine temple ever discovered, this one room structure dates from the 12th century B.C. Later, during the 12th and 11th centuries, the temple was twice rebuilt and enlarged (see plans). Stratum XII, the earliest phase, is the one shown in the photograph where we see plastered benches and a beaten lime floor. The stone walls are from the two later temples (strata XI and X). The two round column bases—about six feet apart—were added in the last phase of the temple. Charred wood found at the bases of the columns was evidence that the stone bases originally held cedar columns which supported the roof. We can easily imagine Samson standing in such a Philistine temple, arms outstretched, straining to topple the columns and destroy the temple with his enemies and himself inside.

TELL QASILE EXCAVATIONS

of the Philistines at a time when they were not only prosperous but when they had already assimilated local Canaanite culture. Their success is reflected in the grain pits, silos, presses, and storerooms, and in the store jars for wine and oil, as well as in the great number of farm tools, including flint sickle-blades. The archaeological finds include remains of a metal industry and several work shops.

No archaeological study of the Philistines would be complete without considering their connection with the new metal of the era, iron. The Bible (1 Samuel 13:19; 17:7) offers only tantalizing hints that the Philistines attempted to maintain a technological superiority over the Israelites in the production and distribution of metals, perhaps including iron. This suggestion is supported by the fact that most of the iron tools and weapons found in Israel before about 1000 B.C. come from sites that show signs of Philistine occupation or influence—for example, the iron knives from Tell Qasile and from the Tell el-Far'ah (South) Philistine tombs. However, the older view that the Philistine introduced iron production into Canaan has been challenged. Apparently, the political upheavals that characterized the late 13th century in the Aegean and eastern Mediterranean disrupted trade in copper and tin, thus providing an incentive to develop other resources such as iron. It is true that only small quantities of iron have been found in Canaan dating to before the 12th century when the Philistines arrived in the area, but the gradual development of iron technology under a variety of influences, including that of the Philistines, is a complex story. Moreover, iron did not become common in Israel until after the eclipse of Philistine culture in the tenth and ninth centuries.

The Philistine material culture, particularly the pottery and cult vessels, does not accord with the negative meaning of the term "Philistine" as it is used today. Philistine ceramic ware demonstrates high artistic and aesthetic abilities. Indeed, Philistine material culture stands out against the bleak background of the world in which they lived.

Philistine pottery in the Holy Land is a large,

A MYCENAEAN IIIC:1 BOWL FROM CYPRUS. It is easy to see the striking similarity of this bowl to its Philistine counterpart (see next page. Several Philistine pottery forms and decorations are clearly derived from Mycenaean prototypes.

ISRAEL DEPARTMENT OF ANTIQUITIES AND MUSEUMS

ISRAEL DEPARTMENT OF ANTIQUITIES

AN ASSEMBLAGE OF PHILISTINE POTTERY. Here we see some shapes and decorative motifs characteristic of the Philistine pottery repertoire.

Back row, left to right:

A KRATER. This large two-handled bowl is one of the most common types found at Philistine sites.

A STIRRUP JAR. This vessel is distinguished by a solid (false) neck; the actual opening into the stirrup jar is through the funnel-like spout on the shoulder.

A "BEER JUG" OR STRAINER SPOUT JUG. In the upper decorative band appear two types of Philistine naturalistic forms: a bird with head turned backward and on the right, a fish.

A TALL NECKED JUG. Richly decorated in red and black, this jug shows Egyptian influence in both its form and decoration; the lotus design on its long neck is clear evidence of Egyptian influence.

A STIRRUP JAR. A repeated bird design circles the lower band of this vessel; the characteristic funnel-like spout on the shoulder has broken off.

Front row, left to right:

A CYLINDRICAL BOTTLE. The black and red geometric design on a white slip is characteristic of this type of bottle, as are the small pierced horizontal handles.

A BOWL. Smaller than a krater, the Philistine bowl, like the krater, is derived from Mycenaean prototypes, this bowl from Ashkelon, with its bichrome tongue motif, is very similar to a Mycenaean IIIC:1b example found at Sinda on Cyprus.

A HORN-SHAPED VESSEL. Two pierced handles on the inner curvature of this vessel indicate that it was carried on a cord.

homogenous group of locally made painted ware, derived from Mycenaean traditions in shape and decoration. We are able to connect this distinctive pottery with the Philistines for a variety of reasons, geographical, stratigraphical and comparative.

The geographical distribution of this pottery corresponds strikingly with the territory occupied and influenced by the Philistines, diminishing as one moves away from Philistia itself.

Stratigraphically, Philistine pottery occurs in levels and deposits which can be dated from the first decades of the 12th century to the late 11th century B.C., a time span closely corresponding to the Philistine settlement and expansion.

A comparative study of the various phases of Philistine pottery is of greatest assistance, however, in understanding the rise and fall of Philistine culture in Canaan. Initially, the pottery reflected the process of crystallization and diffusion of Philistine culture in Canaan. Then we see a gradual assimilation of local material culture. Eventually Philistine ware disappeared altogether.

The story begins with the appearance of a locally produced variant of monochrome Mycenaean III C:1 ware (reflecting Philistine origins) at a few sites, especially Ashdod and Tel Miqneh, around 1200 B.C. Not long after this, we find the first Philistine ware *per se*, with its rich variety of motifs in bichrome decoration of black and red on a heavy white slip background. In the last quarter of the 12th century, we already notice a slight decline in the overall quality of the ware and some departure

ISRAEL DEPARTMENT OF ANTIQUITIES AND MUSEUMS

GEOMETRIC DESIGNS are the customary decoration of horn-shaped vessels, usually applied in red, or red and black, on a white slip. A mirror allows us to see the small pierced handles. Through these handles a cord was probably strung in order to sling the vessel over a shoulder or around a neck.

from original Mycenaean shapes and decoration. Then in the second half of the 11th century, a steep decline set in, with some hybrid Philistine and local types appearing, while other Philistine forms slowly assimilated into local styles. This transformation can be seen particularly in the bowls and kraters. The white-slipped, bichrome decoration gradually died out, often replaced by the red slip, hand burnishing, and dark brown decoration more characteristic of Canaanite ware. Not long after 1000 B.C., when David humbled the once-powerful Philistine military machine, the distinctive features of Philistine pottery faded away completely.

The shapes and decorative motifs of Philistine pottery were a blend of four distinct ceramic styles: Mycenaean, Cypriot, Egyptian, and local Canaanite. The dominant traits in shape and almost all the decorative elements were derived from the Mycenaean repertoire, and, as we have said, point to the Aegean background of Philistine pottery Philistine shapes of Mycenaean origin include bell-shaped bowls, large kraters with elaborate decoration, stirrup jars for oils and unguents, and strainer-spout beer jugs; the latter no doubt served as centerpieces at many a Philistine party. A few of the many decorative motifs are stylized birds, spiral loops, concentric half-circles, and scale patterns. Although Philistine vessels were richly decorated with motifs taken from the Mycenaean repertoire, these motifs were rearranged and integrated with other influences to create the distinctive "signature" known as Philistine.

Cypriot influence in Philistine pottery is most striking in the bottle and the horn-shaped vessel. An elongated cylindrical body tapering to a narrow curved neck gives the horn-shaped vessel its name. Both Cypriot and Philistine examples represent cheaper copies of similar vessels made of ivory and alabaster, and appear during the Late Bronze Age (13th century B.C.) and continue through the Iron Age (early 12th century B.C.).

Egypt makes its most visible contribution to the Philistine repertoire with the tall-necked jug. The long, slightly bulging neck is a common feature of the Egyptian ceramic tradition. The stylized lotus

ISRAEL DEPARTMENT OF ANTIQUITIES AND MUSEUMS

FLASK FROM MEGIDDO. Called a "pilgrim" flask, this Philistine pottery vessel is decorated with straight and wavy radial red and black lines and a Maltese cross in the center. Small loops project from either side of the flask which dates to about 1100 B.C.

MUSEUM OF FINE ARTS, BOSTON: OTIS NORCROSS FUND

MYCENAEAN POTTERY RING. Although the provenance of this cult vessel, called a *kernos*, is unknown, it probably originated in Cyprus, where *kernoi* are most numerous. Similar *kernoi* have been found in Israel at Beth Shean, Beth Shemesh, Megiddo, and elsewhere. The pictured *kernos* dates to the last phase of Mycenaean culture, about 1200 B.C. *Kernoi* are hollow rings, decorated with small vessels, fruits, animals and birds. This one is decorated with a bull's head and miniature vases and bowls, all common symbols of fertility.

Although no one knows for sure how a *kernos* was used, probably during the course of a religious ritual some liquid was poured into the hollow ring (perhaps through one of the objects on the ring), shaken up, and then poured out.

motif which appears on Philistine pottery was taken directly from Egyptian prototypes. The tall-necked jug is not, however, exclusively of Egyptian inspiration; on the contrary, it is an outstanding example of the eclectic nature of Philistine pottery: It is Egyptian in the shape of the neck and in the neck decoration, Aegean in the decorative motifs on the main band of body decoration, and Canaanite in the shape of the body. All three elements are blended beautifully into a single pottery type. The role of Canaanite pottery in the Philistine repertoire is limited, but clear: the Philistine potter applied his own decorative motifs to long-established Canaanite pottery shapes.

The unique style of Philistine pottery is the result of the Philistine potter's success in integrating ceramic traditions from his Aegean homeland with influences from the Cypriot, Egyptian, and local Canaanite pottery groups to which he was exposed.

Philistine cult vessels provide us with insights into Philistine ritual and beliefs. They also demonstrate how Philistine craftsmen wove their Aegean traditions with strands from Egypt and Canaan, as well as with their own ideas to create innovative and distinctive cult objects.

Take, for example, the *kernos* or pottery ring. The *kernos* form itself reflects Aegean influences. A *kernos* is a hollow pottery ring about 10 inches in diameter on which hollow objects like birds or pomegranates are set. We are not sure how it was used but probably a liquid of some kind was poured into the hollow ring, shaken about, and poured out in the course of a religious ritual. The well-known Gezer Cache included a Philistine *kernos* with an attached bird, a pomegranate, and bird vessel. But it also contained a faience fragment bearing the cartouche of Ramesses III, thus dating this cache to the first half of the 12th century B.C. The beautiful white-slipped, bichrome objects belong to the earliest phase of the Philistine style.

A distinctive Philistine cult vessel is the one-handled

ISRAEL DEPARTMENT OF ANTIQUITIES AND MUSEUMS

"ASHDODA." THIS SEATED female figurine found in a Philistine stratum at Ashdod is a unique complete example of a well-known Philistine cult object. "Ashdoda's" body merges into a four-legged throne. Her flat armless torso and molded breasts outlined in black form the back of the throne. Elongated triangles—a typical Philistine artistic form—and black horizontal bands decorate the white surface of the figurine. The features of Ashdoda figurines—the head, the curved body forming a throne and the legs—are Mycenaean concepts that were borrowed by the Philistines and adapted to their style of design and color.

ISRAEL DEPARTMENT OF ANTIQUITIES AND MUSEUMS

"ASHDODA" HEAD. Roughly made, this fragment from Ashdod is one of many "Ashdoda" type cult objects found in excavations throughout the Mediterranean area.

ISRAEL DEPARTMENT OF ANTIQUITIES AND MUSEUMS

LION-HEADED *RHYTON*. This one-handled ritual drinking cup, or *rhyton*, found near the Tell Qasile temple, is an impressive example of Philistine decorative art. It has bulging eyes and cheeks and a flattened nose; its open jaws show tongue and fangs. Red and black painted designs accentuate the features.

Animal-headed *rhyta* have a long history in the Mycenaean Minoan repertoire. Processional scenes painted on New Kingdom tomb walls in Egypt show envoys, probably from Crete or the Aegean islands, bearing gifts of precious metal, including lion-headed *rhyta*, to the Egyptian functionaries.

TELL QASILE EXCAVATIONS

BIRD-HEADED BOWL. Light and graceful, this terra-cotta bowl was one of many which were originally elevated on high stands in the Tell Qasile temple complex dating to the first half of the 12th century B.C. The bird bowl demonstrates the talent of Philistine craftsmen who adapted local traditions to create their own distinctive cult objects.

A MOURNING FEMALE figurine holds her head in grief. This terra-cotta figurine, almost 3 3/4 inches (10 cm) tall, is assumed to have come from the 12th- to 11th-century B.C. cemetery of Tell ‘Aitun, where some tombs contained Philistine pottery.

The figurine was originally mounted on the rim of a krater, a large, two-handled bowl. The base of the figurine retains the negative impression of the krater rim.

Executed with a combination of applique modeling and incision, the figure has a rough naturalistic style. A long open dress reveals the naked body. The raised arms continue the line of the long-sleeved garment.

Several features distinguish this mourning woman from Canaanite figurines: the modeling in the round, the dress, the position of the hands, and the mounting on the krater rim. Similar mourning figures of Mycenaean origin have been found at Perati on the east coast of Greece (see p. 166), and at Rhodes, Crete and Cyprus.

lion-head *rhyton*, a ritual or drinking cup; examples have been found at a variety of sites. The Philistine pottery *rhyton* is the last echo of a long Mycenaean-Minoan tradition of metal and stone animal-head *rhyta*. These vessels have been found in the shaft graves at Mycenae, at Knossos on Crete, and have been pictured on New Kingdom tomb walls in Egypt. From a later period (13th to early 12th century B.C.) comes an ivory plaque from the treasury at Megiddo on which are incised two *rhyta*, one lion-headed and the other gazelle-headed, carried by two servants in a procession (see photograph in “The Finds That Could Not Be,” BAR, January/February 1982).

In the Philistine temple at Tell Qasile, three high cylindrical cult stands were found. Each had a bowl topped with a bird’s head. Although the bird representation has a long history and is well attested in the local Canaanite repertoire, its recurrence in different facets of Philistine culture is striking. Various types of terra-cotta vessels found at many Philistine sites are formed in the likeness of birds. Painted birds are a distinctive feature of Philistine pottery. The ships of the Sea Peoples depicted at Medinet Habu have bird figureheads. The motif is considered emblematic of Philistine decorative art.

Another cult stand, found at Ashdod, features five musicians around its base (see photograph in “The Finds That Could Not Be”). Four are modeled in the round and stand in windowlike openings. The fifth and central figure was formed by a combination of techniques. The figure’s outline was cut out, then the individual features were molded and added. Each of the figures in the Ashdod stand plays a musical instrument: cymbals, double pipe, frame drum, and stringed instrument that is probably a lyre. We are reminded of the passage from 1 Samuel 10: “After that thou shalt come to the hill of God, where is the garrison of the Philistines; and it shall come to pass when thou art come thither to the city, that thou shalt meet a company of prophets coming down from the high place with a *nevel* (large lyre) and a *tof* (frame drum) and a *halil* (double pipe) and a *kinnor* (lyre) before them: and they shall prophesy.” The musicians represented on the stand were probably part of a Philistine cult, their role similar to that of the “Levites which were singers” in the temple of Jerusalem (2 Chronicles 5:12–13).

Female pottery figurines also reflect Philistine cult origins and beliefs. The “Ashdoda” is the only complete example of a well-defined type that was common from the 12th to the eighth century B.C. The Ashdoda figure is probably a schematic representation of a female deity and throne. It is clearly related to a grouping known throughout the Greek mainland, Rhodes and Cyprus—a Mycenaean female figurine seated on a throne, sometimes holding a child. These Mycenaean figurines are thought to represent a mother goddess.

Hints of Philistine mourning customs can be gleaned from the terra-cotta female mourning figurines from Philistine contexts at sites such as Tell ‘Aitun and Azor. Most of this material comes from burials. These figurines stress hand gestures. Sometimes both hands hold the top of the head. On others, one hand is placed on the head and the other on the breast. Such figures are often attached to the rims of Philistine kraters. Similar mourning figures on similar kraters are closely associated with the burial customs and the cult of the dead found in the Aegean world at the end of the Mycenaean period. Here is another clear Aegean component of Philistine culture, this time in funerary rites.

ISRAEL DEPARTMENT OF ANTIQUITIES AND MUSEUMS

ANTHROPOID COFFIN LID. Found at Beth Shean in Israel's Jordan River Valley, this clay coffin lid dates to the time of Saul, the second half of the 11th century B.C. About 50 anthropoid coffins were found at Beth Shean. The majority are molded in a naturalistic style, with their faces clearly outlined. In contrast, on this lid and on four others, no facial outlines are delineated. The lid is the face—a fact that gives these lids, aptly called "grotesque," a bizarre, caricature-like effect. The face on this lid is boldly stylized: it has a high-ridged nose and deep horizontal-groove mouth; the chin is barely indicated; the arms and hands are disproportionately small and stick-like.

The distinctive feature of this particular lid is the applique headdress which is remarkably similar to the headdresses of the Philistine warriors depicted in the Medinet Habu reliefs (see pp. 143, 145, 147). Although other anthropoid coffins have been found in Canaan and in Egypt, none of those has this unique headgear—a clear indication that the bodies buried in these anthropoid coffins were Sea Peoples, probably Philistines.

Burial customs are generally a sensitive indicator of cultural affinities, and Philistine burial customs reflect the same fusion of Aegean background with Egyptian and local Canaanite elements that distinguishes every other aspect of their culture. As yet no burial grounds in any of the main Philistine cities, such as Ashdod, have been found; however, several cemeteries that can be related to Philistine culture on the basis of tomb contents have been explored. In some cases the Philistines perpetuated the indigenous funerary customs and tomb architecture; in others, they employed foreign modes of burial, such as the cremation interment found at Azor.

Two other features of Philistine burials are illuminating—the use of anthropoid clay coffins (an Egyptian custom) and interment in rock-cut chamber tombs whose design is Mycenaean in origin.

Anthropoid coffins are built roughly in the outline of a body; the lid is formed in the shape of a head. At Tell el Far'ah in the Negev, Petrie found two complete anthropoid coffins in chamber tombs he called "the tombs of the lords of the Philistines." These coffins were built up by the coil technique, which was often used in making large vessels. The lid was cut out of the leather-hard clay before firing so that it exactly fit the opening. The lids were ineptly modeled with faces in what has aptly been termed the "grotesque" style, with only a schematic outlining of facial features and arms. Although the anthropoid coffins were adopted by the Philistines directly from the Egyptians, their use among the Philistines did not become common. The tombs

AN ANTHROPOID COFFIN, uncovered by the author, lies undisturbed in the grave where it was placed more than 3,000 years ago (opposite). Burial in anthropoid coffins like this one at Deir el-Balah, south of Gaza, was an Egyptian custom adopted by the Philistines who later occupied this site. The form is similar to a large storage jar, but it accommodates the human shape it contains—flat base, narrow at the feet, gradually widening for the trunk and shoulders, and rounded at the head. This coffin is about six feet long and about six feet in circumference. Small storage jars placed near its head served as grave markers.

A face appears on the coffin lid. The face is framed by rows of indentations representing a curly Egyptian style wig. It is clearly outlined—almost like sculpture in the round. The arms and face are molded in a naturalistic style.

When they opened the coffin, the archaeologists beheld a poignant and dazzling sight (inset). Inside lay two skulls just barely touching. Gold and carnelian earrings and pendants that once adorned the woman rested beside the skulls. Alongside the skeletons were bronze and alabaster vessels. Above the large bronze platter was an alabaster cosmetic spoon shaped in the form of a nude "swimming girl." To the right of the spoon was a bronze mirror. Scarabs of faience and carnelian and seals helped to date this burial to the 13th century B.C., the reign of Ramesses II.

NATIONAL MUSEUM, ATHENS

BOWL WITH STYLIZED MOURNING FIGURINES. This deep bowl, called a ***lekane***, was found in a Mycenaean cemetery at Perati on the east coast of Greece. Dating roughly to 1200 B.C., the figurines are probably prototypes of the mourning figurine found at Tell 'Aitun in Israel.

From the center of each of the two handles, a cylindrical stem rises to support a shallow cup that adheres to the ***lekane*** rim. Each solid clay figurine wears a long dress and is attached to the rim of the vessel with a peg in its foot. In the classic gestures of women mourners in ancient art, the hands of these figures express pain, grief and despair: they clutch their heads and tear their hair.

The similarities between these Mycenaean figures and the Philistine example elsewhere in this article demonstrate the transfer of Mycenaean culture to the eastern Mediterranean basin by the Sea Peoples. Although the style of the Philistine figurine is naturalistic compared to the schematic Mycenaean figures, all have certain features in common: they are mounted on the rims of deep vessels found in burials; they wear long dresses; and their hands clutch their heads in classic gestures of mourning.

themselves consist of a stepped dromos (or passageway) leading to a rectangular chamber with shelves cut into the rock for placing the deceased and his or her burial goods. This tomb type was common throughout the area of Mycenaean influence.

At Beth Shean, about 50 anthropoid coffins were discovered in 11 funeral deposits in the Northern Cemetery, dating from the 13th to the 11th centuries B.C. Of this number, only five have lids and other features that link them to the "grotesque" style encountered at Tell el-Far'ah. The distinctive feature of the Beth Shean "grotesque" lids is the appliqué headdress, which consists of plain horizontal bands, rows of knobs, zigzag patterns, and vertical fluting. These patterns are arranged differently on each lid. However, one lid portrays a headdress crowned by vertical fluting, identical to the "feathered" cap worn by the Peleset (Philistines), Tjekker, and Denyen on the Medinet Habu reliefs of Ramesses III. This headgear provides decisive evidence that the bodies buried in the grotesque coffins at Beth Shean were Sea Peoples, quite possibly Philistines. The Bible (1 Samuel 31:8–13; 1 Chronicles 10:9–12) relates that Beth Shean was occupied by the Philistines after Saul's defeat at Gilhoa in the late 11th century B.C. The grave goods associated with these "grotesque" headdress coffins at Beth Shean confirm a date in the second half of the 11th century, the time of Saul.

Although there is no doubt that Philistines used clay anthropoid coffins, the great majority of clay coffin burials discovered in Palestine belong to a period preceding the Philistines, when Egyptian officials and garrison troops were stationed in Egyptian strongholds. The Egyptian "middle class," in Egypt as well as in Canaan, frequently used clay coffins, in which grave goods of Egyptian, Mycenaean, Cypriot and Canaanite origin were buried.

The Egyptian stronghold and associated cemetery discovered by the author at Deir el-Balah is typical of a period of Egyptian domination, followed by Egyptian-influenced Philistine occupation of the site. The cemetery yielded an outstanding assemblage of some 40 complete coffins as well as Egyptian faience, alabaster, and gold burial items. The cosmopolitan character of those buried at Deir el-Balah is evidenced by the collections of pottery grave goods of Egyptian, Canaanite and Aegean types, dating from the late 14th through the 13th centuries B.C. A Philistine settlement succeeded the Egyptian stronghold at Deir el Balah. Although no Philistine burials have yet been discovered, it seems likely that the Philistines at this site at least occasionally adopted the Egyptian practice of burial in a clay coffin, as they clearly did both at Tell el-Far'ah and at Beth Shean. Clay coffin burials are simply one more instance of the Philistines adopting and adapting Egyptian cultural traits after their mercenary service in or near Egyptian strongholds during the sunset of the Egyptian empire.

Thus, new discoveries in the Aegean and the Levant have transformed our view of the Philistines and have provided us with a detailed portrait of these Biblical people. We are now entering a new phase of research which may eventually allow us to distinguish the culture of the Philistines from other Sea Peoples. The new excavations at the Tjekker port of Dor, and the continuing work at Akko (possibly a Sherden site), may enable us to discover cultural distinctions between these two related peoples and the Philistines. While the search for the Philistines continues, the search for other Sea Peoples in Canaan has just begun. ■

The author and the editors wish to acknowledge the valuable assistance of Jehon Grist in the preparation of this article.

This article, written especially for *Biblical Archaeology Review*, is based on materials contained in Professor Trude Dothan's recently published book, *The Philistines and Their Material Culture* (Yale University Press, 1982).

Related Reading

Dothan, M., and Freedman, D. N. *Ashdod I* (*Atiqot* VII), Jerusalem, 1967.

Dothan, M. *Ashdod II–III* (*Atiqot* IX–X), Jerusalem, 1971.

Dothan, T. *Excavation at the Cemetery of Deir el-Balah* (*QEDEM* X), Jerusalem, 1979.

Dothan, T. *The Philistines and Their Material Culture*. New Haven, 1982.

Malamat, A. "The Struggle against the Philistines." In *The History of the Jewish People*, edited by H. H. Ben-Sasson, pp. 80–87. Cambridge, Mass. 1976.

Mazar, A. *Excavations at Tell Qasile* (*QEDEM* XII), Jerusalem, 1980.

Mazar, B. "The Philistines and Their Wars with Israel." In *The World History of Jewish People*, Vol. 3, Judges, edited by B. Mazar, pp. 164–179. New Brunswick, 1971.

Sandars, N. K. *The Sea Peoples: Warriors of the Ancient Mediterranean*. London, 1978.

Vassos Karageorghis, "Exploring Philistine Origins on the Island of Cyprus," BAR, March/April 1984.

Trude Dothan, "Ekron of the Philistines, Part I," BAR, January/February 1990; Seymour Gitin, "Ekron of the Philistines, Part II," BAR, March/April 1990.

Lawrence E. Stager, "When Canaanites and Philistines Ruled Ashkelon," BAR, March/April 1991 (see p. 168 of this book).

Bryant G. Wood, "The Philistines Enter Canaan," BAR, November/December 1991.

Itamar Singer, "How Did the Philistines Enter Canaan? A Rejoinder," BAR, November/December 1992.

Hershel Shanks, "The Philistines and the Dothans: An Archaeological Romance, Part 1," BAR, July/August 1993; "The Philistines and the Dothans: An Archaeological Romance, Part 2," BAR, September/October 1993.

Carl S. Ehrlich and Aren M. Maeir, "Excavating Philistine Gath: Have We Found Goliath's Hometown?" BAR, November/December 2001.

Tristan Barako, "How Did the Philistines Get to Canaan? One: by Sea," BAR, March/April 2003; Assaf Yasur-Landau, "How Did the Philistines Get to Canaan? Two: by Land," BAR, March/April 2003.

Tristan Barako, "Philistines Upon the Seas," BAR, July/August 2003.

Trude Dothan, "Philistine Fashion," BAR, November/December 2003.

Seymour Gitin, "Excavating Ekron," BAR, November/December 2005.

Hershel Shanks, "Queen of the Philistines," BAR, September/October 2010.

When Canaanites and

Philistines Ruled Ashkelon

LAWRENCE E. STAGER

CARL ANDREWS, COURTESY LEON LEVY EXPEDITION

CARL ANDREWS, COURTESY LEON LEVY EXPEDITION

ASHKELON. THE SUMMER OF 1990. The sixth season of the Leon Levy Expedition, sponsored by the Harvard Semitic Museum. In the waning days of the season, on the outskirts of the Canaanite city, we excavated an exquisitely crafted statuette of a silver calf, a religious icon associated with the worship of El or Baal in Canaan and, later, with the Israelite God, Yahweh. The calf lay buried in the debris on the ancient rampart that had protected the city in the Middle Bronze Age (c. 2000–1550 B.C.).

The calf was housed in a pottery vessel in the shape of a miniature religious shrine, which itself had been placed in one of the storerooms of a sanctuary on the slope shortly before the destruction of the seaport in about 1550 B.C. The date is secure. Other pottery found in the sanctuary dates to the terminal phase of the Middle Bronze Age (MB IIC, c. 1600–1550 B.C.).

A merchant approaching the Canaanite city from the Mediterranean on the road leading up from the sea would have been dwarfed by the imposing earthworks and towering fortifications on the northern slope of the city. About 300 feet along his ascent from the sea, he might have paused to make an offering at the Sanctuary of the Silver Calf, just off the roadway to the right—nestled in the lower flank of the rampart. Farther up the road to the east, the merchant would have entered the vast metropolis of Ashkelon through the city gate on the north.

The silver calf was nearly complete and assembled when we found it. Only one horn was missing, and only the right foreleg was detached from the rest of the body. Less than 4.5 inches long and 4 inches high, the calf nevertheless weighs nearly a

A DAUNTING SLOPE outside Ashkelon's northern gate would have dissuaded many an attacker bent on conquest. At bottom center (where the people are clustered) are the excavated rooms of the sanctuary of the silver calf (inset).

The approximately 40-degree slope is not a natural feature but rather an artificial earthwork that was the base of an enormous fortification system throughout much of Ashkelon's history. The ramparts date to Middle Bronze II (2000–1550 B.C.) and were rebuilt four times in that period alone. The earliest layer of the slope was capped with mudbricks. The later three were capped with rows of rough field stones; tamped earth or mud plaster, about 4 inches thick, covered the stones and gave the slope a smooth exterior surface.

pound (14 oz.). It is a superb example of Canaanite metalwork. The delicate and naturalistic rendering of the features leave no doubt about the quality of the craftsmanship—or about the age and sex of the small animal: It is a young male calf, yet old enough to have developed horns. The body is made of bronze; only 2 to 5 percent is tin, the rest, copper. It was cast solid, except for the horns, ears and tail and the right foreleg and left hindleg. These two legs were cast separately and joined to the rest of the calf by tenons (projections) and riveted in place. The sole surviving horn, the ears and the tail were made of forged copper* and inserted into the body. Tenons also extended below the hooves. These were obviously used to mount the statuette on a small platform or dais, which perished or disappeared in antiquity. The calf was once completely covered with a thick overleaf of pure silver. Deep grooves running along the back and underside of its bronze body and around its neck still contain remnants of the silver sheet. Some of the silver overleaf has also survived on the legs, head and tail.

*Forged copper is heated, hammered and cooled until the desired shape is attained.

The ceramic model shrine that housed the calf is a cylinder with a beehive roof. It has a knob on top of the roof and a flat bottom. A doorway raised slightly above the floor is just large enough for the calf to pass through. Hinge scars on the door jambs indicate where a separate clay door had once been fitted into place.

The silver calf was just one of the many splendors of Ashkelon during this period, the apex of Canaanite culture in the Levant. During the first half of the second millennium B.C., Askhelon was one of the largest and richest seaports in the Mediterranean. Its massive ramparts formed an arc of earthworks extending over a mile and a half and enclosing a city of more than 150 acres, with probably 15,000 inhabitants, nestled beside the sea. On the north side of

DRAWING OF THE DEFENSIVE SLOPE at Ashkelon, showing the slope's major defensive features: A mudbrick tower, now badly deteriorated, of the Middle Bronze IIC period (1600–1550 B.C.) is at upper left. Another massive mudbrick tower, at upper right, was built by the Philistines in Iron Age I (1200–1000 B.C.). In front of the Philistine tower lie thick layers of artificial fills that formed the slope, or glacis, of the Philistine rampart. Rising behind it are remnants of Hellenistic fortifications, made of medium-sized ashlar blocks of sandstone.

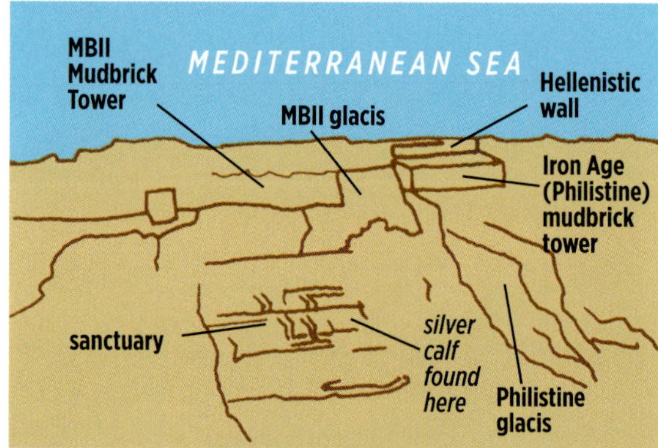

THE ARTIST'S RENDITION (below), with its exaggerated, "fish-eye" angles, depicts how Ashkelon's northern gate might have appeared in the 16th century B.C. A visitor, perhaps a seafaring trader from Phoenicia, might well have paused at the Sanctuary of the Calf at the base of the slope (center) to present an offering of thanks for a safe journey and then made his way up the slope to the impressive twin-towered gate. The sanctuary was not directly below the gate but below and to the right of it—perhaps because the path up the slope was at an angle rather than head-on to the gate, thus making the climb easier.

The excavations here are casting new light on Canaanite and early Israelite religious practices and are helping solve one of the most controversial issues in Biblical archaeology: When did the Philistines arrive on the shores of Canaan?

DRAWING BY ANDREW HERSCHER

RICHARD CLEAVE, COURTESY LEON LEVY EXPEDITION

ASHKELON ON THE SEA. An arc of earthworks one-and-a-half miles long encloses the immense 150-acre ancient city. Built over a 3,500-year span, from 2000 B.C. to 1500 A.D., the protective rampart defines the flat, semicircular mound on which the ancient city stood. Today the Yadin National Park, named after famed Israeli archaeologist Yigael Yadin, who died in 1984, lies inside the 150-acre mound.

the city, where we excavated, the gates and fortifications had been rebuilt at least four times during the 150 years of the Middle Bronze IIB-C periods (1700–1550 B.C.).

This magnificent city was probably destroyed by the Egyptians in the aftermath of the "Hyksos expulsion." The Hyksos were an Asiatic people, probably Canaanites (some of whom might have originated in Ashkelon), who had imposed Canaanite hegemony over much of Egypt during the Second Intermediate Period (c. 1650–1550 B.C.), until the Egyptians managed to expel them forcibly, pursuing them back into Canaan.

The silver calf from Ashkelon is a very early, rare example of bovine iconography in metal. Bull or calf symbolism expressed in metal and other media was associated with El or Baal, leading deities in the Canaanite pantheon. This tradition provided the progenitors of later Biblical iconography that linked

ABUTTING THE MEDITERRANEAN SEA in modern-day Israel, Ashkelon was a center, in turn, of Canaanite, Philistine, Phoenician, Roman, Byzantine and Islamic cultures. It was a member of the Philistine pentapolis, or league of five cities, and appears frequently in the Bible. Samson killed 30 men there in a rage (Judges 14:19); David, after he heard of the deaths of Saul and Jonathan, cried, "Publish it not in the streets of Ashkelon" (2 Samuel 1:20); and Zephaniah predicted that "Ashkelon shall become a desolation" (Zephaniah 2:4).

CARL ANDREWS, COURTESY LEON LEVY EXPEDITION

FIRST GLANCE. Shelby White, writer and connoisseur of ancient Near Eastern art, points to a metal calf minutes after its discovery within a sanctuary at the base of Ashkelon's north slope. The diminutive figurine (4.5 inches long and 4 inches high) electrified the excavators and became the highlight of the 1990 dig season. Lying shattered in pieces around the calf are remnants of the pottery shrine that housed the calf. The sanctuary was destroyed, together with much of the city, probably by the Egyptians in about 1550 B.C.

The calf, cast of solid bronze, was found remarkably well preserved; only the right foreleg had become detached from the rest of the body and the left horn was missing. The right foreleg and left hindleg were cast separately and riveted into the body. The remaining horn, the ears and the tail were of forged copper and were also inserted into the body. Grooves along the calf's back and underside and around the neck still contain silver, as do parts of the legs, head and tail, leading excavators to conclude that the figurine was once completely covered by a sheet of silver.

Yahweh, the Israelite God, with golden and silver calf-images.

During their formative period (before about 1200 B.C.), the early Israelites borrowed heavily from Canaanite culture, even while, at the same time, they distanced themselves from their neighbors. When, in about 925 B.C., the kingdom split in two, with Israel in the north and Judah in the south, Jeroboam, the first king of the northern kingdom installed "golden calves" in the official sanctuaries at Dan and Bethel. The association of Yahweh with such images was obviously acceptable there. However, prophets like Hosea and rival priests from Jerusalem (the capital of the southern kingdom) condemned calf symbolism as idolatry. The words of Hosea not only provide us with a polemic against calf iconography, they also tell us how these images were made and how they were revered:

> "Ephraim [the northern kingdom] was ...guilty of Baal-worship; he suffered death. Yet now they sin more and more; they cast for themselves images; they use their silver to make idols, all fashioned by craftsmen. It is said of Ephraim: 'They offer human sacrifices and kiss calf-images'" (Hosea 13:1–2, Revised English Bible).

With but this taste of Canaanite Ashkelon, let us pass on to Philistine Ashkelon. That is the Ashkelon of the Bible.

Both Biblical and cuneiform texts make it clear that Ashkelon was a Philistine city during most of the Iron Age (c. 1200–586 B.C.). During that time it was a member of the famous Philistine Pentapolis* that also included Ekron, Gaza, Gath and Ashdod.

*See Trude Dothan and Seymour Gitin, "Ekron of the Philistines, Part 1: Where They Came From, How They Settled Down and the Place They Worshiped In," and "Ekron of the Philistines, Part 2: Olive-Oil Suppliers to the World," BAR, January/February and March/April 1990, respectively.

ADAPTED FROM A DRAWING BY PIRHIYA BECK

When the Philistines (or an earlier vanguard of their ethnic tradition) arrived in coastal Canaan is a hotly debated issue, to which we will return later.

In 604 B.C. Ashkelon, like its sister-city Ekron, was destroyed by King Nebuchadrezzar (also called Nebuchadnezzar) and his neo-Babylonian army. Less than 20 years later (in 586 B.C.) Nebuchadrezzar would destroy Jerusalem and the Temple built by King Solomon.

The last Philistine king of Ashkelon, Aga', and his sons, as well as sailors and various nobles, were exiled to Babylon, just as many Jews were after the fall of Jerusalem. Unlike the Jews, however, we hear nothing about the return of the Philistines to their native land. Those that remained behind later lost their ethnic identity, although the region they once occupied and dominated culturally, was still identified as Philistia, or Palestine, by the Romans hundreds of years later; today, many Arabs call themselves Palestinians, echoing their Philistine namesakes of the distant past.

When my predecessor at Ashkelon, the British archaeologist John Garstang, readied his expedition in 1920, he supposed that Philistine Ashkelon was a comparatively small site, occupying only the south mound known as al-Hadra, a mere 15 acres. He had no idea that, even there, the Philistine cities lay buried under 12 to 15 feet of later civilizations. Digging from the top of the mound, Garstang soon despaired of ever reaching anything earlier than the Hellenistic period. After two seasons of excavation (1920–1921), he abandoned Ashkelon for a less complicated site.

During that same two-season period, however, Garstang's young assistant, W. Phythian-Adams was rather more clever. He succeeded in locating both earlier Philistine and Canaunite levels.

Phythian-Adams nibbled away at the north (Grid 38) and west (between Grids 50 and 57) sides of al-Hadra with two step trenches. These small-scale excavations documented a continuous sequence of occupation from about 2000 B.C. (beginning of Middle Bronze IIA) to the modern era. Unfortunately, Phythian-Adams recorded the location of these two step trenches, one no bigger than a telephone booth, only by the designation of the plot number on the official Ottoman land registry. These numbers identify fields approximately 300 feet long. Nevertheless, it was our very good fortune to have established our two main trenches next to his during our opening season. Once we discovered this, we were reassured that here Iron and Bronze Age levels lay below later cultural remains.

What we did not know, until last season, was how big Philistine Ashkelon really was. Over 2,000

CARL ANDREWS, COURTESY LEON LEVY EXPEDITION

ITS SHRINE REPAIRED, the Ashkelon silver calf stands beneath the proud gaze of author Stager, Ashkelon's chief excavator. The last people to have viewed the calf and shrine as they now appear were Canaanite worshippers living nearly 3,600 years ago.

The opening of the shrine is just wide enough for the calf to pass through. A clay door once covered the opening. The excavators believe the calf was displayed emerging from the shrine, much like the calf or bull depicted in the drawing on a second-millennium B.C. cylinder seal from Acemhöyük, in Anatolia (see illustration).

The Hebrew Bible is filled with invective against calf worship, most famously in the incident of the Golden Calf (Exodus 32). The prophet Hosea said derisively of the northern kingdom of Israel: "They offer human sacrifices and kiss calf images" (Hosea 13:2). The Canaanites associated calf or bull images with the worship of El or Baal, the most important deities in their pantheon of gods. Many scholars believe the Israelites emerged from Canaanite society a little before 1200 B.C.; scholars conjecture that the Israelites' abhorrence of calf worship stems from their need to distance themselves from Canaanite religious practice.

The Massive Middle Bronze Fortifications—How Did They Work?

Numerous theories have attempted to explain the function of the immense sloping defensive structures that enclosed many ancient cities in the Middle Bronze Age II (2000–1550 B.C.). Why so wide at the base? The rampart at Ashkelon, for example, is more than 50 feet high and more than 75 feet at the base.

At one time, most scholars attributed these formidable MB II fortifications to the "Hyksos," the enigmatic and supposedly non-Semitic people from the north, who, with their superior weapons of war, invaded and conquered Canaan and Egypt in the 17th century B.C. The Hyksos had chariots, even at this early date. Ashkelon's excavator, British archaeologist John Garstang, believed that Ashkelon's earthworks, like those of the "Lower City" of Hazor, surrounded, not a city, but a huge chariot park. Storing chariots and their horses required a wide, protected area; hence the huge earthworks. The inhabited portion of Ashkelon, Garstang thought, was confined to a small mound inside the wide arc of the earthen embankments.

Other scholars proposed that the earthworks were related to chariotry, but for the opposite purpose: to keep them out rather than in.

Yigael Yadin dispelled both notions. His excavations at Hazor showed that the city extended throughout the lower portions of the site and was surrounded by impressive earthworks that formed the base of the fortification system. The earthworks, in other words, surrounded not a chariot park but an entire city. We now believe this to be true at Ashkelon as well. As for the other theory—that the earthworks were meant to repel chariots—Yadin pointed out that chariot warfare took place not around cities but in open plains away from cities.

Yadin believed the earthworks at Hazor were built to counter the battering ram, also once thought to have been introduced by the Hyksos. This seems highly unlikely, however, since we know that in later periods, the besiegers, such as the Assyrian king Sennacherib at Lachish* in 701 B.C. and the Romans at Masada in 73 A.D., actually *built* sloping siege ramps in order to move their battering rams into position for attacking weak points in the fortification line, such as the city gate. So I doubt that these huge earthworks were intended to counter the use of battering rams; they might have even aided in their use.

Archaeologists Peter Parr and G. R. H. Wright have proposed a more banal function for the sloping ramparts: to counter erosion of the tell, or artificial hill, formed by superimposed layers of settlement. The tell of some cities reached a considerable artificial height by the second millennium B.C. But surely, there must have been more energy-efficient and less costly ways of countering erosion than by installing tons and tons of earthen embankments around the site.

I would like to propose another solution. I agree with Yadin that the MB II ramparts were a defense against siege warfare. But these thick sloping embankments, often surrounded by a ditch or dry moat, were designed, not to counter battering rams; rather they were built in response to another very ancient city-conquering technique—tunneling, mining and sapping—in common use even in the medieval period, in fact right up to the invention of gunpowder.

While the city was under siege, a team of excavators from the attacking army would begin their tunnel at some distance from the fortification line they wished to undermine. Their object was to cause the fortifications to collapse or to sneak beneath them and then to surface inside the city, usually at night, to launch a surprise attack. It might take days, even weeks, for the "moles" to reach their objective. Once under the fortifications they might widen the tunnel in order to collapse the defenseworks above, or if that failed, to stoke the widened tunnel with combustibles, which would then be burned in order to precipitate collapse, while assault troops penetrated the breach above ground.

Obviously, the thick earthen ramparts of Ashkelon and many other Canaanite cities posed a serious obstacle to this siege technique. The amount of debris the tunnelers would have had to remove before reaching the wall line and towers was so great that this would give scouting parties, sent out by the besieged city, adequate time to spot the sappers and trap them or smoke them out. The ditch which surrounded many such ramparts was, whenever possible, dug to bedrock. This prevented the sappers from beginning their tunnel beyond the ditch and would give the scouts of the besieged city a better chance at spotting the entrance to a tunnel.

Tunneling through an MB II rampart was not only slow but also quite dangerous: The sand and soil fills, such as were used at Ashkelon, would have been extremely unstable. The tunnels would have been extremely susceptible to collapse (we know from experience just how unstable the balks or standing sections are at Ashkelon after more than one collapse).

When I presented this hypothesis to the premier military historian of the ancient Near East, Professor Israel Ephal of the Hebrew University, he was quick to accept the idea and then informed me that there was even an Akkadian word, *pilšu*, that describes just such a siege technique, and it was already in common use by the early second millennium B.C. Thus the sapping or tunneling technique was known and used precisely at the time we find massive fortifications appearing in Syria and Canaan.

My conclusion is that the construction of immense sloping structures at the base of the city wall was not introduced by the Hyksos as foreign invaders. Indeed, the "Hyksos" were really Canaanites, anyway, as we now know from Manfred Bietak's excavations at Tell-ed-Dab'a, the Hyksos capital of Avaris in the Egyptian Delta. This fortification technique was an indigenous innovation of Canaanite cities to counter the besiegers' tactic of tunneling to undermine the battlements or to enter the city clandestinely. —LAWRENCE E. STAGER

*See David Ussishkin, "Answers at Lachish," BAR, November/December 1979; Hershel Shanks, "Destruction of Judean Fortress Portrayed In Dramatic Eighth-Century B.C. Pictures," BAR, March/April 1984; and David Ussishkin, "Defensive Judean Counter-Ramp Found At Lachish in 1983 Season," BAR, March/April 1984.

feet north of al-Hadra, we found Philistine fortifications—a massive mudbrick tower 34 feet by 20 feet and a huge glacis-type* rampart. These protected a Philistine seaport not of 15 acres, but of over 150 acres. These fortifications were built in about 1150 B.C. Ashkelon, like Ekron and Ashdod (also recently excavated), was a large, heavily fortified city of the Philistines. Farther north at Dor, a city of the Sikils (according to the Egyptian "Tale of Wen-Amon"), excavations have revealed not only the Sea Peoples' harbor but also their fortifications and glacis of the 12th century B.C.[1]

In contrast to the Israelites, especially the rustic ridgedwellers of the central hill country, the Philistines of the plain appear to have been far more urbane and sophisticated, thus belying the dictionary definition of a Philistine as a person who is lacking in or smugly indifferent to culture and aesthetic refinement. This negative portrayal derives ultimately from the Bible, of course, written by bitter enemies of the Philistines. When the early Israelites were using coarse, unpainted pottery, for example, the Philistines were already decorating their pottery with imaginative bichrome motifs and figures, such as fishes and birds.

Our staff zoo-archaeologists, Dr. Paula Wapnish and Professor Brian Hesse of the University of Alabama in Birmingham, have begun to document a rather dramatic shift in domesticated species at the end of the Late Bronze Age (13th century B.C.) and the beginning of the Iron Age (12th century B.C.). The shift is from sheep and goats to pigs and cattle. This shift occurred at Ashkelon and other coastal sites, but not in the central highland villages of the same period dominated by Israelites—settlements like Ai, Raddana and Ebal.[2] From a strictly ecological perspective, this seems surprising. The oak-pine-and-terebinth woodlands that dominated the central hill country of Canaan, where the earliest Israelite settlements of about 1200 B.C. are to be found, are ideally suited for pig production, especially because of the shade and acorns.

*See Neil Silberman, "Glossary: A Question of Defense," BAR, May/June 1989.

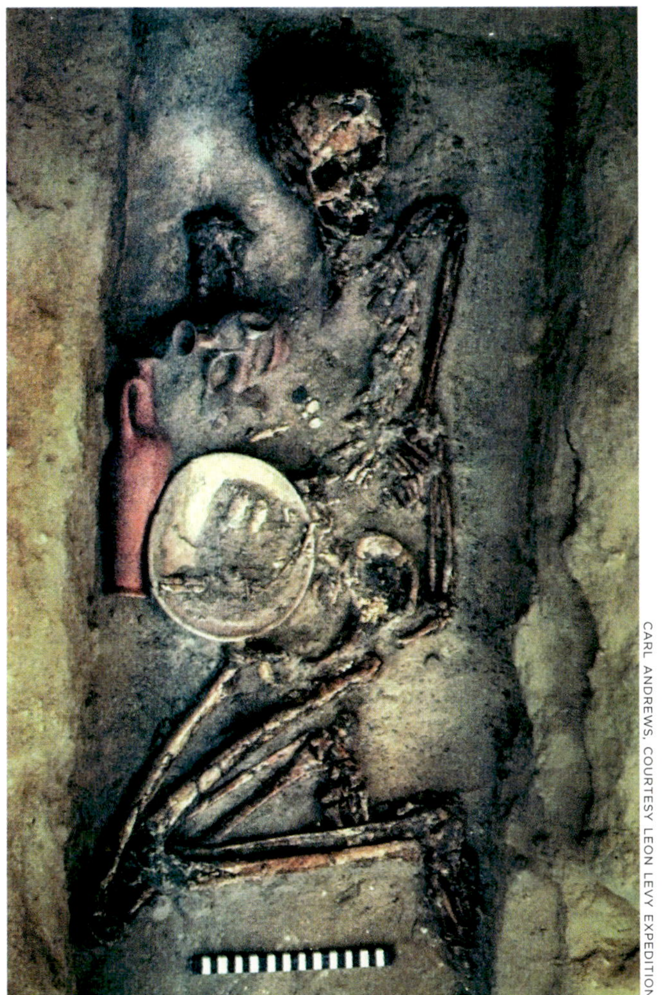

CARL ANDREWS, COURTESY LEON LEVY EXPEDITION

ILAN SZTULMAN, COURTESY LEON LEVY EXPEDITION

THE CANAANITE WAY OF DEATH. An adolescent Canaanite girl lies in a flexed position in a mudbrick-lined vault covered with wooden boughs and coated with white plaster, dating to about 1500 B.C. At her shoulder the excavators found two toggle pins, for fastening a garment; three Egyptian scarabs and an ivory roundel lay on her midsection. The burial also contained Syrian and Cypriot pottery.

The photo above shows the other items found in the burial: a Red-Polished Syrian flask (center, rear); two Base-Ring juglets (right) imported from Crete, which may have contained opium; and two bowls, seen as found in the photo at left, one with a food offering of a lamb or goat chop and a small bird (perhaps a dove or a partridge).

The scarabs and the Cypriot pottery imports helped excavators date the burial to about 1500 B.C., indicating that Ashkelon had revived after the Egyptians destroyed parts of the seaport about 50 years earlier. The custom of burying within the city, rather than in a cemetery outside it, and the mudbrick-lined vault are continuations of Middle Bronze II (2000–1550 B.C.) Canaanite burial traditions.

FROM ATLAS ZUR ALTAGYPTISCHEN KULTUREGESCHICHTE BY W. WRESZINSKI

FROM YIGAEL YADIN, *THE ART OF WARFARE IN BIBLICAL LANDS*, VOL. II

When Did the Philistines Arrive in Canaan? Multiple Clues Help Unravel the Mystery

The question of when the Philistines arrived in Canaan—and more generally when the Sea Peoples (of which the Philistines were one) arrived in the Levant—and just where they came from is finally being answered.

One key is an Egyptian wall relief (drawing opposite, top) on the temple of Karnak, in Thebes. Long thought to have been commissioned by Pharaoh Ramesses II (1279–1212 B.C.), the relief has recently been shown to depict a series of campaigns conducted in Canaan in 1207 B.C. by Merenptah (1212–1202 B.C.), son of Ramesses II.* The scene shown here is of the siege of Ashkelon, identified as such by the hieroglyphics at top center. The desperate inhabitants beg for mercy while the battle rages below them. An oversize pharaoh dominates the right portion of the scene. What is crucial in this scene is that the inhabitants are depicted with the same dress as undoubted Canaanites in other, adjacent reliefs—and without the distinctive headgear and clothing with which the Philistines and other Sea Peoples are depicted in other Egyptian reliefs. The Philistines, we must therefore conclude, had not yet arrived in Canaan in 1207 B.C.

When they did arrive is shown by a second Egyptian wall relief, at Medinet Habu (shown in reconstruction opposite, bottom). The relief dates to about 1175 B.C.,

*See Frank J. Yurco, "3,200-Year-Old Picture of Israelites Found in Egypt," BAR, September/October 1990 (see p. 40 of this book).

JAMES WHITRED

Monochrome Pottery

TERRY SMITH

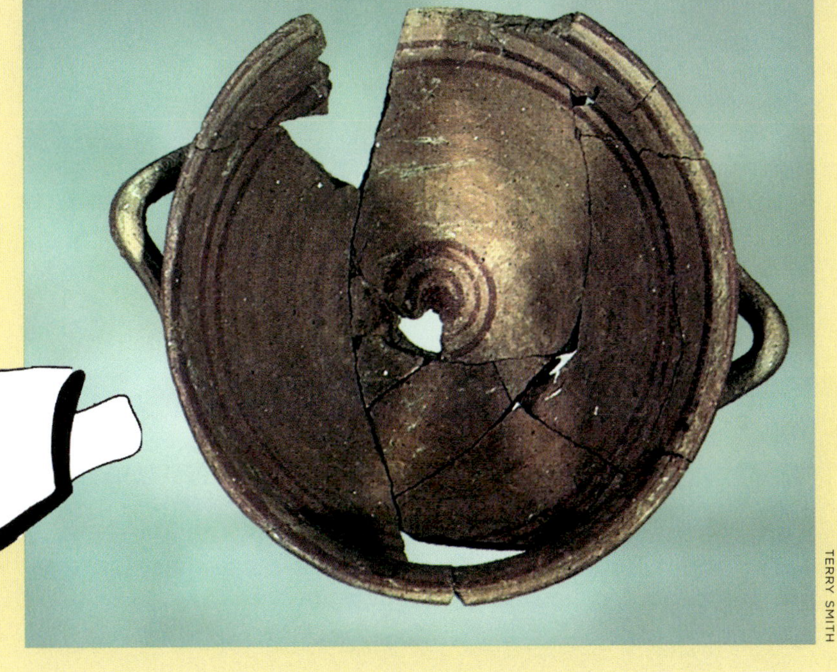

TERRY SMITH

Bichrome Pottery

JAMES WHITRED

JAMES WHITRED

during the reign of Ramesses III (1182–1151 B.C.), and depicts a naval battle between Egyptian ships (left) and those of the Sea Peoples, including the Philistines (center and right), called Peleset in the hieroglyphics that accompany the relief. The Sea Peoples can be identified by their distinctive headgear, which consist of feathered headdresses.

At about the same time the battle recorded at Medinet Habu was taking place, a new type of pottery was making its appearance in Canaan. Known as Mycenaean IIIC1, or monochrome, pottery, it is Mycenaean in style but made of local clays. In Canaan, examples have been uncovered at Ashdod and Ekron, and now at Ashkelon. The photo on the preceding page (top) shows a portion of floor beneath a public building with columns that contained monochrome pottery. As the name implies, monochrome pottery is decorated with only a single color (black or red), such as in the sherds and on the inside of the carinated bowl (previous page, bottom), all dating to about 1175–1150 B.C. The profile drawing shows the carination, or the sharply angled body, of the bowl; the left half of the drawing shows the outside of the bowl, while the right half is a cutaway view showing the bowl's thickness. The most commonly found decorations on the outside of Philistine monochrome pottery are antithetic spirals (that is, mirror-image spirals set next to each other—as in the center photo on the previous page) and horizontal bands; less common were net-patterned lozenges and wing motifs; on the interiors, they feature horizontal bands and spirals.

One level higher in the floor, dating to the latter half of the 12th century B.C., were examples of the next stage of pottery evolution, called Philistine bichrome. These are decorated in two colors, red and black, as in the pictures above. The top photo shows a bichrome bell-shaped bowl with wing motif uncovered in 1920–21 by the British archaeologists John Garstang and W. Phythian-Adams. Bichrome pottery frequently features antithetic spirals, red and black checkerboard patterns, birds and, rarely, fish.

Author Stager notes that after about 1175 B.C. the locally made monochrome pottery in Canaan began to diverge in style from the monochrome pottery that was being manufactured in the Aegean. Coupled with the evidence provided by the two Egyptian wall reliefs discussed above, Stager concludes that the Philistines were Aegean peoples—specifically Mycenaean Greeks—who came to Canann *en masse* in about 1175 B.C.

One reason why such a hog-acorn economy did not thrive in the early Israelite environment must ultimately be rooted in very early religious taboos that forbade the consumption of pork. If so, these findings would nullify the hypothesis of anthropologist Marvin Harris that "kosher" rules can be explained primarily by ecological considerations.[3] These findings would also contradict those scholars who argue for a much later date for the introduction of these dietary restrictions.

As noted earlier, when the Philistines arrived on the coast of Canaan is still a vexed question, although it is becoming increasingly clear where they came from. Two leading experts in the definition of Philistine culture, Professors Trude and Moshe Dothan, have argued that a generation before the Philistines themselves arrived, a pre-Philistine group of Sea Peoples landed on the coast of Canaan. The arrival of the Philistines is marked, in their view, by the appearance in Canaan of what has become known as Philistine bichrome ware, a distinctive red and black decorated pottery. An earlier monochrome pottery has been identified by them with an earlier generation of pre-Philistine Sea Peoples.[4]

Unlike the Dothans, I believe this earlier monochrome pottery indicates the earliest phase of Philistine settlement in southern Canaan, just as it serves as the hallmark of new groups of Sea Peoples settling all along the Levantine coast and in Cyprus in the first half of the 12th century B.C. Trude Dothan has provided us with a detailed typology of the hybrid pottery style known as Philistine bichrome ware. Her analysis leaves little doubt that this distinctive red and black decorated pottery, as well as many of its shapes and motifs, derives ultimately from the Mycenaean Greek world, with more limited inspiration from Cypriot, Egyptian and Canaanite sources. However, recent excavations at three of the five members of the Philistine Pentapolis—Ashdod, Ekron (Tel Miqne) and now Ashkelon—indicate the direct antecedent of this bichrome ware was a monochrome pottery even closer to Mycenaean Greek pottery prototypes than the bichrome ware.[5] Moreover, the monochrome pottery was made in Canaan, as we know from the clays.

At Ashkelon in Grid 38 (lower) we have documented stratigraphically the sequence from monochrome ware (Mycenaean IIIC:1) to bichrome ware (Philistine). Beneath the floors of a large public building with thick stone column drums was an earlier building. On its floor lay the earliest Philistine pottery yet discovered at Ashkelon; carinated bowls with strap handles and bell-shaped bowls, decorated with monochrome antithetic spirals, horizontal bands, net-patterned lozenges and tongue and wing motifs on the exterior and with horizontal bands and spirals on the interior.

When did the Philistines arrive *en masse* on the shores of Canaan? An early contingent of Sea Peoples fought with the Libyans against the Egyptian pharaoh Merneptah (1212–1202 B.C.), as we know from the famous Merneptah Stele, but the Peleset, or Philistines, were *not* among them. Merneptah quelled another revolt in 1207 B.C., also recorded on the Merneptah Stele, led by the Canaanites of Ashkelon, Gezer, Yanoam and the Israelites. That there were Canaanites, rather than Sea Peoples, in Ashkelon at this time is shown by wall reliefs once assigned to Ramesses II—now properly dated to his son Merneptah—apparently depicting his Canaanite campaign.* The people inside the ramparts of Ashkelon are depicted in these reliefs as Canasnites, not as Sea Peoples. Moreover, at that time Mycenaean and Cypriot pottery was still being *imported* into the Levant. So the Sea Peoples apparently did not arrive in Canaan until after the reign of Merneptah.[6]

Not until the reign of Ramesses III (1182–1151 B.C.) do we find the locally made Mycenaean-style pottery in the Levant diverging from the earlier and purer Mycenaean prototypes. This reflects a change from trade items coming from comparatively few production centers in the Mediterranean world to locally manufactured pottery at a number of regional centers.

In his famous inscription known as the "War Against the Sea Peoples," Ramesses III describes the Philistine approach to Canaan and his subsequent victory over them. He refers to the Philistines by their name as written in Egyptian hieroglyphics, "Peleset." In accompanying reliefs on the walls of the temple at Medinet Habu, Ramesses III depicts the Philistines, as well as other well-armed Sea Peoples. These reliefs date to about 1175 B.C. These Philistines should be identified with the monochrome pottery that appears in Canaan at about this time.

In short, although Philistine bichrome ware was once thought to herald the arrival of the Philistines early in the reign of Ramesses III (c. 1180–1175), it now appears that the bichrome pottery was dated a bit too early. The monochrome pottery that appears a generation earlier actually marks the first appearance of the Philistines in Canaan, during the reign of Ramesses III.[7]

A closer look at this pottery will also help solve the riddle of Philistine origins.

*See Frank J. Yurco, "3,200-Year-Old Picture of Israelites Found in Egypt," BAR, September/October 1990 (see p. 40 of this book).

JAMES WHITRED, COURTESY LEON LEVY EXPEDITION

When tested by neutron activation analysis,* the early monochrome Mycenaean IIIC pottery proved to have been made from local clays, whether at Ashdod and Ekron in Philistia or at Enkomi, Kition and Old Paphos on Cyprus.[8] Almost none of it was imported. Although we must always be cautious about inferring new peoples from pots, I think it can be argued in this case that when this locally made Mycenaean pottery appears in quantity in the eastern Mediterranean, it indeed marks the arrival of the Sea Peoples. Their path of destruction along the eastern Mediterranean coast can be traced from Cilicia, in southwest Turkey, at such sites as Miletus and Tarsus, to the Amuq (or Plains of Antioch), south to Ibn Hani (the seaside resort of the kings of Ugarit in the 14th and 13th centuries B.C.), in Syria; farther south to coastal Canaan at Acco; and on down the coast through Philistia.[9]

As these groups of peoples migrated throughout the eastern Mediterranean coast, their potters no longer shared a common tradition. Thus, it makes little sense to try to put the Mycenaean IIIC styles into an interregional sequence, since local styles quickly diverged from a common template, influenced as they were by very different local surroundings.[10]

When the Philistines first arrived in southern Canaan (c. 1175 B.C.), they made Mycenaean-style pottery using the local clays. Later, in about 1150 B.C., they assimilated Canaanite, Egyptian and other motifs, making the hybrid that archaeologists have for years called "Philistine" pottery. Perhaps we should now call it second-generation Philistine pottery. In fact, the Philistines arrived on the coast and settled in the Pentapolis a generation or more before the production of the bichrome pottery that bears their name.

What we have outlined archaeologically and dated to the early part of Pharaoh Ramesses III's reign is described in very vivid terms by Ramesses III himself in his "War Against the Sea Peoples":

> "Dateline: Year 8 under the Majesty of Ramesses III [c. 1175 B.C.]: ...The foreign countries [Sea Peoples] made a conspiracy in their islands. All at once the lands were removed and scattered in the fray. No land could stand before their

*Neutron activation analysis can detect some of the rarest elements present in pottery. By comparing the chemical "fingerprint" of the potsherd to that of various clay sources, it is often possible to determine the provenance of pottery. See Maureen F. Kaplan, "Using Neutron Activation Analysis to Establish the Provenance of Pottery," BAR, March 1976.

arms, from Hatti, Kode [Cilicia], Carchemish, Arzawa and Alashiya [Cyprus] on, being cut off at [one time]. A camp [was set up] in one place in Amor [Amurru]. They desolated its people, and its land was like that which has never come into being. They were coming forward toward Egypt, while the flame was prepared before them. Their confederation [of Sea Peoples] was the Philistines, Tjeker [=Sikils], Shekelesh, Denye(n) and Weshesh lands united."[11]

As a logical inference from the archaeological evidence, we may add the following: If the makers of the local monochrome Mycenaean pottery (IIIC:1) settling along the coast from Cilicia in Anatolia to Cyprus and Israel are not Mycenaean Greeks themselves, then we must conclude that they studied their potmaking in Mycenaean workshops. And then they somehow convinced all of their "barbarian" consumers that this pottery was what they should use. Throwing caution to the wind, I am willing to reject these possibilities and state flatly that the Sea Peoples, including the Philistines, were Mycenaean Greeks.

I am willing to speculate even further: When we do discover Philistine texts at Ashkelon or elsewhere in Philistia (and it's only a matter of time until this happens), those texts will be in Mycenaean Greek (that is, in Linear B or some related script). At that moment, we will be able to recover another lost civilization for world history.

We partially excavated two public buildings that were used in both the monochrome and bichrome phases of the Philistine occupation of Ashkelon. These two public buildings produced more than 150 enigmatic artifacts—thick cylinders of unbaked clay, slightly pinched at the waist. More than one row of these cylinders were found lying on the floors of both buildings. Whatever the function of these cylinders, it appears that the same type of activity was carried on in both the monochrome and bichrome phases of these 12th-century B.C. buildings.

As we were excavating these strange cylinders at Ashkelon, at nearby Tel Miqne (which the excavators identify as the Philistine city of Ekron) the diggers were finding the same strange objects at their site. Could they be tablets prepared for inscribing? Would we be able to find the first real evidence of Philistine writing? At both Ashkelon and Miqne, the dig directors eagerly tried to find the first signs of Philistine writings on these unbaked "tablets." But, alas, not a trace was found!

We then shifted to a more banal reading of the evidence. The alignment of the clay cylinders next to walls suggested that they had been dropped from vertical looms. Yet they looked unlike any loomweights we had ever seen. They were unperforated; Levantine loomweights had holes through which the vertical strand of thread from the loom was attached.

HUMBLE, YET TELLING in their implications, 150 cylinders of unbaked clay (see below) lay on the floors of two 12th-century B.C. buildings (see opposite).

Excavators of the Philistine city of Ekron (Tel Miqne) also found small cylindrical objects very similar to those at Ashkelon. Thinking that perhaps they were clay writing tablets of some kind, both teams of excavators were hoping to find the first. ever examples of Philistine writing on these cylinders, but soon had to settle for a more mundane explanation of the objects' function: Tiny remnants of fibers, not visible to the human eye but found in the dirt nearby, indicated that the small clay objects were loomweights used in weaving. Their shape—pinched at the waist and not perforated—argues for a Mycenaean Greek origin for the Philistines: While perforated loomweights were common elsewhere, unperforated weights such as those at Ashkelon and Ekron have been discovered in Cyprus at Kition and Enkomi (both known to have been settled by the Sea Peoples of Mycenaean Greek origin) and indeed even in Mycenae itself.

CARL ANDREWS, COURTESY LEON LEVY EXPEDITION

JAMES WHITRED, COURTESY LEON LEVY EXPEDITION

A MEDITERRANEAN WANDERER. Found in the excavations at Ashkelon, this terra-cotta mold (left) and an impression made from it (opposite) depict Odysseus (also known by his Latinized name, Ulysses), the hero of Homer's *Odyssey*, battling the sea monster Scylla. Dating to the Roman period (first–second centuries A.D.), the impression shows Odysseus' spear pointing to the right. The sea monster's tail whips in front of Odysseus' face; heads of oarsmen can be seen below the spear and the head of the helmsman can be seen above the spear butt. The *Odyssey* describes the scene: "I put on my glorious armor and, taking up two long spears in my hands, I stood bestriding the vessel's foredeck at the prow, for I expected Scylla of the rocks to appear first from that direction."

The *Odyssey* is the tale of Odysseus' ten-year-long trek home from the Trojan War. Greek mythology is filled with tales of heroes wandering the eastern Mediterranean world after the war. Stager observes that these tales, as well as the founding myths of many Near Eastern cities (which claim to have been founded by figures from Aegean lands) contain more than a kernel of truth: He believes, for example, that the land of Canaan was settled by Mycenaean Greeks in the 12th century B.C. As this terra-cotta mold shows, the tale of Odysseus' wandering was known in Ashkelon as late as the first or second centuries A.D.

Egon Lass, research associate and grid supervisor, finally solved the mystery. His job includes systematically collecting samples from every square yard of excavated floors or surfaces at Ashkelon, and then wetsieving them. In this way, Lass discovered that occupational debris from the floors with the strange, lined-up clay cylinders contained concentrations of fibers, fibers that could not be detected with the naked eye during excavation, but that appeared only after wet-sieving. Since these cylinders were associated with the weaving industry, they probably were loomweights. The thread was tied around the pinched waist, which was why they were not perforated with holes.

This homely clue looms (forgive the pun) large for determining the cultural homeland of the Philistines and other Sea Peoples.

To the pottery evidence, we can now add the even more persuasive evidence of the lowly loomweights found in abundance at both Ashkelon and Miqne-Ekron. Surely these artifacts made of unbaked clay, yet quite different from the local Levantine perforated type, were not imported from abroad, but were made and used by immigrant weavers.

In this same period (early 12th century B.C.), Achaeans or Mycenaeans are thought to have arrived *en masse* on Cyprus (Alashiya).* At two of the Cypriot settlements, Kition and Enkomi, this same type of unperforated loomweight (or "reels" as the excavators there called them) were found in abundance (along with the perforated Levantine ones) in rooms where weaving was being done. The most striking evidence for the origin of the Philistines and other Sea Peoples, however, is the appearance of cylindrical unperforated loomweights in the Mycenaean homeland itself, at centers such as Tiryns, Pylos and Mycenae. When the great archaeological pioneer Heinrich Schliemann was digging at Mycenae, he found numerous cylinders of unbaked clay, but was puzzled about what they were used for. By the time he finished work at Tiryns, where they were also quite common, he rightly surmised that "apparently they were used as weights for looms."[12] In this as in so many other instances, we have learned to take Schliemann's hunches seriously.

Another clue to the Greek connection is the name of one of the Sea Peoples mentioned in Ramesses III's inscription, the Denyen, who have often been equated with the Danaoi of Homeric tradition. The latter term, frequent in the *Iliad*, is used interchangeably in Homer with "Achaeans," who were, of course, the Greeks.

Despite this Greek connection with Danaoi and the archaeological evidence of Philistines in Canaan, scholars have been hesitant to identify all the Sea Peoples with the Mycenaean Greeks. The Greeks are usually considered a minor constituent of the "barbarian" hordes that comprised the Sea Peoples. Modern connotations of "Philistine" (inspired, no doubt, by Biblical pejoratives) have not put scholars

*See translation of Ramesses III inscription, in which Alashiya is one of the countries overwhelmed by the Sea Peoples.

LAWRENCE E. STAGER, COURTESY LEON LEVY EXPEDITION

in a frame of mind that allows easy acceptance of these Sea People "barbarians" as elevated Greeks. But that is what the archaeology suggests. Nor has our uphringing in the classics helped; indeed it has probably hindered us from recognizing that the heroes of the *Iliad* and the *Odyssey*—the "good guys"—just might be akin to the "bad guys"—namely, the Sea Peoples.

According to Greek epic traditions, which give us the same story from the Greek perspective, some time after the Trojan War (the most widely accepted traditional date for the fall of Troy is about 1183 B.C.), several heroes were celebrated as shipwrecked wanderers trying desperately to return home to mainland Greece. The classic homecoming story is the *Odyssey*. Before Menelaus (who started the whole thing when he married Helen of Troy) returned to his native Sparta after the war, he wandered to Cyprus, Phoenicia, Egypt and Libya. During these difficult, but lucrative, wanderings, Menelaus accumulated much wealth, including such sumptuous items as "two silver bathtubs, and a pair of tripods, and ten talents of gold"—all given to him as "gifts" (however reluctantly) by an Egyptian from Thebes (*Odyssey* IV, 128–129).[13]

Odysseus himself, the hero of the *Odyssey*, got into trouble in Egypt, when Zeus "put it into [Odysseus'] head to go with roving pirates to Egypt." Odysseus' roguish companions plundered the fields of the Egyptians, captured women and children and killed the men. But the Egyptians did not sit idly by; they mounted a counterattack. According to the *Odyssey*, many of the Greek pirates were killed; others were led into captivity and made to work at forced labor. Luckily, Odysseus (for some unstated reason) was sent to Cyprus (*Odyssey* XVII, 425–445).

The adventures of Odysseus were still celebrated in Ashkelon in the Roman period, as I realized after piecing together what little remained of a pottery mold for making plaques. The mold depicted a warrior with spear and shield in hand standing before the mast. Below him were oarsmen and, to his right, a steersman. The key to the scene, however, is the tail of some kind of sea monster that whips up beside the defending warrior. The scene on the mold recalls the hair-raising episode of Odysseus and the six-headed sea monster Scylla (or Skylla) described in the *Odyssey* (Book XII, 80ff.). Shortly before six of his men were devoured by Scylla, Odysseus ordered his crew to "Sit well, all of you, to your oarlocks, and dash your oars deep into the breaking surf of the water, so in that way Zeus might grant that we get clear of this danger and flee away from it. For you, steersman, I have this order; so store it deeply in your mind, as you control the steering oar of this hollow ship..." The visual imprint of Homer's words lay before us in this terra-cotta mold, with oarsmen and steersman clearly depicted but in Roman style of the first or second century A.D. The story was apparently celebrated in Ashkelon by people who still recalled their Greek heritage hundreds of years later.

Greek legends preserve many "homecoming" stories. In one of these epics (the fragmentary *Nostoi*[14]) some of the Greek heroes never make it back home after the Trojan War. Instead, they wander about the eastern Mediterranean, often with large followings of refugees, founding cities as they go. These founding legends have been preserved at local shrines dedicated to the founding hero.

Among the more remarkable founding stories dealing with what the German scholar Fritz Schachermeyr called the "Achaean Diaspora" are accounts of the colonization of Pamphylia and Cilicia in Asia Minor and Phoenicia on the coast of Canaan—from Colophon in the north to Ashkelon in the south.[15]

According to later legends, many Greeks left Troy for parts south under the leadership of one seer named Amphilochus and another named Calchas. At Clarus near Colophon, one Mopsus, who would become the founding hero of Ashkelon, defeated Calchas in a riddle contest. Tradition has preserved several different riddles that led to Calchas' defeat; here is one of them:

"[Another] question propounded by Calchas was in regard to a pregnant sow, how many pigs she carried, and Mopsus said, 'Three, one of which is a female'... When Mopsus proved to have spoken the truth, Calchas died of grief."[16]

Riddles were very serious business indeed! Having replaced the original seer Calchas, Mopsus went on to lead his people across the Taurus Mountains into Pamphylia, where he founded two important cities: Aspendus and Phaselis. Mopsus then led other Achaeans on through Cilicia, founding Mallus and Mopsuestia (Mopsus' hearth). From Cilicia, Mopsus marched down the coast all the way to Ashkelon, where, according to the fifth-century Lydian historian Xanthus, Mopsus threw the statue of the mermaid goddess Atargatis (=Tanit/Ashtarte/Asherah) into her own sacred lake. Mopsus, according to this tradition, died in Ashkelon.[17]

According to Richard Barnett, Mopsus is the "first figure of Greek mythology to emerge into historical reality."[18] He says this because a bilingual inscription from the eighth century B.C., written in hieroglyphic Luwian and in Phoenician, was found at Karatepe in Cilicia. In this inscription, Azatiwatas, servant of the king of the Danuniyim (Homer's Danaoi), traces his lineage through the "house of MPŠ (=Mopsus)," indicating that there may have been a kernel of truth behind these Greek founding legends. I mentioned above that one of the cities Mopsus founded was Mopsuestia, which means Mopsus' hearth. Hearths were well known in Aegean and Anatolian cultures, but not in Canaan. Recently however, Israeli archaeologist Amihai Mazar discovered a small raised hearth in a public building adjacent to a Philistine temple at Tel Qasile.[19] Even more recently Trude Dothan and Seymour Gitin have found a sequence of circular, sunken stone-lined hearths in a monumental building at Philistine Miqne,* apparently another Greek element introduced into Canaan by the Philistines, or Sea Peoples.

This archaeological and textual analysis has led me to the inescapable conclusion that two very different cultures and peoples—one Semitic (comprised of Canaanites and Israelites); the other Greek—lived side by side in parts of Canaan.

In the context of these sometimes hostile, sometimes friendly neighbors, we are better able to understand some Biblical heroes as well as villains.

From this perspective it is not so fanciful to imagine Goliath (1 Samuel 17), the Philistine champion whom young David slew with his slingshot, as a mighty, well-armed warrior, similar to Achaeans like Achilles and Odysseus. At the very least, Goliath was equipped much more like an Achaean warrior, complete with bronze greaves on his legs, than like a Canaanite or Israelite soldier (for whom greaves were totally alien).

The adventures of the mighty Samson also reflect a Greek connection. Although the Bible identifies him as an Israelite hero from the tribe of Dan, he does not fit the mold of a typical Biblical Judge of the period, nor is he a leader of Israelite armies like the other Judges. He is instead an individual champion about whom many a tale was told. As recognized by many 19th-century Biblical scholars, Samson is much more like a Greek hero—specifically like Herakles—than a Biblical Judge.[20] In an insightful phrase in *Paradise Lost*, John Milton refers to our hero as the "Herculean Samson."

Samson is the only riddle-teller in the Bible. At his wedding feast to an unnamed Philistine woman from Timnah, Samson propounded this rather bad riddle to the 30 young men at the feast:

"Out of the eater came something to eat,
Out of the strong came something sweet."

Judges 14:14

To know the answer to the riddle you must know that a year earlier Samson had killed a lion with his bare hands. When he passed by the spot on his way to his wedding, he found that a swarm of bees had made their home in the lion's carcass. He scooped out the honey and ate it with his hands.

The guests of course did not know this, so they could not guess the answer to the riddle. After much cajoling, however, Samson finally tells his Philistine bride the answer, which she promptly reveals on the last day of the feast to the male guests. And they answered:

"What is sweeter than honey,
And what is stronger than a lion?"

Samson then responded (with a trace of barnyard humor):

"Had you not plowed with my heifer
You would not have guessed my riddle!"

Judges 14:18

Unlike the Greek seer Calchas, who died of grief when his riddle was answered, Samson simply pays off his bet of 30 linen tunics and 30 sets of clothing by going down to Philistine Ashkelon and killing 30 of its men. He strips them and gives their wardrobes to the guests who had answered the riddle.

Samson is also famous for his seven magical locks

*See photo in "Ekron of the Philistines, Part 1: Where They Came From, How They Settled Down and the Place They Worshiped In," BAR, January/February 1990.

of hair. The Biblical writers transformed Samson into a Nazarite, a man dedicated to God. But, although he does not cut his hair, Samson hardly qualifies as the usual Nazarite: He drinks strong drink whenever he likes. Samson's long locks endow him with superhuman strength, however. When shorn, he is, the Bible says, much weaker, "like any man" (Judges 16:17). There is a parallel in Greek epic: Scylla cut her father's hair while he slept, thus removing his invincibility. The king was then captured by King Minos.[21]

The riddle, the magic locks and a hero of superhuman strength were not the stuff of Canaanite or Hebrew lore; they were, however, very much a part of the later Greek, and probably Mycenaean-Minoan, world.

The adventures of Samson took place in the foothills of Canaan, the Shephelah, an intermediate zone of economic, social and cultural exchange between Greeks and Israelites, between Philistines and Hebrews. This border zone with its hybrid cultural elements is reflected not only in the stories we have examined but in the archaeology as well. It is significant, I think, that archaeologists using material culture data have always been confused about the ethnic and cultural affinities of the inhabitants of this intermediate zone during Iron Age I (1200–1000 B.C.). Was Beth Shemesh, on the edge of the Shephelah, for example, an Israelite or a Philistine settlement during stratum III, the Iron I stratum? The signals are confusing and disagreement abounds.

The ancient inhabitants were probably no less confused, for this was taboo territory, the meeting-ground of alien cultures.

Indeed, there is some uncertainty and confusion about the very identity of Samson's tribe, Dan. Were the Danites originally Israelites or did they trace their origins to the Danaoi, the Greeks of Homeric epic?

According to Yigael Yadin, Cyrus H. Gordon and Allen H. Jones, the Danites of the Bible were identical with the Homeric Danaoi, the Egyptian Denyen (in Ramesses III's inscription), the Danuna (in the Amarna Letters of the 14th century B.C.) and the *DNNYM* (in a Phoenician inscription from Karatepe).[22] According to Yadin's reading of the Biblical text, Dan "dwells on ships" (Judges 5:17). Unlike other Israelite tribes, Dan lacks a genealogy (Genesis 46:23; cf. Numbers 26:42). Yadin therefore concludes that Dan was not one of the original Israelite tribes in the early confederation; nevertheless, "Dan shall judge his people as one of the tribes of Israel" (Genesis 49:16). Yadin went even further and attempted to locate the Denyen/Danaoi/Danites in the area around Tel Aviv in the 12th century B.C., where he specifically identified the earliest settlement at Tel Qasile, stratum XII, with these immigrants. Eventually the Danites migrated north and established themselves at Laish/Dan in the north (Judges 18), by which time they were thoroughly integrated into the Tribal League of Israel during the period of the Judges.

While at first glance this hypothesis is extremely appealing, there are many reasons for rejecting it upon further reflection. First and foremost, texts relating to the Sea Peoples give us no indication about the location of the Denyen in the Levant. In the Amarna letters the Danuna seem to be somewhere north of Ugarit in modern Syria. By the time of the Egyptian "Tale of Wen-Amon" (about 1050 B.C.), the Tjeker (or Sikils), occupied the seaport of Dor and surrounding territories.[23] Slightly earlier, the Onomasticon of Amenope (about 1100 B.C.) lists Philistines (Peleset), Sikils and Sherden—all Sea Peoples—living on the coast of the Levant. If this list is in geographical order, then the Philistines represent southern Canaan; the Sikils, the Dor region; and the Sherden, the Acco area.[24] In none of these texts are the Denyen even mentioned; however, this might be expected if in fact they migrated to Laish/Dan before 1100 B.C., as Avraham Biram, the excavator of Laish/Dan, believes they did. Unfortunately, for the Danite=Danaoi hypothesis, the earliest settlement at Laish/Dan which could plausibly be linked to the Danites (stratum VI) has yielded very little Philistine pottery; rather it is characterized by collared-rim store jars and pits—artifacts and features commonly associated with the early Israelites.[25] Furthermore, the Biblical texts relating to the Danites are open to other interpretations. The key text for Yadin—"And Dan, why did he remain in ships?" (Judges 5:17)—can also be interpreted to mean those Danites who served as clients on the ships of the Phoenicians or even the Sea Peoples.** In other words, the Danites were in a client/patron relationship with one of the seafaring peoples of the Levant, but this does not imply that the Danites themselves were Sea Peoples, or Phoenicians. As the Samson story indicates, the Danites were an Israelite tribe located on the western periphery of early Israel even before they moved north to Laish/Dan but were probably under the heavy influence of their coastal Sea Peoples neighbors.

The Samson saga represents a literary genre that Harvard Professor Frank Cross has labeled a "border epic" where two very different cultures—early Greek and Israelite—met on the coast of Canaan. The historical milieu, as I have reconstructed it first from archaeology and then assisted by texts, is a dynamic

**See Lawrence E. Stager, "The Song of Deborah—Why Some Tribes Answered the Call and Others Did Not," BAR, January/February 1989.

one in which these two very different cultures encounter each other, interact and transform their respective traditions.

[1]Personal communication from Ephraim Stern, Professor of Archaeology, Institute of Archaeology, Hebrew University.

[2]See Brian Hesse, "Animal Use at Tel Mique-Ekron in the Bronze Age and Iron Age," *Bulletin of the American Schools of Oriental Research* (*BASOR*) 264 (1986), pp. 17–27; also his report on the 1985 faunal remains from Ashkelon in *Ashkelon 1*, forthcoming, Harvard Semitic Museum Archaeology and Ancient History series (Cambridge, MA: Harvard Univ. Press).

[3]Marvin Harris, *Cows, Pigs, Wars and Witches: The Riddles of Culture* (New York: Random House/Vintage, 1975), pp. 35–57.

[4]Trude Dothan, *The Philistines and Their Material Culture* (New Haven, CT: Yale Univ. Press, 1982); for their most recent statement, see Trude Dothan, "The Arrival of the Sea Peoples: Cultural Diversity in Early Iron Age Canaan," pp. 11–22, and Moshe Dothan "Archaeological Evidence for Movements of the Early 'Sea Peoples' in Canaan," pp. 59–70, both in *Recent Excavations in Israel: Studies in Iron Age Archaeology*, ed. Seymour Gitin and William G. Dever Annual of the American Schools of Oriental Research 49 (Winona Lake, IN: Eisenbrauns, 1989).

[5]We need not imagine, as some scholars once did, that non-Mycenaean motifs of Philistine bichrome ware were acquired during the peregrinations of the Philistines around the eastern Mediterranean (e.g., Cyprus and Egypt) before landing in Canaan. All of these sources of inspiration were right at hand in Canaan itself. Even bichrome decoration itself was known in Phoenicia during the 13th century B.C. and has been found at Ashkelon (this LB IIB bichrome should not be confused with the earlier LB I bichrome, which originated in Cyprus).

In her most recent assessment, Trude Dothan ("The Arrival of the Sea Peoples") has made a fine typological distinction between the Mycenaean IIIC:1 decoration, which she characterizes as Simple Style, and the Philistine bichrome decoration, which she associates with the Elaborate Style known in other parts of the eastern Mediterranean. With this distinction she implies in a more subtle way than before two "waves" of Sea Peoples: The pre-Philistine group makes and uses Simple Style, they are then either augmented or replaced by the later group, the Philistines, who produce Elaborate Style pottery.

It would be an extraordinary development, indeed, if a pre-Philistine group of Sea Peoples preceded in establishing new and impressive cities and then were displaced at each of the Pentapolis sites by the Philistines a decade or two later. It seems much more likely that the relatively minor developments in style from monochrome simple to bichrome elaborate represent changes within the potting tradition of the same people and culture as the second generation of Philistine potters assimilate some of the local Canaanite and other traditions. In other words, Philistine bichrome pottery represents a regional style that developed in south Canaan. It seems likely that other immigrant groups of Sea Peoples settling in the northern coastal Levant, in Cyprus and in the central Mediterranean—for example, Sardinia, Sicily and Italy—might develop distinctive regional styles as they come in contact with different indigenous cultures.

[6]Lawrence E. Stager, "Merenptah, Israel and Sea Peoples: New Light on an Old Relief," *Eretz-Israel* 18 (1985), pp. 61–62.

[7]See Stager, "Merenptah, Israel and Sea Peoples." Using other lines of reasoning, both Amihai Mazar ("The Emergence of the Philistine Material Culture," *Israel Exploration Journal* 35 [1985], pp. 95–107) and Itamar Singer ("The Beginning of Philistine Settlement in Canaan and the Northern Boundary of Philistia" *Tel Aviv* 12 [1985], pp. 109–122) reached similar conclusions.

[8]F. Asaro, Isadore Perlman and Moshe Dothan, "An Introductory Study of Mycenaean IIIC:1 Ware from Tel Ashod," *Archaeometry* 13 (1971), pp. 169–175; Asaro and Perlman, "Provenience Studies of Mycenaean Pottery Employing Neutron Activation Analysis," in *The Mycenaeans in the Eastern Mediterranean, Acts of the International Archaeological Symposium* (Nicosia, Cyprus: Department of Antiquities, 1973), pp. 213–224; Jan Gunneweg, Trude Dothan, Perlman and Seymour Gitin, "On the Origin of Pottery from Tel Miqne-Ekron," *BASOR* 264 (1986), pp. 3–16.

[9]See Stager, "Merenptah, Israel and Sea Peoples," p. 64, n. 37 for bibliography of sites through 1985. To this list we should add Dothan, 1989.

[10]See Dothan, 1989.

[11]John A. Wilson, transl. in *Ancient Near Eastern Texts* (*ANET*), ed. James B. Pritchard (Princeton: Princeton Univ. Press, 1969), p. 262.

[12]Heinrich Schliemann, *Tiryns: The Prehistoric Palace of the Kings of Tiryns* (New York: Scribner's, 1885), pp. 146–147. For Kition, see Vassos Karageorghis and M. Demas, *Excavations at Kition: The Pre-Phoenecian Levels*, vol. V: Part 1 (Nicosia: Cyprus Dept. of Antiquities, 1985), for example, pl. 20:1087; pl. 34:1020, 1024; pl. 57:1024; pl. 117:5150–5156; pl. 195:5149–5156.

[13]All references to Homer's *Odyssey* follow the translation of Richard Lattimore, *The Odyssey of Homer* (New York: Harper & Row, 1965).

[14]Stubbings, "The Recession of Mycenaean Civilization," *Cambridge Ancient History*, (*CAH*), eds. I.E.S. Edwards, C.J. Gadd, N.G.L. Hammond and E. Sollberger (Cambridge, UK: Cambridge Univ. Press, 3rd edition 1975), vol. II, part 2: *History of the Middle East and the Aegean Region c. 1380–1000 B.C.*, pp. 354–358.

[15]Fritz Schachermeyr, *Griechische Frühgeschichte: ein Versuch, frühe Geschichte wenigstens in Umrissen verständlich zu machen* (Vienna: Osterreichischen Akademie der Wissenschaften, 1984), pp. 181–190.

[16]Strabo, *The Geography*, XIV, 1.27.

[17]Schachermeyr, *Griechische Frühgeschichte*, pp. 183–185.

[18]Richard D. Barnett, "The Sea Peoples," *CAH*, vol. II. part 2, pp. 363–365, and "Phrygia and the Peoples of Anatolia in the Iron Age," *CAH*, vol. II, part 2, pp. 441–442.

[19]Amihai Mazar, *Excavations at Tell Qasile: Part One, The Philistine Sanctuary: Architecture and Cult Objects*, Qedem 12 (Jerusalem: Hebrew Univ. Press, 1980).

[20]See citations and discussion in George Foote Moore, *A Critical and Exegetical Commentary on Judges* (International Critical Commentary) (New York: Scribner's, 1895), pp. 364–365.

[21]Othniel Margalith, "Samson's Riddle and Samson's Magic Locks," *Vetus Testamentum* (*VT*), 36 (1986), pp. 225–234.

[22]Yigael Yadin, "'And Dan, why did he remain in ships?'" *Australian Journal of Biblical Archaeology* 1 (1968), pp. 9–23; Cyrus Gordon, "The Mediterranean Factor in the Old Testament," *VT*, Suppl. 9 (1962), pp. 19–31; Allen H. Jones, *Bronze Age Civilization: The Philistines and the Danites* (Public Affairs Press: Washington, D.C., 1975); Hershel Shanks, "Danaans and Danites—Were the Hebrew Greek?" BAR, June 1976.

[23]See John A. Wilson, *ANET*, p. 28, for Wen-Amon, where Dor is called a "town of the Tjeker (=Sikil)." Recently Dr. Avner Raban, of the Center for Maritime Studies at Haifa University, has discovered the remains of the ancient harbor used by Wen-Amon in the 11th century B.C. at Dor (see Raban, "The Harbor of the Sea Peoples at Dor," *Biblical Archaeologist* 50 (1987), pp. 118–126.) The terrestrial archaeologist at Dor, Professor Ephraim Stern, considers the fortification system with glacis to have been built initially by the Sea Peoples, and specifically by the *Sikils* (personal communication). Shortly before the fall of Ugarit at the hands of the Sea Peoples, the *Šikalayū*, "who live on ships," were raiding and kidnapping along the coast, according to one Akkadian letter found at Ugarit (RS 34.129). Among the last tablets written there the last king of Ugarit despairs, saying: "The enemy ships are already here, they have set fire to my towns and have done very great damage in the country"

(RS 20.238). These seafarers and pirates (the *Šikalayū* = "Sikils") later moved down the coast and settled in the region of Dor.

Several scholars misidentified the *Šikalayū* with the Sea Peoples group known as Shekelesh (e.g. G.A. Lehmann, "Die Šikalayū—ein neues Zeugnis zu den 'Seevölker'—Heerfahrten im späten 13 Jh. V. Chr. [RS 34. 129]," *Ugarit Forschung* 11 [1979], pp. 481–494).

Anson Rainey was the first scholar to identify correctly the *Tjeker* of Egyptian sources with the *Šikalayū* of Ugarit. The *tj* of *Tjeker* should be phoneticized *s* (samakh); and of course, Egyptian *r* can equal *r* or *l* in Semitic. The gentilic *Šikalayū* actually masks the ethnicon *Sikil* (see Rainey, "Toponymic Problems," *Tel Aviv* 9 [1982], p. 134; for the best interpretation of the text, see Gregory Mobley, "The Identity of the *Šikalayū* [RS 34.129]," *BASOR* [forthcoming]).

Thus the Sea Peoples, who established themselves at Dor in the early 12th century B.C.—namely, the *Sikils*—closely resemble the *Sikelor* of later Greek sources, the people who gave their name to Sicily, just as the *Sherden*, another group of Sea Peoples, bequeathed their name to Sardinia, and the Teresh/Tursha to first Tarsus and later to the Etruscans of Italy. According to the dispersal of proper names and the evidence of immigrant Mycenaeans, it would appear that during the "colonization" of the coastal Levant and Cyprus, fissiparous groups of Sea Peoples bearing the same ethnicons settled the coastal regions of the central Mediterranean and bequeathed their names to several peoples and places there.

[24] Moshe Dothan, "Archaeological Evidence for Movements" and his "Sardine at Akko?" in *Studies in Sardinian Archaeology: Sardinia in the Mediterranean*, vol. 2, ed. Miriam Balmuth (Ann Arbor: Univ. of Michigan Press, 1986), pp. 105–115.

[25] Avraham Biran, "The Collared-rim Jars and the Settlement of the Tribe of Dan," in Gitin and Dever, *Recent Excavation*, pp. 71–96.

Related Reading

Lawrence E. Stager, "The Fury of Babylon: Ashkelon and the Archaeology of Destruction," BAR, January/February 1996 (see p. 378 of this book).

Daniel M. Master and Lawrence E. Stager, "Buy Low, Sell High: The Marketplace at Ashkelon," BAR, January/February 2014.

For more about the Philistines, see Trude Dothan's article on page 142 of this book and the Related Reading.

How Iron Technology

EDITORIAL PHOTOCOLOR ARCHIVE, STAATLICHE MUSEUM, BERLIN

Changed the Ancient World

And Gave the Philistines a Military Edge

JAMES D. MUHLY

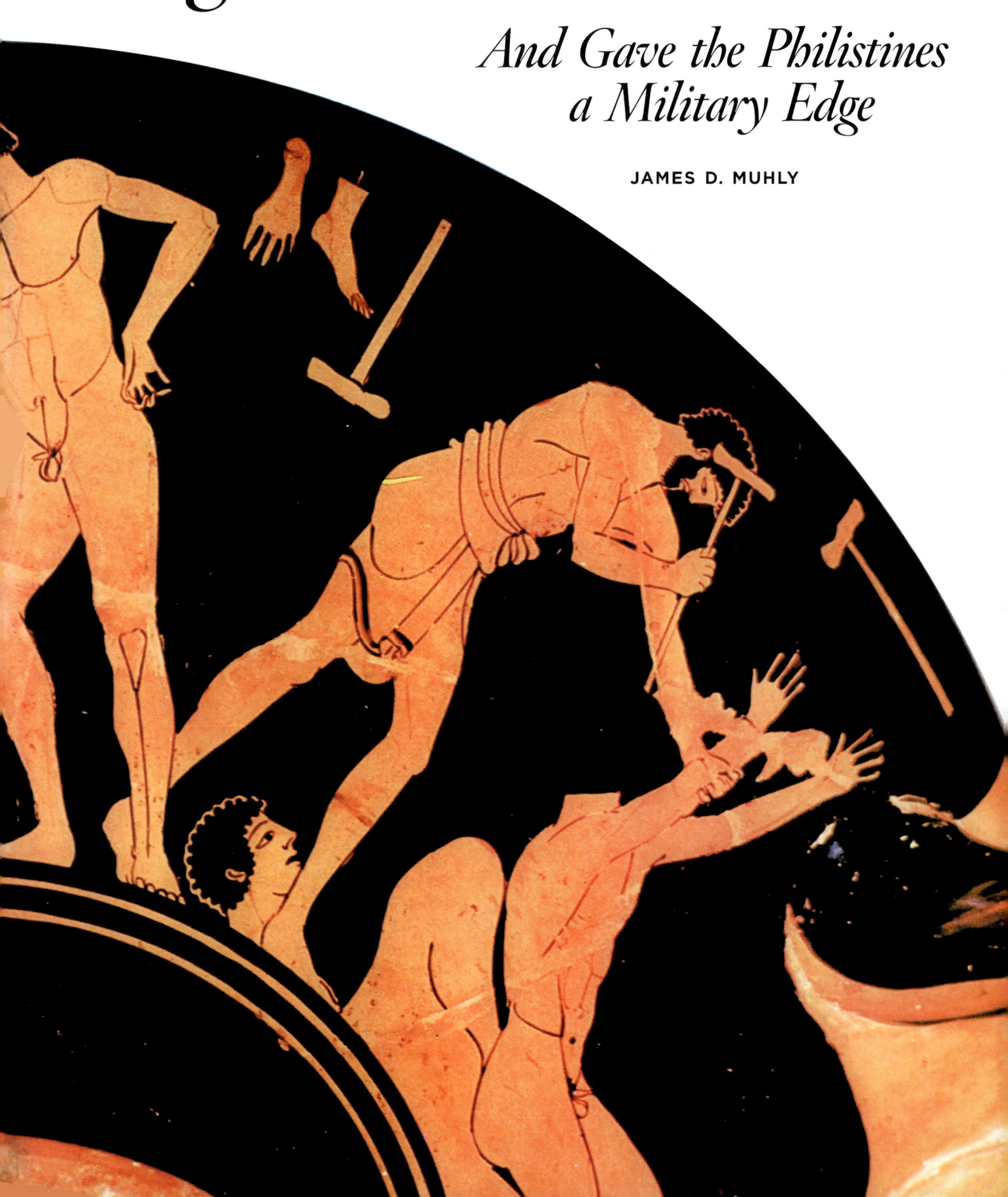

MODERN HISTORIANS DIVIDE THE ROUGHLY 3,000 year-period beginning approximately 3200 B.C. into two major segments—the Bronze Age and the Iron Age. The Bronze Age I extends from about 3200 B.C. to 1200 B.C.* Thereafter it is the Iron Age.** This is some indication of the enormous importance (as well as the date generally) of the discovery of iron technology in the eastern Mediterranean.

Archaeology and modern science are now beginning to clarify how this fundamental change occurred, and in so doing a new dimension has been added to our understanding of Biblical history in general as well as to our understanding of particular Biblical passages.

As a result, we may even be able to answer the much-mooted question: Did the Philistines have an iron monopoly that enabled them, at least for a time, to dominate the Israelites? Answering this question will involve us in a consideration of the famous passage from 1 Samuel:

> "There was no smith to be found in all the land of Israel, for the Philistines had said to themselves, 'The Hebrews might make swords or spears!' So all Israel would go down to the Philistines to repair any of their plowshares, mattocks, axes or sickles. The price was a palm for plowshares and mattocks and a third of a shekel for picks and axes or setting an ox-goad. So at the time of the battle of Michmash neither sword nor spear was available to any of the soldiers who were with Saul and Jonathan—only Saul and Jonathan had them." (1 Samuel 13:19–22; *Anchor Bible* translation)

Until about 1200 B.C., bronze was the predominant metal in the ancient world—for a very simple reason. The melting point of copper is about 1100°C. The melting point of iron is 1530°C. This roughly 400° difference was crucial in terms of the capabilities of ancient technology.

From at least the fifth millennium B.C. copper was worked as a molten metal.† In the fourth millennium, an arsenical alloy of copper was developed in the Middle East. This alloy usually contained from two to four percent arsenic. The best examples of this alloy come from the famous hoard of over 400 copper objects from the cave of Nahal Mishmar on the west bank of the Dead Sea.

The Bronze Age, beginning in about 3200 B.C., witnessed the introduction of an alloy known as bronze, consisting of about 90 percent copper and 10 percent tin. During the Bronze Age, an elaborate bronze casting technology was developed. Many bronze casting molds have been found throughout the Bronze Age world, often matching the surviving objects cast from them. The entire casting operation is depicted on the walls of Egyptian New Kingdom tombs, the most famous of which is that of the vizier Rekhmire (first half of the 15th century B.C.). Larger objects were sometimes cast in the sand, rather than in molds, as we know from the Bible passage describing Hiram's manufacture of the bronze utensils to be used in Solomon's Temple.

> "All these furnishings made by Hiram for King Solomon for the Temple of Yahweh were of burnished bronze. He made them by the process of sand casting in the Jordan area between Succoth and Zorethan." (1 Kings 7:45–46, *Jerusalem Bible* translation)

A temperature of 1200°C to melt copper could be attained in an ancient furnace by the use of a bellows and tuyères‡ that supplied the necessary forced draft of air. But the melting point of iron, 1530°C, seems to have been beyond the capability of an ancient furnace.

This does not mean that iron was not used at all. On the contrary, iron objects are known from as early as the fifth millennium B.C. But until the coming of the Iron Age, iron was an exotic, semi-precious metal used, for example, in jewelry. We even have examples of an iron bezel in a gold ring from Late Bronze Age Greece. Iron was also used for the manufacture of ceremonial weapons. An iron battle axe from Ugarit (about 1400 B.C.) and

*The Bronze Age is subdivided into Early Bronze (3200–2000 B.C.), Middle Bronze (2000–1550 B.C.) and Late Bronze (1550–1200 B.C.). Each of these is also further subdivided.

**The Iron Age is subdivided into Iron Age I (1200–1000 B.C.), Iron Age II (1000–586 B.C.), and, sometimes, Iron Age III (586–330 B.C.).

OVERLEAF: FOUNDRYMEN ON an Attic vase cast a life-size bronze statue. This foundry scene, the most detailed to survive from the ancient world, decorates an early fifth century B.C. vase known as the Berlin Foundry Cup. It shows a construction technique, the piece casting of a life-size bronze statue, that simply would not have been possible when working with iron. On the left is the furnace in which bronze was melted; the young man peering out from behind it is probably working the bellows. The objects hanging to the right of the furnace are interpreted as votive offerings to ensure the successful outcome of the casting, but the presence of the saw has never been explained. On the far right, a foundry worker taps the mold with a hammer to release the statue from its mold. Between this worker's feet is the statue's head, ready to be joined to the bronze body.

†Pure copper metallurgy developed to a high degree, not only in the old world from Eastern Europe to Pakistan but even in North America.

‡A tuyère is an opening in a furnace through which a blast of air enters, facilitating combustion.

ZEV RADOVAN, COURTESY ISRAEL MUSEUM

a dagger from the tomb of Tutankhamen in Egypt (about 1350 B.C.) are examples.

These early iron objects were not cast, because the iron could not be heated to a molten state; instead they were wrought. The iron was forged, after smelting, while it was in a semi-solid spongy state.

Pure iron worked in this way is not very utilitarian. Indeed, plain wrought iron is decidedly inferior to tin-bronze, being both softer and less durable. The work-hardened edge on a bronze cutting instrument is far superior to anything that can be produced in plain wrought iron.

Thus for the 2,000 years of the Bronze Age (3200–1200 B.C.) bronze was the predominant metal in the ancient world. This is especially ironic, if I may be pardoned the pun, because iron was so much more widely dispersed than copper. But, from the viewpoint of Bronze Age technology, these vast iron deposits were relatively worthless.

Moreover, not only was copper less common than

COPPER CEREMONIAL OBJECTS belong to a magnificent hoard of more than 400 copper pieces found in the Judean wilderness near the Dead Sea. Hidden in a cave in Nahal Mishmar, the hoard dates to the Chalcolithic period (fourth millennium B.C.). The beauty and workmanship—unique for its time but extraordinary at any time—make this the earliest and most important collection of metal artifacts found anywhere in the world.

The objects may have been used in cult rituals at a nearby temple. At the center is a "crown"; to the right is a standard with ibex heads; other implements include mace heads and scepters.

The Nahal Mishmar hoard demonstrates the exceptional sophistication of copper metallurgy that had developed in fourth millennium Palestine. The objects were made by what is called the "lost wax" process. Wax was carved in the shape of the artifact, a clay mold was then built around the wax model; the wax was melted away and, finally, molten copper, sometimes with an admixture of arsenic, was poured into the cavity.

ROBERT MADDIN

IRON TOOLS AND WEAPONS from Middle Eastern sites: a) knife found in a tomb at Tell el Far'ah (south); b) Tell el Far'ah (south) arrowhead; c) Tell Jemmeh knife; d) Tell Jemmeh hoe; e) chisel from Al Mina in northern Syria.

iron, but tin, the second component of bronze, was indeed quite scarce. In the Mediterranean world, alluvial tin, or cassiterite, is known from the Eastern Desert of Egypt. While there is geological evidence for its presence in these areas, there is no evidence of its ancient exploitation. Apart from Egypt, alluvial tin is known only from regions as far away as southern England (Cornwall) in the West and Afghanistan in the East. The Biblical reference to tin from Tarshish (Ezekiel 27:12) is not very helpful in locating ancient tin deposits because we cannot locate Tarshish.

At the end of the Late Bronze Age, there was a worldwide upheaval of destructions, invasions and migrations. Whether the crises were related to one another is unknown. But these upheavals plunged the world into a Dark Age of poverty and isolation. This was the time when Troy was destroyed, when the Dorians moved into Greece from the northwest, when the Phrygians migrated to Anatolia, when the Sea Peoples, including the Philistines, attacked (but were repelled by) Egypt and finally settled on the Palestine coast, and when the Israelites occupied Canaan. At this time, Mycenaean sea power ended, the Hittite empire collapsed, the great city-states in Syria were destroyed, and the Arameans migrated into Mesopotamia and Syria. These destructions marked the end of the great empires of the Late Bronze Age and of the palace economies that developed around the urban centers associated with these empires.

The Late Bronze Age, until the very end, had been a time of prosperity and extensive international trade. Late Bronze Age levels of excavations, wherever they are located, characteristically uncover substantial quantities of "imported" pottery, frequently painted and decorated. But all this came to an end in the waning years of the Late Bronze Age. International trade routes were permanently disrupted and local communities withdrew into themselves. No longer could vast supplies of copper, and especially tin, be brought over long distance by land and sea. During the Bronze Age, according to the most recent scholarship, the tin used in Middle Eastern bronze came all the way from Afghanistan. Although the proof for this statement has not been fully supplied, it does suggest the kinds of production problems that ensued following the disruption of international commerce. Copper supply dwindled and tin became almost unavailable.

In the archaeological levels from the first part of the Iron Age, precious metals are no longer found and imported materials are extremely rare. There were, of course, areas where Bronze Age culture, including metalworking, survived, but this was the exception, not the rule.

As is so often the case in human history, necessity became the mother of invention. While bronze was easily available, there was no necessity for the development of iron technology. In short, the inception of the Iron Age came about in response to a materials shortage, a crisis created by the disruption of international trade routes. When bronze became scarce, those smiths living in areas that had not been invaded and devastated were forced to fall back on local resources and to make do with what was available nearer to home. Iron metallurgy developed against this background.

Not only were iron deposits more likely than

ROBERT MADDIN

AN IRON PICK from Har Adir in the upper Galilee. This tool's remarkable state of preservation belies its date—from the 12th or early 13th century B.C. On the top we see it as it was excavated; on the bottom, after cleaning and preservation. This pick is especially noteworthy because it is one of only two artifacts from this period that have undergone metallurgical analysis. In the bottom photo, the arrow far left points to the tiny metal chip removed for this scientific study. The right arrow indicates where hardness readings were made. The hardness readings and the results of metallographic examination show that the pick was made of carburized iron (steel) that had been quenched and then tempered.

copper to be available locally, but iron was more easily extracted from the earth. Iron ore deposits, even when found in association with copper deposits, tend to be on the surface and therefore their extraction does not require any elaborate mining technology. Copper ores, on the other hand, tend to be located in veins running deep into the ground and often require a network of underground shafts and galleries in order to be mined. Archaeologists have found a number of early copper mines, some going back to the fifth millennium B.C., but no ancient iron mines, perhaps because iron was mined on the surface.

The famous Biblical description of the riches of the Promised Land reflects the fact that copper mining requires underground shafts and galleries but iron mining utilizes surface deposits. In addition to its agricultural wealth, the land of Canaan was "a land where the stones are of iron, where the hills may be quarried for copper." (Deuteronomy 8:9, *Jerusalem Bible* translation). Actually, ancient Palestine has only limited deposits of iron ore,* but the Biblical author accurately described the conditions under which the two metals could be found.

While local accessibility and ease of extraction might be thought to have given iron the edge (again, excuse the pun), only the scarcity of bronze provided the goad for the development of iron technology.

Perhaps this is understandable because iron technology is difficult and complicated. As we have seen, in antiquity iron could not be heated to the melting point, so it had to be wrought or forged in a semi-solid spongy mass (or bloom, as it is called). Moreover, this porous mass of agglomerated iron had trapped within its interstices quantities of impurities called gangue, consisting basically of silica. In order to consolidate the metal, it was necessary to hammer or forge the red-hot bloom, thus forcing out or extruding the unwanted gangue. But even when this was done, the resultant pure iron was soft compared to bronze.

The essential factor in the technological development of iron metallurgy was the introduction of up to .8 percent carbon into the red-hot iron, accomplished by a kind of osmosis through prolonged contact with glowing charcoal in the forging furnace. The introduction of this carbon transformed iron from an exotic, semi-precious metal into a metal that would give its name to the age. For carburized iron (iron to which carbon has been added) is, in fact, steel.

The technology is not simple, however. When red-hot carburized iron (or steel) is suddenly cooled off by plunging it into a vat of cold water (quenching), the result includes the formation of material called martensite. Martensite is earth's second-hardest substance. Only a diamond is harder.

*There are a number of minor deposits—in the Makhtesh southwest of the Dead Sea, in the Galilee and in the Wadi Arabah—but the only major ore deposit is that at Mugharat el Wardeh in the vicinity of Ajlun, about 20 miles north-northwest of Amman, a deposit that would be exploited today were it not so inaccessible.

The problem is that martensite, though extremely hard, is also very brittle. An object of pure martensite will shatter upon impact.

When carburized iron is quenched, however, the result is not pure martensite. Usually only the outer layers of the object will be converted into martensite; the inner layers will be composed of pearlite, consisting of alternate layers (or lamellae) of ferrite (pure iron) and cementite (a compound of iron and carbon). Just how much martensite will be produced depends upon mass and temperature.

In order to relieve the brittleness of the metal, it was necessary to reduce some of the martensite through tempering; that is, reheating the iron, at temperatures above 150°C, in order to decompose some of the martensite and thus reduce the brittleness of the metal. This resulted in an elaborate trade-off of hardness versus durability that became the hallmark of advanced iron metallurgy.

The technology of working with iron thus became far more complex than anything connected with copper or bronze, and it all had to be learned empirically. No Iron Age smith was aware even of the existence of carbon, an element not identified until the end of the 18th century A.D.; he only learned empirically of its effect. But once these ancient smiths learned that iron subjected to the elaborate heat-treatment of carburization, quenching and tempering was far superior to bronze, a new age was ushered in. Iron was no longer a curiosity but one of the most useful resources in the crust of the earth.

The Iron Age became the age of the blacksmith. The village blacksmith standing at his forge before an anvil, holding a lump or bar of red-hot iron in a pair of tongs, was a metalworking scene unknown to the inhabitants of the Bronze Age world. But this scene became common when iron emerged as the dominant metal, largely replacing the casting technology used for copper and bronze.

A vivid artistic representation of a smithy appears on a sixth century B.C. amphora from Athens (see cover photo on p. 141). An assistant, who is partially obscured by a furnace, holds a red-hot bar of metal with a pair of tongs while the blacksmith stands in front of the anvil, raising a sledge-hammer with a wedge-shaped head, ready to strike the bar. Two bearded men holding staffs sit and respectfully observe. Lying on the floor and hanging on the wall are a saw, tongs, a vase, a garment, a knife, a chisel, a sheathed sword and sledge-hammers with wedge-shaped heads and with double concave heads.

The first recorded reference to the profession of blacksmith comes in an archival text from the reign of the Assyrian king Ninurta-tukulti-Assur, about 1132 B.C.[1]

The work of the blacksmith is vividly described in the Bible. For example, in Isaiah 44:12, we learn about the manufacture of iron idols:

> "The blacksmith works on it over the fire and beats it into shape with a hammer. He works on it with his strong arm til he is hungry and tired; drinking no water, he is exhausted." (*Jerusalem Bible* translation)

The same image is projected in Ecclesiasticus 38:29–31, part of a section dealing with trade and crafts:

> "So it is with the blacksmith sitting by his anvil;
> he considers what to do with the iron bloom,
> the breath of the fire scorches his skin,
> as he contends with the heat of the furnace;
> he batters his ear with the din of the hammer,
> his eyes are fixed on the pattern;
> he sets his heart on completing his work,
> and stays up putting the finishing touches."
> (*Jerusalem Bible* translation, but reading "iron bloom" instead of "pig iron")

Indeed, the red-hot iron furnace came to be used metaphorically for Egypt, from which God delivered the Israelites. Solomon prays to Yahweh on behalf of his people: "They are your people and your heritage whom you brought out of Egypt, that iron furnace." (1 Kings 8:51; *Jerusalem Bible* translation). The image is repeated in Deuteronomy 4:20 and in Jeremiah 11:4.

Bronze of course continued to be used in the Iron Age, especially for purposes for which iron was unsatisfactory. The basic difference between bronze and iron technology determined, to a very great extent, the ways in which the two metals were used. With bronze it was possible to make large, elaborate and intricate castings from the molten metal in shapes impossible to duplicate by forging a bar of iron. A life-size statue was almost commonplace in bronze, but unheard of in iron. Iron came to be used for objects of rather simple shape and design, requiring great hardness and strength. This meant cutting and chopping instruments such as axes, adzes and chisels,* digging instruments such as hoes and plowshares, and, above all, weapons. Because of its hardness and its ability to take and hold a sharp cutting edge or point, iron was ideal for swords, spearheads, knives, daggers, and even arrowheads. Thus, iron soon became the metal of war, producing the iron armory described in Job 20:24. But all of this was possible only with the use of carburized iron (or steel) and the development of

*See 13th century B.C. iron sickle illustrated in "The Israelite Occupation of Canaan," BAR, May/June 1982.

COURTESY CAIRO ARCHAEOLOGICAL MUSEUM AND EGYPTIAN DEPARTMENT OF ANTIQUITIES

A GOLD DAGGER (top) and an iron dagger, each with its own scabbard. These exquisite weapons were found among the treasures buried with King Tutankhamen about 1350 B.C. Gold daggers are known from other contexts, going back to the Royal Cemetery of Ur (c. 2500 B.C.), but this iron dagger is unique in the Bronze Age world (and for this reason the Egyptian government allowed the gold dagger to travel about the world as part of the exhibition of The Treasures of Tutankhamen, but insisted that the iron dagger remain in Cairo). The best description of the iron dagger is that of Howard Carter, the excavator of the tomb, first published in 1922: "The haft of the dagger is of granulated gold, embellished at intervals with collars of Cloisonné work of colored rock crystal; but the astonishing and unique feature of this beautiful weapon is that the blade is of iron still bright and resembling steel!"

It is assumed that the blade of this dagger is made of meteoritic iron, but no technical study of it has ever been made.

HIRMER VERLAG, COURTESY ALEPPO MUSEUM

A CEREMONIAL BATTLE AXE from Ugarit (c. 1400 B.C.). Atop the bronze socket of this elegant weapon, cast in a mold and inlaid with gold, is a crouching wild boar. The blade was probably wrought or hammered from a piece of meteoritic iron, as were many iron artifacts of this period. No proper metallographic analysis has been made of this blade, but based on available information, metallurgist H. G. Richardson said of the axe: "It is not a formidable weapon in any sense—size, weight, hardness or inherent soundness. In a finish fight the bronze socket would be far more dependable than the iron blade."

THE METROPOLITAN MUSEUM OF ART, ROGERS FUND, 1931

EGYPTIAN METAL WORKERS MELT METALLIC COPPER. This painting decorates the wall of Vizier Rekhmire's tomb from the 15th century B.C. on the west bank of the Nile near Thebes.

Each hearth has a light blue center, representing either ashes or a floor of clay or stone. The two figures above remove a clay crucible of molten metal from the hearth. The vase above them may contain a copper/tin mixture or water to douse the hot lifting rods.

Between the two lower figures are a vase and a pile of charcoal. The men use foot bellows to direct a forced draft of air onto the hearth in order to increase the intensity of the fire. Although this technique has now been studied in some detail, the best description of it is still that of Norman de Garis Davies (*The Tomb of Rekhmire at Thebes*, 1943): "The hearth, when in use, was fed with air from two pairs of bellows, each of which was operated by a man who threw his weight from one bag to the other. When he stepped off a depressed bag he raised its upper side by means of a string, and while it was filling again he was deflating its fellow. The air from the bag under pressure was discharged into the heart of the fire through a pipe of reed, ending near the fire in a pottery nozzle [tuyère]. The bellows consisted of a red leather bag mounted on a white object of the same size and shape, which may be a flat stone or another bag.... No valve is shown, but air may have entered through a hole which the operator closed with his heel. The upper bag was tied horizontally round the middle with cord to enable it to stand the distension better."

a technology involving quenching and tempering.

In the Bible, iron is a symbol of strength. In Job 40:18 we are told of Behemoth, the brute whose bones are "as hard as hammered iron." And in Daniel 2:40 we read the prophecy of the four kingdoms:

> "There will be a fourth kingdom, hard as iron, as iron that shatters and crushes all. Like iron that breaks everything to pieces, it will crush and break all the earlier kingdoms." (*Jerusalem Bible* translation)

The sharpness of the edge of an iron dagger is assumed in these lines from a Babylonian Wisdom text known as *The Dialogue of Pessimism*[2]: "Woman is a pitfall—a pitfall, a hole, a ditch. Woman is a sharp iron dagger that cuts a man's throat."

The problem of tracing the development and spread of iron technology should be an ideal one for archaeology in combination with modern science. More than 40 years ago, R. J. Forbes, then the world's leading specialist in ancient technology, observed: "If there ever was a problem of ancient metallurgy in which the technical aspect can give us the correct solution it is that of the coming of the Iron Age."[3]

Today, archaeologists in cooperation with metallurgists, can discover a great deal of information from a small metal sample taken from an ancient iron artifact. After the archaeologist excavates an iron object, the modern metallurgist can determine hearth temperatures reached at the different stages of production such as forging or tempering. From a study of the penetration of carbon into the iron object, the metallurgist can make rough calculations of the length of time the object was held in the charcoal fire and even at what temperature in order to achieve that particular carbon penetration. Very recently we have learned to use even corrosion product in new analytical techniques developed at the University of Pennsylvania. The problem is that permission to take the necessary samples from ancient artifacts has proven quite difficult to obtain. Some modern countries refuse to authorize such research because it involves taking a small sample of metal from the ancient artifact. The exceptions are Israel and Cyprus.

For the past five years Professors Robert Maddin and Tamara Stech and I (all colleagues at the University of Pennsylvania) have been working together on a detailed program involving the scientific study of early metal artifacts throughout the eastern Mediterranean, concentrating on objects that could be dated within the limits of the crucial transition period from 1200 to 900 B.C. (from the end of the Bronze Age to the full Iron Age). Metallurgical analyses of individual artifacts have

Grim Episode from Homer's *Odyssey* Evokes Early Steel-Making Techniques

This chilling scene on the neck of a Proto-Attic amphora from the early seventh century B.C. portrays the encounter of Odysseus with the giant, Polyphemus, who was called the Cyclops because he had a single eye in the middle of his forehead. Odysseus and his men, trapped in the cave of Polyphemus, managed to escape by getting the giant drunk on wine and then, after he had fallen asleep, blinding him by thrusting a glowing olive wood pole into his eye socket. Homer describes the result in a passage of gruesome intensity (*Odyssey*, IX: 389–94):

> "The blast and scorch of the burning ball singed all his eyebrows and eyelids, and the fire made the roots of his eye crackle. As when a man who works as a blacksmith plunges into cold water a great axe or adze which hisses aloud, 'doctoring' it, since this is the way that steel is made strong, even so Cyclops's eye sizzled about the beam of the olive." (Translation after that by Richard Lattimore)

The *Odyssey*, although it incorporates older material, was first written down in the late eighth century B.C. Homer's description of Polyphemus's agony is the earliest literary description of the quenching of carburized iron, or steel. So graphic a simile could only have been created by someone who had himself watched the blacksmith at work. It is such passages that make the study of the Homeric poems so complex and yet so important for understanding the transition from bronze to iron and the beginnings of the Iron Age. Homer, in the *Iliad* and the *Odyssey*, wrote about a period (during and after the Trojan War) at the end of the Late Bronze Age, and bronze is the metal used by his heroes, both Greek and Trojan. But in vivid descriptive passages, such as this one of the Cyclops, Homer frequently draws upon material from his own daily world, the world of the eighth century B.C. In such passages iron suddenly appears as the metal in common use.

The Polyphemus passage is also important for what it tells us about the development of iron technology. The fact that it was possible to harden a material by plunging it into cold water was obviously a puzzle to Homer. The Greek word that describes this peculiar property of carburized iron (and only carburized iron, because quenching would not change the properties of wrought iron) is translated here as 'doctoring' but is etymologically related to English words such as pharmacy. Homer and the inhabitants of Dark Age Greece must have seen the transformation of carburized iron through quenching as something bordering on the magical. They did not understand the exact nature of the physical change created by the act, but they recognized that somehow the metal had been transformed.

HIRMER VERLAG, COURTESY ELEUSIS MUSEUM

added significantly to the largely archaeological surveys that follow. After five years of study, we can state that iron technology probably first developed in the Eastern Mediterranean, with Greece and Cyprus playing the dominant roles, and that the introduction of iron metallurgy into Israel came about through contacts with the Aegean world and the migrations of the Philistines and other Sea Peoples.

The development of iron metallurgy occurred in areas where a surviving tradition of Bronze Age metalworking was combined with an ability to respond to the new pressures of a difficult, even hostile environment. This can clearly be seen in the Aegean, where the concentration of 12th century iron artifacts comes from just those areas where the Late Bronze Age Mycenaean heritage is most apparent, areas that somehow managed to avoid the devastations and destructions that marked the end of the Late Bronze Age throughout the eastern Mediterranean. Examples are the sites of Perati in East Attica, Mouliana in Crete, Lefkandi in Euboea and the Kamini cemetery on the island of Naxos.

With the introduction of a strong Aegean element into Cyprus, probably the result of the arrival of Greek colonists in the early 12th century B.C., comes the first use of iron on Cyprus, followed there by the rapid development of iron technology. Again, this occurs at Cypriot sites, such as Kition,

ROBERT MADDIN

A CRUCIBLE in which bronze was heated to molten temperatures. Found at Ayia Irini, a Late Bronze Age (15th century B.C.) site on the island of Kea, Greece, this clay crucible still bears flakes of pale green bronze. Under its thick rim at right is a spout through which the bronze was poured into a mold.

that maintained strong elements of continuity with the culture of the Late Bronze Age, and at sites in the southwestern part of the island that witnessed the first arrival of the Greek colonists.

The influence of these Greek colonists can be seen in the pottery and the architecture as well as in the iron artifacts of 12th century Cyprus. Contemporaneous iron objects from Cyprus and from the Aegean suggest a common cultural and ironworking heritage for that area. For instance, consider the one-edged curved knife of iron having a hilt of bone or ivory fastened with three bronze rivets, examples of which have been found at numerous eastern Mediterranean sites. The combination of metals may be a result of the fact that bronze rivets, unlike iron ones, could be cold-worked, thus preventing damage to the delicate ivory hilt. But the combination suggests a certain continuity between bronze and iron cultures and supports the contention that iron technology developed in areas where Bronze Age culture, including a bronze metalworking industry, survived.

Such iron knives with bronze rivets have been found in 12th to early 11th century contexts throughout the Aegean and the eastern Mediterranean, from Perati in Attica to Hama in Syria, almost always* uncovered in association with typical Mycenaean IIIC1 pottery of the 12th century B.C. (or its local imitations). Such an iron knife was recently found at the Philistine site of Tell Qasile, again in a 12th century B.C. context and at a site having very strong connections with Cyprus, especially Kition, and with the Aegean.

From the so-called "500" cemetery at the Philistine site of Tell el-Far'ah (south), another site with strong Aegean connections, come several 12th century B.C. iron objects, including a dagger from Tomb 542. We have not studied this dagger, but an iron knife with one bronze rivet from Tomb 562, dating from the 11th century B.C., proved to be made of carburized iron presenting a metallurgical structure that strongly suggested deliberate carburization.

From Cyprus we have even better evidence for the development of a sophisticated iron technology. In 1971 the Swedish metallurgist Erik Tholander analyzed a curved iron knife from a tomb at Idalion and found it to be made of quench-hardened steel. We have now confirmed Tholander's results, working with another sample from the same knife, and have at the same time greatly expanded the evidence for the use of carburized iron from sites scattered all over the southern half of the island, including Kouklia-Skales (Palaepaphos), Amathus, Idalion and Kition, as well as from Lapithos in the north. All this evidence for carburization comes from 11th century B.C. contexts.

We have very little metallurgical evidence for the state of ironworking technology in the 12th century B.C. We do have a number of surviving iron objects from Canaanite, Philistine, and Israelite sites,[4] but with two exceptions, no scientific studies have been carried out on any of these 12th century pieces. One exception is a knife from Tell Qasile which proved, unfortunately, to be totally corroded. The other exception is somewhat extraordinary—an iron pick found in 1976 by a young Israeli archaeologist, David Davis, excavating on behalf of the Israeli Department of Antiquities at Har Adir, near Sasa in the Upper Galilee. The iron pick is in a remarkable state of preservation and clearly dates to the early 12th, perhaps even the 13th century B.C. We are working with the excavator on the publication of this pick, which to date remains unpublished, but even now we can state that our metallurgical analysis of the iron indicates that the manufacturer of the pick had knowledge of the full range of ironworking skills associated with the production of quench-hardened steel. The pottery from the site associated with the pick reflects close connections with the island of Cyprus.

Thus the 12th and 11th century iron objects

*The exception is an iron knife from Hama which was not found in this Mycenaean IIIC1 context.

that have been found throughout the eastern Mediterranean all come from sites that have in common an international milieu, and more particularly some sort of contact with the Aegean and Cyprus. The archaeological evidence also indicates some degree of continuity, perhaps even the survival of metalworking traditions, from the more sophisticated world of the Late Bronze Age. The only exceptions to these general propositions are the Early Israelite sites located just to the north of Jerusalem Ai, Khirbet Raddana, and Tell el-Ful (ancient Gibeah where an 11th century iron plowshare was found). At these sites iron appears in a context independent of any evidence for contact with the outside world. They also represent new settlements with no Bronze Age metalworking traditions.

An essentially Bronze Age culture continued to survive in the Aegean at a number of sites—the Ionian islands, the southeastern part of the Greek mainland (eastern Attica and Euboea), and in some of the larger islands such as Crete, Rhodes and Naxos. This was also true in Cyprus. In Palestine this same continuity can be seen in the northern Canaanite cities, like Megiddo (stratum VIIA) and Taanach (period IB) in the Jezreel Valley, and at Beth-Shean (stratum VI).**

Both in the northern and central parts of Palestine, the Israelites were initially limited to the occupation of isolated sites in the hills (such as Izbet Sartah)† because they could not conquer the rich cities in the plain below. The sons of Joseph complained to Joshua that:

> "The highlands are not enough for us, and what is more, all the Canaanites living in the plain have iron chariots, and so have those in Beth-Shean and its dependent towns, and those in the plain of Jezreel." (Joshua 17:16, *Jerusalem Bible* translation)

Joshua replied that:

> "A mountain shall be yours; it is covered with woods, but you must clear it, and its boundaries shall be yours, since you cannot drive out the Canaanite because of his iron chariots and his superior strength." (Joshua 17:18, *Jerusalem Bible* translation)

This tradition is found throughout the Conquest narratives. The Israelites, as a loose confederation of tribes, lacked the military technology necessary to conquer the fortified Canaanite cities of the plain. The technological superiority of the Canaanites is dramatized in this passage from Joshua by the emphasis upon their possession of "chariots of iron." Jabin, the king of Canaan who reigned at Hazor, is said to have possessed a force that included 900 chariots of iron. (Judges 4:3)

These passages from Joshua and Judges referring to "iron chariots" and "chariots of iron" present some problems—both metallurgical and chronological. No one actually had chariots of iron. The *Jerusalem Bible* translates one passage of Judges 4 as chariots "plated with iron." In Joshua, it translates simply "iron chariots." The translation "plated with iron" is really an interpretation without textual support. The words "plated with" were simply supplied by the translator. It is extremely difficult to plate with iron. These "chariots of iron" must be regarded as a poetical and psychological description of the latest in military hardware, combining chariots, the most formidable aspect of all Late Bronze Age armies, with iron, the latest addition to the military arsenal and a metal that was just starting to make its impact upon the military world of the Early Iron Age. The actual use of iron must have been confined to fittings, such as the hubs of the chariot's wheels, perhaps even parts of the wheel itself. (The same explanation probably applies to the iron bedstead of Og, king of Bashan, in Deuteronomy 3:11.) Such iron chariot fittings have been recovered at Taanach, but

ROBERT MADDIN, COURTESY DR. VASSOS KARAGEORGHIS, EPISKOPI MUSEUM, CYPRUS

TWO FRAGMENTARY TUYÈRES, or hollow clay nozzles through which blasts of air entered a Late Bronze Age furnace, flank a crucible fragment. Industrial debris like this found at Bamboula on Cyprus is often discovered during the course of an excavation; it is evidence that some metallurgical operation was conducted at the site, probably involving the melting and casting of copper or bronze.

**See "The Israelite Occupation of Canaan," BAR, May/June 1982, by Yohanan Aharoni.

†See "An Israelite Village from the Days of the Judges," BAR, September/October 1978, by Aaron Demsky and Moshe Kochavi (see also p. 108 of this book).

COURTESY MANFRED BIETAK AND THE ARCHAEOLOGICAL INSTITUTE OF AUSTRIA

unfortunately in an uncertain archaeological context.

The chronological problem unsolved in these Biblical references to chariots of iron is that they appear to date to the 12th century at the latest. The excavator of Hazor, Yigael Yadin, dates the Israelite destruction of Hazor to about 1230 B.C. A 13th century date for this destruction is now universally accepted.* Yet the use of iron for offensive weapons cannot be documented before the 12th century, and really not before the 11th. Perhaps in one way or another, the Conquest Narratives describe the world of the 12th to early 11th century B.C., although some events may have occurred earlier.

In any event the present evidence indicates that iron technology developed in Palestine in the 12th century at the earliest, stimulated by the arrival of the Philistines and other Sea Peoples who brought with them the inspiration, and perhaps even the new technology from the Aegean area. We have already examined the evidence for the development of iron technology in the Aegean area as well as the impressive recent evidence for the extensive use of iron in 12th to early 11th century Cyprus.

Trude Dothan has recently examined in these pages the Aegean origins of the Philistines.** We may therefore be brief here: According to the Bible the Philistines came from Caphtor (Amos 9:7), long identified as the Biblical name for the island of

*See Aharoni, BAR, May/June 1982.

**See Dothan, "What We Know About the Philistines," BAR, July/August 1982 (see also p. 142 of this book).

LIMESTONE MOLDS. In about 1740 B.C., metal workers at Tell el-Daba in the Eastern Nile Delta cast a variety of copper tools and weapons in these molds. In the stone at left, two chisels and an axe head are clearly outlined. The stone at right includes a knife, a saw and a chisel, and at bottom are two thin harpoons and an adze. Harpoons were used to catch fish and hippopotamus, a popular local dish.

The metal craftsmen at Tell el-Daba were Canaanites originating most likely from the area of Byblos, an eastern Mediterranean port with a long tradition of copper tool production. In the late Middle Kingdom (c. 1750–1700 B.C.), intensive trade linked the two harbor cities of Byblos and Tell el-Daba and led to the establishment of a major settlement of Byblites at Tell el-Daba. (The dates and interpretation used in this caption are those of the excavator of Tell el-Daba, Manfred Bietak.)

Crete. Other traditions (Zephaniah 2:5 and Ezekiel 25:16) link the Philistines with the Cherethites, identified as Cretans. The connections between Cyprus and the Philistines are most apparent in the characteristic Philistine style of pottery. The Aegean elements in Philistine pottery, long recognized as being influenced by Mycenaean IIIC1 ceramic traditions, clearly came not from Greece itself, but from the local imitations of Mycenaean wares produced at 12th century B.C. sites in Cyprus. Amihai Mazar has recently excavated three superimposed Philistine temples at Tell Qasile dating from the first half of the 12th century to the middle of the 11th century. (Drawings of plans of these temples appear in "What We Know About the Philistines," see p. 142 of this book) He also uncovered a *favissa* of cult objects associated with the second of the three temples. There are very close connections between these Philistine temples and the Philistine cult objects, on the one hand, and a series of so-called shrines or temples excavated recently in Cyprus (Kition), the Greek Islands (Phylakopi or Melos) and the Greek mainland (Mycenae), on the other hand. Thus it seems reasonable to conclude that the Philistines introduced advanced iron technology into Palestine. What still remains unclear is the formative history of that technology.

In a recent issue of BAR, Yohanan Aharoni argued that "thus far no substantial archaeological evidence indicates that iron had been widely used in Philistia before it was widely used at Israelite sites."† This statement in fact misses the point. Aharoni failed to distinguish between the *kinds* of iron artifacts found at Philistine and Israelite sites. Philistine political control of the area of southern Palestine dates from the end of the 12th century B.C. at the earliest. Iron artifacts from the 11th century are to be found at Israelite as well as Philistine sites, but *all of the weapons*—swords, daggers, spearheads—are found at Philistine sites.

This archaeological picture is entirely consistent with the literary tradition preserved in 1 Samuel 13:19–22, quoted at the beginning of this article. In this passage we are told that there were no smiths in the land of Israel because the Philistines were fearful that the Hebrews might make swords or spears. So the Israelites had to come to the Philistines to get their farm implements repaired.

Aharoni rightly points out that the Biblical passage makes no mention of iron—nor of an iron-working monopoly for that matter. But the Israelites obviously had metal farm implements that needed repairing. On the basis of the surviving artifactual evidence, it is reasonable to assume that, by the end of the 11th century B.C. (the time of the reign of Saul), these farm implements were made of iron.

In contrast to the farm implements found at Israelite sites, an important collection of 11th century iron objects, including three daggers and five knives, has been found at Tel Zeror, a site with strong Cypriot connections in the Late Bronze Age. Tel Zeror also had close connections with the Sea Peoples at nearby Tell Dor, known from the Wenamun tale to have been inhabited by the Tjekker (one of the Sea Peoples). Indeed, the inhabitants of Tel Zeror may well have been Sea Peoples (perhaps Philistines).

Aharoni has argued that the absence of iron artifacts in Philistine levels at Ashdod, the most important Philistine site to be excavated in modern

†See Aharoni, "The Israelite Occupation of Canaan," BAR, May/June 1982.

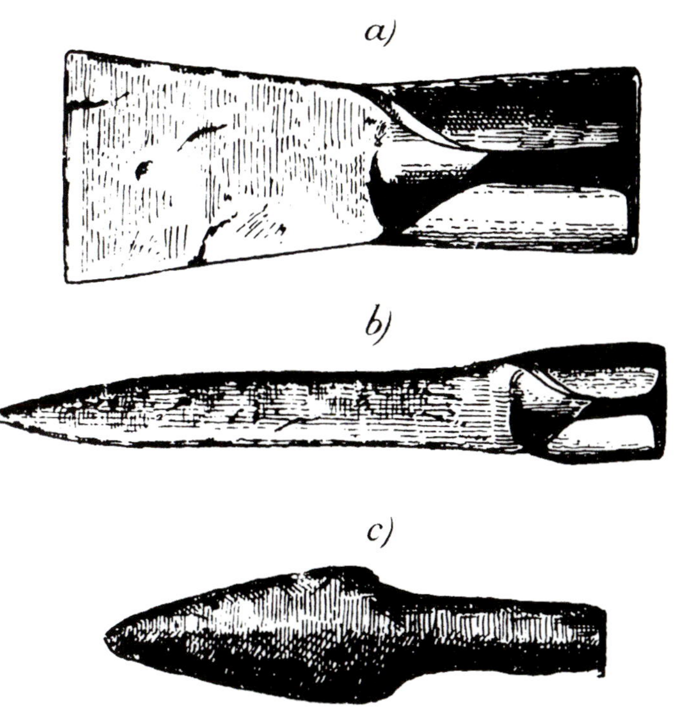

GOTTLIEB SCHUMACHER, TELL EL-MUTESELLIM, VOL. I

IRON IMPLEMENTS found in a 10th century blacksmith's workshop at Megiddo: a) a hoe; b) a plowshare; and c) an ox goad.

times, indicates that the Philistines had no role in the development of early iron metallurgy. This overlooks the fact that at Tel Mor, which served as the harbor for ancient Ashdod, Moshe Dothan (who also excavated Ashdod) found extensive evidence for 12th century B.C. metalworking activity, including tuyères, crucibles and copper spatter, the bits and droplets of copper that fall out when molten copper is poured into a crucible.‡ True, this all relates not to iron, but to the casting of molten copper, but it indicates the sort of background usually associated with the development of iron metallurgy. Dothan also found iron slag from the 10th century B.C. In addition, at Ashdod itself, Dothan found a single-edged knife from about 1000 B.C. and a large blade-like object and an axe from the end of the 10th century B.C.

What is puzzling—and still difficult to understand—is the distribution of carburized as opposed to noncarburized iron. For example, the iron objects from Philistine Ashdod mentioned above are not carburized at all.

We have analyzed iron objects from several other sites in Palestine, but unfortunately these objects do not include the 12th to early 11th century iron

‡Our analysis of this material led to the conclusion that Tel Mor served as a recycling or reprocessing center for the impoverished bronze industry of the 12th century B.C.

objects from Megiddo. At Taanach, we did extensive work on 10th century iron objects; most showed some degree of carburization. Yet the evidence was not consistent and objects that one would have expected to be made of steel, such as a chisel, were made of wrought iron. Of the two plowshares from Taanach that we examined, one was made of carburized iron, the other was not. We have no explanation for this inconsistency. At Tell Jemmeh, near Gaza, a site we would naturally associate with the Philistines, iron objects probably dating to the 10th century (although some modern investigators date them later) show little or no evidence of carburization. These objects, along with the ones from Ashdod, certainly provide no support for any claim to Philistine superiority in the technology of ironworking. Yet the 11th century iron knife from Tomb 562 at Tell el-Far'ah (south) showed evidence for carburization, while two others from the contemporaneous Tomb 220 did not—again the same inconsistency as at Taanach. From Tomb 240, probably of the 10th century, an iron dagger presented excellent evidence for carburization.

Clearly, our sample base is still too small to provide data for meaningful conclusions. We can present good arguments for the role of the Philistines in the early development of iron technology, but these arguments can, at present, only be supported, not substantiated by the existing analytical evidence.

Having looked at the objects themselves, let us now consider what little evidence we have relating to ironworking installations. It is sad but true that until the last 20 or 25 years most field archaeologists focused their attention on the excavation of monumental public and administrative buildings, on religious and ceremonial centers, and on cemeteries where there was a good chance of finding rich burial goods. Thus, we still know little about domestic architecture and the routine of daily life, and practically nothing about the industrial centers of the ancient world. Moreover, sometimes what are in fact pottery kilns for firing pottery have been mistakenly described as metalworking installations. Published examples of this error include the so-called "furnaces" from Beth Shemesh stratum IV (room 490) and stratum III (room 441), and from Tell Deir Alla (phase B).*

In the early part of this century, Sir Flinders Petrie excavated some "furnaces" at Tell Jemmeh near Gaza. These furnaces probably date to the 9th to 8th centuries B.C. As Petrie correctly observed, they were forging furnaces, not smelting furnaces. It would be helpful to know more about these discoveries, but unfortunately Petrie published only the briefest account and nothing is left of the remains at the present time.

During the first excavations at Megiddo, 1903–1905, Gottlieb Schumacher identified a blacksmith's workshop consisting of a small room very likely from the Solomonic period. Again, few details were published, apart from references to the discovery of ash and slag and a substance identified as iron ore. Associated with the workshop was a hoard of iron artifacts including a hoe (a), a plowshare (b), and an ox-goad (c). This hoard is very similar to the one from Taanach that we have studied, but, alas, the Megiddo hoard seems to have vanished, so there is no possibility of subjecting it to metallurgical analysis.

To summarize and conclude, the evidence is strong that iron technology developed in the Aegean and was probably brought to Palestine by the Sea Peoples, and perhaps by the Philistines themselves. Based on excavated evidence, it appears that the Philistines did have a monopoly of sorts on ironworking, as reflected in the passage from 1 Samuel. Iron weapons are found at Philistine sites only; at Israelite sites we find iron agricultural implements, as reflected in the literary tradition preserved in the Bible.

In my view, however, the Philistine ironworking monopoly was political, not technological. What is described in the passage from 1 Samuel is not a Philistine technological monopoly supported by metalworking secrets known only to the Philistines. At least at the present, we have no evidence of Philistine ironworking technological superiority; indeed, the evidence regarding deliberate carburization of iron at Philistine sites is inconsistent, some artifacts showing deliberate carburization and others, quite late, showing no carburization. The restrictions imposed on the Israelites could thus only have been accomplished as a result of Philistine political control. In order to overthrow Philistine political domination, the tribally organized Israelites finally agreed to band together, to elect Saul as king, and to present a united front against the Philistine pentapolis. Finally, in the early 10th century, King David broke the dominion the Philistines had exercised over much of Palestine.

Our analysis indicates that a common typology of iron artifacts is found throughout Palestine, dating at the latest to the end of the 10th century B.C. But at this point in our research we cannot say whether there was a common ironworking technology. At

*The "furnaces" at Tell Deir Alla have been related to the passage in 1 Samuel 13:19–22, as representing one of the places where the Israelites went down to have their metal implements repaired, but the published plans indicate that what was excavated there were pottery kilns of the channel type, best known from second millennium sites on the island of Crete.

present, the scientific evidence for the early history of ironworking technology is confined to Cyprus and Israel, and even there it is incomplete and inconsistent. We know much more than we did five years ago, but we still have much to learn. We know nothing, for example, about the early period of ironworking in Greece, Turkey or Syria. We have not examined a single piece of iron from Lebanon and we are just beginning to learn something about iron technology in Jordan.

Clearly what is needed is a major international research project designed to explore all facets of the history of early ironworking throughout the ancient world. Until now, our group at the University of Pennsylvania has supplied the entire body of existing scientific evidence relating to ironworking in the eastern Mediterranean during the years 1200–800 B.C. We have, I believe, demonstrated the enormous potential of this research. Whether our project will grow and expand, whether our efforts will encourage other scholars to undertake work in this field remains to be seen.

But we have already advanced beyond the time when Biblical scholars could analyze passages like 1 Samuel 13:19–22 in blissful ignorance of everything except philology. The Biblical authors had a multi-faceted view of their world—of its domestic and industrial life as well as its monuments and ceremonies. It is time that modern scholars attempt to reach the same level of competence. We must strive to recreate, through all the means at our disposal, a world that was taken for granted by its contemporary inhabitants.

[1] Ernst Weidner, "Ausden Tageneines assyrischen Schattenkonigs," *Archiv fur Orientforschung*, Vol. X, pp. 148.

[2] W. G. Lambert, *Babylonian Wisdom Literature*, Oxford University Press, 1960, pp. 146–147, lines 51–52.

[3] R. J. Forbes, "The Coming of Iron," *Jaarbericht... Ex Orient Lux*, 910 (1944–48 [1952]), pp. 207–14.

[4] Trude Dothan, *The Philistines and Their Material Culture* (Yale University Press, 1982), p. 92, Table 1; and Jane Waldbaum, *From Bronze to Iron* (Gotebörg, Sweden: 1978).

We received a number of letters from experienced blacksmiths in response to this article. Read them and Muhly's responses in the Queries and Comments section of the May/June 1983 issue of BAR.

Related Reading

Thomas E. Levy and Mohammad Najjar, "Edom and Copper," BAR, July/August 2006.

Thomas E. Levy and Mohammad Najjar, "Condemned to the Mines," BAR, November/December 2011.

New Light on the Edomites

ITZHAQ BEIT-ARIEH

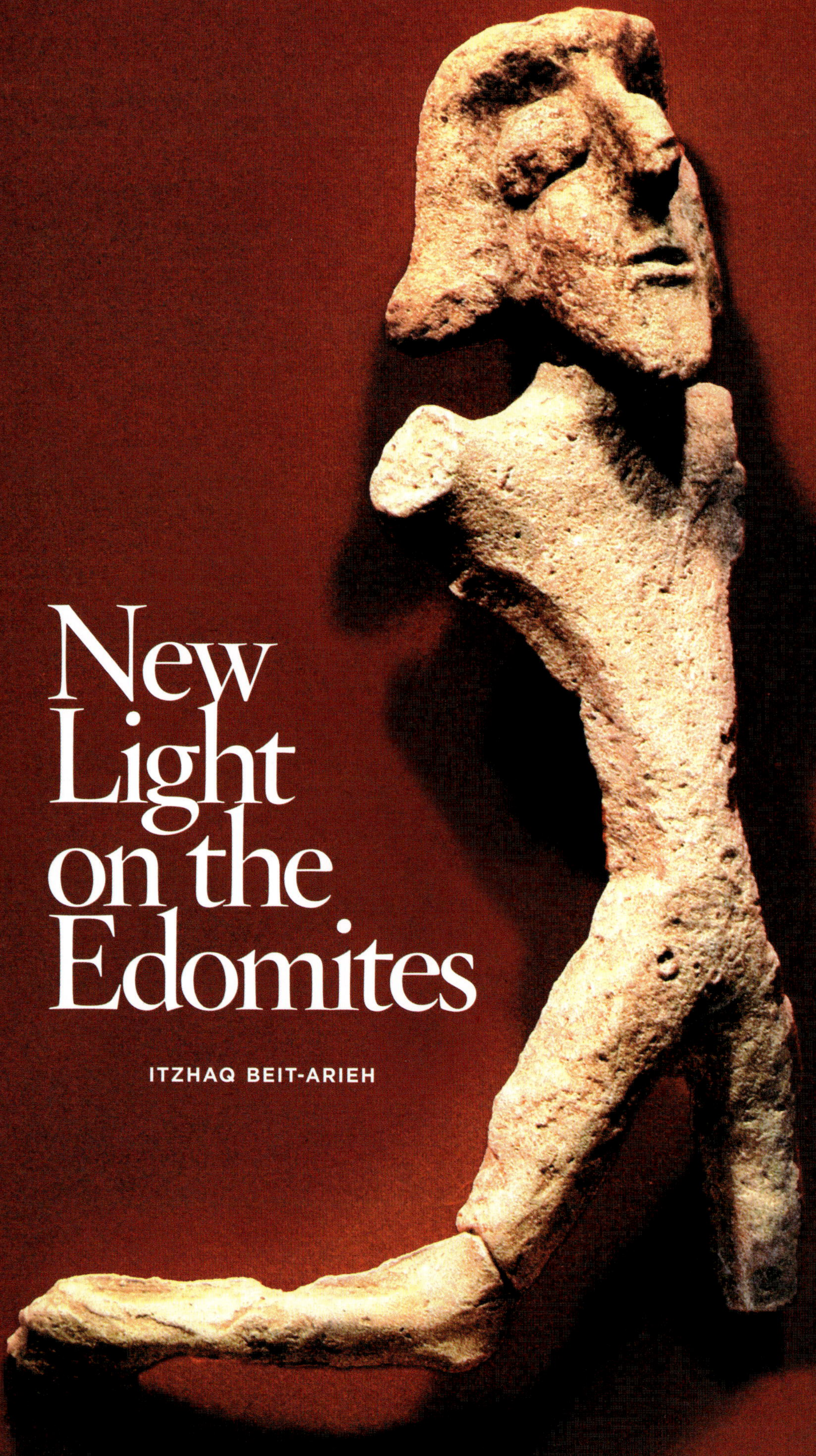

AVRAHAM HAY

Winter is sometimes the best time to dig in Israel's Negev desert—and sometimes the worst. In summer the heat can be stifling; while in winter, cold windy days at times prevent any outdoor work. It was the winter of 1979 when I began to excavate Tel Ira, a site in the eastern Negev.*

As BAR readers know, modern archaeologists never excavate a site in isolation. Any site must be understood in the context of the entire area or region of which it is a part.

So naturally we conducted a detailed survey of the region around Tel Ira. Not surprisingly, we discovered literally scores of small archaeological sites that had previously been unknown.

One morning in January we were riding in our Jeep about five miles east of Tel Ira, slowly climbing the deeply fissured side of a hill above the Malhata Valley, looking for new sites. Our experienced eyes easily detected archaeological remains on the highest part of the flat-topped hill. We quickly drove the remaining way up the hill and jumped out of the Jeep.

Scattered about the site were large quantities of pottery sherds, all from the end of the Iron Age period, the ubiquitous archaeological indication of occupation in the Israelite period.

But as we collected the sherds, we also found some rarer objects—fragments of clay figurines and reliefs. I had been an archaeologist for 22 years. I had excavated more than 20 sites and surveyed vast areas. But never before had I seen a site with figurines and reliefs strewn about the surface.

I knew that obviously the site should be excavated, not simply surveyed on the surface. The funds needed for excavation were, fortunately, not large, but, in the restricted world of archaeological financing, five years would pass before we were able to obtain funding even for a small-budget excavation.

In 1984 we began the excavation of the site—named Horvat Qitmit, the ruins of Qitmit.** With help from the army, our small team from Tel Aviv University's Institute of Archaeology† has now completed 13 short periods of excavation at the site.

The excavation is not yet complete, however, and the research and analysis of the finds has barely begun, but enough is already known—and the material is so exciting—to justify what must be regarded as a preliminary report to BAR readers.

We now know that we are uncovering the first Edomite shrine ever excavated. Moreover, this Edomite shrine is located not in Edom but in ancient Judah, a fact, as we shall see, that has very considerable geopolitical significance,

Until barely 50 years ago, our sole information about the Edomites came from the Bible. We knew of the land of Edom east of the Jordan and south of the land of Ammon and Moab. We also knew that the Edomites were the hated enemy of the Israelites.

In the Biblical genealogies, Jacob's twin brother Esau is the ancestral founder of the Edomites (Genesis 36). Jacob and Esau struggled even in the womb (Genesis 25:22). When Rebecca, their mother, pregnant with twins, inquired of the Lord, she was told:

"Two nations are in your womb,
Two separate peoples shall issue from
your body;
One people shall be mightier than the other,
And the older shall serve the younger."

Genesis 25:23

Esau was the firstborn, red and hairy. He became a hunter who sold his birthright to Jacob for a mess of pottage. By trickery, Jacob also obtained his dying father's blessing, making Jacob master over Esau in fulfillment of the prophecy given Rebecca. When Esau learned what had happened, he was furious and sought to kill Jacob. Warned by his mother, Jacob fled to the land of her brother Laban.

When Jacob returned more than 20 years later, the two brothers were reconciled in tearful embrace. But they never really got along together, despite—or perhaps because of—their fraternal relationship.

Unlike Jacob, Esau took wives from among the Canaanite women. Esau then took his family to settle in another country.

A KNEELING MAN. This 6-inch-high figurine with a stick-like body was found in the enclosed area of the *bamah* at Qitmit. Fragments of additional figurines found nearby suggest that he was one of a dozen or so in the vicinity of the *bamah*. It is possible that he may be kneeling in prayer.

The ruins at Qitmit constitute the first Edomite shrine ever excavated, and thus contribute enormously to our understanding of Edomite religious practices. Located in the heart of the Judahite settlement of the eastern Negev, Qitmit provides evidence of the Edomite conquest of this Judahite territory at about the time of the fall of Judah in 586 B.C., or a few years later.

*On behalf of the Institute of Archaeology, Tel Aviv University, and the Israel Department of Antiquities.

**I named the site after a small wadi at the foot of the site, named Wadi Qatamat in Arabic and Nahal Qitmit in Hebrew. "Qatamat" in Arabic means dusty, ashy sand. The Hebrew name is derived from the Mishnah and means ashes.

†The expedition was directed by the author and included students of Tel Aviv University's Institute of Archaeology, as well as a number of volunteers. The scientific team included Dani Weiss and Dani Goldschmidt, area supervisors; Liora Freud, area supervisor and registrar; Joseph Kapelyan, surveyor and drawer of finds; Moshe Weinberg and Avraham Hay, photographers. The pottery restoration was carried out in the institute's laboratory by Naomi Nedav, Mira Barak, Yona Shapira and Rahel Pelta.

"Esau took his wives, his sons and daughters, and all the members of his household, his cattle and all his livestock, and all the property that he had acquired in the land of Canaan, and went to another land because of his brother Jacob. For their possessions were too many for them to dwell together, and the land where they sojourned could not support them because of their livestock. So Esau settled in the hill country of Seir—Esau being Edom" (Genesis 36:6–8).

The powerful animosity between the Israelites and the Edomites is reflected in the divine admonition in Deuteronomy 23:7: "You shall not abhor an Edomite for he is your kinsman." The abhorrence made the divine command necessary.

From the viewpoint of the Biblical historian, the source of much of Israel's antagonism toward Edom could lay in the Edomites' refusal to allow the Israelites to pass through Edom on their way to the Promised Land following the Exodus from Egypt, or more probably, the antagonistic relationship between the two neighbors may have had an influence on the telling of the Biblical story.

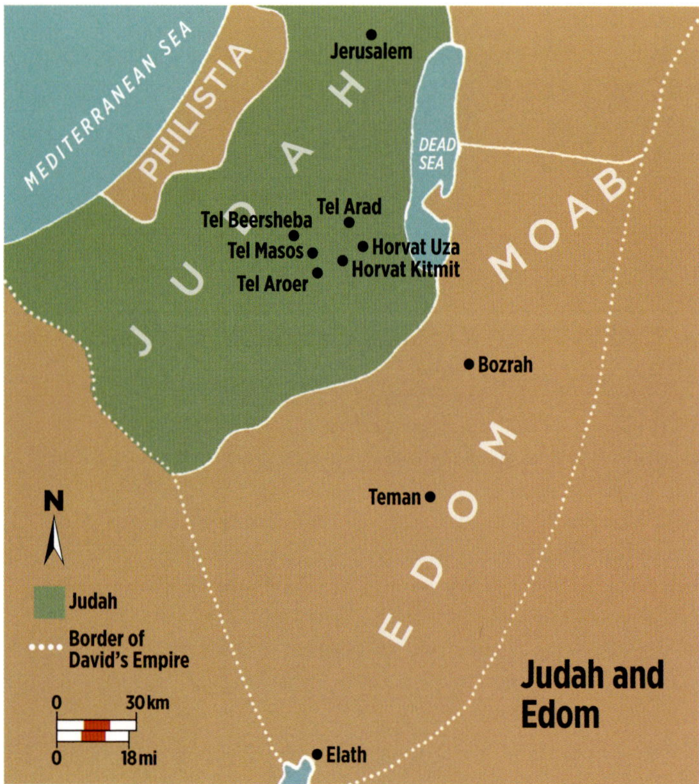

BOUNDARIES OF RIVAL KINGDOMS. Mortal enemies, the Israelites and Edomites fought one another from the time of Saul (c. 1020–1004 B.C.) until the conquest of Edom during David's reign (c. 1004–965 B.C.). Israelite rule over Edom lasted until the reign of Joram, king of Judah, when the Edomites successfully rebelled and established their own king (2 Kings 8:20). Reconquered during the reign of the Judahite king Amaziah (798–769 B.C), the Edomites once again freed themselves during Ahaz's rule (733–727 B.C.). The Edomites subsequently flourished until the Babylonian destruction of Judah in 586 B.C.

After leaving Kadesh-Barnea (which bordered on the land of Edom), the Israelites sent a message to the king of Edom:

"Thus says your brother Israel: 'You know all the hardships that have befallen us; that our ancestors went down to Egypt, that we dwelt in Egypt a long time and that the Egyptians dealt harshly with us and our ancestors. We cried to the Lord and He heard our plea, and He sent a messenger who freed us from Egypt. Now we are in Kadesh, the town on the border of your territory. Allow us then to cross your country. We will not pass through fields or vineyards, and we will not drink water from wells. We will follow the king's highway, turning off neither to the right nor to the left until we have crossed your territory.'

"But Edom answered him, 'You shall not pass through us, else we will go out against you with the sword.'

"'We will keep to the beaten track' the Israelites said to them, 'and if we let our cattle drink your water, we will pay for it. We ask only for passage on foot—it is but a small matter.'

"But they replied, 'You shall not pass through!'

"And Edom went out against them in heavy force, strongly armed. So Edom would not let Israel cross their territory, and Israel turned away from them" (Numbers 20:14–21; see also Judges 11:17).

So the Israelites were forced to take another, more circuitous route.

According to Joshua 24:4, the Lord gave Esau—that is the Edomites—the hill country of Seir: "I gave Esau the hill country of Seir as his possession, while Jacob and his children went down to Egypt" (Joshua 24:4).

The land of Edom extended from the Wadi* el-Hasa (Nahal Zered in the Bible, which runs into the Dead Sea) on the north to the mountain slopes north of Eilat on the south. Edom's western border was the Arabah, the rift that extends south from the Dead Sea to the Red Sea. On the east, Edom's border was the desert. The country sits on a high

*A wadi is a dry river or streambed that flows only as a result of flash floods in winter.

plateau, 3,500 feet above sea level. The adjacent Dead Sea is nearly 1,300 feet *below* sea level. The climate of the area is desert-like, although it has some water sources and certain areas are suitable for dry (that is, unirrigated) farming.

Israel and Edom fought with each other throughout the period of the Israelite kingdom. Saul, the first king of Israel, we are told, waged war against Edom (1 Samuel 14:47). His successor, King David, defeated the Edomites, and they consequently became his vassals (2 Samuel 8:13–14).

Israel apparently ruled Edom throughout David's reign, as well as during Solomon's reign. As late as the reign of King Jehoshaphat (870–846 B.C.), we are told that "there was no king in Edom" (1 Kings 22:47).

In the reign of Jehoshaphat's son Joram (sometimes written Jehoram), the Edomites successfully rebelled and set up a king of their own (2 Kings 8:20): "Thus Edom fell away from Judah to this day" (2 Kings 8:22).

In the reign of Amaziah (798–769 B.C.), Edom again came under Judah's control; Amaziah, we are told, "defeated 10,000 Edomites in the Valley of Salt, and he captured Sela in battle" (2 Kings 14:7; see also 2 Chronicles 25:11–12). Amaziah's son Azariah (or Uzziah) apparently completed the reconquest of Edom, for we are told that he restored Eilat to Judah and built it up (2 Kings 14:22).

Unwilling to accept a situation in which it was cut off from the maritime traffic of the Red Sea (as a result of the loss of Eilat), Edom managed to throw off the Judahite yoke during the reign of King Ahaz, at least to the extent that Edomites again settled Eilat—again the Bible adds, "to this day" (2 Kings 16:6).

For the next 150 years or so—at least until the Babylonian destruction of Judah in 586 B.C.—Edom flourished economically and enjoyed the high point of its political power. At the same time, the northern kingdom of Israel was conquered and destroyed by the Assyrians; and the southern kingdom of Judah was under increasing pressure, first from the Assyrians and then from the Babylonians. Edom, on the other hand, by means of shrewd diplomacy and cautious political policies managed to avoid getting involved in the aggressive campaigns of the superpowers and, despite the conquests of Assyrians and Babylonians in the region of Edom, managed to preserve its geographical integrity.

The implacable feelings of enmity and hatred between Israel and Edom—the result of this long history of strife and warfare—is clearly reflected in the prophecies of Israel's greatest prophets. The

Head of a Goddess

The horned headdress, which is the divine crown *par excellence* in the ancient Near East, identifies the figure as a deity. A comparison with the various statuettes found at Qitmit makes it possible to identify this particular head as the head of a goddess rather than of a god.

The head, including the prominent knob on top and the neck, is wheel-made. It is fashioned in the shape of the well-known rattle found at many Iron Age sites.

Pieces modeled by hand were then applied to mark the facial features, hairdress and horns. Traces of their untidy application are visible on the back of the head, the chin and the neck. The face is painted red, and the hair is black.

The asymmetry of the face is particularly noticeable in the unequal eyes; they were incised on bits of clay that were then applied to the face. Again, there is no symmetry in the eyebrows and locks of hair. This lack of symmetry is also evident in the modeling of the mouth, which gives the face a lively expression enhanced by a captivating smile.

A divine mitre with three horns is quite rare and is known only on metal statuettes representing armed goddesses said to have come from Syria or Phoenicia. One such figurine was found in Galilee. However, none of these statuettes comes from controlled excavations. Hence the head from Qitmit may be of importance in reevaluating these metal pieces.

The meaning of the third horn is not clear. Some scholars consider it to be a remnant of the uraeus worn on the forehead by the Egyptian pharaohs. Another possible explanation would seek its origin in the third horn on the headdress of the "Syrian goddess," known from Syrian cylinder seals of the second millennium.

Any attempt to identify the goddess meets with difficulties, as the statue is incomplete and her attributes are unknown. Moreover, there is no certainty that she was

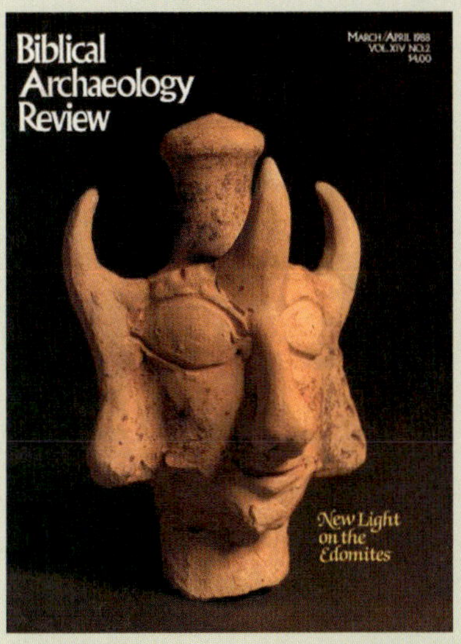

the sole deity worshipped at the site. Any tentative attempt at identifying the goddess would have to rely on comparisons with similar statuettes and on other objects, found at the site, that may be considered part of her cult. —PIRHIYA BECK

ITZHAQ BEIT-ARIEH

Figurine Fragments Led to Discovery of Edomite Shrine

While conducting an archaeological survey in the eastern Negev, Itzhaq Beit-Arieh made an extraordinary find on a flat-topped hill overlooking the Malhata Valley, a site that he would later name Horvat Qitmit. Mized with the numerous, common, pottery sherds strewn over the landscape, among which were some Edomite pottery sherds, he found fragments of clay figurines and reliefs, artifacts that he had never before seen on the surface of sites in this archaeologically rich area.

Excavation of the site revealed even more of the cultic objects. Those shown here *in situ* (opposite, top) include an ostrich, a hand and a dagger, at center, from left to right respectively.

Heads from human figurines (right) and fragments from larger statues (shown on p. 214) were also among the finds. The heads exhibit similar features that were mostly hand-modeled and attached to the heads separately, although some heads were produced from molds. Some of the figures consist of a head and torso only, with the lower limbs replaced by a triangular wedge, as in the example at upper center. The wedge was probably used to insert such figures into a slot on a cult stand or on some other object.

The discovery of relatively great amounts of Edomite pottery, the Edomite script, and these objects—some of which are similar to figurines that have been found in the land of Edom—led the excavator to propose that Horvat Qitmit was an Edomite cult-center. The first Edomite cult-center ever excavated, it is dated to about the time of the Babylonian destruction of Jerusalem in 586 B.C.

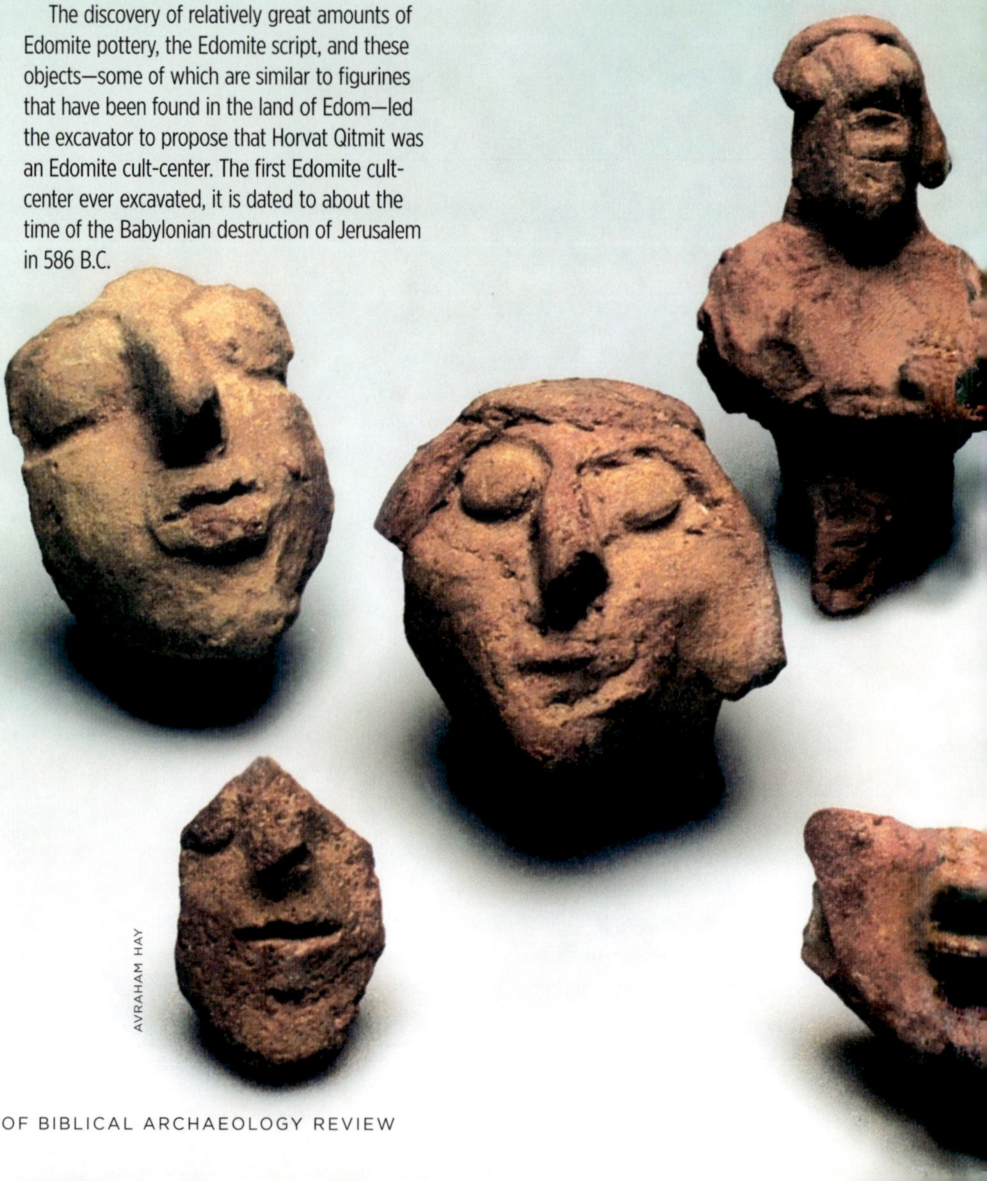

AVRAHAM HAY

MOSHE WEINBERG

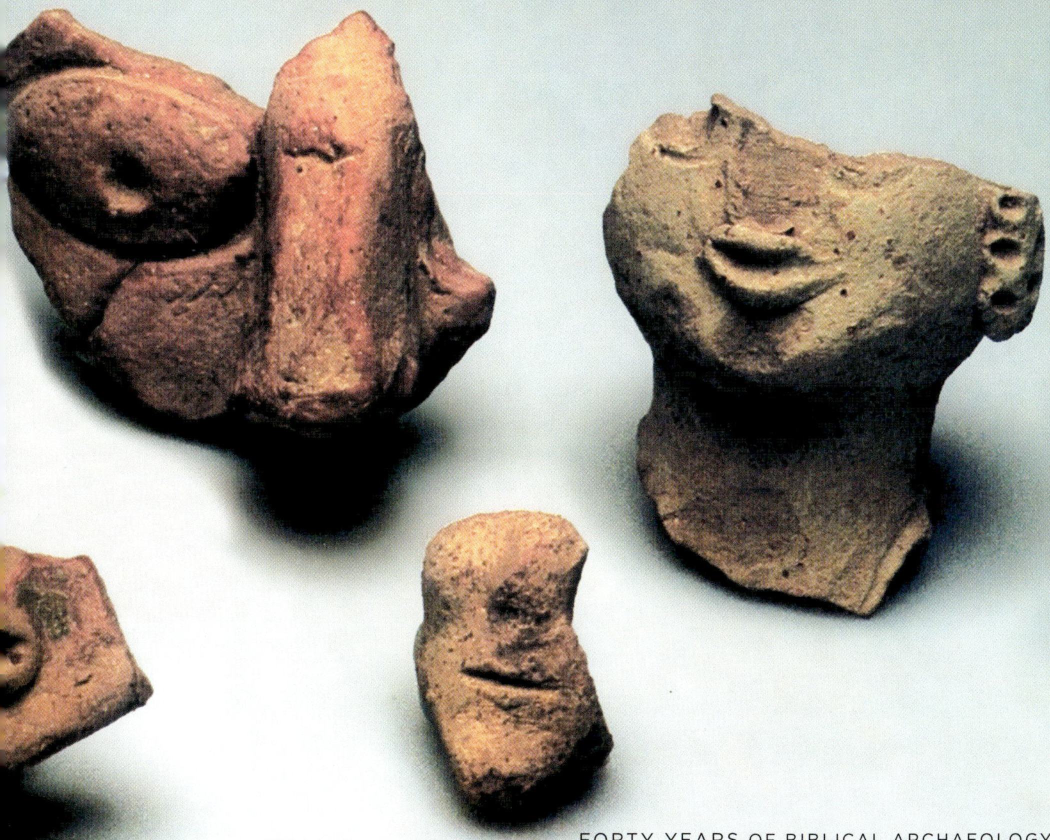

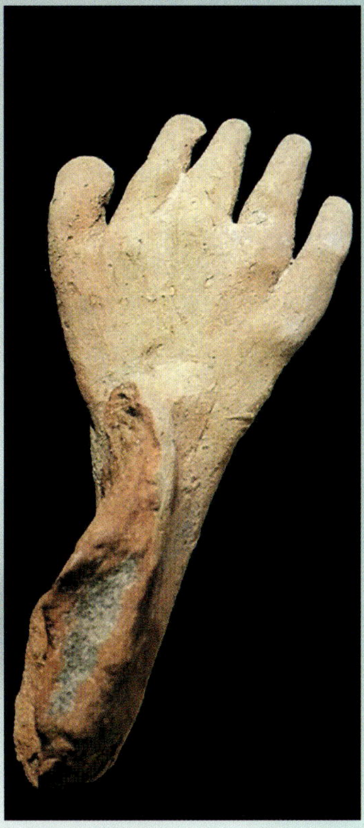

AVRAHAM HAY

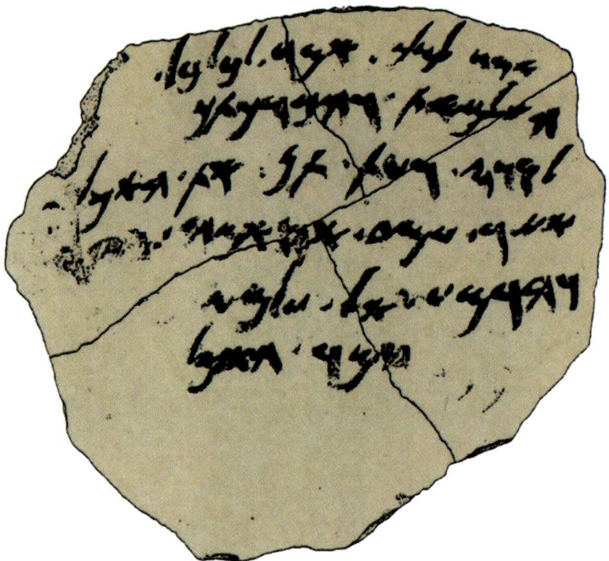

ADA YARDENI

EDOMITE OSTRACON from Horvat 'Uza, a Judean fortress in the eastern Negev. The discovery of this ostracon provided the first clear evidence of Edomite penetration into the Negev. The fortress probably fell into the Edomites' hands at about the time of the Babylonian conquest of Judah (c. 586 B.C.), the time to which the ostracon is dated. Six lines of writing, in the Edomite script and language, form the following, virtually complete message on the 4 1/2-inch by 3 3/4-inch pottery sherd "(Thus) said Lumalak (or <E>limelek): Say to Blbl! / Are you well? I bless you / by Quas. And now give the food (grain) / that Ahi'ma (or o).../ And may U[z] iel lift [it] upon (the altar?).../ [lest] the food become leavened (?)." This short letter was probably addressed to the Edomite commander of the fort by a high Edomite official. After a standard salutation and invocation of the blessing of the Edomite god Qos (Quas), the message commands the recipient to give some food, possibly unleavened dough, to the bearer of the ostracon.

prophet Jeremiah in his prophecy concerning the nations says of Edom:

> "And Edom shall become an astonishment. Every one that passes by it will be astonished and will hiss at all the plagues thereof. It shall be like the overthrow of Sodom and Gomorrah and the neighbor cities thereof, says the Lord. No man shall abide there, neither shall any son of man dwell therein" (Jeremiah 49:17–18).

The prophet Ezekiel pronounced judgment on Edom with these words: "Thus said the Lord God: I will stretch out my hand against Edom and cut off from it man and beast, and I will lay it in ruins" (Ezekiel 25:13).

The Edomites did not come to Judah's aid when the Babylonians attacked Jerusalem in the early sixth century B.C.—thus there was no limit to Israel's enmity. Listen to the prophet Obadiah:

"Thus said my Lord God concerning Edom:
I will make you least among nations,
You shall be most despised.
Your arrogant heart has seduced you,
You who dwell in clefts of the rock,
In your lofty abode.
You think in your heart,
'Who can pull me down to earth?'
Should you nest as high as the eagle,
Should your eyrie be lodged 'mong the stars,
Even from there I will pull you down
—declares the Lord

• • •

"For the outrage to your brother Jacob,
Disgrace shall engulf you,
And you shall perish forever.
On that day when you stood aloof,
When aliens carried off his goods,
When foreigners entered his gates
And cast lots for Jerusalem,
You were as one of them.
How could you gaze with glee
On your brother that day,
On his day of calamity!
How could you gloat
Over the people of Judah
On that day of ruin!
How could you loudly jeer
On a day of anguish!
How could you enter the gate of My people
On its day of disaster,
Gaze in glee with the others
On its misfortune
On its day of disaster,

And lay hands on its wealth
On its day of disaster,
How could you stand at the passes
To cut down its fugitives!
How could you betray those who fled
On that day of anguish!
As you did, so shall it be done to you;
Your conduct will be requited!"

Obadiah 1:1–4, 10–15

Other prophets, such as Isaiah, Joel, Amos and Malachi, also vented their wrath on Edom.

The earliest archaeological evidence for the Edomite tribes in the land of Edom was discovered by the American rabbi-archaeologist Nelson Glueck* in the 1930s and 1940. In his surveys east of the Jordan, Glueck identified as Edomite some sites he dated to the 13th to 12th centuries B.C. This was the same period when other Semitic peoples—such as the Moabites and the Ammonites (east of the Jordan) and the Israelites (west of the Jordan)—were consolidating their tribal units into what we might call proto-nations. Glueck correctly identified some of the pottery as Edomite, but it is dated to a much later period—the eighth to seventh centuries B.C. The archaeological evidence from the 13th to 12th centuries in the territory of Edom is rather sparse, but it does point to some kind of early occupation.[1]

This archaeological evidence is supplemented by an Egyptian papyrus document (Papyrus Anastasi VI) dating to the end of the 13th century B.C., in which an Egyptian official, who is overseeing the frontier, reports on certain Shasu tribes in Edom. According to this report, "[We] have finished letting the Shasu tribes of Edom pass the fortress (of) Mer-ne-Ptah Hotep-hisr-Maat. Life, prosperity, [and] health, which is [in] Tjeku...."

This report, one of a group that served as models for schoolboys, presents the form in which an official on the eastern frontier of Egypt would report the passage of Edomite tribes into the better pasturage of the Delta.

Strangely enough, that is the only extra-Biblical source that sheds light on the Edomites in this period.

The next extra-Biblical reference to Edom comes from Assyria 400 years later. The gap can possibly be explained by the fact that there were no campaigns against Edom either by the Assyrians or by the Egyptians during this period. After this gap, several Assyrian rulers refer to Edom or Edomite kings in their victory inscriptions. Adad-nirari (reigned 810–783 B.C.) mentions Edom in his list of conquests. Tiglath-Pileser III (745–727 B.C.) campaigned in Syria-Palestine and subdued a number of rulers who paid him tribute, including Qosmalaku, king of Edom (spelled U-du-mu-a-a in Akkadian cuneiform). In 712 B.C., Sargon II fought against a coalition of states in the region, including Ashdod, Judah, Moab and Edom.

After his famous campaign against Judah in 701 B.C., Sennacherib tells us that Aiaramu, king of Edom, was among those who paid tribute to him. During the reign of Esarhaddon (680–669 B.C.), Qosgabri, king of Edom, is mentioned among the 12 kings of the region who contributed money toward the construction of Esarhaddon's royal palace in Nineveh. This same king of Edom is mentioned again during the reign of Esarhaddon's successor, Ashurbanipal (668–633 B.C.). The beginning of this same king's name (Qosg...) was also found on a seal impression excavated at Uum el-Biyara.**

In a series of Hebrew letters recovered from the excavation of the fortress at Arad by the late Yohanan Aharoni, the Edomites are also mentioned. Aharoni notes that the letters came from stratum VI and suggest that this stratum was destroyed by the Edomites in 595 B.C.† According to Aharoni, the letter mentioning the Edomites is addressed to the Judahite commander of the Arad fort, who is ordered to send soldiers to reinforce the garrison at Ramat Negeb in the eastern Negev, because an attack by the Edomites is anticipated—"lest the Edomites come," to use the language found on the Hebrew ostracon (an inscribed pottery sherd).

That Edom appears so frequently in inscriptions connected with the Assyrian and Babylonian military campaigns testifies to Edom's importance as a political power in the eastern Mediterranean world at this time. In the seventh century B.C., Edom was apparently at the height of its cultural and political development. To its neighbor Judah, Edom no doubt loomed as a menace threatening Judah's very existence, especially as Assyrian power declined (late seventh century B.C.) and as Babylonian pressure on Judah mounted, toward the end of the seventh century.

Pottery from this period that can be identified as Edomite was first identified by Nelson Glueck at Tell el-Kheleifeh, on the northern shore of the Gulf of Eilat‡ There Glueck excavated a fort built in the eighth century B.C. and destroyed in the

*See Floyd S. Fierman, "Rabbi Nelson Glueck—An Archaeologist's Secret Life in the Service of the OSS," BAR, September/October 1986.

**The seal impression reads: LQOSG[BR] MLK'[DM], "Belonging to Qosg[br] King of E[dom]."

† See Anson F. Rainey, "The Saga of Eliashib," BAR, March/April 1987.

‡ Gary D. Pratico, "Where is Ezion-Geber? A Reappraisal of the Site Archaeologist Nelson Glueck Identified as King Solomon's Red Sea Port," BAR, September/October 1986.

ITZHAQ BEIT-ARIEH

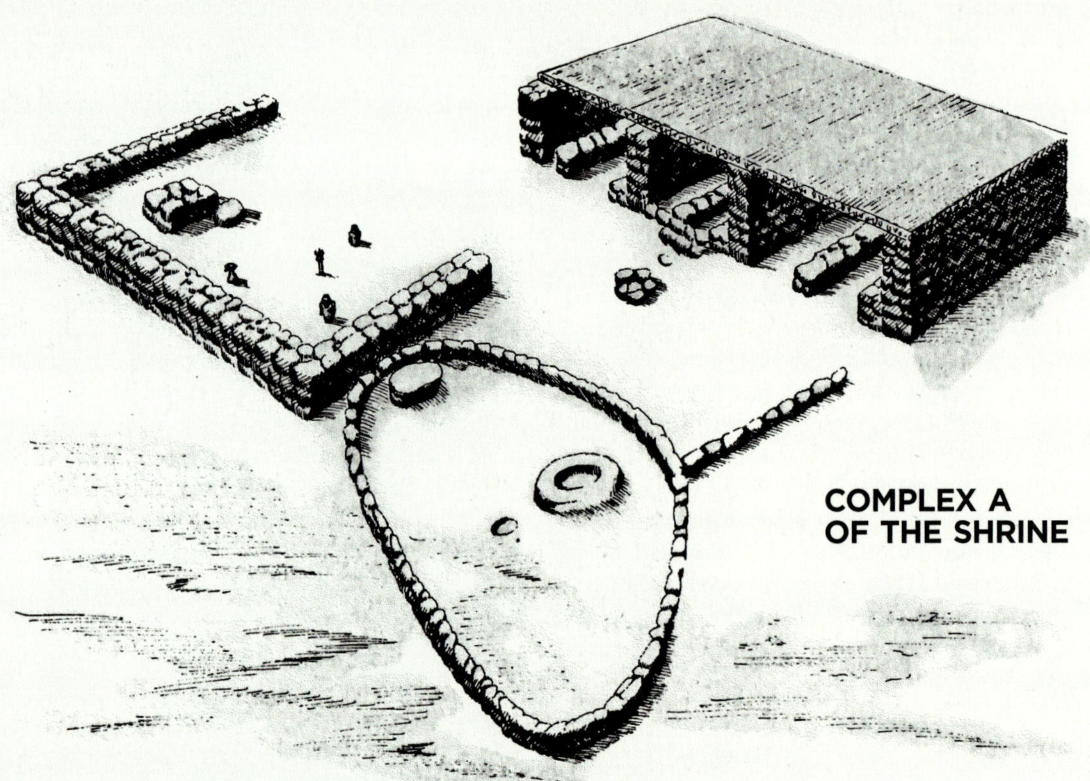

COMPLEX A OF THE SHRINE

JUDITH DEKEL

ITZHAQ BEIT-ARIEH

ITZHAQ BEIT-ARIEH

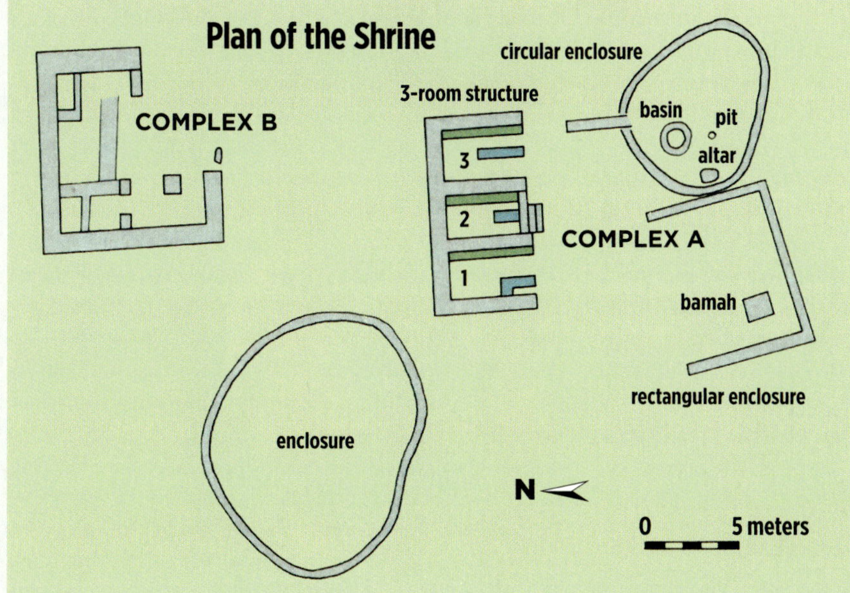

Cultic Center at Qitmit

The Qitmit site contains two areas with structures (see plan). The southern area (Complex A) has been excavated; the northern area (Complex B) is still being excavated. To the west, outside these two areas, are two oval enclosures (one is omitted on the plan). Complex A consists of a three-room, rectangular structure; a circular enclosure with a basin, small pit and altars; and a *bamah* bounded on three sides by stone walls. The three-room structure (in foreground of photo, opposite) measures 34 by 18 feet and has two steps (lower center in photo) leading up to the center room. A layer of ashes a foot deep covered the crushed chalk floor in each of the three, 6½-by-13-foot rooms. During a second phase of construction, some of the structure's walls were doubled in thickness (green areas on plan), and 3-foot-high podiums (blue areas), topped by broad, flat stone slabs, were added to each room. These podiums may have supported statues or cult vessels used in some ceremony.

The *bamah*, a low platform of fieldstones, measures 3 by 4 feet. It is preserved to a height of 16 inches. Large chunks of dislodged plaster were found scattered about the bounded area of the *bamah*. This plaster had been used to fill in the fissures in the bedrock of the enclosure in order to create a smooth surface on which various cult objects could be placed.

A basin and small altar (above) are the principal structures in Complex A's circular enclosure. The round, 3-foot-wide basin, center foreground, is plastered on the inside, over its rim and on the outside as well; it was probably used for water storage. The 31-inch-high altar, beside the man, undoubtedly served for animal sacrifices. A close-up of the altar (left, center) reveals details of its construction: It consists of a flat flintstone, 31 by 24 inches, set on a base of smaller stones. Stone slabs line the upper part of a 3-foot-deep pit beside the basin (see plan). The author thinks it may have served as a drain-pit for spillover water from the basin, or for blood from animal sacrifices performed on the altar.

Artist Judith Dekel has reconstructed Complex A as it may have appeared (below, opposite). Some cult stands, such as the one on p. 216 and the three-horned statue seen on the cover (see p. 207), stand near the *bamah*, ready to be used in ceremonies we can only imagine.

GRASPING AT AIR, a life-size hand (below), at the end of a flexed arm, curls around a missing object. Originally part of a warrior statue, the hand may once have held a weapon. A dagger, decorated by knobs at the end of its hilt (left), was attached originally to a warrior statue. Such statues, which stood about 2 feet high, are thought to have served as surrogates for the people who placed them in the temple.

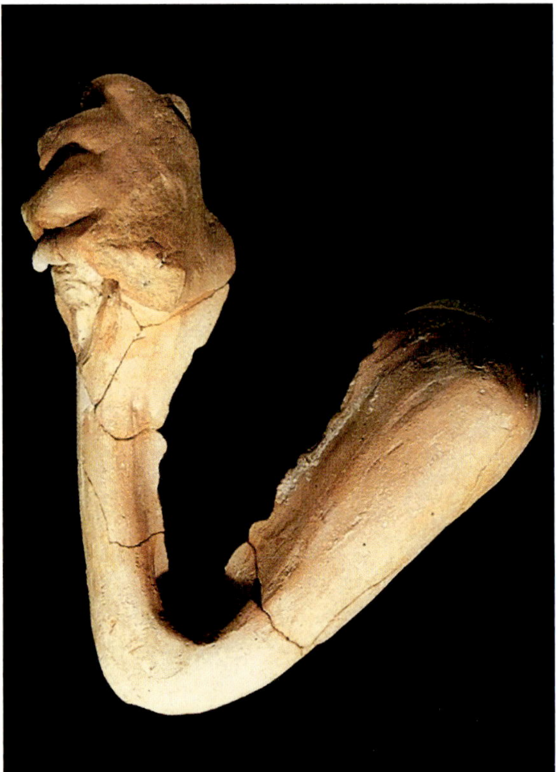

early sixth century B.C. In stratum IV, Glueck found a large quantity of pottery painted with geometric designs, some with triangular knobs and some undecorated plain pottery of distinct shape, all of which markedly differed from contemporaneous Judahite pottery. Glueck denominated this distinctive pottery repertoire as Edomite, and the designation has withstood the test of time.

Similar pottery has now been found at a number of sites on the Edomite plateau, confirming that this pottery is specific to this area. Especially important is an excavation directed by Dr. Crystal Bennett of the British School of Archaeology at Buseirah, which is apparently the Edomite city of Bozrah, mentioned several times in the Bible as the capital of Edom.* A number of archaeological surveys in the area of ancient Edom have also recovered quantities of Edomite pottery. On the basis of this considerable evidence, we can now say that Edomite pottery is richly diverse and technically accomplished.

Edomite pottery has also been found in both the eastern and western Negev in Israelite strata from the seventh and the beginning of the sixth centuries B.C. These sites include Arad, Horvat 'Uza, Tel Malhata, Tel Ira, Tel Masos and Tel Aroer in the eastern Negev and Tel Sera and Tel Haror in the western Negev. Edomite pottery has been found as far west as the fort at Kadesh-Barnea in the southwest Negev highlands, and in an Iron Age site recently excavated at Hasevah in the Arabah.

At most of these Negev sites, only small quantities of Edomite pottery were found, primarily painted sherds. At three sites, however—Tel Malhata, Tel Aroer and Tel Ira—larger quantities of pottery including some complete undecorated vessels were recovered.

Not only Edomite pottery, but Edomite writing has now been identified. Unfortunately, all these inscriptions are in very fragmentary condition. For this reason their contents tell us very little, but they do tell us a great deal about the paleography of

*Other sites in the area of Edom where Edomite pottery has been found include Umm el-Biyara (perhaps Biblical Selah), Tawilan and a small site named Ghrareh, about 12 miles south of Petra.

the Edomite script and about the structure of the Edomite dialect.

The largest Edomite inscription yet found is on an ostracon from Tell el-Kheleifeh. It is a fragmentary list of names. First identified as Edomite script by Professor Joseph Naveh of the Hebrew University in Jerusalem, it is basically a west Semitic script that reflects the influence of contemporaneous Aramaic script. By the eighth to seventh centuries B.C., this Aramaic script had already begun to penetrate the region along with the Assyrian military campaigns.

Other sites in the Judahite Negev also yielded Edomite inscriptions—two at Tel Aroer and one at Horvat 'Uza. At Tel Aroer, an inscribed seal and a small Edomite ostracon fragment were found. At Horvat 'Uza, we found a complete Edomite ostracon.[2]

The discovery of Edomite pottery and inscriptions at sites in the Judahite Negev naturally raises questions. Obviously, there was some connection between Judah and Edom during the seventh and the beginning of the sixth centuries B.C. Perhaps it consisted of the ordinary commercial relations common between neighboring countries. On the other hand, the Edomite pottery and inscriptions found in the Judahite Negev may have belonged to Edomites who had settled as minority elements among the dominant Judahite population. It might even be possible to interpret the Edomite pottery and inscriptions as evidence of an Edomite conquest of parts of the Judahite Negev.

Based only on the materials I have mentioned, it would be difficult to choose among these three possibilities, possibilities which, incidentally, are not mutually exclusive. But our recent excavation of Horvat Qitmit has convinced me that at least part of the Judahite Negev was at times conquered and occupied by the Edomites.

From the outset, when we first discovered Horvat Qitmit, we knew of its Edomite connection, for some Edomite sherds from the seventh and sixth centuries B.C. were found on the surface among large quantities of other pottery. The fragments of clay figurines and reliefs that were scattered on the surface clearly indicated that this had been a cultic site, destroyed some 2,600 years ago.

After partially excavating the site, we have determined that there was only one archaeological stratum, consisting of two phases.

The site comprises two much-eroded building complexes. The two building complexes are approximately 65 feet apart without any apparent connection. Thus far we have excavated only the southern

A SEA OF SHERDS challenges the patience and keen eyes of the restorers. The uniqueness of many of the artifacts at Qitmit complicated the restoration task, because the restorers had no example to guide them.

AVRAHAM HAY

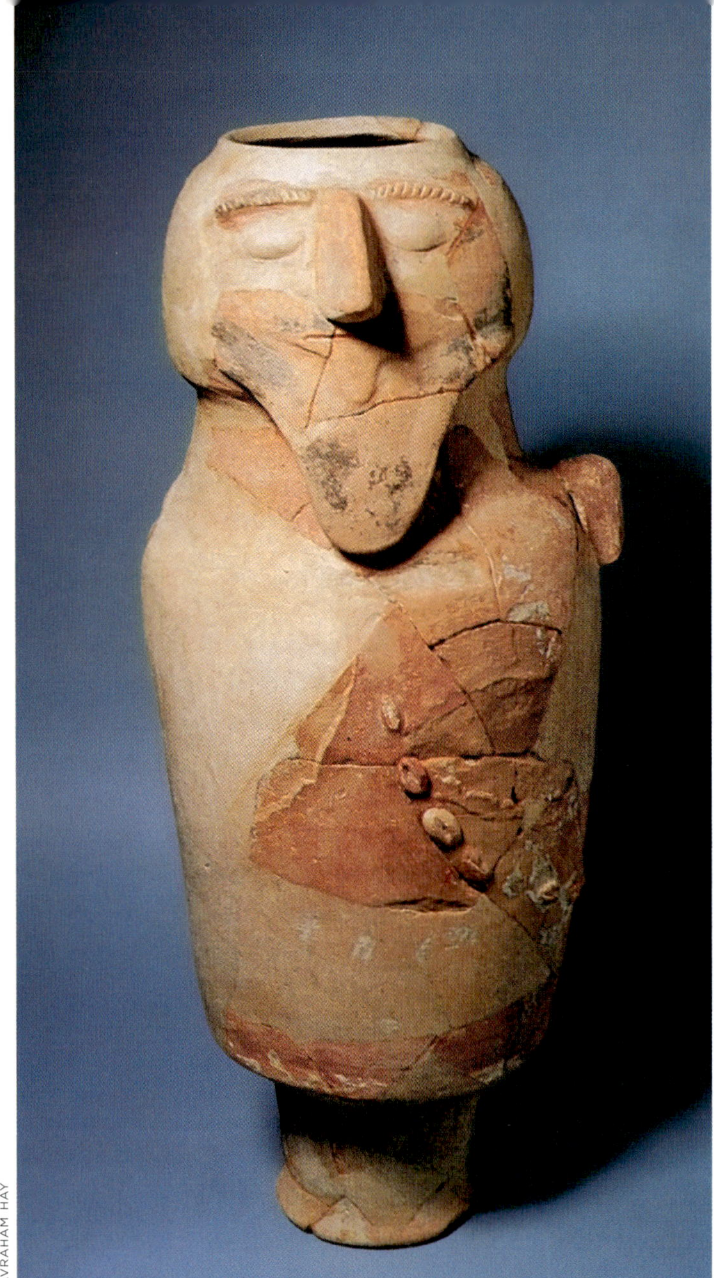

AVRAHAM HAY

ANTHROPOMORPHIC CULT STAND. Still showing traces of the original decorations painted in red and black, this stand bears a heavy-lidded face with a well-trimmed beard. Ritual offerings may have been put in a bowl that was then placed over the hole in the top of the head. This is one of a large number of wheel-made, cylindrical pottery stands found at Horvat Qitmit. An artist depicts them on p. 212 as they may have appeared when in use.

complex (Complex A), which seems to have contained the main part of the temple.

The temple structure in Complex A consists of three contiguous rectangular rooms, each approximately 6 1/2 by 13 feet. Each room opens to the south (the direction of Edom) across its entire width. The middle room is approached by two steps. In the building's second phase, some of the walls were doubled in thickness (green on the plan) and podiums approximately 3 feet high were added inside each of the three rooms (blue on the plan). The podiums are topped by broad, flat stone slabs.

What purpose did these podiums serve? No structural function is apparent. We may speculate that statues and cult vessels connected with some sacrificial ritual were placed on them.

The crushed chalk floor in each of the three rooms was covered with a layer of ash about a foot thick. On the floor and in the layer of ash, we found huge quantities of pottery sherds, as well as the bones of sheep and possibly goats. Some of the bones even have scratch marks from having been chewed.

About 35 feet south of this temple building was an area enclosed on three sides by straight walls—on all sides except the north; that is, this area opened toward the temple structure. Inside the enclosure was a *bamah*, a low platform (preserved only to a height of about 16 inches). The *bamah* was built of medium-size fieldstones set on bedrock. The *bamah* measured about 4 feet by 3 feet.

Fissures in the bedrock within the enclosure had once been filled with plaster to create a smooth surface; large chunks of dislodged plaster were found strewn about the enclosure area.

Another enclosure, this one circular, was located east of the rectangular enclosure, to complete the structure of Complex A. Inside the circular enclosure, we found a small altar made of flintstones set on a stone base, together with a basin made of fieldstones next to the altar. The basin measured about 3 feet in diameter and was plastered on the inside and over its outer rim. A pit nearly 3 feet deep was hewn out of the bedrock a few feet south of the basin. Animals were no doubt sacrificed on the altar. The basin was probably for water storage. The pit probably served as a drain-pit for the spillover water from the basin or for the blood drained from the animal sacrifices.

The complex as a whole probably served as a diverse cultic center, including not only areas for animal sacrifice, but also for ritual meals, the offering of prayers and the performance of other rites. This is confirmed by the extraordinary finds, mostly from the rectangular enclosure area. There we recovered not only everyday pottery vessels, but also various cultic objects, clay statues and figurines.

The cultic objects included a large quantity of wheel-made, cylindrical, cult stands, mostly painted with designs in red and black. Some of these cult stands were fenestrated (with windows). Others had zoomorphic or humanoid figurines attached to the solid bases or placed on projecting ledges, forming scenes of a cultic nature. The figurines are sometimes hollow and sometimes solid, and they include humans, cattle, sheep and birds. One of the figurines is a human-headed sphinx with a bearded face.

AVRAHAM HAY

POTTERY CHALICES DECORATED with pomegranates were among the cultic vessels found at Horvat Qitmit. An intact pomegranate juts down from the right side of one chalice, at center, which also exhibits traces of six more pomegranate decorations that once encircled the vessel. Fragments of another such chalice, left, and pomegranates, right, are also shown. The pomegranate, found throughout the Near East, probably symbolized fertility because of its numerous seeds.

Some of the human figurines portray only the torso, with the lower half of the body represented by a triangular wedge that was evidently inserted in slots in the cult stands or in some other object.

The faces on the human figurines are quite similar. Most are finished by hand, but a few are made from a mold. Some of the human features of the anthropomorphically shaped stands, such as noses and hands, are practically life size. Altogether they have a remarkable sculptural quality.

According to Professor Pirhiya Beck, who is currently studying the iconography of these cult stands, the warrior figures represent the people who placed them in the temple to serve as their surrogates; there the surrogates would constantly worship the Edomite god, calling down his blessing on the person represented by the figurine.

Human figures in the shape of vessels (anthropomorphic vessels) have been found at contemporaneous Israelite sites (for example, at Gezer and Beth-Shemesh), but none is parallel to the Qitmit figurines, except a fragment from Tel Erani. The Tel Erani fragment has a bearded head equal in size to the heads on our stands from Horvat Qitmit. This fragment appears to have once been attached either to a vessel or perhaps even to a cult stand. Cult stands with scenes using human and animal figures are known in the ancient Near East as early as the third millennium B.C. The best known is the famous stand from Tel Ta'anakh from the Late Bronze Age. Another example, found in the Iron Age level at Ashdod, features human figures—musicians, in this case—in the fenestrations.*

Other cultic vessels from Qitmit include three pottery chalices decorated with pomegranates. One of the chalices has an intact pomegranate with traces of six more pomegranates that were once at tached around the outside of the vessel. The pomegranate motif was widespread in the ancient Near East from very early times and often appears in a ritual context, probably representing fertility because of the pomegranate's many seeds.

We also found miniature altars decorated at the top with rounded knobs, and fragments of

*For photographs and discussions of these two stands, see LaMoine F. DeVries, "Cult Stands—A Bewildering Variety of Shapes and Sizes," BAR, July/August 1987.

perforated incense-burning cups of a kind commonly found at Transjordanian sites, particularly at Tell el-Kheleifeh. This latter type of altar has three short legs and holes in the walls.

Another noteworthy find from the rectangular enclosure was a stone seal on which was depicted a figure dressed in a long gown, with one hand raised heavenwards in a gesture of supplication or blessing. Similar representations have been found on numerous seals throughout the Near East dating from different periods. This seal probably belonged to one of the Edomite priests who served at Qitmit. To the priests, or perhaps to the worshippers, belonged numerous bronze finger-rings and crescent-shaped earrings found in our excavation.

Five inscribed sherds, parts of whole vessels and of a cult stand, were also found in the excavation, one in Complex A and four in Complex B. All of the inscriptions are unfortunately very fragmentary. Two, however, belong to a single text that was incised after firing. It probably came from a cult stand. What remains of the text is a single line that, standing alone, yields no meaning; however, it does contain the name of the principal Edomite god Qos (*QWS*). The paleography of the script on all the sherds is similar to contemporaneous inscriptions from eastern Transjordan, and thus may reasonably be assumed to be in the Edomite script.

But the most extraordinary of our finds from Horvat Qitmit was a three-horned goddess figurine, also found in the rectangular enclosure. One curved horn was placed at each side of the head, and a third sprouts from the middle of the goddess's forehead. Professor Beck has described this goddess in greater detail in the sidebar on page 207.

In my earlier discussion of the Edomite pottery from the seventh to early sixth centuries B.C., I noted that it was found in large quantities at Transjordanian sites within the territory of Edom, as described in the Bible. This same pottery has been found in small quantities at nearly all sites in the Biblical Negev, in strata dating to the late seventh to early sixth centuries B.C. At Horvat Qitmit, however, the proportion of Edomite pottery is several times greater than at other Negev sites. This must be regarded as the determining factor in the site's cultural attribution. In short, Qitmit was an Edomite cult-center, and the area around it must have been controlled by the Edomites. Qitmit cannot be explained either on the basis of ordinary trade relations or as a small community of Edomites living in a Judahite settlement. Moreover, Qitmit existed for some time, as reflected in its solid construction and its two phases.

Qitmit was constructed during the last days of the kingdom of Judah. It may have continued in use for some years after the Babylonian destruction of Jerusalem and the exile of the Judahite population.

What can we make of this Edomite shrine in the heart of the Judahite settlement of the eastern Negev? It attests to the continued struggle between Judah and Edom since the peoples emerged as nations, a struggle amply reflected in the Bible. The Biblical evidence must reflect the historical reality of the period of the Judahite kingdom. From the Biblical evidence and the evidence from Qitmit, it may fairly be assumed that Edom invaded and conquered extensive Judahite territory in the eastern Negev some time near the fall of Jerusalem, either before or after, taking advantage of Judah's weakness. This Edomite invasion of the eastern Negev was a prelude to the further expansion of Edomite settlement into the Hebron highlands, the southern Shephelah.* and the northern Negev. Finally in the Hellenistic period (337–37 B.C.), and probably already in the Persian period, the Edomite position in Judah was "legitimized." This formerly Judahite area, now settled by the Edomites, became officially known as "Edumea" or Idumea. The Edomite cult-center at Horvat Qitmit represents an important stage of this Edomite expansion into Judah.

*The Shephaleh is the Biblical term for the low hilly area between the Judean mountains and the coastal plain.

[1] More recent evidence contradicts Glueck's conclusion that the land of Edom was unoccupied between the beginning of the second millennium B.C. and the end of the 13th century B.C. Glueck's conclusion, which is no longer accepted, supported a late date for the Israelite conquest of Canaan because prior to the 13th century the area was unoccupied. The Bible records that the Israelites met resistance from several peoples in this area on their march to Canaan. In the last decade, as a result of extensive archaeological surveys in Jordan, many sites dating to Middle Bronze II and Late Bronze periods have been discovered in the land of Edom, Moab and Ammon. Glueck's conclusion must therefore be modified. (See James A. Sauer, "*Transjordan in the Bronze and Iron Ages*: A Critique of Glueck's Synthesis," *Bulletin of the American Schools of Research* 263 [1986], pp. 1–26; see also John J. Bimson and David Livingston, "Redating the Exodus," BAR, September/October 1987, pp. 40–53, 66–68; and Baruch Halpern, "Radical Exodus Redating Fatally Flawed," BAR, November/December 1987, pp. 56–61.)

[2] Itzhaq Beit-Arieh and Bruce Gesson, "An Edomite Ostracon from Horvat 'Uza," *Tel Aviv* 12 (1985), pp. 96–101.

Related Reading

Rudolph Cohen and Yigal Yisrael, "Smashing the Idols: Piecing Together an Edomite Shrine in Judah," BAR, July/August 1996.

Itzhaq Beit-Arieh, "Edomites Advance into Judah," BAR, November/December 1996.

Thomas E. Levy and Mohammad Najjar, "Edom and Copper," BAR, July/August 2006.

5

David and Solomon

The very existence of these storied kings is questioned by some, and their accomplishments diminished by others. The following articles show what archaeology has contributed to the debate.

The glory days. The golden age. The United Monarchy. The reigns of David and Solomon. Some modern scholars, however, (often referred to as "Biblical minimalists") have challenged not only the grandeur of the United Monarchy, but also the very nature of David and Solomon's kingdom, and even the kings' existence. As always, BAR turned to the archaeology and the experts to sort fact from fiction.

MARCH/APRIL 1994
"David" Found at Dan

Avraham Biran, the director of the Tel Dan excavation where the "David" stela was found, was, perhaps surprisingly, modest about it. I wonder if that was because he himself had little to do with its discovery; it was found not by excavation but in secondary use in a later wall at the site. The team surveyor, Gila Cook, saw the writing on a stone in the wall just as the sun hit the inscription at the precise angle to highlight it.

When I talked to Avraham about writing an article on the inscription, he insisted that the article must also include other spectacular finds discovered at the site. I agreed. After our usual editing process, however, Biran decided he did not want his name to appear as author because, as we edited the opening, it might seem that he was bragging. The result was that it was printed without an author, as it appears here, but "based [on the scientific report] and other materials supplied by Professor Biran." Biran died in 2008, just one month shy of his 99th birthday.

JANUARY/FEBRUARY 2006
Did I Find King David's Palace?

The name "David" had never before appeared in an ancient inscription, which had provided much ammunition to the Biblical minimalists who questioned whether the king of Israel had in fact been a historical figure. The initial response to the find by some of the minimalists ran the gamut from other strained readings to a claim that the inscription had been forged. In any event, all now recognize that the inscription in fact refers to *Beth David* (the dynasty of David) a mere 100 to 150 years after David died. The name "'David' [was indeed] Found at Dan."

The title of Eilat Mazar's 2006 article cautiously ends with a question mark. She knew that unless she excavated an inscription reading "This is King David's Palace," the doubters would be out there with their knives. And indeed they have been.

But with the passage of time—and more excavation—the doubts have receded. Then in January/February 2014 Nadav Na'aman, a highly respected senior scholar at Tel Aviv University (the center of the doubters), published an article in BAR in which he concluded that the building that "Eilat Mazar unearthed and identified as the residence of King David is indeed a suitable candidate for this building." We print this article following Eilat Mazar's article as a bonus, not counting it in the 40 articles that comprise these volumes.

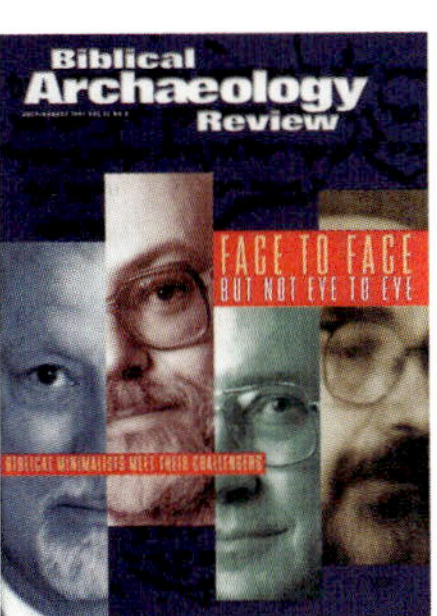

JULY/AUGUST 1997
Cow Town or Royal Capital?—Evidence For Iron Age Jerusalem

Eilat Mazar's article (with Nadav Na'aman's addendum) focuses on one building. Is it or isn't it? Another article by Nadav Na'aman—and this one counts in the 40—focuses more broadly: Was Jerusalem the administrative center of a state or merely a tribal center (as some Biblical minimalists contend)? Na'aman assembled the archaeological as well as textual evidence. He concluded that David and Solomon regarded themselves as kings and were so regarded by their neighbors and that Jerusalem was the governing and administrative center of their kingdom.

"David" Found at Dan

Inscription crowns 27 years of exciting discoveries

IT'S NOT OFTEN THAT AN archaeological find makes the front page of the *New York Times* (to say nothing of *Time* magazine). But that is what happened last summer to a discovery at Tel Dan, a beautiful mound in northern Galilee, at the foot of Mt. Hermon beside one of the headwaters of the Jordan River.[1]

There Avraham Biran and his team of archaeologists[2] found a remarkable inscription from the ninth century B.C.E. that refers both to the "House of David" and to the "King of Israel." This is the first time that the name David has been found in any ancient inscription outside the Bible. That the inscription refers not simply to a "David" but to the House of David, the dynasty of the great Israelite king, is even more remarkable.

"King of Israel" is a term frequently found in the Bible, especially in the Book of Kings. This, however, may be the oldest extra-Biblical reference to Israel in Semitic script. If this inscription proves anything, it shows that both Israel and Judah, contrary to the claims of some scholarly Biblical minimizers, were important kingdoms at this time.

Together with his colleague Professor Joseph Naveh of the Hebrew University, Professor Biran promptly wrote a scientific report on the inscription, which was published in the *Israel Exploration Journal*.[3] This special article for BAR readers is based on that report and on other materials supplied by Professor Biran.

Let us start with some background. In the first season at Tel Dan—27 years ago, in 1966—Biran and his team uncovered on the slope of the mound a small potsherd incised with four letters in ancient Hebrew script. Although inscriptions are quite rare in excavations in Israel, the excavators were not really surprised. In the previous year, a ninth-century B.C.E. Aramaic inscription incised on the base of a bowl had been discovered quite by accident on the surface of the site. The late Professor Nahman Avigad, who published the inscription, read it as "of the butchers." The bowl on which it was inscribed had probably belonged to the cooks or butchers in the royal household of Dan.[4]

The four-letter Hebrew inscription on the potsherd was dated to the eighth century B.C.E., about a century after the "butcher" inscription. The four letters read *l'mṣ* (לאמץ). The first letter is the common preposition meaning "belonging to"; the last three letters are a name: Amotz. This was the name of the father of the prophet Isaiah (Isaiah 1:1; 2 Kings 19:2; 2 Chronicles 26:22, etc.), who prophesied in the eighth century B.C.E. The jar did not belong to Isaiah's father—the name was fairly common—but the discovery of an eighth-century B.C.E. inscription with a well-known name naturally caused considerable excitement for the members of the expedition and raised hopes of finding more.

Two years later, in 1968, while excavating a seventh-century B.C.E. building, Biran found a sherd

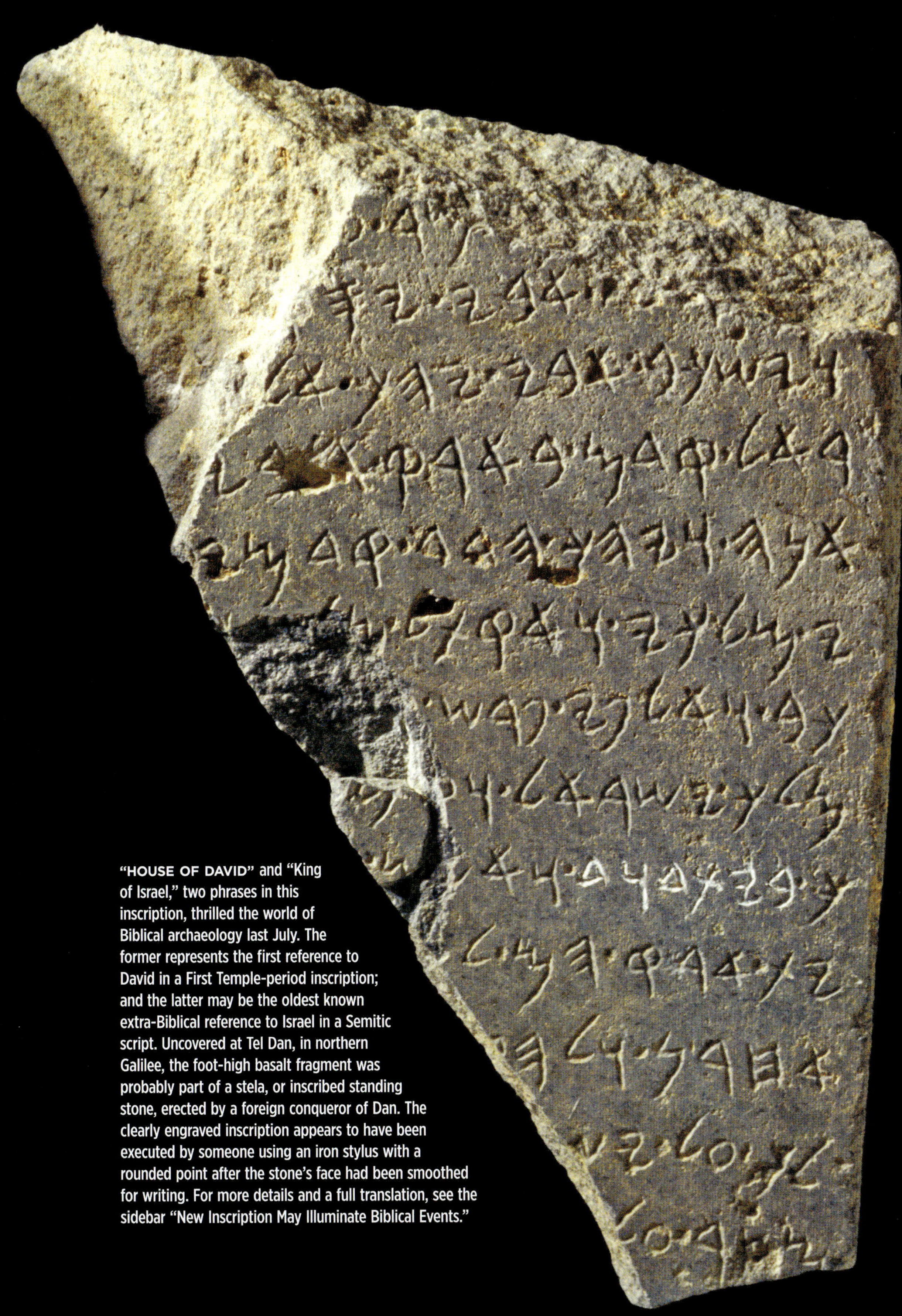

"HOUSE OF DAVID" and "King of Israel," two phrases in this inscription, thrilled the world of Biblical archaeology last July. The former represents the first reference to David in a First Temple-period inscription; and the latter may be the oldest known extra-Biblical reference to Israel in a Semitic script. Uncovered at Tel Dan, in northern Galilee, the foot-high basalt fragment was probably part of a stela, or inscribed standing stone, erected by a foreign conqueror of Dan. The clearly engraved inscription appears to have been executed by someone using an iron stylus with a rounded point after the stone's face had been smoothed for writing. For more details and a full translation, see the sidebar "New Inscription May Illuminate Biblical Events."

ZEV RADOVAN

inscribed with seven letters in Phoenician script. It read *lb'lplṭ* (לבעלפלט), meaning "belonging to Baalpelet." The name Baalpelet means "may Baal rescue." As Baal was a pagan god, it is unlikely that Baalpelet the jar owner was an Israelite.

We have no idea who this Baalpelet was. Twenty years later, however, on the northern part of the mound, Biran found another ostracon inscribed with the letters *l* and *ṭ*, probably the last letters of the same name. Baalpelet may have been a prominent member of the Dan community, if having two jars inscribed with his name is any indication. Alternatively, the name may simply have been popular in the seventh century B.C.E.

THE TEL DAN EXCAVATION, seen in the foreground, began in 1966. Israel's longest ongoing dig, Tel Dan continues to produce remarkable discoveries. In the upper left, the foothills of Mt. Hermon rise from the cultivated plain.

"OF THE BUTCHERS" says the Aramaic inscription on the 4-inch-wide base of this pottery bowl. Incised after the bowl was fired, the ninth-century B.C.E. inscription suggests that the bowl belonged to the butchers or cooks of the royal household at Dan. The bowl was found by accident on the surface of the mound the year before excavation began. The drawing shows the inscription, with dashed lines indicating reconstructed portions.

Eight years later, in 1976, in a disturbed level of occupation (thus, it cannot be precisely dated by stratigraphy), the Tel Dan team found an unusual bilingual inscription—in Greek and Aramaic—incised on a stone, mentioning the "God who is in Dan." This inscription conclusively established that the site was Biblical Dan.

Another ten excavation seasons passed without a hint of an inscription. Then, in 1986, in a layer of violent destruction attributed to the Assyrian conquest of northern Israel by Tiglath-pileser III in 733/732 B.C.E., a stamped jar handle was found, bearing the letters *l'mdyo* (לעמדיו). The seal that made the impression had belonged to someone named *Immadiyo*, that is, "God is with me." The *-yo* (יו) element in the name is a shortened form of Yahweh (the personal name of the Israelite God) used in the northern kingdom, Israel.* Immadiyo is thus a Yahwistic name that may reflect Immadiyo's, or his parents', devotion to the Israelite God.

In 1988, they uncovered another Yahwistic name on an eighth-century B.C.E. jar handle: *zkryo* (זכריו), meaning "God (Yahweh) remembers" or "May God (Yahweh) remember." This is a very common name in the Bible, perhaps more easily recognizable by transliterating it with vowels: Zecharya or, even more recognizably, Zechariah or Zachariah (the same name in Hebrew). Another Biblical form of the name is Zecharyahu, especially in Judah. Young's Bible concordance lists 27 different men named Zechariah in the Bible, and two named Zachariah. In the New Testament, Zechariah was the name of John the Baptist's father (Luke 1).

One of the Biblical Zechariahs was the son of Jeroboam II; he succeeded his father to the throne of Israel (in about 753 B.C.E.) and held it for a bare six months. At that time Dan was included in the kingdom of Israel. It is tantalizing to imagine that perhaps the seal belonged to a king, King Zechariah of eighth-century B.C.E. Israel. The date of the seal impression and the date of the king's reign do seem to fit.

In addition to these inscriptions, the Tel Dan team made many other important discoveries: the unique triple-arched gate, the Mycenaean tomb, the

*The shortened form of Yahweh used in names in the southern kingdom, Judah, was *-yahu*.

DUBY TAL

MARK OF OWNERSHIP. "Belonging to Amotz" (*l'mṣ*) says the four-letter inscription in paleo-Hebrew on this small sherd from a jar. Although this is the same name as the father of the prophet Isaiah (Isaiah 1:1), the name was fairly common in the eighth century B.C.E., the date of this sherd. The discovery of this inscription in 1966, the first year of the excavation at Tel Dan, raised expectations for the dig's future.

UNUSUALLY LARGE PHOENICIAN script, deeply incised before firing of the original vessel, forms the inscription on the potsherd at lower right. The inscription reads, "belonging to Baalpelet" (*lb'lplṭ*). The name means "may Baal rescue," referring to the pagan god Baal, so it may not belong to an Israelite. Excavated from a seventh-century B.C.E. building in 1968, the ostracon measures about 10 inches wide and 9 inches high.

Another ostracon (below) with the letters *l* and *ṭ* together, probably the end of the same name, turned up 20 years later in the northern part of the mound (see photograph). Whether this ostracon and sherd both refer to the same person, or whether it was simply a popular name, remains unknown.

scepter head and the Israelite gate complex.* None was more dramatic, however, than the inscription uncovered last summer referring to the "House of David" and the "King of Israel."

In a sense the find can be attributed to the fact that the Israel Government Tourist Corporation and the Antiquities Authority had decided that Tel Dan was a site worthy of a major conservation and restoration project, so that, after nearly a generation of excavation, the site can be properly presented to visitors. As part of this project, which began in 1992, the archaeologists removed the debris from the eighth-century B.C.E. Assyrian destruction level—the destruction of Tiglath-pileser III, as previously mentioned—outside the city-gate complex. The purpose was simply to remove this destruction debris. But, as so often happens in an excavation, the unexpected occurred. As the destruction debris was being removed, an intriguing new ninth-century B.C.E. gate was uncovered; it formed an additional outer gate leading to the city-gate complex.

The previously known city-gate complex consisted of an outer gate that opened into a rectangular pavement (about 28 feet long and 65 feet wide), on the other side of which stood the major, or inner, gate. In this plaza, just as one approached the inner gate, a low platform had been uncovered several years ago (see photo, p. 232). It had sockets at three of the four corners (the fourth socket was missing) that apparently once supported a canopy over the platform. The platform was probably either for the city's ruler, to greet a parade of dignitaries along a

*For the gates and tomb, see John C. H. Laughlin, "The Remarkable Discoveries at Tel Dan," BAR, September/October 1981; for the scepter head, see Avraham Biran, "Prize Find: Tel Dan Scepter Head," BAR, January/February 1989. Also see Hershel Shanks, "BAR Interview: Avraham Biran—Twenty Years of Digging at Tel Dan," BAR, July/August 1987.

DEFINITELY DAN. PROFESSOR Biran's 1976 discovery of this 6-by-10-inch limestone tablet confirmed the identity of the site he was digging. The bilingual inscription in Greek (top three lines) and Aramaic (bottom line) refers to a person named Zoilos who made a vow to the "god who is in Dan," or, in an alternative reading, to the "god of the Danites." Found in Tel Dan's sacred area, this votive inscription dates to the late third or early second centuries B.C. based on the style of the scripts.

beautifully paved processional route, or a pedestal for the statue of a deity. To the right was a bench where perhaps the elders sat—to judge cases, to make deals or to welcome a royal procession.

In 1992, as part of the conservation-preservation project, Biran made an unexpected find when the layer of destruction in this area was removed. A decorated capital that may have adorned the top of one of the columns of the canopied structure above the platform was excavated (see photo, p. 233).

The next surprising find was a set of five standing stones in a niche just inside the outer gate. At either end of this row of standing stones lay large, carefully hewn, rectangular blocks. These blocks apparently belonged originally to part of the structure that sheltered the standing stones. The nature of these stones and their location—along the city wall in the plaza of the city-gate complex—together with a cache of some 25 pottery vessels found west of the standing stones, suggests that they may be sacred pillars, the *massebot* often mentioned in the Bible. This suggestion is further buttressed by the votive nature of the vessels: nine oil lamps, three of which have a pedestal and seven spouts; five three-legged cups (possibly for incense); four flat and five deep bowls; and numerous other stands. All of these artifacts are known to have cultic functions.

In short, this evidence suggests that the plaza between the outer and inner gates had a small "gateway" sanctuary that could be considered a *bamah* (often translated "high place") of the kind mentioned in 2 Kings 23:1–20. That Biblical passage describes the seventh-century religious reforms instituted by King Josiah. Like King Hezekiah before him, Josiah wanted to centralize all worship of the Israelite God Yahweh in the Jerusalem Temple. To ensure this, Josiah destroyed the outlying *bamot* (plural of *bamah*). In this connection, the Biblical text specifically mentions "*bamot* of the gates" and one that was at the "entrance" (*petach*) of a gate (2 Kings 23:8). The *bamah* at Dan may have been this kind of structure.

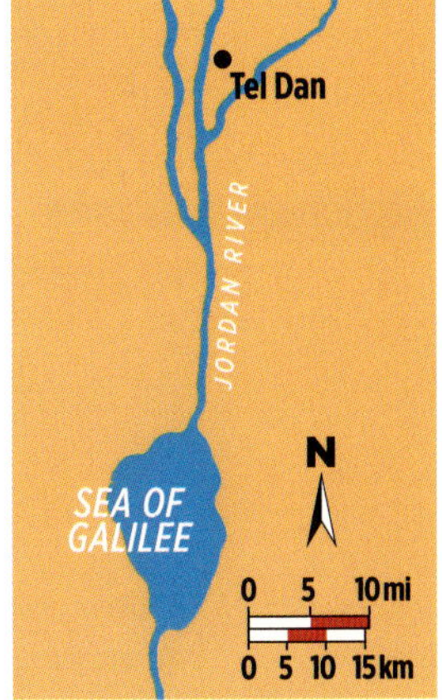

TEL DAN lies by the headwaters of the Jordan River, near Israel's northern border.

In 1993, Biran and his team continued clearing the area outside the outer gate of the city-gate complex, because they knew that the paved plaza extended there, both to the east and to the south. There they uncovered approximately 475 square yards of pavement outside the outer city gate. Then on the east they hit a wall that had undergone considerable change, including the construction of a water channel through it in the Roman period. On the northern side of this wall, they found the "House of David/King of Israel" inscription, but that is getting ahead of the story.

South of this plaza outside the city-gate complex was a row of five unworked stones (one was missing). On either side of this row of stones lay a squared stone, on top of which was a stone pivot

Stamped Jar Handles Provide More Inscriptions

Jar handles stamped with the owner's name have turned up several times in the Dan excavation. The destruction layer attributed to the conquest of northern Israel in 733/732 B.C.E. by the Assyrian king Tiglath-pileser III yielded such an inscription in 1986 (top). The paleo-Hebrew script reads *l'mdyo* (belonging to Immadiyo). The name means "God is with me." The element *yo* or *yau* was the form used in the northern kingdom of Israel for Yahweh, the Israelite God.

Another eighth-century B.C.E. example (bottom), found in 1988, bears the name *zkryo* in paleo-Hebrew script. Transliterated with vowels, this spells Zechariah or Zachariah (meaning "God [Yahweh] remembers" or "May God [Yahweh] remember"). Twenty-seven people in the Bible have this name, and one of them is King Zechariah of Israel, who reigned for six months in about 753 B.C.E. It is tantalizing to think that the jar may have been royal property, but this must remain in the realm of conjecture.

set inside the door socket. It seemed that they had discovered another gate, still farther out from the other one, and that this was its threshold (see box, pp. 234–235). The two hemispherical stone pivots, made of local black basalt, once held square wooden doorposts, as reflected in the square hole in each of them. Thus the doors resting on the hemispherical pivots could be opened and closed with ease. The function of this new outer gate—an outer outer gate—is still unclear.

The biggest surprise was, of course, the inscription. The team's surveyor, Gila Cook, first noticed it. There, in secondary use *in* a wall, on the east side of the plaza, beneath an eighth-century B.C.E. destruction level, she saw a basalt stone protruding from the ground. As the rays of the afternoon sun glanced off this stone, Gila thought she saw letters on it and called Biran over. When he bent down to look at the stone, he exclaimed: "Oh, my God, we have an inscription!" The stone was easily removed and, when turned toward the sun, the letters sprang to life. In their words, "It was an unforgettable moment."

The piece of basalt was a fragment of what must have been a large monumental inscription. The sidebar "New Inscription May Illuminate Biblical Events" contains a drawing of the 13-line inscription, a transcript in modern Hebrew letters and an English translation. In the translation, the words and letters in brackets have been reconstructed on the basis of surviving parts of the inscription. A dot over a letter in the modern Hebrew transcription indicates that the letter has only partially survived.

Parts of 13 lines have been preserved, but not a single one is complete. In the first line, only three letters have survived. In the second line are five letters and part of a sixth; in the last line, only five letters; and the widest line has a mere 14 letters.

On the other hand, the surviving letters are clearly engraved and easy to read. The script is in Old Hebrew letters, sometimes called paleo-Hebrew, the kind of letters used before the Babylonian destruction of the First Temple in 586 B.C.E. When the Jews returned from the Babylonian exile, they brought back the square Aramaic script still used today.

Dots separate the words, as was then customary. In line 9, where "House of David" appears, however, the two Hebrew words *bytdwd* are not separated by a dot, but written together, like HouseofDavid. The dynastic name of the kingdom of Judah, whose founder was King David, was apparently regarded as one word.

Note that the first letter (farthest to the right) in line 9, just before the reference to the House of David, is the last letter of *melech*, the Hebrew

A CHARIOTEER ADORNS this beautifully preserved krater, one of several Late Bronze Age Mycenaean imports found in a well-built tomb at Dan. Other funerary offerings included gold and silver jewelry, bronze swords and ivory cosmetic boxes. The tomb and its contents date to the heyday of Canaanite Laish in the 14th or 13th century B.C.E. and testify to the city's prosperity and extensive relations before its conquest by the Israelite tribe of Dan (Joshua 19:47; Judges 18:29).

word for king, so the previous line probably ended with the other two letters of the word for king. In short, there was probably a reference to "the king of the House of David." Perhaps the missing part even gave his name.

In line 8 is a reference to *melech yisrael*, the king of Israel, so the text mentions both the northern kingdom of Israel and the southern kingdom of Judah and the king of each. Unfortunately, the kings' names, if they were ever there, have not survived.

In line 5, however, is the name Hadad. Hadad was a storm god, especially popular among the Arameans east of the Jordan. "Hadad went in front of me," the text reads. This is apparently a victory stela erected in Dan by an Aramean king devoted to Hadad.

Line 4 reads: "...rael formerly in my father's land." Apparently the two letters that were at the end of

A LABYRINTHINE GATE COMPLEX confronted the ancient visitor who wished to enter the Israelite city of Dan in the First Temple period, as shown in this isometric reconstruction (right). After entering via the recently discovered outer outer gate and paved plaza (see box, pp. 234–235), the visitor would pass through the outer gate into a small plaza containing five standing stones constituting a shrine (opposite) and a low platform of hewn limestone blocks covered by a canopy, which may have served as a throne or held a cult statue (below).

Next the visitor would pass through the four-chambered inner gate, which measures almost 100 feet wide and 60 feet through its passage and dates to the ninth century B.C.E. The two rooms on each side of the entryway probably housed the guards.

Continuing to follow the pavement, the visitor would come at last to the 55-by-40-foot upper gate, beyond which lay the city itself.

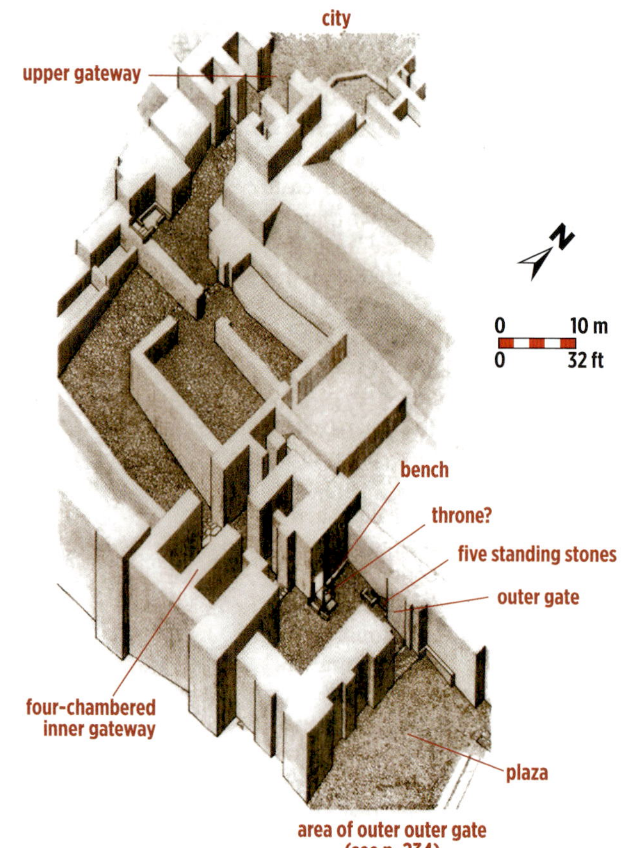

THIS LOW PLATFORM of hewn limestone blocks covered by a canopy may have served as a throne or held a cult statue. Round, carved, socketed bases—two beside the platform on the left and one on the right—indicate that posts were inserted into the holes to support the canopy over the platform. A presumed fourth base has disappeared. This platform may perhaps be explained by, and in turn illustrate, a passage in the Bible: "Then the king arose and took his seat in the gate ... and all the people came before the king" (2 Samuel 19:8). To the right of the platform, a stone bench, perhaps for the elders of the city, lines the wall for about 16 feet.

line 3 were "Is" so that the original text read "Israel formerly in my father's land." There may even have been a reference to the cities of Israel.

In lines 6 and 7, the author of the text boasts that he "slew [some apparently large number of] chariots and 2,000 horsemen." Then the following lines contain references to the king of Israel and, presumably, the king of the House of David.

Thus this appears to be a victory stela erected in Dan by an Aramean, a devotee of Hadad, who is boasting of his military victory over Israel and perhaps also Judah. That this is an Aramean victory stela is confirmed by the fact that the language is Early Aramaic, related to, but slightly different from, Hebrew. The author of the text was probably not the Aramean king, but rather a military commander of the king's, because in line 6 we find a reference to "my king." On the other hand, lines 2 and 3 refer to "my father" and line 4 refers to "my father's land," indicating royalty of some sort. Perhaps the military commander who erected the stela was himself a royal personage, possibly a king who was subordinate to the king of Aram who ruled from Damascus. The Bible actually mentions two such subordinate kingdoms, Maacah (2 Samuel 10:6, 8; 1 Chronicles 19:7) and Rehob (2 Samuel 10:8). Although Maacah and Rehob were more than a hundred years before the Dan stela was written, these kingdoms may still have existed in the period of the stela.

In 1 Kings 15:16–22 (a parallel account appears in 2 Chronicles 16:1–6), we learn of a war between King Baasha of Israel and King Asa of Judah. Asa took all the gold and silver from the Jerusalem Temple and from his own palace and presented it to Ben-Hadad, king of Aram, as a gift, with a note requesting Ben-Hadad's help. Ben-Hadad responded by attacking cities in the northern kingdom of Israel, and captured several of them, including Dan (1 Kings 15:20).

Does this Biblical episode provide the historical background of the Dan stela? Did Ben-Hadad, the Aramean, erect this victory stela after capturing Dan?

The answer depends on (1) whether the date of the stela is contemporaneous with this episode, and (2) whether the two texts "fit" with one another.

The Biblical episode can be dated to the first half of the ninth century B.C.E., about 885. (Baasha's reign extended from 906 to 883 and Asa's reign from 908 to 867.)

How was the stela dated to the ninth century B.C.E.? One way to date the inscription is paleographically—by the shape and stance of the letters. On this basis, Joseph Naveh dated the inscription to the ninth century. The evidence comes from other inscriptions that have been previously dated. In the

DROOPING LEAVES, a motif well known from Assyrian ivories, decorate this foot-high limestone capital found in 1992. Another decorative element appears above the leaves. The capital may have adorned the top of a column supporting the canopied structure that protected the low platform between the outer and inner gates.

FIVE SMALL STONES, perhaps Biblical *massebot*, stand in a niche against the city wall, just inside the outer gate. Large, well-hewn, rectangular blocks flank the standing stones, indicating that a structure may have sheltered the stones. The discovery of some 25 votive pottery vessels nearby supports the idea of a cultic function for these stones.

ninth century, Aramaic script and Phoenician script had not yet gone their separate ways, so comparisons to inscriptions in both scripts are relevant. Unfortunately, however, most extant ninth-century inscriptions, like the famous Mesha stela, which is most similar to the Dan inscription, come from the latter half of that century. Only the Phoenician Nora inscription* and an inscription from Cyprus come from the early ninth century. So, the Dan inscription can be dated paleographically to about the middle of the century, but might fall within a range of some decades earlier or later.

An archaeological analysis, however, suggests a date in the first half of the ninth century. The stela fragment that bears the inscription was used in a wall that was destroyed by Tiglath-pileser III in 733/732 B.C.E., so the stela must have been erected before this date. But that doesn't help much.

The pottery from the level beneath the stela fragment narrows the range. While the amount of pottery found there was small, none of it was later than the first half of the ninth century! This suggests that the stela was broken up around that time, so that it would have been erected sometime during the first half of the ninth century B.C.E. It must have stood at least some time before being destroyed and used secondarily in the wall. A date early in the ninth century fits nicely with the date of the Biblical episode (about 885 B.C.E.).

But an examination of the two accounts—the one in the Bible and the other on the fragmentary inscription—suggests caution. Obviously, the reconstruction of the text presents many difficulties and many possibilities. Note that in line 9, Naveh and Biran have reconstructed an "I" before "slew," so that the author of the text does the slaying. That is their best guess, although other reconstructions are possible. If the reconstruction of "I" is correct, it appears that the author of the victory stela is claiming a victory over Judah (the House of David), who is his enemy, as well as over Israel. If that is so, it would conflict with the Biblical episode, in which the Aramean king was allied with the king of Judah, having been bribed with a gift of gold and silver. Thus the stela may be describing some other military engagement in

*See Joan G. Scheuer, "Volunteer's Report: Searching for the Phoenicians in Sardinia," BAR, January/February 1990; and Edward Lipinski, "Epigraphy in Crisis—Dating Ancient Semitic Inscriptions," BAR, July/August 1990.

Destruction Debris Yields Plaza, New Gate and Inscription

The clearance of destruction debris from the conquest of Dan by Assyrian king Tiglath-pileser III in 733/732 B.C.E. brought forth a wealth of new discoveries in 1992 and 1993. The plan (below) shows the relationship of a newly cleared plaza and a hitherto undiscovered outer outer gate to the previously known outer and inner gates. It also marks the findspot of the "House of David" inscription.

In the upper photo, the newly cleared plaza, measuring 475 square yards and paved with stones, lies in front of the outer gate, at lower right. In the southeast corner of the plaza (lower photo), four unworked stones and one missing stone mark the threshold of the new outer outer gate. This threshold also appears in the upper photo at the edge of the paved plaza, at center, to the left of the man. At each end of this threshold, a large recumbent stone with a socket holds a hemispherical stone pivot made of black basalt. Wooden doorposts once fitted into the square holes in the pivots, allowing the gate doors to swing easily open and closed.

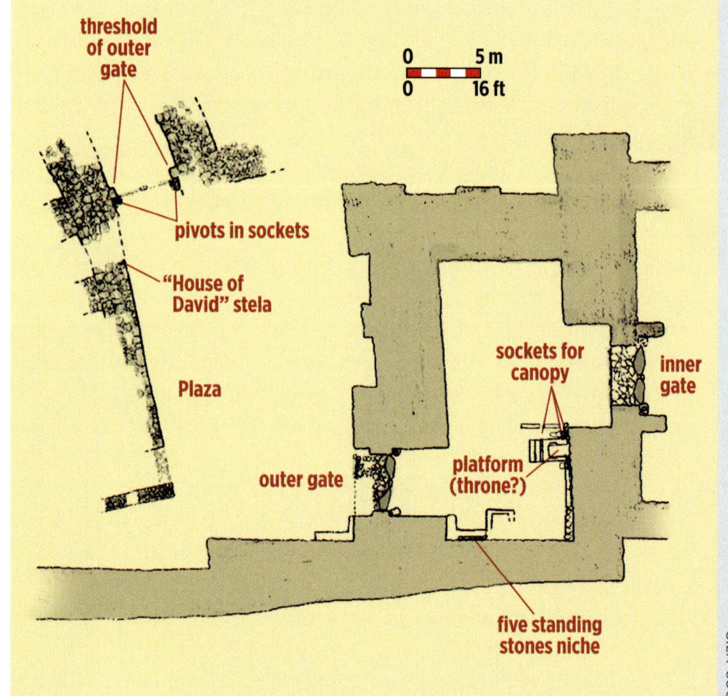

GILA COOK

New Inscription May Illuminate Biblical Events

Tel Dan surveyor Gila Cook first spotted the "House of David" inscription in the glancing rays of the afternoon sun. She called over excavation director Avraham Biran, who, when he saw it, exclaimed, "Oh, my God, we have an inscription!" The photos show the fragmentary stela as it was found (below) and shortly after removal (opposite).

Broken in antiquity and reused as building material, the stela lay in a wall beneath the eighth-century B.C.E. destruction debris from Tiglath-pileser III's conquest. The inscription's 13 partially preserved lines in the Early Aramaic language, written in paleo-Hebrew script of the ninth century B.C.E., uses dots to separate the words (drawing, opposite). Based on associated pottery fragments and evidence from the inscription itself, Professor Biran suggests the stela was erected in the first half of the ninth century B.C.E. Biran and his colleagues continue to search for additional fragments of the stela.

In the translation, the material in brackets represents suggested reconstructions. Fortunately, the phrases "House of David" (the dynastic name of the kingdom of Judah) and "king of Israel" (often used without a specific name in the Books of Kings) need no reconstruction. The inscription seems to commemorate the victory of an Aramean king over the kingdoms of Israel and Judah. One of the Aramean king's military commanders probably erected the stela, for it speaks of "my king" (line 6). In view of the date and the location in Galilee, among other factors, the stela may describe events in the war of Ben Hadad I against King Baasha of Israel in 885 B.C.E. (1 Kings 15:16–22; 2 Chronicles 16:1–6). In any case, it shows that Israel and Judah were important kingdoms in the ninth century B.C.E. When the Israelites reconquered Dan, they apparently destroyed the stela and used its pieces in the wall.

Transcription		Translation
[ ]מר.ע[ ]	(1)	...
[ ].אבי.יסק[.]	(2)	...my father went up
וישכב.אבי.יהך.אל[. .יש]	(3)	...and my father died, he went to [his fate...Is-]
ראל.קדם.בארק.אבי[.]	(4)	rael formerly in my father's land...
אנה.ויהך.הדד.קדמי[.]	(5)	I [fought against Israel?] and Hadad went in front of me...
י.מלכי.ואקתל.מנ[הם. .ר]	(6)	...my king. And I slew of [them X footmen, Y cha-]
כב.ואלפי.פרש.[ ]	(7)	riots and two thousand horsemen...
מלך.ישראל.וקתל[ת. .מל]	(8)	the king of Israel. And [I] slew [...the kin-]
ך.ביתדוד.ואשם.[.א]	(9)	g of the House of David. And I put...
ית.ארק.הם.ל[ ]	(10)	their land...
אחרן.ולה-[.מ]	(11)	other...[...ru-]
לך.על.יש[ראל.]	(12)	led over Is[rael...]
מצר.על[.]	(13)	siege upon...

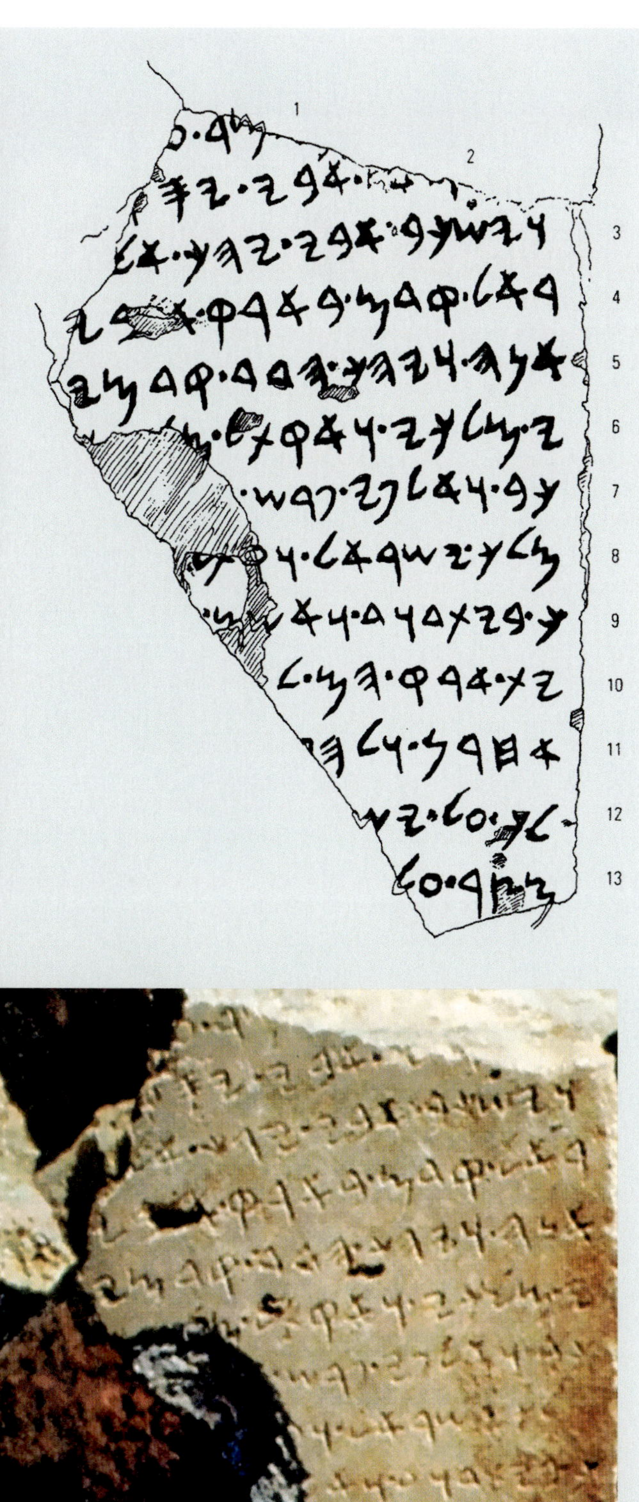

which both Judah and Israel were allied against Aram.

There were probably several battles or wars in the ninth century B.C.E. between Aram and Israel. Not all were recorded in the Bible. Indeed, several other possibilities are mentioned in the Bible.[5] For the time being, the matter must remain in the realm of learned conjecture.

In any event, at some point Israel must have regained control of Dan, perhaps when King Ahab rebuilt the city after its destruction by Ben-Hadad I in 885 B.C.E. When the Israelites regained control of the city, the Aramean victory stela was destroyed. The only thing we can be sure of is that it was broken and that one of the fragments was used in a wall bordering a plaza in the city-gate complex.

As stated earlier, this is now the oldest extant Semitic reference to Israel. The "king of Israel" is also referred to in the famous Mesha stela, which, according to most experts, dates to later in the ninth century. The immensely important Merneptah stela, dated to 1207 B.C.E., also refers to Israel, but the text is in hieroglyphics. The Tel Dan inscription is therefore the oldest appearance in Semitic script of the name Israel—at least for now. Who knows when a new inscription that challenges this claim will be found.

All images courtesy Avraham Biran and Hebrew Union College-Jewish Institute of Religion unless indicated.

[1] See the following BAR articles: Avraham Biran, "Prize Find: Tel Dan Scepter Head," BAR, January/February 1989; Hershel Shanks, "BAR Interview: Avraham Biran—Twenty Years of Digging at Tel Dan," BAR, July/August 1987; John C. H. Laughlin, "The Remarkable Discoveries at Tel Dan," BAR, September/October 1981.

[2] From the Nelson Glueck School of Biblical Archaeology of the Hebrew Union College-Jewish Institute of Religion.

[3] Avraham Biran and Joseph Naveh, "An Aramaic Stele Fragment from Tel Dan," *Israel Exploration Journal* 43 (1993), pp. 81–98.

[4] See *Palestine Exploration Quarterly* 100 (1968), pp. 42–44.

[5] For a discussion, see Biran and Naveh, "An Aramaic Stele Fragment from Tel Dan," *Israel Exploration Journal* 43 (1993), pp. 95–98.

Related Reading

Hershel Shanks, "Face to Face: Biblical Minimalists Meet Their Challengers,' BAR, July/August 1997.

Philip R. Davies, "What Separates a Minimalist from a Maximalist? Not Much," BAR, March/April 2000.

"Debate: Minimalists on Parade," BAR, January/February 2005.

"The Devil Is Not So Black as He Is Painted," BAR, May/June 2010.

Yosef Garfinkel, "The Birth & Death of Biblical Minimalism," BAR, May/June 2011.

Strata: "How Many?" BAR, January/February 2012.

Did I Find King David's

EILAT MAZAR

THERE CAN BE LITTLE DOUBT that King David had a palace. The Bible tells us that Hiram of Tyre (who would later help King Solomon build the Temple) constructed the palace for David: "King Hiram of Tyre sent envoys to David, with cedar logs, carpenters and stonemasons; and they built a palace for David" (2 Samuel 5:11). Nine years ago I wrote an article in BAR suggesting where, in my opinion, the remains of King David's palace might lie.[1] I proposed looking in the northern part of the most ancient area of Jerusalem, known as the City of David.

I was struck by this idea while engaged in other research on the archaeology of Jerusalem. I had noticed the findings of the well-known British archaeologist Kathleen Kenyon, who dug here in the 1960s. In her Area H, at the northern end of the City of David, Kenyon discovered a section of a massive public structure that she considered

Palace?

BETTMANN/CORBIS

PRECEDING PAGES: IN this composite electronic image, a statue of King David seems to hover above a building that may have been his palace. In any event, it is a portion of an impressive Iron Age public building from the time of King David that was discovered this past year in Jerusalem by archaeologist Eilat Mazar (inset photo at bottom left). (The statue was carved between 1395 and 1405 by Claus Sluter as part of the Well of Moses in the Chartreuse de Champmol monastery in Dijon, France.) The building is at the north end of the City of David, the oldest inhabited part of Jerusalem.

In a BAR article nine years ago, Mazar speculated that David likely would have built his palace in this very area. At the time she did not have the financial backing to test her case, but a lecture at a Jerusalem think tank led to her making contact with a donor who agreed to underwrite an excavation.

Mazar was not the first to make important discoveries in this part of Jerusalem. British archaeologist Dame Kathleen Kenyon (photo above), who excavated there in the 1960s, found a portion of a large structure that she thought was part of a casemate wall (two parallel walls divided by perpendicular walls) built by King Solomon in the tenth century B.C.E. Mazar wondered whether Kenyon's discovery was actually part of David's palace—a possibility Kenyon apparently never considered because she thought the area was north of Jerusalem's walls in the tenth century B.C.E. Writing again in our pages, Mazar explains in the accompanying article why her new discovery is the best candidate for David's palace. *Photo of area by Eilat Mazar; photo of statue by Erich Lessing/Art Resource, N.Y.*

to be part of a new casemate wall* built by King Solomon. She dated the wall, on the basis of the pottery associated with it, to the tenth century B.C.E., the time of King David and King Solomon, according to the Bible. Kenyon was quite knowledgeable about Jerusalem pottery of the First Temple period, and, although she could not distinguish with assurance between pottery sherds of the tenth and the ninth centuries B.C.E., she was quite capable of distinguishing pottery sherds from those centuries (which belong to the period archaeologists call Iron Age IIa) from sherds of the eighth and seventh centuries B.C.E (Iron Age IIb). The pottery sherds she excavated in Area H were not of the later types. Perhaps this casemate wall, I speculated, was part of David's palace.

In 1995, not long before he passed away, I spoke with my grandfather, Professor Benjamin Mazar of Hebrew University, about my idea. I told him I thought there was a high likelihood of finding remains from King David's palace near Kenyon's Area H. Aside from the archaeological discoveries there, the site fit quite well with the notice in 2 Samuel 5:17, which describes David in the City of David *going down*, or descending (*yered*), from his residence to the citadel or fortress (*metzudah*). The citadel or fortress to which he descended was of course the Canaanite/Jebusite stronghold, the Fortress of Zion (*Metzudat Tsion*; see 2 Samuel 5:7) that he had conquered a short time earlier. It is clear from the topography of the City of David that David could have gone *down* to the citadel only from the north, as the city is surrounded by deep valleys on every other side. It also makes sense that the Jebusite stronghold would have been located at the high point in the City of David, that is, in its northernmost section. From here, the fortress would not only command all areas of the city but would also provide for the defense of the city on its only vulnerable side—the north, which had no natural defense. If this was in fact the case, one can infer that after conquering the city, David's palace was constructed north of this citadel (David went down to the fortress) and *outside* the northern fortifications of the city.

Although Kenyon most probably correctly dated the remains of the monumental structure she exposed in Area H, she never considered the possibility that King David built his palace *outside* the bounds of the fortified city. It therefore never occurred to her that this structure might have belonged to David's palace.

Speaking of "the restricted area of site H, north

*A casemate wall consists of parallel walls subdivided by perpendicular walls.

GARO NALBANDIAN

"DAVID WENT DOWN TO THE FORTRESS" when he feared an attack by the Philistines, according to 2 Samuel 5:17. Where did he go down from? This photo helps provide the answer. It is taken looking north, facing the spur known as the City of David, the oldest settled portion of Jerusalem; beyond it is the Temple Mount, where David's son Solomon built the Temple. Marked on the photo are Area H, where Kathleen Kenyon found parts of what Mazar has now identified as a large public structure; to the south of it is the massive Stepped-Stone Structure, a portion of hillside blanketed with large blocks that must have supported a major building on the slope above it (see photo, p. 249); the Gihon Spring, ancient Jerusalem's only source of fresh water; and the Kidron Valley, east of the city. Author Eilat Mazar suggests that the Stepped-Stone Structure was part of the same complex as David's palace. Her suggestion may seem odd at first—why would David have built his royal residence beyond Jerusalem's fortified walls? Because there was no room within the small walled city, Mazar answers. The palace required no protection in normal times; when a threat loomed, David and his entourage could quickly "go down," as the Bible says, to the city's fortress a few feet to the south.

of the line of the east-west complex that divides occupation of the Jebusite period from that which is probably tenth century B.C.,"[2] Kenyon earlier wrote that here "there was a very important building, which could well have been defensive, and which was subsequently added to, either in the late Jebusite or early Israelite period."[3]

In short, Kenyon did not consider the possibility that David's palace would have lain beyond the fortification line outside the city. She knew that by David's time, the city had already been settled for two thousand years and had been surrounded by a wall for nearly a thousand years. The city was already very cramped. Nevertheless, Kenyon put David's palace *inside* the city: "David must have cleared a space within the Jebusite town, but the size of this residence is unlikely to have been great, for anything grandiose would have taken too much space within the restricted area of the Jebusite-Davidic city."[4]

To my mind, however, choosing a site for his palace adjacent to the northern side of the Jebusite fortress would have been a very logical step for someone who was already planning a northern expansion of the city—an expansion for the Temple on what was to become the Temple Mount, for which David bought land from Araunah the Jebusite (2 Samuel 24:18-25). In peaceful times, the palace inhabitants would not be exposed to danger, and in the unlikely event of a threatening military assault, such as a Philistine offensive, the palace could be abandoned and the occupants could *descend* to the stronghold within the barricaded city. And in fact that is what 2 Samuel 5:17 (and the chapter generally) refers to when it says that David went down to the fortress to protect himself against the Philistines, who attacked after he had been crowned king of all Israel.

David had made a bold alliance with Hiram the Phoenician, king of Tyre, who built him a new palace in Jerusalem. When the Philistines heard that David was now the newly crowned king of all Israel, they rose up to attack him. Upon hearing of the attack, David abandoned his new palace and *descended* to the stronghold (2 Samuel 5:17).

When I told my grandfather of my idea about the possible location of David's palace, he was enthusiastic about it. "Where, exactly," he asked me, "did Kenyon find the piles of ashlars [nicely hewn rectangular stones] together with the proto-Aeolic (sometimes called proto-Ionic) capital? Wasn't it right next to the place you're talking about?" Indeed, it was. When I ran to check Kenyon's reports, I

DAVID HARRIS

A FOUNDING FATHER of Israeli archaeology—and the grandfather of author Eilat Mazar—Benjamin Mazar is shown near the southern wall of the Temple Mount, an area he excavated extensively in the 1970s (the silver dome of the al-Aqsa mosque is visible above the wall). The elder Mazar, a former president of Hebrew University and a perceptive Bible scholar as well, encouraged his granddaughter's efforts to locate David's palace.

Below is a drain tile stamped with the name Eusebius. The tile was part of a Byzantine-era (fourth-seventh century C.E.) house (now called by archaeologists the House of Eusebius) discovered in the 1920s in the northern portion of the City of David. Eilat Mazar made her discoveries underneath the area where the house had been found.

FROM EXCAVATIONS ON THE HILL OF THE OPHEL

confirmed that ashlar stones and an elegant proto-Aeolic capital had been found literally at the foot of the scarp at the southeastern edge of the structure in Area H. And this was just the kind of impressive remains that one would expect to come from a tenth-century B.C.E. king's palace. (This was the case, for example, at Megiddo.)[5]

One of the many things I learned from my grandfather was how to relate to the Biblical text: Pore over it again and again, for it contains within it descriptions of genuine historical reality. It is not a simple matter to differentiate the layers of textual sources that have been piled one atop the other over generations; we don't always have the tools to do it. But it is clear that concealed within the Biblical text are grains of detailed historical truth.

By the time I published my first article (in Hebrew) on these ideas, my grandfather had died. I wanted to publish as quickly as I could because so much construction was taking place that I worried the site might be built over. Only by publishing my ideas could I hope that someone would raise the necessary funds to excavate the site.

To be frank, it would take a certain amount of courage, as well as money, to support this excavation. My position, to put it mildly, had not received sweeping support from the archaeological community. Indeed, quite the opposite was the case; the prevailing opinion was that no significant ruins remained to be discovered at the top of the City of David. In addition to Kenyon, R.A.S. Macalister and J. Garrow Duncan had excavated at this and adjacent sites between 1923 and 1925, reaching bedrock in many places. They left the impression that, aside from a few walls and the debris of large stone masonry, there wasn't much left to look for. Moreover, bedrock in this area is quite near the surface. Many scholars therefore concluded that it was not worth resuming excavations at this site.

It was not until almost a decade after my first publication that we found a donor and supporter. Throughout all this time, my friend Bouky Boaz worked with me, going to meetings and talking to potential donors. Four years ago I became a senior fellow at the Shalem Center, a research institute in Jerusalem for Jewish and Israeli social thought. At one point, I gave a lecture on my ideas to a seminar there, and the president of the center, Daniel Polisar, was so impressed that he decided to try to help. On a trip to New York he mentioned the project to the chairman of the Center's board of trustees, Roger Hertog. Mr. Hertog courageously took up the challenge to finance the excavation of the site.

We began excavations in mid-February 2005 on behalf of the Shalem Center and under the academic auspices of the Institute of Archaeology of the Hebrew University of Jerusalem. We also enjoyed the full cooperation of the Elad Association, which runs the visitors' center in the City of David, in which the excavation site is located. Almost from the start, ancient remains, preserved beyond all expectations, were unearthed. Surprisingly, I felt very much at ease throughout the entire excavation. Perhaps what helped me most was the recognition of the importance of what we were doing. I decided I would be silent about the palace theory. I would let the stones speak for themselves. Either they would corroborate the palace theory or refute it.

It soon became clear that Macalister and Duncan had "visited" almost the entire area of the dig, which covered more than 3,000 square feet. In most places they had left walls in place. Only occasionally did they take apart walls down to bedrock.

About 5 feet below the surface, we were surprised to find Byzantine remains (fourth-seventh century C.E.), but nothing later. I really have no explanation for the absence of any later remains. One may speculate that they were destroyed by still later construction, but nonetheless it is surprising.

From the Byzantine period, we uncovered a structure that had previously been exposed by Macalister and Duncan. We uncovered a small part of it, however, for the first time. A single room that had survived the centuries had a plain, white mosaic floor belonging to a multi-roomed house that Macalister and Duncan called the House of Eusebius, a name imprinted on one of the drain tiles in the house (see bottom photo, opposite). The House of Eusebius no doubt belonged to someone of considerable wealth. The house was built in typical Byzantine style, with a central peristyle courtyard just like the Byzantine houses discovered in Benjamin Mazar's excavations at the foot of the Temple Mount.[6]

The House of Eusebius was built directly on top of remains from a large building from the Second Temple period (late first century B.C.E. and first century C.E.). It was apparently built as a residence, but all that survived was part of the basement whose floor contained a number of water installations. Particularly impressive were a large (17 by 10 feet) plastered pool, a plastered room covered by an arch and a plastered ritual bath (*miqveh*) with

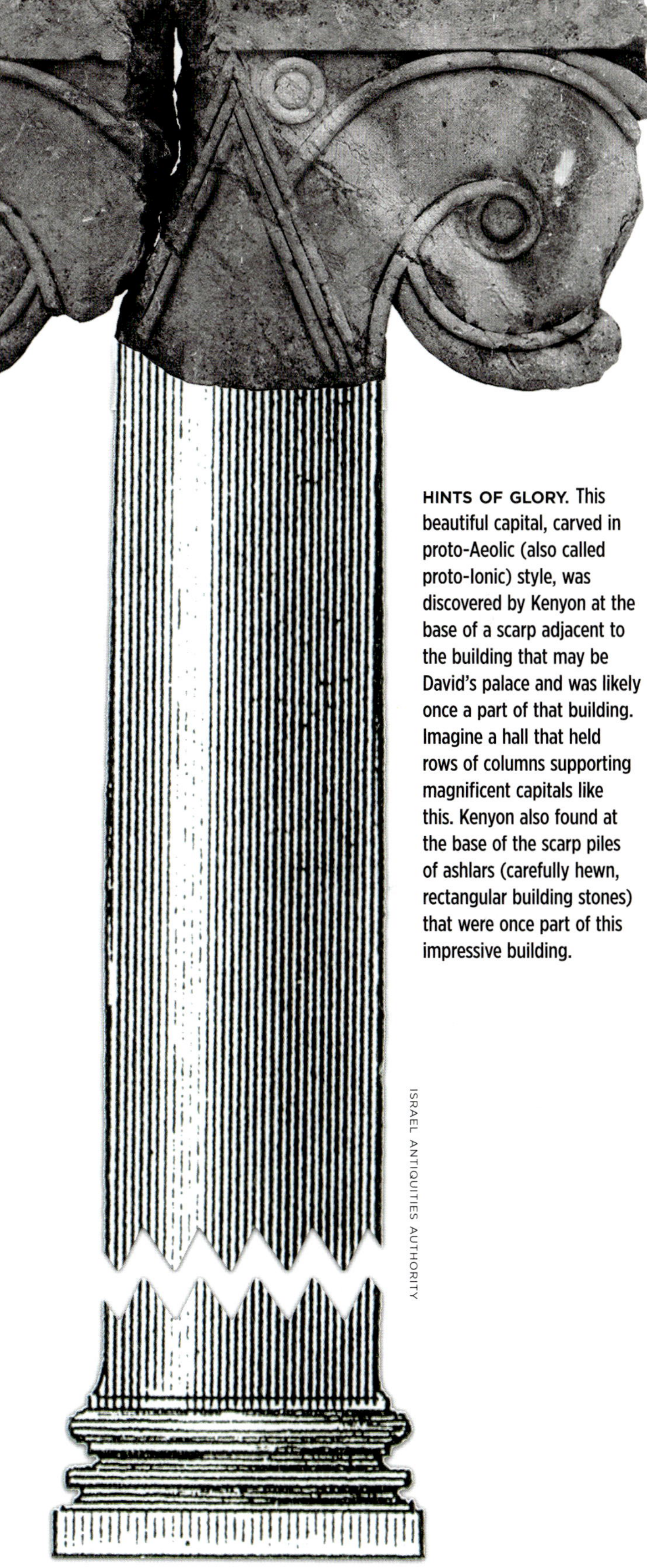

HINTS OF GLORY. This beautiful capital, carved in proto-Aeolic (also called proto-Ionic) style, was discovered by Kenyon at the base of a scarp adjacent to the building that may be David's palace and was likely once a part of that building. Imagine a hall that held rows of columns supporting magnificent capitals like this. Kenyon also found at the base of the scarp piles of ashlars (carefully hewn, rectangular building stones) that were once part of this impressive building.

ISRAEL ANTIQUITIES AUTHORITY

View shown on page 246
View shown on page 245
View shown on pages 238–239

FIT FOR A KING. An overview (opposite) of Eilat Mazar's excavation area looking to the east, with the closely packed houses of the village of Silwan in the distance. Marked on the picture are the angles of the other site photos that appear in this article. The photo at right, taken to the west, shows a massive wall.

Mazar has dubbed the large public building she is excavating the Large-Stone Structure. She suggests it may well have been built by King David as his palace. The name recalls the Stepped-Stone Structure (see photo on p. 249), a massive retaining wall slightly south and east of the Large-Stone Structure, which is believed to have supported Jerusalem's ancient fortress and which Mazar now suggests was part of the palace complex. Mazar believes David's palace was purposefully built close to the northern wall of the fortress so that its residents could swiftly find refuge in the fortress in case of impending attack.

EILAT MAZAR

steps. Within the arched room was an assemblage of pottery testifying to the date of its last use—70 C.E., the year in which the Romans destroyed Jerusalem.[7]

The structure from the Second Temple period also incorporated some quite large stones from an even earlier structure. And, indeed, the Second Temple period remains sat on an earlier structure characterized by large, impressive stones. Some of these large stones had even been re-used in the construction of the still-later Byzantine house.

We began calling this early building under (and earlier than) the Second Temple remains the Large-Stone Structure. The name stuck, and we still call it that—at least until the time comes when we are able to identify it more specifically.

We also found part of the Large-Stone Structure in the excavation of Macalister and Duncan. They interpreted what were in fact the remains of the Large-Stone Structure as a Jebusite wall that had been destroyed by King David and left in ruins. Since Macalister and Duncan believed it was a wall that had been destroyed, they didn't bother to "peel back" the large stones that were found strewn over the entire area of the excavation and therefore couldn't have seen what we discovered when we removed the stones. We found giant walls from the Large-Stone Structure between 6 and 8 feet wide extending in every direction beyond the area of our excavation!

The eastern side of the Large-Stone Structure follows the upper eastern f ortification line of the City of David. About 15 or 20 feet below it on the south is the famous Stepped-Stone Structure. The Stepped-Stone Structure is the largest Iron Age structure in Israel, as tall as a 12-story building, built on the side of the hill. It now seems to be part of the same building complex as the Large-Stone Structure. Most scholars believed that the Stepped-Stone Structure supported an artificial platform on top of which stood the Fortress of Zion (2 Samuel 5:7), which has not survived. Now it seems that the Stepped-Stone Structure also supported the Large-Stone Structure.

YITZHAK HARARI

The northeastern side of the Large-Stone Structure was built directly on a 20-foot-high manmade rock cliff uncovered by Kenyon. At the foot of the cliff, Kenyon discovered the debris of ashlar stones and the proto-Aeolic capital. They had fallen from the Large-Stone Structure.

The Large-Stone Structure, now seen as a massive structure built on a high scarp, was not just any public building, but a structure that was clearly the product of inspiration, imagination and considerable economic investment. This is clear not only from the large, impressive stones from which it was constructed but also from the 5-foot-long proto-Aeolic capital that must have once been part of the building. This exemplar is the most beautiful and elegant proto-Aeolic capital ever found in Israel, surpassing those from Samaria and Megiddo. Imagine the column that supported this capital. Then imagine the building in which such columns stood.

Moreover, the area had not been previously

A SOLITARY FIGURE, standing in the area of the northeast corner of the Large-Stone Structure, conveys a sense of the scale of the building discovered by Mazar. She and her team had dug through remains from the Byzantine and Second Temple periods and found a large area of bedrock that had been leveled to create an area that pre-dates the construction of the Large-Stone Structure. Mazar's discovery also helps explain Kenyon's earlier finds in this area: The building blocks and the proto-Aeolic capital, it is now clear, had tumbled from the Large-Stone Structure.

settled. The site was apparently *outside* the walls of the Canaanite city. How do we know this? Beneath the Large-Stone Structure the bedrock had been previously leveled or, where cavities were too deep, filled with crushed limestone and made level. The leveled bedrock with the limestone fill created a broad flat open area that existed quite independently. No structural ruins of any kind were found that related to it. It is certainly one of the most interesting features of our excavation. It dates to the earliest construction stage of the site—before the Large-Stone Structure. It seems that before the Large-Stone Structure was built the site was an open, flat area, a testimony to the careful planning invested in its creation. Perhaps it was some sort of cult site used for worship.

We are not yet sure of the date of this open area. It is clearly earlier than the Large-Stone Structure and probably goes back to the Late Bronze Age (about 1500 B.C.E.) or even the Middle Bronze Age (about 1800 B.C.E.).

Lying on this open flat area was earth fill that helped us date the last use of this open site. The fill was mixed with large quantities of datable pottery sherds, mostly from cooking pots. (The fill also contained animal bones that have not yet been analyzed.) The big surprise was the date of this pottery. Some of it was from the Middle Bronze Age and a few sherds were from the Late Bronze Age, but the majority were from Iron Age I (12th-11th centuries B.C.E.).

The pottery from Iron Age I is quite different from the pottery of Iron Age IIa (tenth-ninth centuries B.C.E.). For example, the ware from Iron Age I is brownish and without slip (a thin layer of clay added after pottery has been turned but before firing) and not burnished (rubbed smooth). In Iron Age IIa, on the other hand, the pottery is often reddish and covered with red slip and is hand burnished; in Iron Age IIb, the burnishing is wheel-made. Moreover, vessels from Iron Age IIa have entirely different profiles from the earlier period.

We found Iron Age I pottery under the Large-Stone Structure in different areas and in impressive quantities.[8] Significantly, it is almost all badly worn. This suggests that these sherds came from the very end of Iron Age I (about 1000 B.C.E.), not earlier. This fill apparently already existed on the open area when the Large-Stone Structure was built. The Large-Stone Structure must have been built after this. How long after? That was the question.

Evidence from the last month of the excavation helped us answer this question. In two rooms in the northern section of the Large-Stone Structure, we discovered a second phase of construction within the building. On the northeast edge of the building there may have even been a third phase, evidently intended to strengthen the structure by the addition of another internal wall. Pottery that relates to these later phases dates to Iron Age IIa. This means that the building had at least two, or perhaps even three, phases over a period of less than two centuries. So the first phase, when the structure was built, must have been close to the beginning of Iron Age IIa, probably around the middle of the tenth century B.C.E., when the Bible says King David ruled the United Kingdom of Israel.

One small clay vessel is particularly important. It is a delicate black-on-red juglet imported from Cyprus (photo above). It is in excellent condition, almost whole. It would not have survived in this condition if it had been subjected to any major upheaval. It seems likely that it was moved when the internal wall was added during the third phase of the building. The lovely red color and style of the juglet clearly dates to the tenth-ninth centuries B.C.E (Iron Age IIa), providing a nice confirmation of our dating of the local pottery to the same date.

We found some pottery from Iron Age IIb (eighth-sixth century B.C.E.) in the northeastern corner of the Large-Stone Structure. This indicates that the building remained in use until the end of the First Temple period (which ended with the Babylonian destruction of Jerusalem in 586 B.C.E.).

The object that was perhaps our most startling find dates to the last period of use of the Large-Stone Structure—from the period just before the Babylonian destruction. It was a seal impression (called a bulla) that once sealed a document, which has long since disintegrated. Like bullae generally, this one is like a flattened ball of clay about the size of a fingernail. The credit for its discovery goes to the hawk eyes of Yoav Farhi, the supervisor of our Area A. He spotted

A DELICATE JUGLET, imported from Cyprus, survived in excellent condition at the Large-Stone Structure, indicating that the area did not suffer from a violent destruction. As at all excavations, pottery was crucial to dating the remains. Mazar has been able to detect three phases of construction of the Large-Stone Structure over less than two centuries, with the earliest dating to about the tenth century B.C.E.—when David would have ruled Israel's United Monarchy from his palace in Jerusalem.

it at the exact moment when the sun's rays illuminated the letters. Without this particular lighting, you can see nothing. Even when the bulla is lit from various directions, only letter fragments are visible. Lighting from a certain specific direction, however, suddenly illuminates all of the letters as if by magic.

The bulla contains three lines of ancient Hebrew script. Yoav quickly deciphered part of a name in the second line—ṢLM (Shalem). I took the bulla home that night. Well into the night, when the children were asleep and the house was quiet, I began to study it. Slowly, I deciphered the name in the first line: Yehuchal. Could it be a Biblical name? I did not recall any Yehuchal in the Bible. Perhaps my reading of the name was wrong. But just to make sure I pulled from the shelf a Biblical encyclopedia. There he was, as large as life—in the book of the prophet Jeremiah: King Zedekiah sent Yehuchal

GABI LARON/INSTITUTE OF ARCHAEOLOGY/HEBREW UNIVERSITY

JUST THE RIGHT angle of sunlight—and the hawk eyes of Yoav Farhi, an area supervisor on Mazar's dig—led to the discovery of this .4-inch-wide bulla, a lump of clay that had sealed an ancient document. Inscribed in three lines, the bulla reads, "Belonging to Yehuchal son of Shelemiyahu son of Shovi." The Book of Jeremiah twice mentions a Yehuchal (Jehucal in English Bibles) son of Shelemiah, indicating that this bulla dates to the late seventh-early sixth century B.C.E. Fittingly, Mazar studied this bulla with the help of a table of ancient letters prepared for an earlier excavation by Yair Shoham—Mazar's late husband and father of their three sons.

(Jehucal in English Bibles) son of Shelemiah to the prophet Jeremiah to pray for the people (Jeremiah 37:3).[9] In the following chapter, we learn that this same man, who was a royal minister, heard the decidedly unwelcome predictions of disaster coming from Jeremiah's lips.[10]

When I opened the encyclopedia and saw the same name in the Bible as was on the bulla, I let out a shriek of surprise that rang out through the still house. Fortunately, the children slept soundly. I felt as though I had just "resurrected" someone straight out of the Bible.

There is something else unusual about this bulla. In full it read: ליהוכלב נשלמיהו בנשבי "Belonging to Yehuchal ben (the son of) Shelemiyahu ben Shovi." Thus we now know the name of Yehuchal's grandfather, as well as his father. Why did Yehuchal mention his grandfather on his seal? This was hardly the standard practice. Perhaps his grandfather was a distinguished, well-known figure in his own right. In Yigal Shiloh's excavation in the 1980s, adjacent to our site, he found 45 bullae in the destruction layer of one of the rooms. But none of the bullae Shiloh excavated mentions the grandfather, only the father.

THE STEPPED-STONE STRUCTURE, the largest Iron Age structure in Israel, covers the northeastern slope of the City of David with a mantle of walls and terraces. So massive an edifice, it is generally agreed, must have supported an imposing structure above it. Many believed that structure was Jerusalem's fortress; Eilat Mazar suggests that the area just to the north, which she believes was the site of David's palace, would have been adjacent to the fortress.

ZEV RADOVAN

Yair Shoham, who published the bullae from Shiloh's excavation,[11] was not only an archaeologist and epigraphist, but also my husband and the father of our three sons. He passed away in 1997. One of the things he left us was an onomasticon of the names on the bullae he had published. I showed our children how I used Yair's table of letters to study and date the bulla we found in our excavation. The form of the letters on the bullae from Shiloh's excavation were the same as on our bulla. And Shiloh's bullae were very solidly dated to the end of the First Temple Period, so we are confident in dating our bulla to the same time. It was a wonderful family experience.

The most famous of Shiloh's bullae belonged to Gemaryahu ben Shafan, the King's scribe and minister at the time of the prophet Jeremiah (Jeremiah 36). Yehuchal is now the second royal minister whose name has appeared on a bulla from the City of David excavations.

In future seasons we hope to continue the exposure of the Large-Stone Structure. But what can we say at this point? Archaeologically, it appears that it was built either at the very end of Iron Age I or at the beginning of Iron Age IIa—either slightly before or slightly after 1000 B.C.E., about when the Bible tells us King David conquered Jerusalem from the Jebusites/Canaanites. Since no remnants of earlier construction were found beneath the building, it seems that this area was outside the Jebusite/Canaanite city.

Could the Large-Stone Structure have been the Jebusite fortress that David conquered, the Fortress of Zion mentioned in the Bible (2 Samuel 5:6-10)? This is unlikely, for it would mean that the citadel did not exist in the Canaanite city during the Middle and Late Bronze Ages and most of Iron Age I, because it was constructed only during the very last days of the Jebusite regime. That is difficult to accept, particularly in light of the character of the construction, which points to an imaginative new initiative with highly sophisticated building techniques, as reflected in the large scale and enormous efforts invested in constructing it.

Since it is unlikely that this was the Jebusite citadel, what else could it be? Perhaps a new temple? But this flies in face of the long tradition, confirmed by the

archaeological evidence, that Mount Moriah, where Abraham almost sacrificed his son Isaac (Genesis 22), became the site of the Temple (see 2 Chronicles 3:1)—namely the Temple Mount, several hundred feet north of our site. It is indeed unlikely that the Large-Stone Structure was the site of a temple.

What is left? Could this be the brainchild of a visionary new ruler who planned to expand the city with a temple to be built on the hilltop to the north? Did King David, now the ally of the Phoenicians, renowned for their building capabilities, authorize them to build a magnificent new palace for him outside but adjacent to the northen boundary of the old Canaanite city, shortly before the construction of the projected new Temple to its north?

The Biblical narrative, I submit, better explains the archaeology we have uncovered than any other hypothesis that has been put forward. Indeed, the archaeological remains square perfectly with the Biblical description that tells us David went down from there to the citadel. So you decide whether or not we have found King David's palace.

[1] Eilat Mazar, "Excavate King David's Palace," BAR, January/February 1997. See also Mazar, "The Undiscovered Palace of King David in Jerusalem—A Study in Biblical Archaeology," in Avi Faust, ed., *New Studies on Jerusalem* (Ramat Gan, Israel: Bar-Ilan Univ., 1996), pp. 9-20 (Hebrew).

[2] Kathleen M. Kenyon, *Digging Up Jerusalem* (New York: Praeger, 1974), p.114.

[3] Kenyon, "Excavations in Jerusalem 1962," *Palestine Exploration Quarterly* 95 (1963), p. 18.

[4] Kenyon, *Digging Up Jerusalem*, p. 103.

[5] Yigal Shiloh, "The Proto-Aeolic Capitals and Israelite Ashlar Masonry," *Qedem* 11.

[6] Eilat Mazar, "The Temple Mount Excavations in Jerusalem 1968-1978 directed by Benjamin Mazar, Final Report, volume II: The Byzantine and Early Islamic Periods," *Qedem* 43. (Volume III, also on the Byzantine period, is about to be published.) We will be able to date the house from the coins we discovered under the mosaic floor and under the drain pipe that funneled water into the cistern serving the building. The building came to an end at the beginning of the Islamic period. We will also be able to date this more precisely after we complete a more in-depth study of the finds. However, we can already say that the pottery found on the mosaic floor was of the finer and metallic Byzantine-ware type, whose appearance is characteristic of the beginning of the Islamic period.

[7] We will be able to deduce the exact construction date of the installations from further in-depth research regarding the numerous coins we found in the walls.

[8] Similar pottery has been found at other Iron I sites, such as Giloh and Shiloh. See Amihai Mazar, "Giloh: An Early Iron Israelite Settlement Site Near Jerusalem," *Israel Exploration Journal* 31 (1981), pp. 1-36 and Israel Finkelstein, ed., "Shiloh: The Archaeology of a Biblical Site," *Tel Aviv* 10, 1993.

[9] The second name on the seal is Shelemiyahu, a variant of Shelemya or, in the English spelling, Shelemiah. In Hebrew, Shelemiyahu simply adds a *vov* to the end of the Shelemyah.

[10] Here the Hebrew text omits an internal *heh* from the name and the English rendering is Jucal.

[11] Yair Shoham, "A Group of Hebrew Bullae from Yigal Shiloh's Excavations in the City of David," in Hillel Geva, ed., *Ancient Jerusalem Revealed* (Jerusalem: Israel Exploration Society and Washington, DC: Biblical Archaeology Society, 1994), pp. 55-61.

After publication, a member of Eilat Mazar's excavation team brought to our attention that BAR's reconstruction of the proto-Aeolic column on page 243 was in error. The capital was likely situated in the entrance of a great structure, rather than atop a column. The Hazor gate reconstruction bears a similar capital in its proper usage (see the photo in the Queries and Comments section of the May/June 2006 issue of BAR).

Related Reading

Hershel Shanks, First Person: "In Defense of Eilat Mazar," BAR, March/April 2008.

Eilat Mazar, "The Wall That Nehemiah Built," BAR, March/April 2009.

Hershel Shanks, "Jerusalem Roundup," BAR, March/April 2011.

Hershel Shanks, First Person: "The Bible as a Source of Testable Hypotheses," BAR, July/August 2011; Hershel Shanks, First Person: "When Is It OK for an Archaeologist to Speculate?" BAR, September/October 2011.

Avraham Faust, "Did Eilat Mazar Find David's Palace?" BAR, September/October 2012.

The Interchange Between Bible and Archaeology

THE CASE OF DAVID'S PALACE AND THE MILLO

NADAV NA'AMAN

EVIDENCE FROM THE BIBLE AND from archaeology must be interpreted independently of each other, but in the end they must be compared and interpreted.

Take Jerusalem: In view of the continuous settlement of Jerusalem from the tenth century B.C.E. until the Babylonian destruction of the First Temple in 586 B.C.E. and, after a short gap, throughout the Persian and Hellenistic periods, local traditions may well have passed orally from generation to generation. And these authentic local traditions might well have reached the authors of the Biblical narratives in the later periods.

With this in mind, I would like to consider our understanding of two major monuments in ancient Jerusalem: (1) The so-called Large Stone Structure (LSS) recently excavated by Hebrew University archaeologist Eilat Mazar and identified by her as King David's palace,* and (2) the Stepped Stone Structure (SSS) extending down the slope from the Large Stone Structure and said to be the Millo, referred to in the books of Samuel and Kings.

The Large Stone Structure and the Stepped Stone Structure are located south of Temple Mount in the oldest part of Jerusalem on a rocky spur known in ancient times and still today as the City of David. Unfortunately, excavation of the City of David is replete with difficulties. Bedrock is high, and late constructions and leveling have removed almost all traces of earlier buildings and scattered the artifacts. Each new city rested its foundations on bedrock and destroyed part of what was left underneath. Archaeology can identify only fragmentary remains and at best establish their date and function; often, erosion and obliteration of much of the evidence by later operations have left fragmented structures and dispersal of the artifacts.

According to the Bible, following David's conquest of the Jebusite "stronghold of Zion," he renamed the place the City of David and fortified it "from the Millo inward" (2 Samuel 5:7–9). Although David fortified the area from the Millo inward, the construction of the Millo itself was assigned to his son Solomon (1 Kings 9:15,24).

David's fortification of the City of David presumably enclosed it with a wall, and there he built a residence, literally a "house," for himself (2 Samuel 5:11). That he built a royal residence is also assumed in the account of his bringing the Ark into the City of David. As he did so, his wife Michal (Saul's daughter) saw him as she looked at him *out of the window* (2 Samuel 6:16), presumably from their residence.

Similarly, the story of David and Bathsheba also assumes that a royal residence was constructed in a

*Eilat Mazar, "Did I Find King David's Palace?" BAR, January/February 2006.

GARO NALBANDIAN

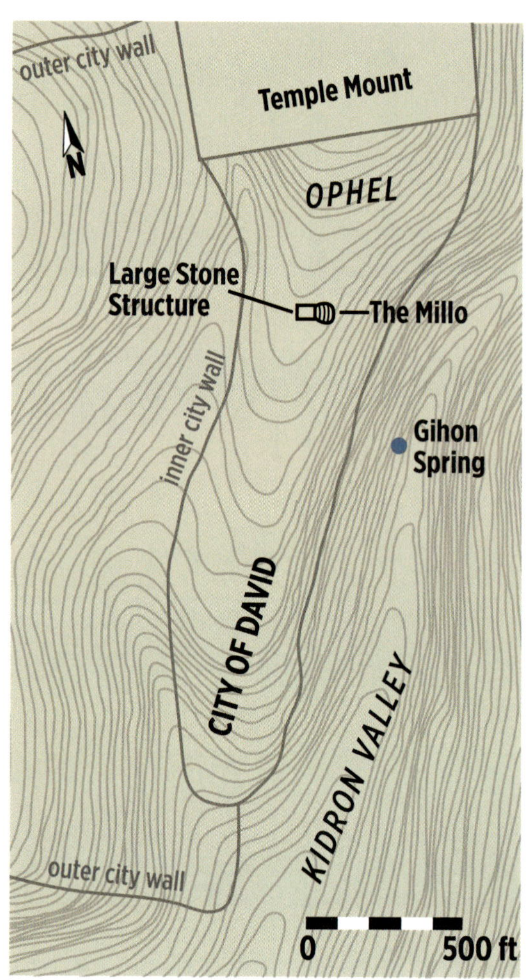

THE CITY OF DAVID, the oldest part of Jerusalem, sits on a 12-acre spur that extends south of the Temple Mount. It is here that David built his palace (the Large Stone Structure), supported by the Millo (the Stepped Stone Structure) extending down the slope. Here too is evidence of the rebuilding of the city wall when Nehemiah returned from the Babylonian exile.

prominent place in the city (2 Samuel 11)—the same prominent place in which Absalom later lay with his father's concubines (2 Samuel 16:22).

Half a millennium later, Nehemiah returned from the Babylonian exile and repaired the wall of the city. When it was completed, he organized a dedication procession; one group, on the east side of the city, after passing the Fountain Gate, went "straight ahead of them." Then "they went up the steps of the City of David, on the ascent to the wall, past the House of David, and up to the Water Gate on the east" (Nehemiah 12:37).

Here too we have a reference to David's house. As Nehemiah's wall has been reconstructed, it passed through a new line near the eastern summit of the city.[1] The House of David must therefore be sought near the Stepped Stone Structure built on the summit of the city's northeastern slope. One of Nehemiah's repair teams mended the wall from a point where "a tower juts out of the house of the king" (Nehemiah 3:25), still another reference to the royal residence. This tower must have been quite prominent because it is mentioned in the work of three of the repair teams (Nehemiah 3:25–27). Within this tower was apparently a court of the guard: One Palal repaired the wall from a point opposite "the tower which projects from the upper king's house which was part of the court of the guard" (Nehemiah 3:25).[2]

The court of the guard, located in the king's house, is mentioned again in Jeremiah 32:2: "Jeremiah the prophet was shut up in the court of the guard which was in the king of Judah's house." The court is frequently mentioned in the story cycle of Jeremiah (Jeremiah 32:8-12; 33:1; 37:21; 38:6,13,28; 39:14–15).[3]

Where was the king's house and the court of the guard?

Based on this Biblical description, I believe King David's residence should be sought on the crest of the City of David, near the Large Stone Structure unearthed by Eilat Mazar.

City of David

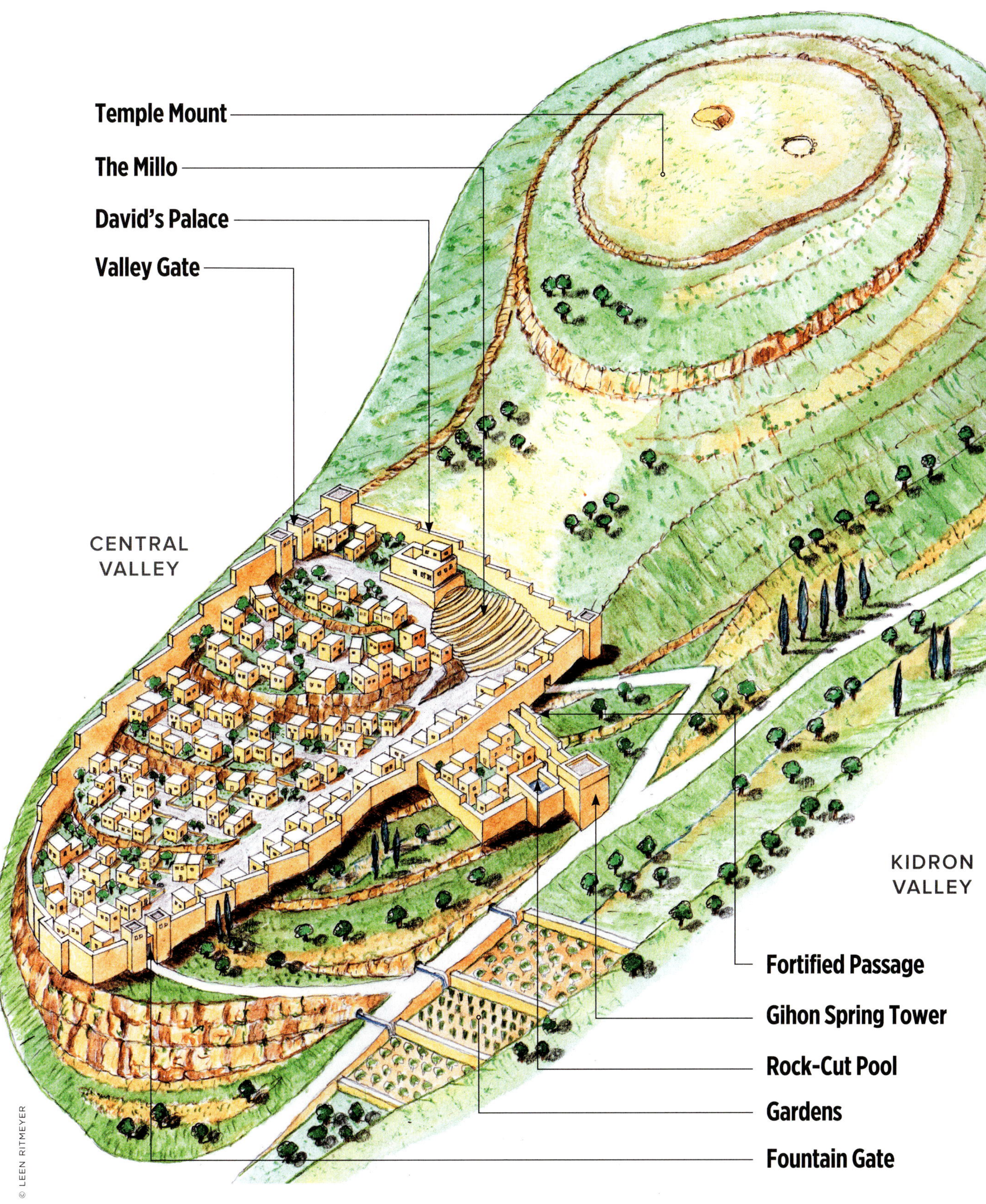

EILAT MAZAR

PLACING THE PALACE. A woman stands in the northeast corner of the Large Stone Structure, which Eilat Mazar identifies as the remains of King David's palace. The Book of Samuel refers to David's royal residence several times (2 Samuel 5:11; 2 Samuel 11; 2 Samuel 16:22). The combination of Biblical and archaeological evidence tends to confirm that Mazar has indeed found the remains of David's palace.

The Millo, our second topic, has always been somewhat of a mystery. "Millo" is the Hebrew term, but it is never translated. Its etymology may be derived from the verb *ml'*, to "fill up." I believe that Millo, a structure built of a fill of stones and earth, is the Biblical name of the Stepped Stone Structure.

This is indicated by an enigmatic Biblical passage involving King Joash (also Jehoash) of Judah who was assassinated by a conspiracy of his servants. They did the dirty deed "in the House of Millo which goes down to Silla" (2 Kings 12:21; 12:20 in English). The House of Millo is a designation of the royal residence located *on top* of the Millo. This account indicates that Joash was assassinated in his palace (compare 2 Samuel 4:5,7; 1 Kings 16:18). Indeed, according to 2 Chronicles 24:25 Joash's servants "slew him on his bed."

That this was the royal residence tends to be confirmed by the fact that two bullae (seal impressions) of Judahite officials mentioned in the Bible (in Jeremiah 37:3; 38:1)—Gedaliah son of Pashhur and Jehucal son of Shelemiah son of Shobai—were discovered in excavations near the Large Stone Structure, near the place where the two officials must have officiated.

It thus appears that the palace built by King David played a central role in the economic and administrative life of Jerusalem at least until the time of Joash (c. 841–801) and even later. Somewhat amazingly, this fact has been ignored in studies of First Temple Jerusalem. The Large Stone Structure, which Eilat

REINFORCING THE PALACE. The Stepped Stone Structure sits on the eastern slope of the City of David. The structures near the bottom of the Stepped Stone Structure are later Israelite houses built centuries after the Stepped Stone Structure was constructed. What the author believes to be David's palace (the Large Stone Structure) was built on the ridge above the Stepped Stone Structure; this photograph was taken before the Large Stone Structure (David's Palace) was excavated by Eilat Mazar.

ZEV RADOVAN

COURTIERS OF THE KING. Seal impressions (bullae) of two of the king's courtiers mentioned in the book of Jeremiah were recently excavated—one (Gedaliah, son of Pashhur, lower left) was found in David's palace itself, the other (Jehucal, son of Shelemiah) was found a few feet away. Both were courtiers in the reign of King Zedekiah (early sixth century B.C.E.), indicating that David's palace was still in use at that time.

INSET: BOTH PHOTOS BY GABY LARON, THE INSTITUTE OF ARCHAEOLOGY, THE HEBREW UNIVERSITY

Mazar unearthed and identified as the residence of King David, is indeed a suitable candidate for this building, or more accurately, for its northeastern wing. A large amount of pottery from the Iron Age and Persian periods (Nehemiah's time) was also unearthed in and near the edifice, indicating continuity of settlement in the area.*[4] Unfortunately, the erosion of the floors of the building and the deplorable state of its preservation prevents the verification of her attractive suggestion of a tenth-century date for its foundation.

One other Biblical reference should be mentioned: According to the Bible, Solomon built his own palace at the time he constructed the Temple (1 Kings 7:1). Of course archaeological access to the Temple Mount is not feasible. In the absence of any archaeological evidence, it is my view that the Temple Solomon built on the Temple Mount was a modest shrine that developed gradually, stage by stage, over many generations, until it became the major Temple of the kingdom.[5] As for Solomon's residence adjacent to the Temple, the reality is that he had two royal residences: one on the Temple Mount and the other in the City of David. This naturally raises the question of their relation. Tentatively, I suggest that the residence in the City of David was the earlier residence and was more important in the early stage of the Judahite monarchy. The residence on the Temple Mount was initially a modest building, originally perhaps a ceremonial palace erected near the shrine that developed gradually over time.** Since the earlier residence initially built by King David was built in a densely inhabited area which placed limitations on its growth, the center gradually shifted to the Temple Mount, which became the seat of the royal palace and the site of the central Temple of the kingdom.[6]

*Eilat Mazar, "The Wall That Nehemiah Built," BAR, March/April 2009.

**For David Ussishkin's view that Solomon's palace was north, rather than south, of the Temple, see "Where Was Solomon's Palace?" in "Jerusalem Roundup," BAR, March/April 2011.

[1] Kathleen M. Kenyon, *Digging up Jerusalem* (London: Benn Ltd., 1974), pp. 181–187; Yigal Shiloh, *Excavations at the City of David I, 1978–1982,* Interim Report of the First Five Seasons, Qedem 19 (Jerusalem: Institute of Archaeology, The Hebrew University, 1984), p. 29; Hugh G.M. Williamson, "Nehemiah's Walls Revisited," *Palestine Exploration Quarterly* 116 (1977), p. 82; Hugh G.M. Williamson, *Ezra, Nehemiah* , WBC 16 (Waco, TX: Word Books, 1985), pp. 200, 208; Joseph Blenkinsopp, *Ezra-Nehemiah—A Commentary*, OTL (London: SCM Press, 1989), pp. 231–232, 237; Hanan Eshel, "Jerusalem under Persian Rule: The City's Layout and the Historic Background," in Shmuel Ahituv and Amihai Mazar, eds., *The History of Jerusalem: The Biblical Period* (Jerusalem: Yad Ben-Zvi, 2000), p. 339 [Hebrew].

[2] While almost all English translations say "court of the guard," the NJPS has "prison compound," no doubt based on the reference in Jeremiah 32:2 as the place where the prophet was imprisoned.

[3] For the court of the guard, see Gary A. Herion, "Guard, Court of the," *Anchor Bible Dictionary* 2 (New York: Doubleday, 1992), 1099a.

[4] For the pottery unearthed in the excavations of the site, see Eilat Mazar, *Preliminary Report on the City of David Excavations 2005 at the Visitors Center Area* (Jerusalem: Shalem Press, 2007); Eilat Mazar, *The Palace of King David: Excavations at the Summit of the City of David, Preliminary Report of Seasons 2005–2007* (Jerusalem: Shoham Academic Research and Publication, 2009).

[5] For the dependence of the original Solomonic shrine on the palace and its gradual growth until it became the state temple, see David Ussishkin, "The Temple Mount in Jerusalem during the First Temple Period: An Archaeologist's View," in J. David Schloen, ed., *Exploring the Longue Durée: Essays in Honor of Lawrence E. Stager* (Winona Lake, IN: Eisenbrauns, 2009), pp. 473–483; André Lemaire, "The Evolution of the Eighth-Century B.C.E. Jerusalem Temple," in Israel Finkelstein and Nadav Na'aman, eds., *The Fire Signals of Lachish: Studies in the Archaeology and History of Israel in the Late Bronze, Iron Age, and Persian Period in Honor of David Ussishkin* (Winona Lake, IN: Eisenbrauns, 2011), pp. 195–202, with earlier literature on p. 195.

[6] This article is an abbreviated and partial account of a much longer paper in *Biblica* 93 (2012), pp. 21–42, titled "Biblical and Historical Jerusalem in the Tenth and Fifth-Fourth Centuries B.C.E." See also Nadav Na'aman, "Five Notes on Jerusalem in the First and Second Temple Periods," *Tel Aviv* 39 (2012), p. 93.

Cow Town or Royal Capital?

EVIDENCE FOR IRON AGE JERUSALEM

NADAV NA'AMAN

BAR READERS ARE ALREADY FAMILIAR with a recent school of Biblical interpretation that denies any historicity to the ancient Israelite kingdom of David and Solomon.[1] I call this the "revisionist" school. Others have described these scholars as "Biblical minimalists"[2] or even "Biblical nihilists."

Jerusalem in the tenth century B.C.E., when David and Solomon were supposed to have lived, was, according to the Biblical revisionists, hardly a town, let alone a city. It was, they contend, still centuries away from being able to challenge any of the dozens of more powerful small autonomous towns in the region. According to two prominent members of this school of thought, University of Copenhagen scholars Niels Peter Lemche and Thomas Thompson, "[Jerusalem] first took on the form and acquired the status of a city, capable of being understood as a state capital, sometime in the middle of the seventh century."[3]

The Biblical evidence that contradicts this view is worthless, they say, because it was written down hundreds of years after the events it describes. The Deuteronomistic history (Deuteronomy through Kings) was composed, according to these scholars, no earlier than the fifth century B.C.E. The histories of David and Solomon were thus written hundreds of years after the deaths of the two kings—assuming they were real people. Therefore, we are told, only non-Biblical sources and archaeological evidence can be used to write a history of early Israel—and, alas, there is not enough material of this kind to write such a history.

The argument of the Biblical revisionists is thus essentially negative: We cannot rely on the Bible. And other evidence varies from scant to nonexistent. Especially for Jerusalem, the archaeological evidence, despite the enormous number of excavations in the city, has provided very little, if anything, from the tenth century B.C.E.

My first response—I shall concentrate on Jerusalem here—is that they are wrong about the archaeological evidence. In the 1980s Yigal Shiloh found a few walls that can be dated to this period.[4] In the 1960s Kathleen Kenyon also exposed a wall fragment from the tenth century.[5] The famous Stepped-Stone Structure may also date to this period.[6] Nevertheless, it is true that tenth-century remains from Jerusalem are few and come only from the ridge south of the Temple Mount known as the City of David; no pottery from this period has been found in other excavated areas of Jerusalem.

KING SHISHAK OF EGYPT, in the fifth year of the reign of the Judahite king Rehoboam (928-911 B.C.E.), "took the fortified cities of Judah and came as far as Jerusalem" (2 Chronicles 12:4). Pharaoh Sheshonq I (945-924 B.C.E.), called Shishak in the Bible, campaigned in Israel and Judah and had a victory stela (right) carved at the temple to Amun in Karnak. Sheshonq also drew up lists boasting of his conquests, among them Arad, Gibeon and Megiddo (where archaeologists have uncovered another victory stela erected by Sheshonq). In this regard, the Bible records a substantively accurate chronology, even if the books of Kings and Chronicles were not put into their final form until hundreds of years after Sheshonq's invasion. How did these memories remain alive so long? Author Nadav Na'aman suggests that scribes, employed by the Jerusalem court, recorded historical events in their annals, which were later used by the Biblical authors to compose Israel's history. Na'aman concludes that the relatively unimportant Rehoboam probably was not responsible for creating the office of court scribe; rather, that office was likely instituted during the united monarchy of David or Solomon, as the Bible relates (see, for example, 1 Kings 4:3).

ERICH LESSING

From this the revisionists conclude that at this time Jerusalem was at most a small provincial town.[7]

The paucity of material from the tenth century, however, can be explained on other grounds. First, the most likely place where Jerusalem's public buildings and important monuments were located is under the Temple Mount, which for obvious reasons cannot be excavated. Thus, the most important area for investigation, and the one to which the Biblical histories of David and Solomon mainly refer, remains *terra incognita*.

But even the area that is, at least partially, available for excavation—the ridge known as the City of David—was continuously settled from the tenth through the early sixth centuries B.C.E. Destructions leave a distinct mark in the archaeological record. Not so continuous occupation, which often leaves only a few remains of earlier building activity. Jerusalem was built on terraces and bedrock; each new city destroyed what was underneath, robbed and reused stones from the earlier buildings, and set its foundations on the solid rock. So we should not expect to find abundant remains of earlier strata. No wonder that the city destroyed by the Babylonians in 586 B.C.E. is the best-known level of the Iron Age city.

For these reasons, it is dangerous to draw negative inferences from the lack of archaeological evidence.

Fortunately, in this case we have a way of testing whether it is legitimate to make any negative conclusions based on the paucity of archaeological evidence. This involves the famous Amarna letters of the 14th century B.C.E., discovered at Tell el-Amarna in Egypt. The letters, written in Akkadian cuneiform, the diplomatic lingua franca of the day, consist of over 300 pieces of diplomatic correspondence between two Egyptian pharaohs (Amenophis III [1391-1353] and Amenophis IV, also known as Akhenaten [1353-1337]) and local rulers in Canaan. The letters are, of course, a treasure trove of information about the period.

Jerusalem, called Urusalim in the Amarna letters,* figures prominently in this diplomatic correspondence. According to the Amarna letters, Canaan was then

*There is no doubt of the equation Urusalim=Jerusalem, based on the geographical description of its location.

under Egyptian hegemony, and Jerusalem was ruled by a local king. The city was the seat of a local dynasty in which governance passed from father to son. In non-Egyptian correspondence these local rulers were also referred to as kings.[8] Egyptian messengers came quite often to the court of Jerusalem. The Jerusalem king sent rich caravans loaded with gifts for the pharaoh.

Jerusalem's territory extended from just south of Bethel in the north to Tel Hebron in the south, and from the Jordan River in the east to the hills of the Shephelah in the west.[9]

It is clear from the Amarna letters that in the 14th century B.C.E. Jerusalem was a capital city from which a considerable territory was ruled (subject to Egyptian oversight). It had a palace and a court with attendants and servants, a temple in which the king played a central role, and an ideology that established him as head of state.

The court also had a scribe, who was in charge of diplomatic correspondence with Egyptian authorities. Six letters were sent by the king of Jerusalem to the pharaoh, exhibiting the diplomatic sophistication of his court and the quality of his scribe.

The picture as revealed by the archaeological record alone, on the other hand, is rather opaque. As with the tenth century, there are hardly any remains from the Late Bronze Age II (14th-13th century B.C.E.). Only a handful of Late Bronze Age II pottery and a few building fragments have been unearthed in the extensive excavations in the Late Bronze Age II city. Scholars would never have guessed from the excavations of Jerusalem that any scribal activity took place there in Late Bronze Age II.

Let's now turn from the Amarna letters to the Bible—in the time of Ezra and Nehemiah, after the return to Jerusalem of the exiles from Babylonia in the fifth century B.C.E. A major fortification wall built under Nehemiah's supervision is described in detail in Nehemiah's memoirs (Nehemiah 3:1-32). There is little doubt that such a wall was in fact constructed, but almost no trace of it has been positively identified in excavations. The city of the Persian period, described so vividly in the books of Ezra and Nehemiah, is known only from fills and building fragments and is mainly identified because it is sandwiched between the debris from the Iron Age and the Hellenistic period.[10] This is another example of the difficulty in recovering strata that developed peacefully and did not end with catastrophe. It is another caution against drawing negative conclusions from negative archaeological evidence.

What I have argued so far is that we cannot judge Jerusalem on the basis of negative archaeological evidence. Is there anything we can say affirmatively about the tenth-century city? The answer is yes, on several counts.

NASHON SNEH/ISRAEL ANTIQUITIES AUTHORITY

LITERACY IN THE UNITED MONARCHY? Inscribed potsherds (ostraca) from the eighth and seventh centuries B.C.E., found in both Israel and Judah, provide evidence for writing in the tenth century B.C.E. These ostraca contain Hebrew characters as well as signs and numerals in hieratic—a cursive form of Egyptian hieroglyphics. Curiously, these hieratic signs do not appear in contemporaneous documents of Israel's neighbors, even though Egypt's relations with Philistia and Phoenicia in the ninth and eighth centuries B.C.E. were much closer than those with Israel. Moreover, no eighth- or seventh-century Egyptian parallels have been found for many of the signs on the Hebrew ostraca. So author Na'aman concludes that the hieratic writing must have entered the Hebrew script in the tenth century. And since the hieratic signs appear on ostraca from both Israel and Judah, the borrowing probably took place before the division of the monarchy into northern and southern kingdoms. If so, writing was introduced into the Jerusalem court in the tenth century, probably in the time of David and Solomon.

First, the Bible. Did the scribes who wrote the histories of David and Solomon have before them original documents from the time of these kings? Or did they compose the history only on the basis of oral traditions? Was there even writing in tenth-century Jerusalem?

Many scholars argue that the Bible's references to the office of the scribe in the courts of David and Solomon, along with various Biblical lists that were possibly drawn from original documents, indicate that the tenth-century court of Jerusalem was indeed literate. Scholars of the revisionist school, on the other hand, assume that writing did not enter the Jerusalem court until the eighth century B.C.E. and that the Biblical history of the united monarchy is no different from the history of premonarchical Israel.

It is true that no extra-Biblical source mentions either David or Solomon. This is not surprising. Detailed accounts of first-millennium international affairs appear for the first time in the ninth century B.C.E. All Syro-Palestinian inscriptions of the tenth century refer to local affairs and shed no light on political events. In other words, even if David and Solomon accomplished the deeds attributed to them in the Bible, no source would have mentioned their names.

There is one exception to the local nature of tenth-century inscriptions: the topographical list of Pharaoh Shishak (945-924 B.C.E.), the founder of Egypt's XXII Dynasty. Toward the end of his reign, Shishak conducted a military campaign in Canaan, primarily against Israel and the non-Judahite parts of the Negev, and left a long list of places conquered by his army—including the town of Arad.

Shishak's campaign is described in 1 Kings 14:25-28. How did the author of the Book of Kings, who probably lived in the late seventh or early sixth century B.C.E., some 300 years after the time of Shishak, know about this military operation? The answer is clear: He must have taken the information from a written text. Otherwise, the memory of the operation would have fallen into oblivion.

The account of Shishak's campaign in Kings indicates that scribes must have been active in Jerusalem's court at least by the late tenth century B.C.E., during the reign of Rehoboam. It is unlikely, however, that scribes were introduced by the relatively unimportant Rehoboam. The Bible relates that the court employed scribes even earlier; royal scribes are mentioned in David's and Solomon's lists of high officials (2 Samuel 8:17, 20:25; 1 Kings 4:3). It would have been scribes who kept the administrative records that are included in the histories of David and Solomon:

- the lists of David's wives and sons (2 Samuel 3:2-5, 5:14-16);
- the list of David's officers (2 Samuel 23:8-39);
- the list of Solomon's high officials (1 Kings 4:2-6);
- the list of Solomon's 12 officers and their districts (1 Kings 4:9-19);
- details of Solomon's building activities in Jerusalem and elsewhere in his kingdom (1 Kings 9:15, 17-18).

Records of this kind are routinely produced by scribes as part of the administrative management of kingdoms. This information might well have been drawn from old written records and used by the Biblical author to describe affairs of state in the time of David and Solomon.

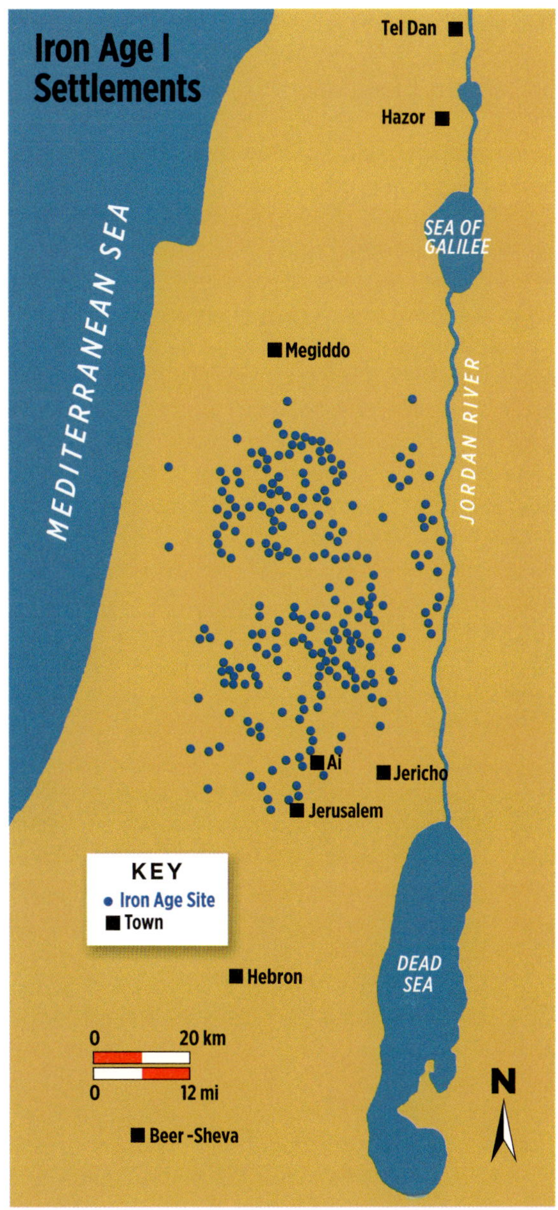

Ostraca from both Israel and Judah dating to the eighth and seventh centuries B.C.E. also demonstrate that writing was an important aspect of the tenth-century court. These ostraca, in Old Hebrew script, contain certain hieratic numerals and signs (hieratic is a cursive form of Egyptian hieroglyphics) that are not found in the documents of Israel's neighbors, but only in Hebrew script. Egyptian relations with the Philistine and Phoenician kingdoms were much closer in the ninth and early eighth centuries than they were with Israel and Judah—so it is hardly conceivable that hieratic signs would have entered *only* the Hebrew script at that time. Moreover, no definite eighth- or seventh-century paleographical parallels have been found in Egypt for many of the hieratic signs found on the Hebrew ostraca. These hieratic signs must have entered the Hebrew script before the division of the monarchy—namely, in the tenth century B.C.E.[11]

From all of this we can reasonably conclude that writing was introduced into the Jerusalem court in the tenth century B.C.E., probably in the time of David or Solomon. Scribes operated in the court of Jerusalem as the king's private secretaries and as officials in the administration of the kingdom.

There is more: The memory of David's founding of Jerusalem as the capital of his dynasty is deeply rooted in Israelite historical traditions. David is described as the conqueror of Jerusalem and the founder of a royal dynasty in Biblical passages written at different times and in a variety of genres—history, prophecy, hymn, liturgy. These accounts tell how David captured the stronghold of Zion, renamed it the City of David, occupied and rebuilt the city (2 Samuel 5:6-9), and transferred the ark of YHWH to his new capital (2 Samuel 6:1-19). A passage from Isaiah recalls David's capture of Jerusalem (which is metaphorically called "Ariel," or YHWH's altar hearth) with the words "Ah, Ariel, Ariel, the city where David encamped!" (Isaiah 29:1). The procession of the ark from its former abode in "the countryside of Jaar" to its permanent abode in Jerusalem is alluded to in a royal psalm (Psalm 132:6-8). The variety of sources and genres strongly suggest a historical basis for these records. Since scholars generally accept the reliability of the Biblical account of Omri's founding of Samaria as the capital of the northern kingdom of Israel (1 Kings 16:24), why should they not believe that the account of David's conquest and occupation of Jerusalem is also basically historical?

Moreover, David's renaming of Jerusalem as "City of David" has distinct parallels in the ancient Near East. It was a common practice to name cities after their founders. For example, Kar Tukulti-Ninurta is named after the Assyrian king Tukulti-Ninurta I; Dur Sharru-ken is named after the Assyrian king Sargon II; and Azitiwadiya is named after its founder, the king of Adana.

Another vital piece of evidence for the existence of the Davidic monarchy comes from the ninth-century B.C.E. stela from Tel Dan, in northern Galilee. The first fragment of this Aramaic stela was discovered in 1993; two other pieces were found in 1994.[12] In lines 7 through 9 of the inscription, the Aramean king, most probably Hazael, king of Damascus, writes: "[I killed Jo]ram son of [Ahab] king of Israel, and [I] killed [Ahaz]iahu son of [Jehoram kin]g of *Beth David*." This indicates that the kingdom of Judah was called *Beth David* (House of David) in the second half of the ninth century B.C.E. We know from other sources that this form of designation—"house of" (*beth*), plus the name of the founder—was typical of the many new west Semitic kingdoms that emerged in the Fertile Crescent in the early first millennium B.C.E. For example, the north Syrian kingdom of Arpad is called *Bit-Agusi*, after the name of Gusi/Agusi; the kingdom of Damascus is called *Bit-Hazaili*, after the name of Hazael; and the kingdom of Israel is called *Bit-Humri*, after the name of Omri.[13] The name *Beth David* for the kingdom of Judah fits perfectly into this ancient Near Eastern usage.

I also believe that we have enough in the Bible to conclude that Solomon must have built a temple, even if it was not as grand as the Bible describes it. We must remember that the author of the Book of Kings lived hundreds of years after the time of Solomon and did not know the exact shape, dimensions or contents of the original temple. He therefore described it after the temple of his own day, assuming a direct continuity between the earliest and latest temples. The original temple would have been much smaller and more modestly decorated; it would have been renovated and gradually expanded during the 350 years of its existence, until it assumed the splendor of the late monarchical period temple. Yet the memory of Solomon as founder of the temple must be authentic, and it is even possible that the historian had seen a Solomonic building inscription from the dedication of the original temple.

Another bit of evidence confirming the existence of the tenth-century B.C.E. united monarchy comes from Isaiah. This eighth-century prophet knew that a united monarchy existed before the division, after Solomon's death, into the northern kingdom of Israel and the southern kingdom of Judah. In an undeniably early passage (late eighth century B.C.E.), Isaiah speaks of a terrible time that is coming, a time so bad that we have not seen its like "since the day that Ephraim left Judah" (Isaiah 7:17). Ephraim is another name for Israel. The prophet is referring to the split-up of the united monarchy.

All this evidence strongly supports the Biblical claims that (a) David conquered Jerusalem and made it his capital, (b) he founded a royal dynasty that ruled from Jerusalem, (c) Solomon built a temple, and (d) a court was established in the new capital with scribes among its officials.

We can also learn a great deal about the united monarchy from the archaeological evidence relating to its emergence. The period before this monarchy is the period of the Judges. In archaeological terminology, the period of the Judges is Iron Age I

(1200-1000 B.C.E.). Recent archaeological surveys have shown that there were about 255 settlements in the central hill country of Canaan in Iron Age I.[14] Even if there was only a modest increase during the time of the united monarchy, there must have been 300 to 350 settlements in the central highlands that were ruled from Jerusalem, as compared to about 30 settlements in Late Bronze Age II. Such a large number of settlements within the monarchy's confines would have required the immediate creation of an administrative apparatus to manage the districts of the new kingdom.

After the split-up, there is no question about the settlement density in the northern kingdom of Israel. The situation in Judah was less dramatic, but not quite so extreme as the Biblical revisionists would have us believe. For example, according to Thompson, "There is... little basis for affirming the existence of a kingdom of Judah in the south [at the time of the split-up described in the Bible]."[15] There was not "sufficient density of population," he says.[16] According to recent archaeological surveys, however, there were at least 34 settlements in the Judahite highlands alone in the tenth century. Following the division of the monarchy, there must have been 35 to 45 sites in the kingdom of Judah, plus a few more sites in the Shephelah and in the Beersheba Valley—more than the number of sites in the kingdoms of Shechem and Jerusalem combined during the Amarna period (14th century B.C.E.).

Thompson unfortunately neither takes into account all of the available evidence nor does justice to the complexity of the problem.

Before concluding, I would like to discuss two other points. First, should the united monarchy be considered a kingdom, like a modern state, or should it more properly be described as a chiefdom? Second, what were the geographical limits of the Davidic "empire"?

A monograph by D.W. Jamieson-Drake[17] is widely cited by the Biblical revisionists for the proposition that Judah did not become a state, and that Jerusalem was not a major administrative center, any earlier than the eighth century B.C.E. Jamieson-Drake bases his conclusion on surveys and excavations in modern Israel; he analyzes the size and distribution of settlements as well as the kinds of social stratification suggested by public works and luxury items. In the tenth and ninth centuries, Jamieson-Drake argues, Judah should be defined as a chiefdom, not even an incipient state: "Judah was a small state in the eighth-seventh centuries, but not before."[18] The Biblical revisionists have reached similar conclusions.[19]

To his credit (and in contrast to other Biblical revisionists), Jamieson-Drake uses clear definitions of "chiefdom" and "state," and he provides clear criteria for the transition from one kind of entity to the other.[20] His conclusions are sound and reasonable, and accord well with the survey conducted recently in the area of the kingdom of Judah.[21] Jamieson-Drake does not dismiss the Biblical descriptions of David and Solomon, but he gives them little credence and suggests that these two kings only set in motion the institutional forces that developed gradually into a full-blown state in the eighth century B.C.E.[22]

While Jamieson-Drake draws a clear line between Biblical and socio-archaeological definitions and data, the line is less clear in the works of his followers. Broadly speaking, they all adopt his conclusion that a state (in the modern sociological sense) centered in Jerusalem emerged in the early eighth century B.C.E. at the earliest. Other Biblical revisionists, however, illegitimately use Jamieson-Drake's socio-archaeological conclusions to dismiss most, or even all, of the Biblical data about tenth-century Israel.[23]

I agree with Jamieson-Drake that Judah was a chiefdom in the tenth and ninth centuries and that it did not become a state until the eighth century. I would suggest that Jerusalem, the center of this chiefdom, was what might be defined as a "stronghold," that is, a fortified residence located in the mountains.

It was common in western Asiatic chiefdoms for tribal chiefs to have their seats in fortified or naturally hilly strongholds. Such forts were sometimes the nuclei around which capital cities later developed. This is how Jerusalem gradually expanded in the ninth century B.C.E., becoming a capital city and the center of a state only in the eighth century.

But its rulers considered themselves kings and were regarded as such by their neighbors and inhabitants. They saw Jerusalem as the governing center of the tenth-century B.C.E. kingdom. The "stronghold of Zion" was the seat of the Davidic dynasty and the ruling elite. Indeed, the City of David was known as "the stronghold of Zion" (2 Samuel 5:7; 1 Chronicles 11:5).

We must always take into account the gap between modern definitions of states and how ancient societies defined themselves. A clear line must be drawn between the two sets of terms. Scholars should state explicitly which terminology they are using. Modern definitions might be the more "scientifically" accurate, but it is equally important to analyze ancient societies according to their own terms and self-perceptions.

The same kinds of considerations are relevant to the geographical extent of the Davidic kingdom: We must distinguish between what was understood at the time as part of the kingdom and how we would characterize it today using modern sociological and anthropological definitions.

According to the Biblical account, David conquered Philistia, Aram, Ammon, Moab and Edom and brought all these kingdoms under his yoke. This great kingdom was short-lived, however, and fell apart immediately after David's death (1 Kings 11:14-25).

Revisionist scholars sometimes assume that such an "empire" could not have existed.[24] But was it really impossible?

Again, let us look at a comparison provided by the Amarna letters. In about 1400 B.C.E. (Late Bronze Age II), Shechem was the seat of a local dynasty. A military offensive by the Shechemite king Lab'ayu extended his kingdom east to the Jordan River and southwest as far as Gezer and Gath in southern Canaan. Lab'ayu mounted this offensive even though his kingdom previously included only about 25 settlements.

Compare this with the situation in David's time. As we have seen, about 255 Iron Age I sites have been discovered in the central hill country of Palestine. Taking into account a moderate increase of settlement, we may assume that the overall number of tenth-century sites in the central highlands was at least 300. Even if we assume that David's kingdom encompassed only the highlands on both sides of the Jordan, the population in his kingdom was many times larger than that of Shechem in the Late Bronze Age II. This abundance of manpower would have enabled David to mobilize an army and conquer large areas. Since David's conquest is described as short-lived, with the "empire" falling apart immediately after the conqueror's death, no established administration would have been set up in the subjugated areas. Only the might of David and the fear of his army would have kept them under his dominion. There are many historical analogies for short-lived conquests of large territories; these conquests also ended with the death of the conqueror. There is therefore nothing impossible about the main outlines of the Biblical account of David's conquest.

Mario Liverani has written about the requirements for the exertion of physical control over a population: "The physical presence of the king in a remote country is sufficient (although necessary) to demonstrate his political control thereon. A victorious raid, even a pacific one, an expedition aiming at knowledge more than at conquest, is the [only] required symbolic achievement—not an effective administrative organization."[25]

This notion of subjugation, which is supported by many historical examples, may well explain the Biblical description of David's great kingdom, provided that at a certain moment in his career he actually reached the remote areas attributed to him. In short, there is nothing impossible about the Biblical description of the extent of David's kingdom, even applying modern concepts of political control.

[1] See the following BAR articles: "'Annual Miracle' Visits Philadelphia," March/April 1996; and Hershel Shanks, "New Orleans Gumbo: Plenty of Spice at Annual Meeting," March/April 1997.

[2] Although Philip Davies, one of the leading Biblical revisionists, has called this term a "sneering epithet," Yale University scholar William Hallo has characterized it as "fairly innocuous" ("Biblical History in Its Near Eastern Setting: The Contextual Approach," in *Scripture in Context*, ed. Carl D. Evans, William W. Hallo and John B. White [Pittsburgh, PA: Pickwick, 1980], p. 3).

[3] Niels Peter Lemche and Thomas L. Thompson, "Did Biran Kill David? The Bible in the Light of Archaeology," *Journal for the Study of the Old Testament* 64 (1994), p. 20.

[4] David Tarler and Jane M. Cahill, "David, City of," *The Anchor Bible Dictionary* (New York: Doubleday, 1992), vol. 2, pp. 52-67.

[5] Kathleen Kenyon, *Digging up Jerusalem* (London: Benn, 1974), pp. 92, 114-115. See also G.J. Wightman, *The Walls of Jerusalem: From the Canaanites to the Mamluks*, Mediterranean Archaeology Supplement 4 (Sydney: Meditarch, 1993), pp. 33-35.

[6] See Yigal Shiloh, *Excavations at the City of David I, 1978-1982, Qedem* 19 (Jerusalem: Hebrew University, 1984), p. 27. However, Tarler and Cahill have recently suggested that the Stepped-Stone Structure was constructed in the 13th-12th century B.C.E. ("David, City of," *Anchor Bible Dictionary*).

[7] See Thompson, *Early History of the Israelite People: From the Written and Archaeological Sources*, Studies in the History of the Ancient Near East 4 (Leiden: Brill, 1992), pp. 331-333; and Lemche, "Is It Still Possible to Write a History of Israel?" *Scandinavian Journal of the Old Testament* 8 (1994), pp. 184-185.

[8] For details, see Nadav Na'aman, "The Contribution of the Amarna Letters on Jerusalem's Political Position in the Tenth Century B.C.E.," *Bulletin of the American Schools of Oriental Research* 304 (1997), pp. 17-27.

[9] Na'aman, "Canaanite Jerusalem and Its Central Hill Country Neighbors in the Second Millennium B.C.E.," *Ugarit-Forschungen* 24 (1992), pp. 275-291.

[10] Tarler and Cahill, "David, City of."

[11] O. Goldwasser, "An Egyptian Scribe from Lachish and the Hieratic Tradition of the Hebrew Kingdoms," *Tel Aviv* 18 (1991), pp. 251-252.

[12] Avraham Biran and Joseph Naveh, "An Aramaic Stele Fragment from Tel Dan," *Israel Exploration Journal* 43 (1993), and "The Tel Dan Inscription: A New Fragment," *Israel Exploration Journal* 45 (1995).

[13] Na'aman, "Beth-David in the Aramaic Stela from Tel Dan," *Biblische Notizen* 79 (1995), pp. 17-24.

[14] See the following articles in *From Nomadism to Monarchy: Archaeological and Historical Aspects of Early Israel*, eds. Israel Finkelstein and Na'aman (Jerusalem: Yad Itzhak Ben-Zvi, 1994): Adam Zertal, "'To the Land of the Perizzites and the Giants': On the Israelite Settlement in the Hill Country of Manasseh," pp. 54-59; Avi Ofer, "'All the Hill Country of Judah': From a Settlement Fringe to a Prosperous Monarchy," p. 102; and Finkelstein, "The Emergence of Israel: A Phase in the Cyclic History of Canaan in the Third and Second Millennia B.C.E.," p. 159.

[15] Thompson, *Early History*, p. 331.

[16] Thompson, *Early History*, p. 331.

[17] D.W. Jamieson-Drake, *Scribes and Schools in Monarchic Israel: A Socio-archaeological Approach* (Sheffield: Sheffield Academic Press, 1991).

[18] Jamieson-Drake, *Scribes and Schools*.

[19] See E.A. Knauf, "King Solomon's Copper Supply," in *Phoenicia and the Bible*, ed. E. Lipinski (Leuven: Peeters, 1991), pp. 171-172, and "From History to Interpretation," in *The Fabric of History: Text, Artifact and Israel's Past*, ed. D.V. Edelman (Sheffield, UK: Sheffied Academic Press, 1991), p. 39. See also Lemche, "Is It Still Possible to Write a History of Israel?" pp. 184-185; and Thompson, *Early History*, pp. 409-411.

[20] Jamieson-Drake, *Scribes and Schools*, pp. 138-145. The chiefdom has been identified as an important stage in the development from a tribal society (sometimes called "segmentary society") to a full-blown state. States are characterized by a greater number of institutions, a larger population, a more complex agricultural system, craft specialization, a defensive organization and a highly diversified administrative apparatus to coordinate social, religious and economic activity.

[21] See Ofer, "Hill Country."

[22] Jamieson-Drake, *Scribes and Schools*, pp. 140-145.

[23] See Knauf, "King Solomon's Copper Supply," pp. 172-184; Philip R. Davies, *In Search of "Ancient Israel"* (Sheffield, UK: Sheffield Academic Press, 1992), pp. 67-70; Lemche, "History of Israel," pp. 168-171, 183-191; and Lemche and Thompson, "Did Biran Kill David?" pp. 15-20.

[24] See G. Garbini, "L'impero di David," *Annali della Scuola Normale Superiore di Pisa* 3:13 (1983), pp. 1-16, and *History and Ideology in Ancient Israel*, trans. J. Bowden (London: SCM, 1988), pp. 21-32; Jamieson-Drake, *Scribes and Schools*, pp. 136-145; Knauf, "King Solomon's Copper Supply," pp. 170-180; Thompson, *Early History*, pp. 331-334, 409-412; and Davies, *In Search of "Ancient Israel"*, p. 69.

[25] Mario Liverani, *Prestige and Interest: International Relations in the Near East ca. 1600-1100 B.C.* (Padova, Italy: Sargon, 1990), p. 59.

Related Reading

Jane M. Cahill, "Jerusalem in David and Solomon's Time," BAR, November/December 2004.

Hershel Shanks, "Newly Discovered: A Fortified City from King David's Time," BAR, January/February 2009.

Hershel Shanks, "Prize Find: Oldest Hebrew Inscription Discovered in Israelite Fort on Philistine Border," BAR, March/April 2010.

Yosef Garfinkel, "The Birth & Death of Biblical Minimalism," BAR, May/June 2011.

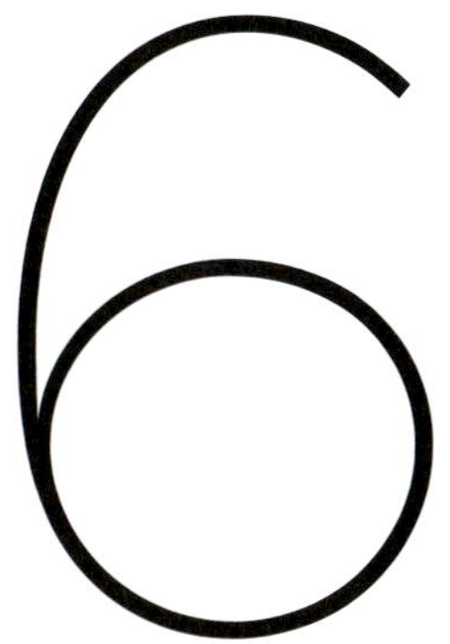

The Temple

Not a stone from Solomon's Temple has been discovered, but archaeologists and artifacts have brought the Biblical descriptions of this magnificent holy structure to life.

The Jerusalem Temple was at the center of ancient Israelite religious life. Destroyed by Babylonian king Nebuchadnezzar's armies in 586 B.C.E., not one stone remains. Yet, all is not lost to history. The Biblical description of Solomon's Temple, also known as the First Temple, and remains of contemporaneous Near Eastern temples, as well as a few controversial artifacts, offer tantalizing glimpses of a former glory.

JANUARY/FEBRUARY 1984
Probable Head of Priestly Scepter From Solomon's Temple Surfaces in Jerusalem

Sorbonne epigrapher André Lemaire reported in BAR on an inscribed ivory pomegranate that he first saw in 1979 in a Jerusalem antiquities shop. And that's the problem: It came from an antiquities dealer. No one knows where it was found. In the language of the trade, it is unprovenanced.

The ivory pomegranate was inscribed "[Belonging] to the Tem[ple of the Lor]d, holy to the priests." After being smuggled out of Israel (following its BAR publication), it was purchased in Switzerland for the Israel Museum for $550,000. Nahman Avigad, one of Israel's most prominent epigraphers, vouched for its authenticity. The Israel Museum displayed it in its own special room and crowds flocked to the museum to see it. Harvard's Frank Cross declared it "priceless."

In 2004 a committee of the Israel Antiquities

Authority (IAA) declared the inscription a forgery. By this time, Avigad had died. Lemaire journeyed to Jerusalem to reexamine the pomegranate; he was more than ever convinced that the inscription on it is authentic. BAR then called a meeting held at the Israel Museum that included Lemaire and the two Hebrew language scholars on the IAA committee that had found the inscription to be a forgery: Shmuel Ahituv and Aaron Demsky. At the meeting in the Israel Museum, where we examined the pomegranate under a microscope operated by Yuval Goren of Tel Aviv University, the key question turned on a single letter (*heh*) in the inscription and whether it "went into the break." If it did, the inscription was genuine; if it stopped short of this break that sheared off part of the pomegranate in antiquity, it was a fake. It was clear that the *heh* did go into the break. Ahituv and Demsky, nevertheless, would not concede that the inscription was therefore authentic.

Both sides filed reports that were published in the *Israel Exploration Journal.** Lemaire relied heavily on the *heh* that went into the break. Ahituv and Demsky, strangely enough, completely ignored it; they discussed the other letters but failed even to mention the *heh.* I wrote a letter to the editor of the *Israel Exploration Journal* (one of whom happened to be Ahituv) pointing this out; I was told that the journal did not print letters to the editor—despite the fact that in some instances they had indeed printed letters to the editor.

More recently, at BAR's request, one of Israel's most prominent photographers, Ada Yardeni, examined the inscription and concluded that it was "possible" that it is a forgery.**

Bottom line: Despite all this, we have decided to include Lemaire's original and still-insightful article. To make your own judgment on the authenticity of the inscription, see "Is This Inscription Fake? You Decide" (September/October 2007), which we print as an addendum to Lemaire's article. Lamaire continues to champion the authenticity of the inscription.

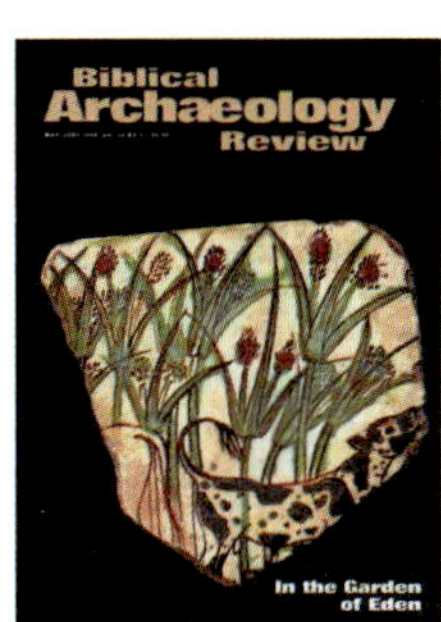

MAY/JUNE 2000
The New 'Ain Dara Temple—Closest Solomonic Parallel

You may wonder why we have placed in this chapter of the book, titled "The Temple," an article about another temple excavated in the early 1980s in northern Syria. It is because this Syrian temple may be the closest parallel to Solomon's Temple of any ancient temple that has yet been discovered. American scholar John Monson described this monumental structure dedicated to a god who left 3-foot-long footprints in the pavement as he strode into his temple. A god or goddess with feet this big was doubtless a giant.

* Shmuel Ahituv, Aaron Demsky, Yuval Goren and André Lemaire, "The Inscribed Pomegranate from the Israel Museum Examined Again," *Israel Exploration Journal* 57 (2007), pp. 87–95.

**Hershal Shanks, First Person: "A New Target," BAR November/December 2014.

Probable Head of Priestly Scepter from Solomon's Temple Surfaces in Jerusalem

Inscription containing name of God incised on ivory pomegranate

ANDRÉ LEMAIRE

BAR RECENTLY PUBLISHED A FASCINATING article by Gabriel Barkay reporting on his excavation of a small rolled silver amulet, dating from the seventh or sixth century B.C. When the amulet was unrolled, it was found to contain the tetragrammaton—the four Hebrew letters *yod*, *he*, *waw*, *he* that form the unpronounceable name of God, sometimes transcribed in Latin letters as Yahweh or Jehovah. (See "The Divine Name Found in Jerusalem," BAR, March/April 1983.)

This truly sensational discovery is said to be the first time God's name has been recovered in an archaeological excavation in the Holy City of Jerusalem.

The claim is technically accurate. However, another artifact containing the Divine Name, or at least a part of it, has recently surfaced in Jerusalem. Not only does this artifact predate the rolled silver amulet by at least 100 years in the First Temple period, but it is also all the more remarkable because it was probably used in the Temple service itself! If so, this is indeed a rare find; for of no other artifact may we say that it was probably used in the Temple service in the Solomonic Temple.

The artifact I refer to is a small inscribed pomegranate fruit made from a single piece of fine ivory; this pomegranate is 1.68 inches (43mm) high and .83 inches (21mm) in diameter, with a flat base into which a small hole was cut. The pomegranate consists of a central ball, or grenade as scholars prefer to call it, and a thin neck that expands into what were originally six petals, four of which have survived. Part of one side of the grenade is broken off. An inscription in paleo-Hebrew letters is incised around the shoulder of the grenade, just below the neck.

One important distinction between the occurrence of the Divine Name on the silver amulet previously reported in BAR and the occurrence of the Name on this small ivory pomegranate is that the silver amulet was excavated in a scientifically

INSCRIBED IVORY POMEGRANATE from the late eighth century B.C., the time of Solomon's Temple. This unique artifact may once have topped a scepter carried by the Temple priests. If it was not part of a scepter, perhaps it was a Temple ornament, an altar decoration or a finial on a throne or cultic box. Carved from one piece of precious ivory, the pomegranate is only 1.68 inches high and 0.83 inches in diameter. Cut into the base is a hole .39 inches (10 mm) deep and .23 inches (6 mm) in diameter.

COURTESY ANDRÉ LEMAIRE

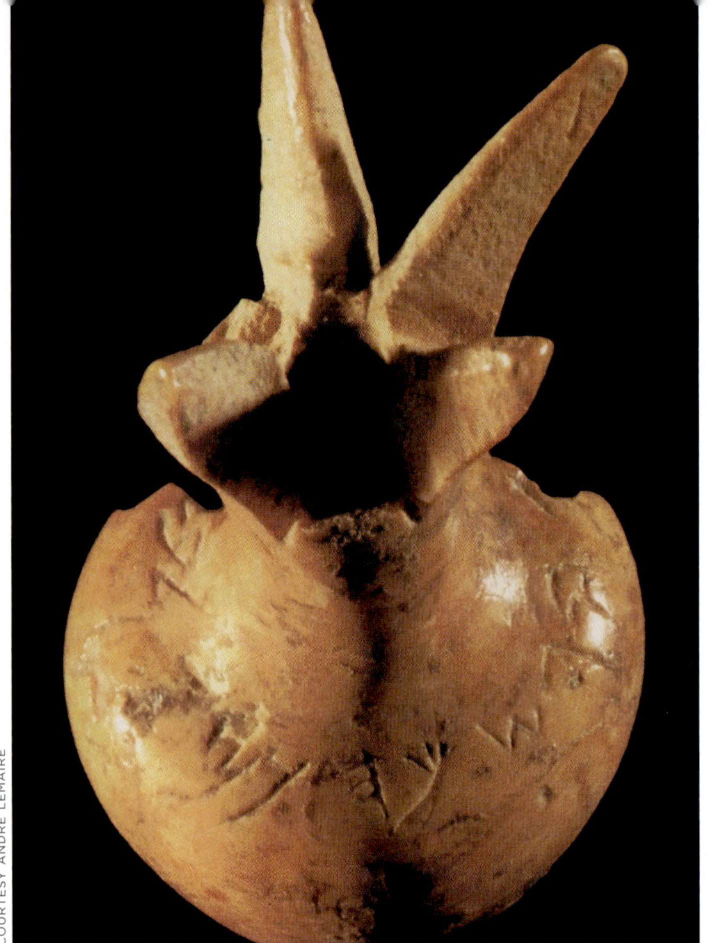

COURTESY ANDRÉ LEMAIRE

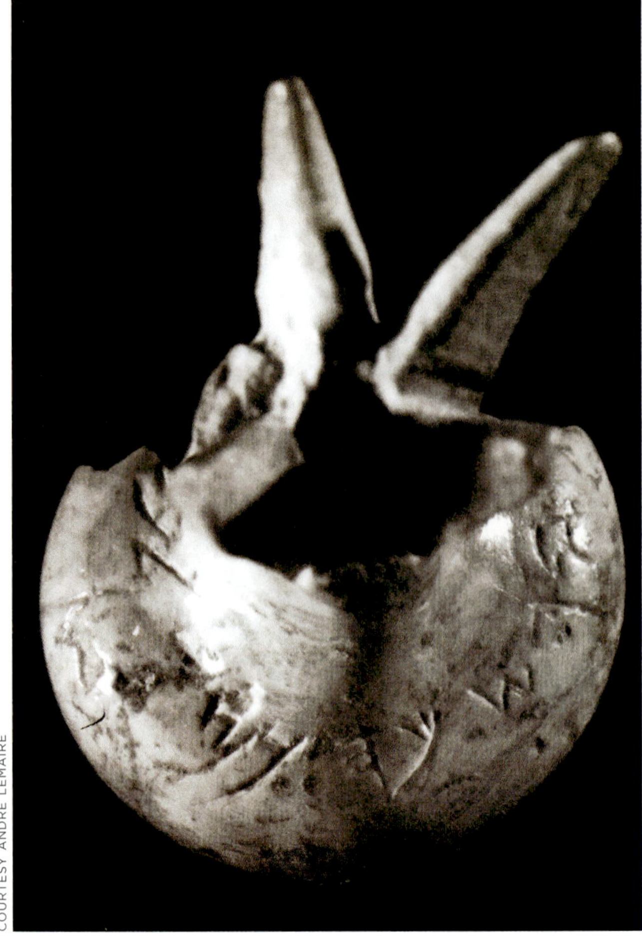

COURTESY ANDRÉ LEMAIRE

THREE VIEWS OF THE INSCRIPTION on the shoulder of the eighth-century B.C. ivory pomegranate. The inscription begins at the upper left, where three letters can be seen separated from the others by a space, and continues around the pomegranate clockwise, interrupted in the back where the pomegranate is broken. The author reads the inscription as follows (bracketed letters are assumed to fill the broken area in the shoulder): *lbẏ[t yhw]ḣ qdš khnm*, which he translates as "Belonging to the Tem[ple of the Lor]d, holy to the priests." The shape of the letters provides the most important clue to the date of the pomegranate. The letters are very similar to the script of the so-called Siloam Inscription, which was cut into the wall of a tunnel King Hezekiah built in about 705 B.C. to bring water from the Gihon Spring inside the walls of Jerusalem.

controlled, professionally directed excavation. The pomegranate was not.

I first saw the pomegranate in July 1979. I had come to Jerusalem to work on a long-term project, a book on the corpus of inscribed northwest semitic seals. Many of these seals are written in paleo-Hebrew script, the ancient alphabet used by the Israelites until after they returned from the Babylonian exile and adopted the so-called square Aramaic script still in use today (see "The Evolution of Two Hebrew Scripts," BAR, May/June 1979). I had come to Jerusalem to check the reading of some paleo-Hebrew inscriptions in the Israel Museum and in the Rockefeller Museum.

As I usually do when I visit Jerusalem, I made the rounds of the antiquities dealers. They know me, and they know what I am looking for—inscribed seals and seal-impressions from the First Temple period. Sometimes they even allow me to take pictures of their wares without buying.

One of the dealers I visited reported that, although he had neither inscribed seals nor seal impressions, he knew someone who had an ivory object with an old Hebrew inscription on it. Of course I was excited about seeing any new paleo-Hebrew inscription, but trying not to appear too eager, I simply told my friend that I would be pleased to look at the object.

Later he called me, and we fixed a time when I would return to his shop to look at the object. I arrived on time. I was invited to the back of the shop where we drank the obligatory tea and chatted about other things. Finally, he took down a box and removed a small ivory pomegranate, which he handed to me. There, incised into the ivory around the neck in a continuous circle, without word separation, was a paleo-Hebrew inscription. Unfortunately, several letters were missing where the grenade had been broken off, but the remaining letters were easy to identify.

I immediately noticed that the shape of the letters was very similar to the letters in the famous Siloam inscription, which was found in the tunnel King Hezekiah of Judah built in about 705 B.C. in preparation for Sennacherib's siege. The tunnel brought water from the Spring Gihon, outside the city wall,

COURTESY ANDRÉ LEMAIRE

to a pool inside the walls of Jerusalem. The inscription on the ivory pomegranate was easily datable on paleographic grounds to the late eighth century B.C.

Since the pomegranate had not been excavated in a scientifically controlled excavation, I knew that I had to be careful: Was it a fake? The ivory pomegranate itself looked genuine. But perhaps the inscription had been incised by a modern forger. To find out, I examined the writing very carefully under a magnifying glass, paying special attention to the edges of the incision. I noticed traces of new incisions at the bottom of some letters, as if someone had tried to clean out caked earth from the incised letters with a small needle. Sometimes a calcic deposit forms on artifacts found in tombs and excavations; perhaps a needle was used to remove calcium deposits from the incised letters. The needle also removed most of the ancient patina from the incised letters, but traces of the same patina that covered the surface of the pomegranate could still be seen in the original incisions. The trace incisions were clearly added after the letters had been incised. This fact and the presence of patina in the incisions confirmed the paleographic evidence that both the inscription and the artifact were genuine.

I photographed the pomegranate and left the shop. When the photographs were developed, I examined the inscription more closely. Despite the lack of word dividers in the inscription, I easily recognized the Hebrew word for holy, *qdš* or *kodesh*.* This was followed by the word for priests, *khnm* or *kohanim*. Then came a blank space. Perhaps this was the end of the inscription and what followed after the space was the beginning of the inscription. After the space were three letters, *lby*. Then came the broken part. It looked like about four letters were missing. Then I dimly saw traces of a Hebrew *he*, followed by the word for holy, as described above. If the space between the *m* and the *l* marks the beginning of the circular inscription, then it reads like this:

lby̆ [xxxx]h̆ qdš khnm

I knew of several paleo-Hebrew inscriptions on vases from Hazor, Arad and Beer-Sheva that contained the word *qdš* or "holy." More significant, however, was an ostracon (No. 18) from Arad that contained

*Hebrew is written without vowels. The second spelling indicates how the Hebrew is pronounced.

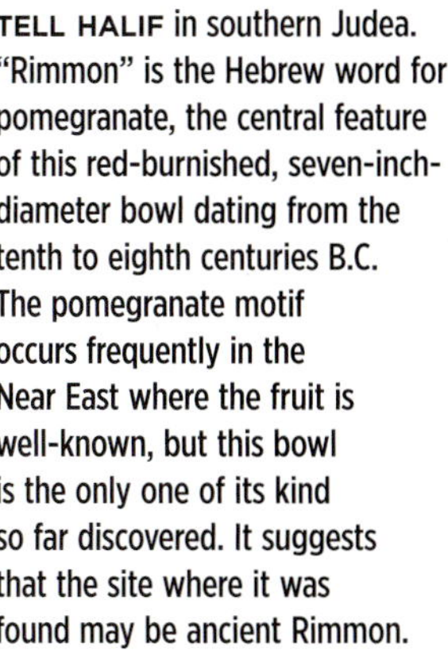
"RIMMON" BOWL FROM TELL HALIF in southern Judea. "Rimmon" is the Hebrew word for pomegranate, the central feature of this red-burnished, seven-inch-diameter bowl dating from the tenth to eighth centuries B.C. The pomegranate motif occurs frequently in the Near East where the fruit is well-known, but this bowl is the only one of its kind so far discovered. It suggests that the site where it was found may be ancient Rimmon.

SIGNHOUSE

COURTESY AMIHAI MAZAR

FROM A PHILISTINE TEMPLE, this pomegranate-shaped pottery vessel resembles the inscribed pomegranate shown to the author in Jerusalem. The Philistine vessel dates to about 1000 B.C. and was discovered at Tell Qasile, a site within the city limits of Tel Aviv.

the phrase *bẏt yhwḣ*, "Temple of the Lord."

Thus, it was very tempting to restore the missing letters as follows:

lbẏ[t yhw]ḣ qdš khnm

"Belonging to the Tem[ple of the Lor]d [Yahweh], holy to the priests."

To anyone familiar with ancient Hebrew inscriptions, this restoration makes eminent good sense and is indeed in many ways obviously correct.

For what purpose was the pomegranate used? Although we cannot be sure, a small hole in the base provides a clue. This hole is about .23 inches (6mm) in diameter and .39 inches (10mm) deep. Apparently, a small rod—about 12 inches (30 cm) long—probably also in ivory, or less likely in wood or metal, was placed in the hole to provide a shaft for a small scepter. In two Assyrian reliefs from Nineveh, we see King Sennacherib (704–681 B.C.) standing in his chariot, holding in his left hand what seems to be a similar small scepter, the head of which is

TSILA SAGIV, COURTESY ISRAEL DEPARTMENT OF ANTIQUITIES AND MUSEUMS

INSCRIBED CARNELIAN SEAL with pomegranates. Two stylized pomegranates lying on their sides with their three petals facing outward decorate this seal at either end of double curved lines. Above and below the lines is an inscription which reads: "Belonging to 'Eliyahu [the son of] Yaqimyahu." (The letters on the seal were purposely reversed so that when the seal was pressed into wet clay, the letters would appear in their proper orientation.) The script closely resembles the script on the ivory pomegranate and on the Siloam inscription; most likely this half inch-long seal was manufactured about 700 B.C. This date precludes the possibility that the 'Eliyahu [Elijah] of the seal is the Biblical prophet, who lived more than 150 years earlier. The seal probably came from Gezer; it was purchased from a Bedouin who lived nearby and claimed it was found at Gezer.

COURTESY OF THE TRUSTEES OF THE BRITISH MUSEUM

ASSYRIAN KING SENNACHERIB holds a pomegranate scepter in his left hand, as he rides in his chariot. This royal procession was carved onto a wall of Sennacherib's palace at Nineveh, where reliefs depicted the events of his reign (704 to 681 B.C.).

COURTESY ISRAEL DEPARTMENT OF ANTIQUITIES AND MUSEUMS

Pomegranate "Priceless" Says Harvard's Frank Cross

"The pomegranate could well be the head of a small scepter or standard," said Professor Frank Cross of Harvard University and one of the world's leading Semitic paleographers, when BAR showed him the new pictures of the ivory pomegranate. "Or it could be an ornament from the Temple or a decoration on an altar or a finial on a throne or cultic box. In any case, it is priceless," Cross added.

There is no doubt as to the object's authenticity, according to Cross. "If it came from around Jerusalem, you would think it came from the Solomonic Temple."

Cross would date the object a few years earlier than the Siloam Inscription, which was inscribed in the late eighth century B.C. in Hezekiah's Tunnel. Based on the shape of the letter forms on the pomegranate, the inscription might be as much as 50 years earlier than Siloam, said Cross.

in the shape of a pomegranate.[1] Similar scepters with pomegranate heads were found in the 1930s by the British Expedition working at Lachish. These scepters date to the Late Bronze Age, more precisely to about the 13th century B.C. So the pomegranate as the head of a scepter is not uncommon.

Why is this ivory scepter so small? The answer lies in the fact that it is ivory; that is, the pomegranate was made from a single piece of ivory, which obviously limited the size.

However, from the object itself and the inscription around it, we can conclude that it was probably used by the priests in the service of the Jerusalem Temple at the end of the eighth century B.C.

Where was the object found? Probably not far from Jerusalem, either accidentally or in an illicit excavation. It is possible that it was found in one of the many tombs carved in the limestone all around Jerusalem. But this is just a guess.

We should not be at all surprised that a pomegranate was used in the Temple in Jerusalem. Pomegranates, along with grapes and figs, are the best-known fruits of the Holy Land. These three fruits are mentioned together in several Biblical passages. In Numbers 20:5, God is asked "Why did

IVORY SCEPTERS WITH POMEGRANATES. Part of a cache of objects found in a temple at Lachish in the 1930s by the Wellcome Marston Archaeological Expedition, these scepters are approximately 9.5 inches long and date to the 13th century B.C.

The ivory pomegranate described in this article may also be part of a scepter; if so, its rod was probably one foot long and the result would have looked much like these graceful scepters.

you make us leave Egypt to bring us to this wretched place [the Wilderness of Zin], a place with no grain or figs or vines [grape] or pomegranates?" And in Deuteronomy 8:8, it is said that the "Lord your God is bringing you into a good land...a land of wheat and barley, of vines, figs and pomegranates."

Several inscribed seals decorated with pomegranates surrounding the name of the owner have been found. These seals date to the eighth to seventh centuries B.C.[2]

In the past few years, several pomegranate-shaped pottery vessels have been found in excavations in Israel. At Tell Halif (Lahav), Professor Joe D. Seger excavated an Israelite tomb, probably from the eighth century B.C., in which he found a bowl with a raised pomegranate in the center. Two pottery vessels in the shape of pomegranates, dating to about 1000 B.C., were found in a Philistine temple excavated by Amihai Mazar at Tell Qasile. These pottery vessels confirm the popularity of pomegranate decorations in the Judean kingdom.

One reason the pomegranate was so popular is that it was probably a symbol of fecundity because of the multitude of seeds contained in the fruit.

According to the Bible, the hem of Aaron's vestment was decorated with pomegranates (Exodus 28:33–34). Four hundred pomegranates decorated the capitals of the two freestanding bronze columns named Boaz and Joachin in front of the entrance to the Temple (1 Kings 7:42, 2 Kings 25:17, 2 Chronicles 4:13 [in some refe rences the number of pomegranates is 100, e.g., 2 Chronicles 3:16 and Jeremiah 52:23]). So we should hardly be surprised that the pomegranate was used in the Temple service.

Thus, archaeological parallels confirm the popularity of the pomegranate, and the Biblical references confirm its association with the Israelite Temple and the priests.

This ivory pomegranate is unique, however, because it was probably used by the priests in the service at the Jerusalem Temple in the late eighth century B.C. If that is true, it is the only sacred object (*qdš* or *kodesh*, holy) that survives from the Temple built by Solomon.

For more details, see A. Lemaire, "Une inscription paleo-hebraique sur grenade en ivoire," Revue Biblique *88 (1981), pp. 236–239.*

[1] See A. Peterson, *Assyrian Sculptures, Palace of Sennacherib*, Plate 29; E. F. Weidner, "Die Reliefs der assyrischen Könige III," *Archiv für Orientforschung* 11 (1936/7), pp. 289–325, especially pp. 308–312.

[2] See D. Diringer, *Le iscrizioni antico-ebraice palestinesi*, Florence, 1934, Table XIX, 24, p. 184, *lhnnyhw//bn 'zryhw*, "Belonging to Hananyahu son of Azaryahu," Vorderasiatische Abteilung der Staatlichen Museen (East Berlin), VA 32; C. Graesser, "The Seal of Elijah," *Bulletin of the American Schools of Oriental Research* 220 (1975), pp. 63–66, now Rockefeller Museum, IDAM 74–1888 (probable origin: Gezer), *l'lyhw/yqmyhw*, "Belonging to Eliyahu (son of) Yaqimyahu"; N. Avigad, "The Chief of the Corvee," *Israel Exploration Journal* 30 (1980), pp. 170–173, *lpl'yhw mttyhw*, "Belonging to Pela'yahu (son of) Mattityahu," private collection; P. Bordreuil and A. Lemaire, "Nouveaux sceau hébreux et araméens," *Semitica* 32 (1982), pp. 21–34, no. 3 *lyknyhw // bn hkl*, "Belonging to Menasseh (son of) Hakal" and no. 5, *lmnśh mlkyhw*, "Belonging to Menasseh (son of) Malkiyahu," (private collection).

Related Reading

Hershel Shanks, "Was BAR an Accessory to Highway Robbery?" BAR, November/December 1988.

"The Pomegranate Scepter Head—From the Temple of the Lord or from a Temple of Asherah?" BAR, May/June 1992.

From July/August 2004 to March/April 2006, BAR ran a column in each issue called "Update: Finds or Fakes?" to keep readers apprised of the latest news about the ivory pomegranate and other alleged forgeries.

Hershel Shanks, First Person: "Jerusalem Forgery Conference," BAR, May/June 2007.

Gabriel Barkay, "The Riches of Ketef Hinnom," BAR, July/August/September/October 2009 (see p. 406 of this book).

Is This Inscription FAKE?

You Decide

COLLECTION ISRAEL MUSEUM, JERUSALEM. PHOTO © ISRAEL MUSEUM, BY NAHUM SLAPAK

The famous Ivory Pomegranate Inscription: Is it a forgery or authentic? You decide. And let us know your decision.

A Hebrew inscription is engraved around the shoulder of the thumb-size pomegranate that reads, "Holy to the priests, (belonging) to the Temple of [Yahwe]h."

For decades the tiny object occupied a special place in Jerusalem's prestigious Israel Museum—the only surviving relic from Solomon's Temple.

The pomegranate was first seen in 1979 in a Jerusalem antiquities shop by one of the world's leading Semitic epigraphers, André Lemaire of the Sorbonne. Based on a lifetime of experience and a careful examination, he pronounced the inscription authentic. It was also examined by Professor Nahman Avigad of The Hebrew University, then Israel's most respected epigrapher, who wrote that "I am fully convinced of ... the authenticity of its inscription ... [T]he epigraphic evidence alone, in my opinion, is absolutely convincing."

With these assurances, in 1989 the Israel Museum acquired the pomegranate for $550,000. All Israel was excited. On the day the pomegranate went on display in a special room of the museum with a narrow light beaming on it from the ceiling, the exhibit was the first item on the evening news in Israel.

In 2004, after two widely publicized inscriptions had been declared forgeries by the Israel Antiquities Authority, the museum decided to revisit the question of the authenticity of the Pomegranate Inscription. A special committee was appointed to reexamine the inscription, using the latest scientific technologies. The committee concluded that the inscription was a forgery!

Lemaire subsequently reexamined the inscription, however, and he was unconvinced. After restudying the inscription under a stereoscopic microscope, he concluded that the pomegranate committee had misinterpreted what it saw and that the inscription was authentic.

In January 2007, at a conference on forgeries convened in Jerusalem by the Biblical Archaeology Society, Lemaire and the two epigraphers on the pomegranate committee, Professors Shmuel Ahituv of Ben-Gurion University and Aaron Demsky of Bar-Ilan University, discussed their differences and decided to look at the object again.

This meeting took place at the Israel Museum on May 3, 2007, where Professor Yuval Goren of Tel Aviv University projected microscopic images of the individual letters onto a screen for all to examine. Alas, the scholars were unable to resolve their differences. They looked through the same microscope, but they saw different things.

Learn how to look at these pictures. Go to www.biblicalarchaeology.org/pomegranate.

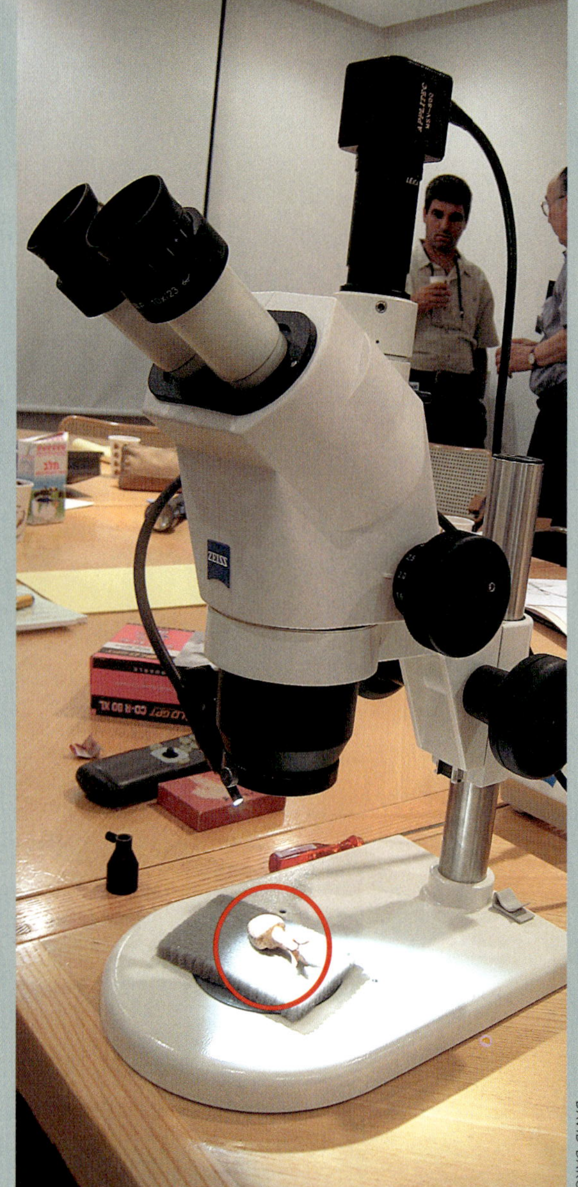

DAVID DAROM

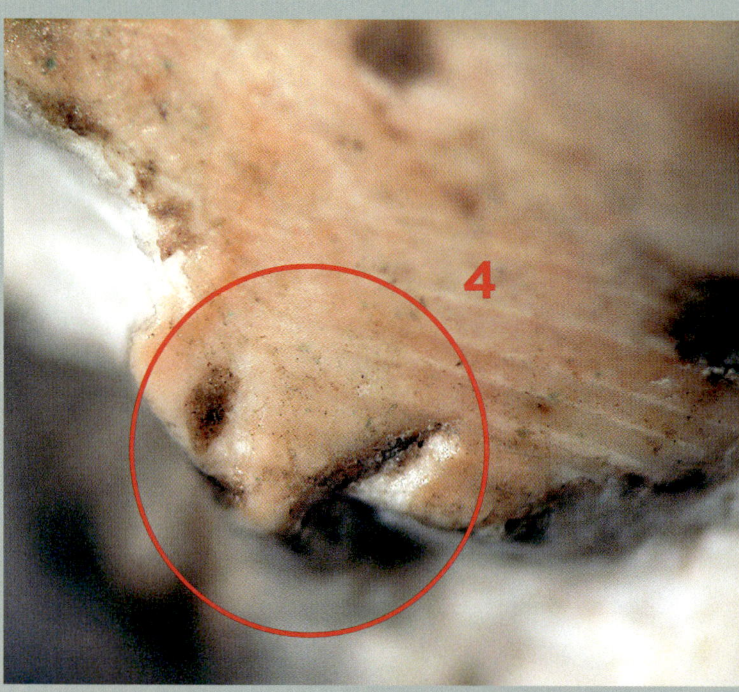

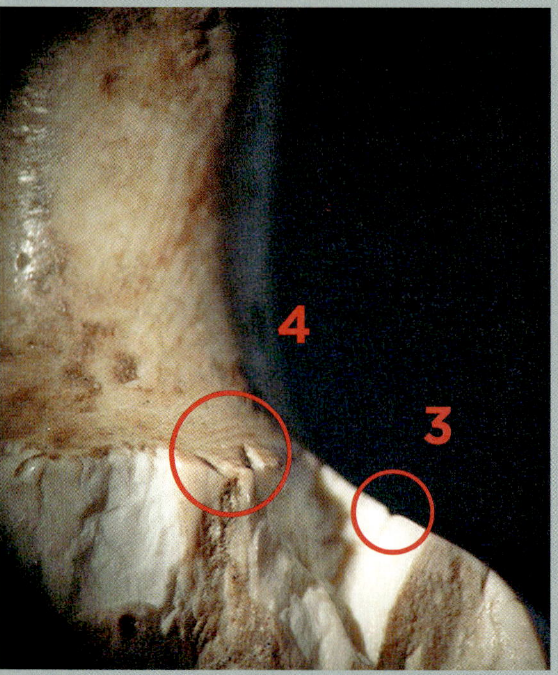

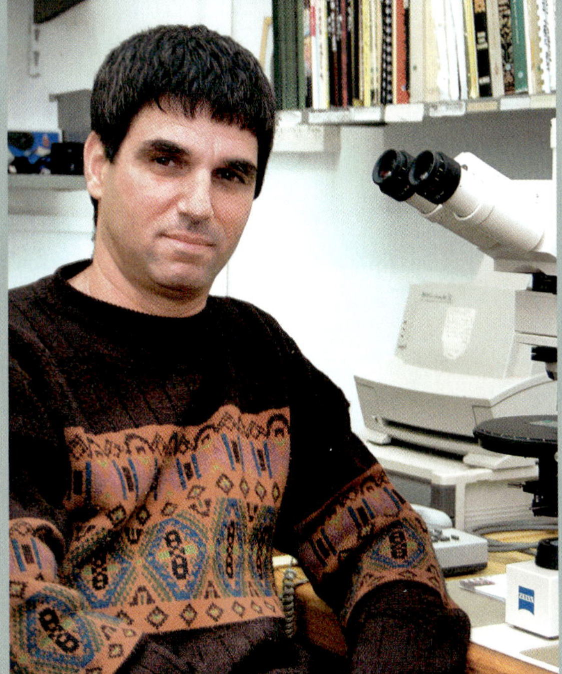

PROFESSOR YUVAL GOREN of Tel Aviv University: BAR publishes "archaeological pulp fiction." Visit **www.biblicalarchaeology.org/pomegranate** for more.

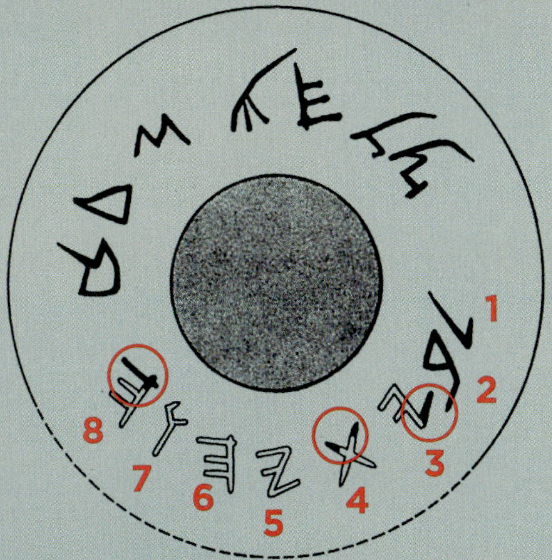

The issue is at once complicated and simple. Much of the ball of the pomegranate broke off in antiquity, and two small modern breaks have made the ancient break even larger. As a result, several letters are completely missing and must be reconstructed. But three letters are *partially* there. It is these three partial letters that are crucial. If these three partial letters artificially stop short of the breaks, as the committee believes, the inscription is a forgery. The forger would apparently have been afraid of breaking off more of the pomegranate if he went into the breaks. If, on the other hand, the partial letters do go into the ancient break, forming a "v" when viewed in section, the inscription is authentic because the inscription must be earlier than the ancient break.

You can now look at the pictures yourself and make up your own mind. Just go to www.biblicalarchaeology.org/pomegranate to read BAR editor Hershel Shanks's report on this May 3 meeting, along with microscopic photographs of the partially surviving letters of the inscription and directions on how to "read" the pictures. You don't need to know ancient Hebrew, and you don't need to be an expert in Hebrew epigraphy. You just need to be able to decide by looking at the pictures whether a stroke of a letter does or does not go into a break in the pomegranate.

Enjoy yourself, and let us know what you think.

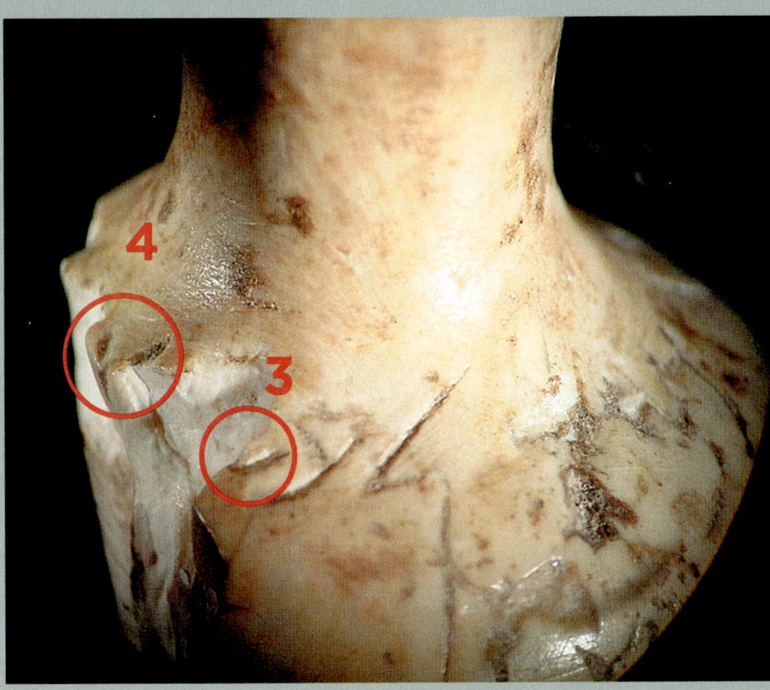

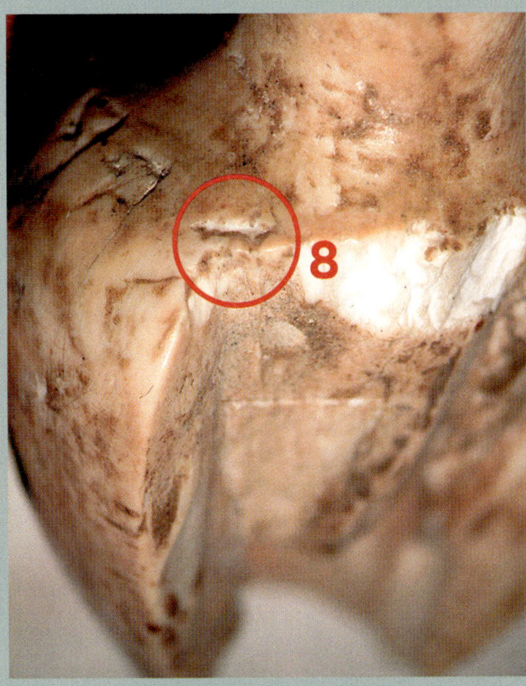

THE NEW 'AIN DARA

JOHN MONSON

A STUNNING PARALLEL TO SOLOMON'S Temple has been discovered in northern Syria.[1] The temple at 'Ain Dara has far more in common with the Jerusalem Temple described in the Book of Kings than any other known building. Yet the newly excavated temple has received almost no attention in this country, at least partially because the impressive excavation report, published a decade ago, was written in German by a Syrian scholar and archaeologist.[2]

TEMPLE CLOSEST SOLOMONIC PARALLEL

For centuries, readers of the Bible have tried to envision Solomon's glorious Jerusalem Temple, dedicated to the Israelite God, Yahweh. Nothing of Solomon's Temple remains today; the Babylonians destroyed it utterly in 586 B.C.E. And the vivid Biblical descriptions are of limited help in reconstructing the building: Simply too many architectural terms have lost their meaning over the ensuing centuries, and too many details are

PRECEDING PAGES: From the rubble-filled courtyard in the foreground to the shrine room in the distance, the ancient temple at 'Ain Dara, Syria, is our closest parallel—in size, date and design—to the Temple built by King Solomon in the tenth century B.C.E. Beautifully preserved despite fire damage and massive looting (for many years, the remains served as a quarry for local builders), the Syrian temple allows us to visualize the magnificent Jerusalem Temple that was utterly destroyed by the Babylonians in 586 B.C.E.

Located on the fertile eastern bank of the Afrin River, in northern Syria, ancient 'Ain Dara was discovered by chance in 1954, when a shepherd exploring a fox's den stumbled across a sculpted lion's head. Archaeologists immediately recognized the lion as part of a city gate. Further exploration led to the discovery of a 6,000-year-old upper and lower city. Built on the highest point of the tell (see plan, below right), the temple (dating from 1300 to 740 B.C.E.) was fully excavated in the 1980s but has received little attention since—despite its correspondences with Solomon's Temple. In the aerial photograph of the upper city (below), the temple remains lie within a circle of columns erected by a restoration team. Photo on the preceding pages by Marie-Henriette Gates.

absent from the text. Slowly, however, archaeologists are beginning to fill in the gaps in our knowledge of Solomon's building project.

For years, pride of place went to the temple at Tell Ta'yinat, also in northern Syria.* When it was discovered in 1936, the Tell Ta'yinat temple, unlike the 'Ain Dara temple, caused a sensation because of its similarities to Solomon's Temple. Yet the 'Ain Dara temple is closer in time to Solomon's Temple by about a century (it is, in fact, essentially contemporaneous), is much closer in size to Solomon's Temple than the sm aller Tell Ta'yinat temple, has several features found in Solomon's Temple but not in the Tell Ta'yinat temple, and is far better preserved than the Tell Ta'yinat temple. In short, the 'Ain Dara temple, which was excavated between 1980 and 1985, is the most significant parallel to Solomon's Temple ever discovered.

The 'Ain Dara temple helps us better understand a number of enigmatic features in the Bible's description of Solomon's Temple. It also figures in the current debate, which has often raged in these pages,** as to the existence of David and

*See, for example, Volkmar Fritz, "What Can Archaeology Tell Us About Solomon's Temple?" BAR, July/August 1987.

**See the following BAR articles: Philip Davies, "What Separates a Minimalist from a Maximalist? Not Much," William Dever, "Save Us from Postmodern Malarkey," and Amihai Mazar and John Camp, "Will Tel Rehov Save the United Monarchy?" March/April 2000; Amnon Ben-Tor, "Excavating Hazor—Part I: Solomon's City Rises from the Ashes," March/April 1999; "David's Jerusalem: Fiction or Reality?": Margreet Steiner, "It's Not There—Archaeology Proves a Negative," Jane Cahill, "It Is There: The Archaeological Evidence Proves It," and Nadav Na'aman, "It Is There: Ancient Texts Prove It," July/August 1998; and Hershel Shanks, "Where Is the Tenth Century?" March/April 1998.

©GEORG GERSTER/PHOTO RESEARCHERS, INC.

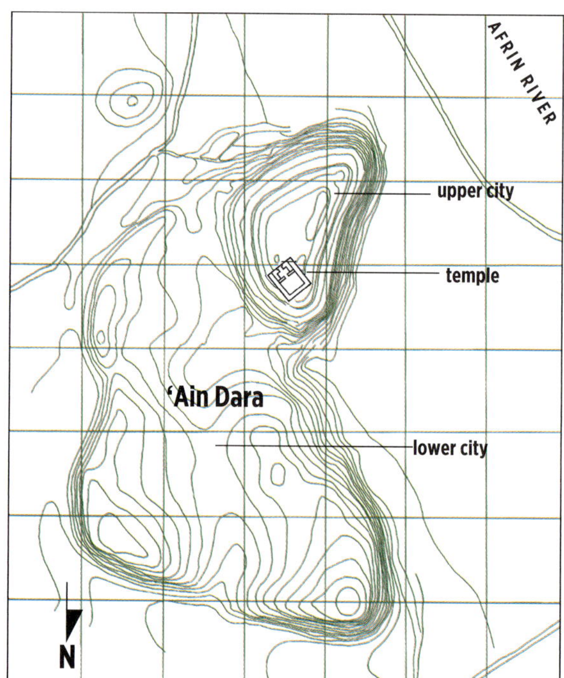

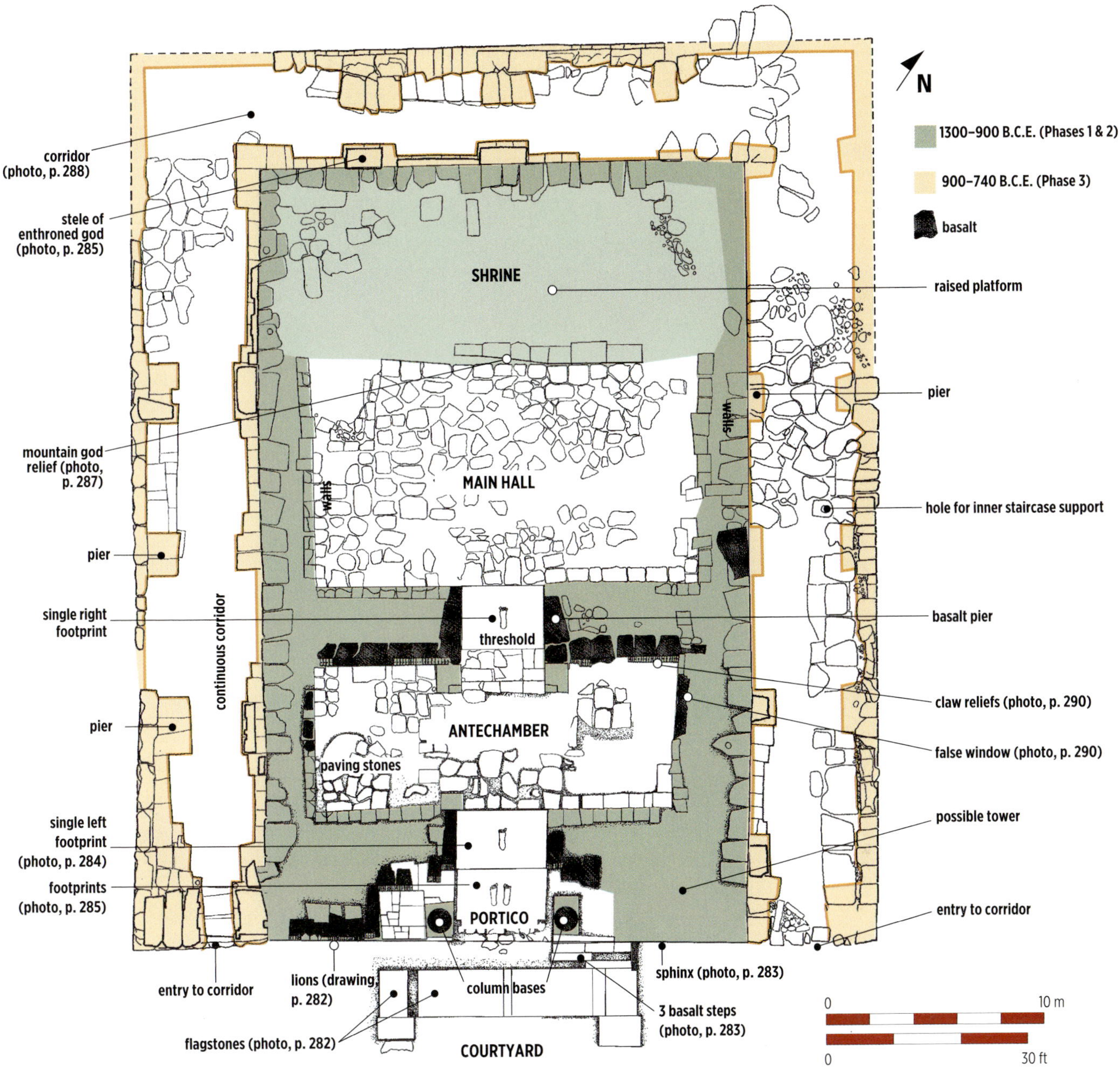

Solomon and their United Monarchy in the tenth century B.C.E. And it is a magnificent structure in its own right. The 'Ain Dara temple has beautifully preserved structural features, including limestone foundations and blocks of basalt. The building originally had a mudbrick superstructure—now lost—which may have been covered with wood paneling. The facade and interior walls are enlivened by hundreds of finely carved reliefs depicting lions, cherubim and other mythical creatures, mountain gods, palmettes and ornate geometric designs.

'Ain Dara lies near the Syro-Turkish border, about 40 miles northwest of Aleppo and a little more than 50 miles northeast of Tell Ta'yinat. The site is large, consisting of a main tell that rises 90 feet above the surrounding plain and an extensive lower city, which covers about 60 acres. 'Ain Dara first attracted attention in 1955, with the chance discovery of a monumental basalt lion. Although the site was occupied from the Chalcolithic period (fourth millennium B.C.E.) to the Ottoman period (1517-1917 C.E.), the temple is undoubtedly the most spectacular discovery at the site. According to the excavator, Ali Abu Assaf, it existed for 550 years—from about 1300 B.C.E. to 740 B.C.E. He has identified three structural phases during this period.

The building was constructed in Phase 1, which lasted from 1300 B.C.E. to 1000 B.C.E. Oriented

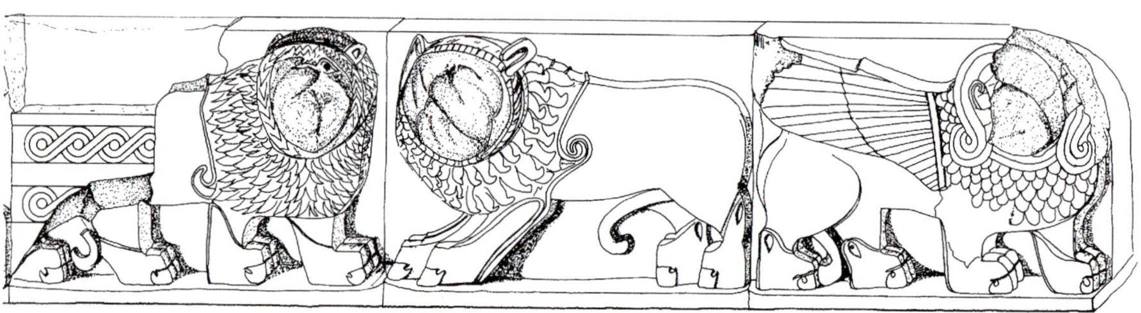

PHOTO BY MARIE-HENRIETTE GATES/ DRAWING BY RENATE BARCSAY-REGNER, DAMASCUS, DEUTSCHES ARCHÄOLOGISCHES INSTITUT

towards the southeast, the temple is rectangular in plan, about 65 feet wide by 98 feet long. Built on a large raised platform, the temple consists essentially of three rooms: a niche-like portico, or porch; an antechamber (sometimes called the *pronaos*); and a main hall (cella, or *naos*), which housed the innermost shrine (in Biblical terms the *debir*, or holy of holies).

In Phase 2 (1000-900 B.C.E.), the period during which the Solomonic Temple was built, the 'Ain Dara temple remained basically the same, except for the addition of basalt piers on the front facade of the building, immediately behind the columns, and in the entrances leading from the portico to the antechamber and from the antechamber to the main hall. Reliefs and a stele were also added to the shrine at the back of the main hall.

In Phase 3 (900-740 B.C.E.), an ambulatory, or hall, consisting of a series of side chambers was added on three sides of the building. The chambers were laid on the pre-existing temple platform, which extended beyond this new construction. The foundations of these chambers are not connected to the main part of the temple, indicating that they are a later addition.[3]

The dating of the two earlier phases was determined not by levels (stratigraphy) or by pottery (the excavation report does not record the stratigraphy and pottery of the temple), but by a comparison of the sculpture with that from other excavated sites.[4]

Like Solomon's Temple, the 'Ain Dara temple was approached by a courtyard paved with flagstones. A large chalkstone basin used for ceremonial purposes stood in this courtyard. (A large basin was also placed in the courtyard of the Jerusalem Temple [1 Kings 7:23-26].) At the far end of the open courtyard, the temple stood on a 2.5-foot-high platform made of rubble and limestone and lined with basalt blocks engraved with lions, sphinxes and other mythic creatures. A monumental staircase, flanked on each side by a sphinx and two lions, led up to the temple portico. The four basalt steps, only three of which survive, were decorated with a carved guilloche pattern, which consists of interlacing curved lines (see photo, opposite). The building itself was covered with rows of basalt reliefs of sphinxes, lions, mountain gods and large clawed creatures whose feet alone are preserved.[5]

Today, only the massive bases remain of the two columns that flanked the open entryway of the

PHOTOS BY A.M. APPA

TO ENTER THE TEMPLE, worshipers would cross the flagstone pavement—made of massive limestone slabs framed with narrow strips of black basalt—in the temple courtyard (photo, far left). Three basalt steps, decorated with a wave-like guilloche pattern, led up to the temple's portico (photo, below; also visible in the photo, far left).

Mythic creatures, carved from basalt, enlivened the walls surrounding the entryway. To the immediate right of the steps is a sphinx (left), with a bull's body, the feathered breast and wings of an eagle, and a human face. To the left of the entry, stood a second sphinx followed by two facing lions—all with damaged faces as shown in the drawing, lower left.

portico. These basalt columns, measuring about 3 feet in diameter, originally supported a roof that protected the portico. The portico entryway follows a common architectural plan known as *distyle in antis*; *distyle* (literally "two columns") refers to the pillars that support the roof, and *antis* (from the Latin for "opposing") refers to the extended arms of the building, which form the portico's side walls and frame the entryway. At either side of this portico are wide square projections that may have supported towers or staircases. Wedged between these two projections, the entryway appears to be simply a niche in the facade of the building, rather than a separate room.

PHOTOS BY A.M. APPA

Sphinxes and colossal lions, carved into the interior walls of the portico, guard the passage into the antechamber. Two large slabs line the portico floor. On these floor slabs are carved gigantic human footprints—each more than 3 feet long. Two footprints appear on the first slab and one left footprint on the second, as if some giant had paused at the entryway before striding into the building. In ancient conception the temple was the abode of the god, which is why these have been interpreted as the footprints of the resident god—or goddess, as we shall see.

Based on the profusion of reliefs and sculptures

DIVINE FOOTPRINTS? THREE 3-foot-long footprints are carved into the limestone slabs lining the floor of the temple portico (above). The delicate carving is designed to look as if the prints were impressed into the stone by an extra-human figure striding into the temple. The single left footprint from the portico appears in the foreground of the photo at left, which looks across the antechamber, over a second threshold to the main hall. A single right footprint (not visible) is carved into this latter threshold.

Throughout the ancient Near East, temples were considered the dwelling places of gods. The Jerusalem Temple, for example, was known in Hebrew as *Beit Yahweh*, the House of Yahweh. These footprints—a very unusual image in ancient Near Eastern art—are probably intended to indicate the presence of the deity who resided in the 'Ain Dara temple.

A stele, or standing stone (right), found in the temple's outermost corridor once depicted an enthroned deity. Only the bottom of the relief has survived, which shows (from left) two legs of a throne and the deity's own two feet, emerging from beneath the hem of a gown. Here the deity is shown in a much more typical manner—wearing pointy-toed shoes (The deities depicted in the reliefs on p. 287 sport similar footwear.)

of lions throughout the building, excavator Assaf attributes the temple to the goddess Ishtar, whose attribute is the lion; hence our use of the feminine.* While the footprints are those of a barefoot human, the deities in all the 'Ain Dara temple reliefs are wearing shoes with curled-up toes (see photos, pp. 285 and 287). So readers must choose their own interpretation.

Large basalt orthostats** engraved with flowery ribbon patterns lined the lower walls of the antechamber. Above them were carvings of immense clawed creatures. The identity of these animals is uncertain as only the claws have survived.

*In the accompanying article in the May/June 2000 issue, Lawrence Stager identifies the deity of 'Ain Dara as Ba'al-Hadad.

**Orthostats are large stones—sometimes undecorated, sometimes bearing complex designs—that are free-standing or that line the lower part of the walls of temples or public buildings. Orthostats carved in the shape of lions or other animals may serve as the base of the doorjambs flanking the entryway to such buildings.

Three steps, decorated with a chainlike carving, lead up from the broad but shallow antechamber (it is 50 feet wide but only 25 feet deep) to the main hall, which forms an almost perfect square (54.5 by 55 feet). At the top of the stairs, a limestone slab serves as the threshold to the main chamber. Whoever was striding into the temple portico left a similarly enormous right footprint on this threshold. The distance between the two single footprints is about 30 feet. A stride of 30 feet would belong to a person (or goddess) about 65 feet tall.

A lion is carved in profile on each of the doorposts of the entryway to the main hall.

At the far end of the main hall is an elevated podium. This was the shrine, or holy of holies, the most sacred area in the temple. A ramp led up to the podium (or dais), which occupied the back third of the main hall. The rear wall of the chamber behind the podium has a shallow niche (*adyton*) in it, perhaps for a statue of the deity or a standing stone. Reliefs depicting various mountain gods lined the podium and the walls of the chamber. The mountain god, too, has a connection with the goddess Ishtar, who, in some incarnations, takes this deity as her lover. This lends further support to the excavator's suggestion that the temple was dedicated to Ishtar.

A wooden screen—now lost—may have once separated the podium from the rest of the main hall: Several holes, or sockets, visible in the left wall (facing the podium) of the main hall and one in the right wall may have supported brackets for the screen.

Certainly one of the most splendid features of the 'Ain Dara temple is the once multistoried hallway that enclosed the building on three sides during Phase 3 (see photo, p. 288). We conclude that it had at least one upper story—and maybe more—based on the thickness and number of large piers, set at regular intervals, which would have provided additional support for the wood and mudbrick construction of the upper floors. (The side chambers in Solomon's Temple, incidentally, had three stories. which decreased in width from lowest to highest [1 Kings 6:5-10].)

These side chambers, which could be entered from either side of the portico, formed a continuous

ERICH LESSING

BALANCING ON A LION'S BACK, the goddess Ishtar appears on this eighth-century B.C.E. stela from Tel Barsib, northeast of 'Ain Dara, Syria. The goddess of love and war, Ishtar was the principal female deity of Mesopotamia. An early-first-millennium poem exalts Ishtar as "goddess of goddesses," "queen of all peoples" and as both a "lion" and "lioness." "Where are your likenesses not fashioned?" asks the poem. "Where are your shrines not founded?" The abundance of lion statuary at 'Ain Dara has led excavator Ali Abu Assaf to identify the temple as a monument to Ishtar.

THE GODS OF ‘AIN DARA. Two horned bull-men flank a mountain god in this relief (above) from the ‘Ain Dara temple’s holy of holies. The deity may be identified by his signature scaled skirt, which is thought to represent the mountain where he dwells.

A stele (right) from the temple’s outer corridor depicts a goddess dressed in a semi-transparent gown. If the temple is indeed dedicated to Ishtar, this stele may represent the goddess, who took a mountain god as her lover. But the fact that this figure wears shoes, and the footprints in the temple threshold are bare, calls into question this identification.

raised hallway that wrapped around three sides of the temple. Sculptures of lions guarded the entrances. Preserved to a height of nearly 5 feet, the corridor walls are lined with more than 80 panels carved with reliefs. In addition, 30 opposing stelae featuring a variety of scenes—a king on his throne (see photo, p. 285), a palm tree, a standing god, offerings—stood on both sides of the corridor. (These are identified as *migra‘ot*, or piers, in 1 Kings 6:6; Ezekiel 41:6.) The exquisite workmanship in the side chambers indicates that they did not function merely as storage space. Indeed, the beautiful carvings indicate they may have had some ceremonial function. But what, precisely, would have been the function of these chambers? Again, readers must provide their own suggestions.

The exterior walls of these outer chambers were

PHOTO BY PETER GRÜNWALD, DEUTSCHES ARCHÄOLOGISCHES INSTITUT, ORIENTABTEILUNG, BERLIN

also decorated with lions and sphinxes, indicating the limited repertoire from which the carvers worked.

As already noted, the 'Ain Dara temple shares many features with Solomon's Temple in Jerusalem. Indeed, no other building excavated to date has as many features in common with the Biblical description of the Jerusalem Temple. Most basically, both have essentially the same three-division, long-room plan: At 'Ain Dara, it is an entry portico, an antechamber and main chamber with screened-off shrine; in Solomon's Temple, it is an entry portico (*'ulam*), main hall (*heikhal*) and shrine, or holy of holies (*debir*).* The only significant difference between the two is the inclusion of the antechamber in the 'Ain Dara plan. With this exception the two plans are almost identical.

If the royal cubit used to build Solomon's Temple

*The most detailed description of Solomon's Temple appears in 1 Kings 6-7. The Book of Chronicles includes a parallel account (2 Chronicles 2-4), but this was written after the First Temple was destroyed. Other references are scattered throughout the Book of Kings and the prophecies of Jeremiah and Ezekiel (especially Ezekiel 40-46). For more on the Temple's design, see the following articles: Victor Hurowitz, "Inside Solomon's Temple," *Bible Review*, April 1994; Volkmar Fritz, "What Can Archaeology Tell Us About Solomon's Temple?" BAR, July/August 1987; Ernest Marie-Laperrousaz, "King Solomon's Wall Still Supports the Temple Mount," BAR, May/June 1987.

BIBLICAL PUZZLE SOLVED. A 15-foot-wide hallway wraps around three sides of the 'Ain Dara temple. In this excavation photo, the back wall of the temple's shrine room appears at right. Two massive basalt stele protrude from the wall (see plan, p. 281). (The closer stele, of an enthroned deity, is shown in detail on p. 285.) The outer corridor wall (at left) was also originally decorated with stele and reliefs.

This corridor is a unique archaeological find in second and first millennium B.C.E. temples. Yet it still has a parallel—in the Bible's description of the Jerusalem Temple: "Against the outside wall of the House—the outside walls of the House enclosing the Great Hall and the Shrine—he built a storied structure; and he made side chambers all around ... The entrance to the middle [story of] the side chambers was on the right side of the House; and a return staircase [?] led up to the middle chambers and from the middle chambers to the third story" (1 Kings 6:5,8).

The thickness of these corridor walls at 'Ain Dara suggests that it, too, may have supported at least one upper story. Holes in the walls of the corridors and in the antechamber may have held a wooden frame for a staircase. Like the corridor in Solomon's Temple, the 'Ain Dara passageway was entered through doors in the facade.

Planning a Temple

‘Ain Dara

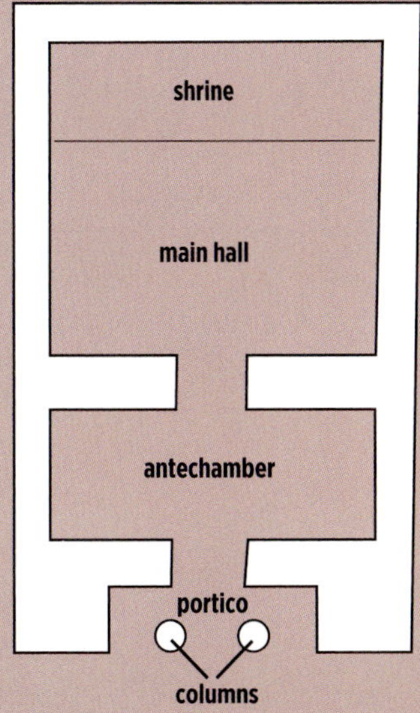

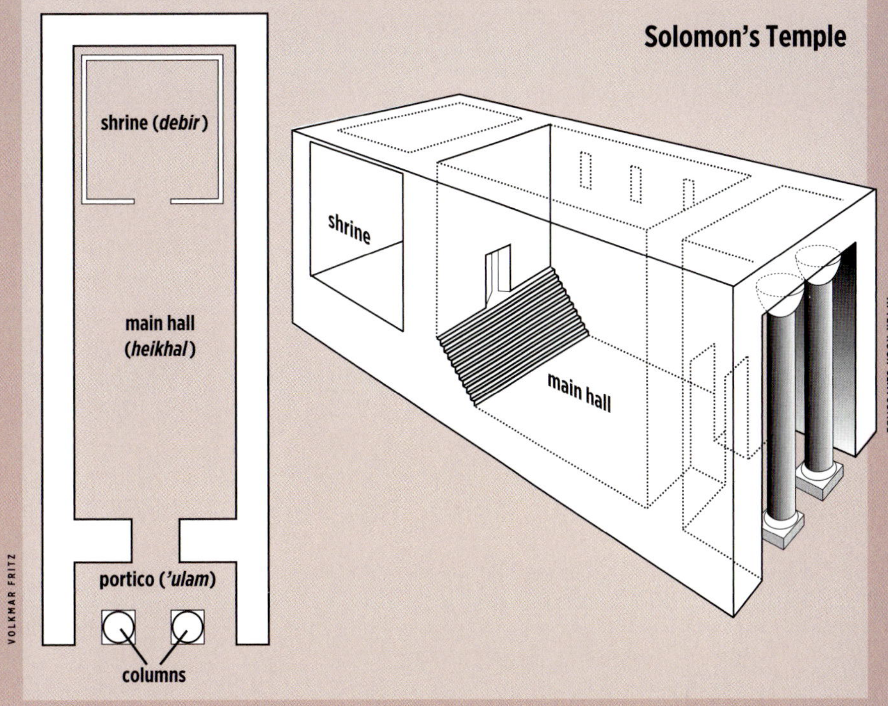

VOLKMAR FRITZ

AFTER HUGH CLAYCOMBE

A common architectural heritage is evident in the plans of Solomon’s Temple and several other temples from northern Israel and Syria. Despite various surface differences, these buildings share the same basic three-room plan, known as the “long-room plan,” which is thought to have derived from Syria in the second millennium B.C.E before spreading south.

Each temple is entered through a portico formed by the extension of the temple’s two side walls. Within each portico stood two columns, which probably supported the roof. At ‘Ain Dara, the shallow portico leads into an antechamber, which in turn leads into the main hall. The other temples shown here had deeper porticos, which opened directly onto the main hall. At the back of each main hall is a shrine room, which could be a niche, as in the Late Bronze Age (1550-1200 B.C.E.) temple at Hazor, in northern Israel; a separate room, as in the eighth-century temple at Tell Ta‘yinat, in northern Syria; a wooden cube set into the main hall, as in Solomon’s Temple; or a screened-off podium, as at ‘Ain Dara. (The outside corridors that wrapped around three sides of the ‘Ain Dara and Solomonic temples are not depicted here.)

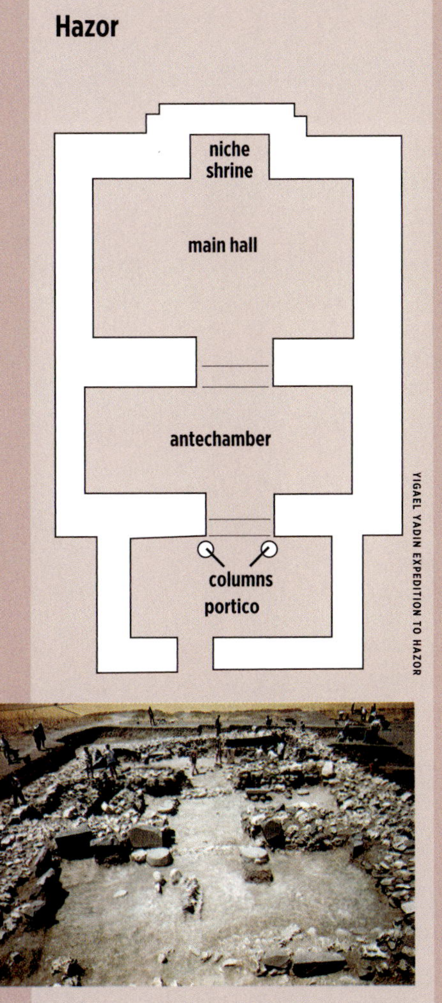

YIGAEL YADIN EXPEDITION TO HAZOR

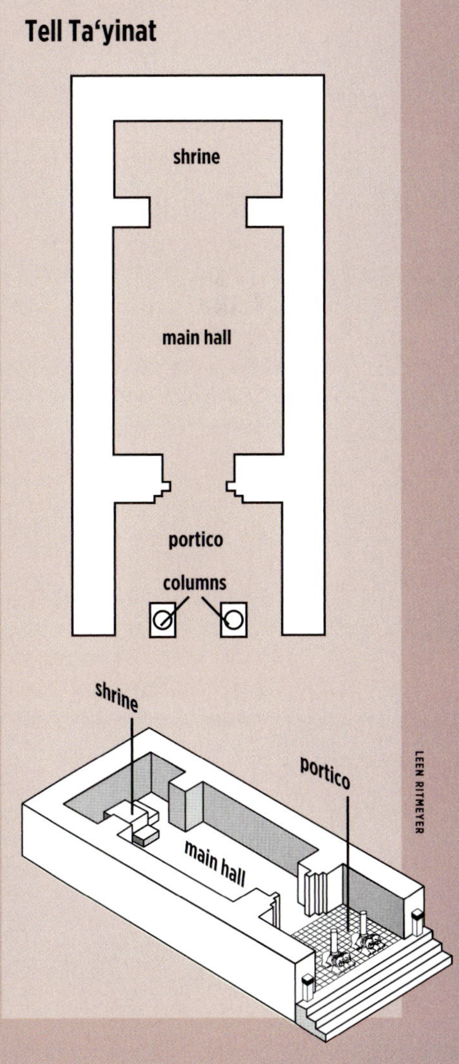

LEEN RITMEYER

PHOTOS COURTESY OF TADATERU NISHIURA, THE TOKYO NATIONAL RESEARCH INSTITUTE OF CULTURAL PROPERTIES

"RECESSED AND LATTICED" windows adorned Solomon's Temple, according to 1 Kings 6:4. Scholars have long wondered just what this enigmatic Biblical description might refer to. Now, author Monson suggests that this recessed and latticed carving (above) from the antechamber of the 'Ain Dara temple may provide the key.

Two rows of horizontal figure eights provide the lattice in this false window. To the right juts out a series of increasingly thick window frames. (The upper and left frames have not survived.)

An ivory (opposite) from Arslan Tash, in northern Syria, depicts a woman gazing out of a small square window with similar receding window frames. The doors of Solomon's Temple, which are described as "five-sided" and "four-sided," may also have been framed by a series of interlocking, receding doorposts.

A tier of basalt slabs engraved with a ribbonlike design runs beneath the windows and around the entire room. Only the carved claws (right) remain of a tier of massive birdlike animals that once perched above this frieze.

was 52.5 centimeters, then the Jerusalem Temple measured approximately 120 feet by 34 feet. The ‘Ain Dara temple is 98 feet long by 65 wide (or 125 by 105 feet including the side chambers). (The Tell Ta‘yinat temple is only 81 feet long.) The ‘Ain Dara temple is thus not only the closest in date but also the closest in size of any temple in the Levant.

Like most ancient temples, both buildings stood at the highest elevation in the city. Both temples were built on a platform and had a courtyard in front with a monumental staircase (*ma‘aleh*, cf. Ezekiel 40:22) leading up to the temple.

In both cases the portico was narrower and shallower than the rooms of the temple. In both cases the portico was open on one side and had a roof supported by two pillars. (Unlike many reconstructions of Solomon's Temple, the pillars Boaz and Jachin were not free-standing; indeed, the comparanda, such as the pillars at ‘Ain Dara, help to establish this. The position of the pillar bases at both ‘Ain Dara and Tell Ta‘yinat indicates they were load-bearing columns.)

In both cases spectacular reliefs decorated the walls, and the carvings in both temples share several motifs: The stylized floral designs and lily patterns, palmettes, winged creatures and lions of ‘Ain Dara may be compared with the "bas reliefs and engravings of cherubim, palm trees, and flower patterns, in the inner and outer rooms" of Solomon's Temple (1 Kings 6:29).

ERICH LESSING

MUSÉE DE LA CIVILISATION, QUEBEC/COURTESY OF THE DIRECTEUR GÉNÉRAL DES ANTIQUITÉS ET DES MUSÉES, SYRIA

The elevated podium at the back of the 'Ain Dara temple, covering a third of the floor area of the main hall and set off from the forepart by a separate screen, is a commanding parallel for the Biblical holy of holies.

Without going into greater detail here, I have determined that the 'Ain Dara temple shares 33 of the roughly 65 architectural elements mentioned in the Bible in connection with Solomon's Temple.

Several additional features of the 'Ain Dara temple help us to better understand aspects of the Biblical Temple as described in the Book of Kings. For example, the Biblical holy of holies is described as a wooden cube measuring 20 cubits on each side (1 Kings 6:20; Ezekiel 41:3-4) in a room 30 cubits high (1 Kings 6:2). It is unclear whether a 10-cubit stairway led up to the holy of holies or whether the shrine was on the same level as the main hall but had a lower ceiling and a space above. The 'Ain Dara temple, as well as other comparanda, clearly indicates that a stairway would have led up to the holy of holies in Solomon's Temple.

The outer ambulatory of 'Ain Dara provides one of the site's most dramatic contributions to our understanding of the Solomonic Temple. According to 1 Kings 6:5, the Biblical Temple was enclosed by something called *sela'ot*, usually translated "side chambers." But until the excavation of 'Ain Dara, the term *sela'ot* defied a convincing explanation. That's because before 'Ain Dara, outer corridors were never attested in a second- or first-millennium B.C.E. temple. I believe that the hallways flanking the 'Ain Dara temple can be none other than the *sela'ot* of 1 Kings 6:5. These walkways at 'Ain Dara are 18 feet wide, as are the Biblical side chambers (when the 5-cubit [about 8-foot] side chamber and 6-cubit [about 10-foot] outer wall of the Biblical Temple are added together). The 'Ain Dara hallway is reached through doors on either side of the temple entrance, which brings to mind 1 Kings 6:8: "There was an entrance to the *sela'ot* on the right side of the temple."

On the basis of the side chambers at 'Ain Dara and in Solomon's Temple, it may be well to re-examine the evidence from other sites. I now suspect that side chambers were quite common. I have already identified seven temples, including Shechem, Megiddo and Alalakh, in which the foundations were wide enough to support multistoried side chambers built against the walls of the temple proper.

Another conundrum in the Biblical description of Solomon's Temple: The Book of Kings refers to the Temple windows as *shequfim 'atumîm* (1 Kings 6:4).

THE FACES OF 'AIN DARA are characterized by almond eyes, rounded noses and half-smiling lips—all sculpted in basalt. The 35-inch-tall face at right originally belonged to one of the hybrid lion creatures that lined the facade of the building. The 22-inch figure at left—perhaps a royal or divine female—wears a diadem studded with rosettes. This face, shown restored, was found in numerous pieces.

PHOTO BY PETER GRÜNWALD, DEUTSCHES ARCHÄOLOGISCHES INSTITUT, ORIENTABTEILUNG, BERLIN

A footnote in the new Jewish Publication Society translation tells us the meaning is uncertain. The windows have variously been described as "recessed and latticed" or "framed and blocked." Some scholars consider any attempt at translation to be an exercise in futility. Lawrence Stager of Harvard University has proposed that the phrase refers to windowlike frames that were stopped up with rubble—that is, *faux* (false) windows.[6] 'Ain Dara offers an intriguing parallel that allows us to take this idea a step further. At least two window frames were carved into the walls of the temple's antechamber (see photo, p. 290). Both windows have a recessed frame on each side; on top, the frame is also indented but is slightly arched. The upper half of each window is filled in with basalt carvings of horizontal rows of figure eights lying on their sides. The lower half is flat with a guilloche pattern running along the bottom. This, I believe, represents the kind of window lattice described in 1 Kings 6:4, thus providing a solution to a riddle that has eluded commentators for generations (compare Judges 5:28; Song of Songs 2:9 and Ben Sirach 42:11).

These faux windows would perhaps have been complemented by true windows close to the ceiling. One additional window frame, in this case an open one, appears in the northeast corner of the 'Ain Dara temple.

The Bible describes "five-sided" (*hamshit*) and "four-sided" (*rebi'it*) doors that led into the main hall and shrine of Solomon's Temple (1 Kings 6:31,33). These, too, have long puzzled commentators (and have led to a number of creative interpretations).[7] In my view, these expressions refer not to the number of surfaces or sides in the door but the number of recesses in the door frame. Even the most basic door frames in the buildings of the ancient Near East often had a single recess, as the necropolis of Silwan in Jerusalem reveals.[8] The doors in more luxurious structures—all over the Mediterranean world and in Mesopotamia—had several recesses in the frame. This is known as rabbeting; in a wooden construction, it is attained by fitting together several receding door frames. This can be replicated in stone on both doors and windows—as shown by the 'Ain Dara temple and the description of Solomon's Temple.

While the 'Ain Dara temple makes its own singular contribution to our understanding of Solomon's Temple, it must also be seen as part of a typology of ancient Near Eastern temples. Architecture, like ancient scripts and pottery, can be organized into chronological sequences and typologies. A century of archaeological research has unearthed a sizable corpus of parallel temples in the Levant that allow for increasingly refined reconstructions. In the years subsequent to the excavation of the Tell Ta'yinat temple, others were discovered at such sites as Megiddo, Zinjirli, Alalakh and Hamath (see map, p. 280). Each of these temples was associated with an adjacent palace, as, of course, was the case with Solomon's Temple (2 Chronicles 2:1, 12). They date to various periods of the second and first millennia B.C.E. and conform very well to the Biblical description of Solomon's regal-ritual center in Jerusalem.[9]

The assemblage of temples has continued to expand during the past two decades. Today we know of at least two dozen excavated temples that may be compared to Solomon's Temple. Most of them are of the long-room type and come from the area north of the Israelite heartland. The Bible itself tells us that Solomon's Temple design was mediated through Hiram of Tyre and other artisans from Phoenicia, the coastal region north of Israel (1 Kings 5:20,32, 7:13-37 [NJPS]).[10] Amihai Mazar has called this temple plan the "symmetrical Syrian temple type."[11] Each has a courtyard in front, a portico, two rooms beyond and an elevated inner room, or holy of holies, at the rear, usually with a niche at the back. Each temple, of course, had its own configuration of secondary features, such as towers protruding from the facade, pillars flanking the entrance, and side chambers. Together they may therefore be regarded as hybrid temples that incorporate a mixture of indigenous and imported architectural forms appropriated for the local religious tradition of each city-state. The Jerusalem Temple includes features that belong to both Canaanite and North Syrian building traditions. Its various components reflect a combination of local traditions and cultural borrowing from farther afield. The influence of the Syrian long-room plan and the iconography of Phoenicia, Syria and Egypt are undeniable. But in the end, neither the Jerusalem Temple nor any of its closest parallels are traceable to a single, monolithic temple tradition.

Chronologically, the 'Ain Dara temple forms a bridge in the temple sequence between the Late Bronze Age (1500-1200 B.C.E.) temple at Hazor (Area H) and the eighth-century B.C.E. Iron Age temple at Tell Ta'yinat. The 'Ain Dara temple corroborates the date of the Solomonic Temple to the early first millennium with a high degree of probability, regardless of the date assigned to the composition of the Biblical text. The Jerusalem Temple thus takes its place comfortably within the typology of Iron Age temples despite the dearth of architectural remains in Jerusalem. Such a broad-based typology is hard to overturn. As it is described in the Hebrew Bible, the Temple of Solomon is a typical hybrid temple belonging to the long-room Syrian type.

Simply put, the date, size and numerous features of the 'Ain Dara temple provide new evidence that chronologically anchors the Temple of Solomon in the cultural traditions of the tenth century B.C.E. The 'Ain Dara temple thus corroborates the traditional date of Solomon's renowned shrine.

[1] Portions of this article have been adapted from "The Temples of 'Ain Dara and Jerusalem," *Text, Artifact, and Image: Revealing Ancient Israelite Religion*, eds. Gary Beckman and Theodore Lewis (New Haven, CT: Yale Univ. Press, forthcoming). I would like to thank Anthony Appa for sharing with me his pictures of 'Ain Dara and his experiences at the site. I am indebted to my mentor, Lawrence E. Stager, for many helpful comments.

[2] Ali Abu Assaf, *Der Tempel von 'Ain Dara*, Damaszener Forschungen 3 (Mainz: Philipp von Zabern, 1990).

[3] Some scholars believe that the Jerusalem Temple was also built in several phases, one of which was the ambulatory; see D.W. Gooding, "An Impossible Shrine," *Vetus Testamentum Supplements* 15 (1965), pp. 405-420.

[4] These other sites are Carchemish, Zinjirli and other Neo-Hittite sites (see Abu Assaf, *'Ain Dara*, pp. 39-41). See more recently Abu Assaf, "Die Kleinfunde aus "An Dara," *Damaszener Mitteilungen* 9 (1996), pp. 47-111.

[5] Here and throughout the temple reliefs we find the "serpentine curve" pattern known from other finds in the Levant, including a basalt bowl from Hazor Temple H (see Yigael Yadin, *Hazor III-IV* [Jerusalem: Magnes, 1961], pl. 122) and most recently a tenth-century pottery vessel from Tel Rehov (see Amihai Mazar and John Camp, "Will Tel Rehov Save the United Monarchy?" BAR, March/April 2000, p. 48).

[6] Lawrence E. Stager, "The Archaeology of the Family in Ancient Israel," *Bulletin of the American Schools of Oriental Research* 260 (1985), pp. 1-35; and "The Song of Deborah: Why Some Tribes Answered the Call and Others Did Not," BAR, January/February 1989.

[7] See Alan Millard, "The Doorways of Solomon's Temple," *Eretz-Israel* 20 (1989), pp. 135*-139*.

[8] David Ussishkin, *The Village of Silwan: The Necropolis from the Period of the Judean Kingdom* (Jerusalem: Israel Exploration Society, 1993), illus. 47, 94, 108.

[9] The association of temple and palace in one building compound has been well attested in Mesopotamia and Egypt. It proved to be a popular layout in the Levant as well, as noted by Ussishkin ("Solomon and the Tayanat Temples," *Israel Exploration Journal (IEJ)* 16 (1966), pp. 104-110; "Solomon's Palace and Building 1723," *IEJ* 16 [1966], pp. 174-186). In 1971 Theodor Busink published all known parallels in one monograph: *Der Tempel von Jerusalem von Salomo bis Herodes: Eine archäologische-historische Studie unter Berücksichtigung des westsemitischen Tempelhaus*, vol. 1, *Der Tempel Salomos* (Leiden: Brill, 1971). Despite the numerous similarities between the Biblical description and Canaanite and Syrian temples, he considered many of the features in the Jerusalem Temple to be Israelite innovations (p. 617)—a point on which we disagree.

[10] Two seminal articles on this subject were written by David Ussishkin; see note 9. For earlier studies, see G. Ernest Wright, "The Significance of the Temple in the Ancient Near East," part 3, "The Temple in Syria-Palestine," *Biblical Archaeologist* (1944), pp. 65-77; Leroy Waterman, "The Damaged Blueprints of the Temple of Solomon," *Journal of Near Eastern Studies* (1943), pp. 284-294.

[11] Mazar's typology is the most comprehensive proposed to date; see "Temples of the Middle and Late Bronze Ages and the Iron Age," in *The Architecture of Ancient Israel*, ed. Aharon Kempinski and Ronny Reich (Jerusalem: Israel Exploration Society, 1992), pp. 161-187. See also Volkmar Fritz, "What Can Archaeology Tell Us About Solomon's Temple?" BAR, July/August 1987. The temples range in date from the third to first millennium B.C.E. and include Munbaqa, Emar, Ebla D, Mari, Chuera, Hayyat, Kittan, 'Ain Dara, Tayinat, Ebla B1, N, Hazor Area A, Hazor Area H, Dab'a, Alalakh I, Hamath, Shechem, Megiddo, Haror, Alalakh VII, IV, Byblos II, Carchemish, Lachish P, Beth-Shean VI and the *temenos* at Dan.

We received a number of letters in response to this article, including a discussion about the height and stride of the deity that dwelled in the 'Ain Dara temple. See Queries and Comments in the September/October 2000 and March/April 2001 issues of BAR.

Related Reading

Leen Ritmeyer, "Locating the Original Temple Mount," BAR, March/April 1992.

Leen Ritmeyer, "The Ark of the Covenant: Where It Stood in Solomon's Temple," BAR, January/February 1996.

Victor Hurowitz, "Solomon's Temple in Context," BAR, March/April 2011.